GOVERNMENT BEYOND THE CENTRE

SERIES EDITORS: GERRY STOKER AND DAVID WILSON

The world of sub-central governance and administration – including local authorities, quasi-governmental bodies and the agencies of public–private partnerships – has seen massive changes in the United Kingdom and other western democracies. The original aim of the **Government Beyond the Centre** series was to bring the study of this often-neglected world into the mainstream of social science research, applying the spotlight of critical analysis to what had traditionally been the preserve of institutional public administration approaches.

The replacement of traditional models of government by new models of governance has affected central government, too, with the contracting out of many traditional functions, the increasing importance of relationships with devolved and supranational authorities, and the emergence of new holistic models based on partnership and collaboration.

This series focuses on the agenda of change in governance both at sub-central level and in the new patterns of relationships surrounding the core executive. Its objective is to provide up-to-date and informative accounts of the new forms of management and administration and the structures of power and influence that are emerging, and of the economic, political and ideological forces that underlie them.

The series will be of interest to students and practitioners in central and local government, public management and social policy, and all those interested in the reshaping of the governmental institutions which have a daily and major impact on our lives.

Government Beyond the Centre
Series Standing Order
ISBN 0–333–71696–5 hardback
ISBN 0–333–69337–X paperback
(*outside North America only*)

You can receive future titles in this series as they are published by placing a standing order. Please contact your bookseller or, in the case of difficulty, write to us at the address below with your name and address, the title of the series and one of the ISBNs quoted above.

Customer Services Department, Macmillan Distribution Ltd
Houndmills, Basingstoke, Hampshire RG21 6XS, England, UK

GBC

GOVERNMENT BEYOND THE CENTRE

SERIES EDITORS: GERRY STOKER AND DAVID WILSON

Published

Richard Batley and Gerry Stoker (eds)
Local Government in Europe

Bas Denters and Lawrence E. Rose (eds)
Comparing Local Governance

Sue Goss
Making Local Governance Work

Clive Gray
Government Beyond the Centre

John Gyford
Citizens, Consumers and Councils

Richard Kerley
Managing in Local Government

Desmond King and Gerry Stoker (eds)
Rethinking Local Democracy

Steve Leach, John Stewart and
Kieron Walsh
**The Changing Organisation and
Management of Local Governance**

Arthur Midwinter
Local Government in Scotland

Christopher Pollitt, Johnston Birchall
and Keith Putman
Decentralising Public Service Management

Rajiv Prabhakar
Rethinking Public Services

Lawrence Pratchett and David Wilson (eds)
Local Democracy and Local Government

John Stewart
The Nature of British Local Government

Gerry Stoker
Transforming Local Governance

Gerry Stoker (ed.)
**The New Management of British Local
Governance**

Gerry Stoker (ed.)
**The New Politics of British Local
Governance**

Gerry Stoker and David Wilson (eds)
**British Local Government in the 21st
Century**

Helen Sullivan and Chris Skelcher
Working Across Boundaries

Tony Travers
The Politics of London

David Wilson and Chris Game
Local Government in the United Kingdom
(5th edn)

Perri 6, Diana Leat, Kimberly Seltzer and
Gerry Stoker
Towards Holistic Governance

Forthcoming

Steve Martin
The Transformation of Public Services

Lawrence Pratchett
Local Democracy in Britain

Local Government in the United Kingdom

Fifth Edition

David Wilson

and

Chris Game

palgrave
macmillan

First edition 1994
Second edition 1998
Third edition 2002
Fourth edition 2006
Fifth edition 2011

Published by
PALGRAVE MACMILLAN

Palgrave Macmillan in the UK is an imprint of Macmillan Publishers Limited, registered in England, company number 785998, of Houndmills, Basingstoke, Hampshire RG21 6XS.

Palgrave Macmillan in the US is a division of St Martin's Press LLC, 175 Fifth Avenue, New York, NY 10010.

Palgrave Macmillan is the global academic imprint of the above companies and has companies and representatives throughout the world.

Palgrave® and Macmillan® are registered trademarks in the United States, the United Kingdom, Europe and other countries

ISBN 978–0–230–24638–6 hardback
ISBN 978–0–230–24639–3 paperback

This book is printed on paper suitable for recycling and made from fully managed and sustained forest sources. Logging, pulping and manufacturing processes are expected to conform to the environmental regulations of the country of origin.

A catalogue record for this book is available from the British Library.

A catalog record for this book is available from the Library of Congress.

10   9   8   7   6   5   4   3   2   1
20   19   18   17   16   15   14   13   12   11

Printed and bound in Great Britain by CPI Antony Rowe
Chippenham and Eastbourne

To Margaret, without whom...

Contents

List of Figures

List of Exhibits

Preface to the Fifth Edition

Readers already familiar with this book will have become used to the appearance of a new edition with almost clockwork precision every four years – a feature that we believe has generally been found helpful. The maintenance of that timetable has owed as much to the enthusiasm and efficiency of our publishers as it has to us, and has also been assisted by the UK's lack of a formally codified constitution (see Chapter 2).

In future, assuming the enactment of the Coalition Government's Fixed-term Parliaments Bill 2010–11, there should be a higher predictability of election dates than in the past, and a greater likelihood of Parliaments lasting for a full five years. In the interests of better government, we personally support this Bill and the reasoning behind it, but we have to admit that, were there to have been fixed five-year Parliaments in the 1990s–2000s, they would have interfered seriously with this book's production schedule.

As it was, the second edition (1998) was able both to evaluate the local government record of the 1979–97 Conservative Administrations and to report the early initiatives of New Labour. The third edition (2002) could assess the Blair Government's first term of office, thanks to the PM, worried apparently about the possible erosion of his party's 179-seat Commons majority, calling an early election in 2001. He did the same four years later, which fitted in conveniently with the book's fourth edition (2006). But then the government's electoral luck started to run out, and ours with it.

As it became increasingly probable that the next election would be in 2010, we faced a tricky choice: stick to the four-year cycle and effectively complete the book without knowing who would form the next government, or wait until 2011, knowing that in the meantime the fourth edition would have lost much, if not most, of its value to potential readers and users. Being British, and indecisive, we went, of course, for a compromise – to write the book in 2009/10 and publish in early 2011 – in the hope that, while it would be both difficult and inevitably deficient, it might prove the least unsatisfactory of the options available.

Because of the kind of book it is, we would guess that only a minority of readers do as the King advised Alice in Lewis Carroll's *Alice in Wonderland*: begin at the beginning and go on to the end, and then stop. If there are any such devotees, though, they will probably be the first to realise how the final draft emerged: more or less in chapter order, over the period before, during and immediately after the 2010 General Election.

Only the final chapters were written in the knowledge of the outcome of that election, and of the early actions and pronouncements of the

Conservative–Liberal Democrat Coalition. All other chapters had to be revised and added to, if post-election material was to be included and necessary factual corrections made. Each such inclusion therefore involved its own mini-compromise: between adding what we considered important new information, and avoiding an indefinite increase in the book's length. We stopped adding and delivered the manuscript at the start of the parliamentary summer recess in late July 2010, and updated thereafter where pagination permitted. It was an imperfect way of proceeding, and we can only hope that most readers will understand our view that other ways seemed likely to be worse.

If it were not already apparent, the assurance that we habitually include at about this point in the Preface is every bit as justified as in previous editions. The book is exactly what it says on the cover: comprehensively revised and updated. No chapter has survived intact, and most contain both new information and new illustrations. Two particularly long chapters in the fourth edition have been split. The sections on Scotland, Wales and English regional governance in the former Chapter 5, on External Structures, now have Chapter 6 to themselves. The former Chapter 9, on Central–Local Government Relations, has been divided into Chapter 10, on the formal framework and setting of the Central–Local Relationship, and Chapter 11, which compares actual practice first to that formal framework and then to some of the academic literature on the topic.

If this particular edition has a single underlying but constantly intruding narrative, it must be cuts, and these apply to the book's production as well as its content. No publisher in these difficult economic times is going to agree to extra chapters without extracting an authorial commitment to make something at least approaching equivalent pages' worth of cuts. It has not been easy, because we have been there before. In the fourth edition we transferred the end-of-chapter sections on Additional Reading to the book's companion website – **www.palgrave.com/politics/wilson**; also some of the illustrative material from earlier editions that was still relevant and of interest without any longer being immediately topical.

We have pursued a similar policy this time. Among the Figures cut from the fourth edition but still accessible on the website are 5.3, 5.4 and 5.6 – the governmental maps of Scotland, Wales and Northern Ireland, which have remained unchanged. The Exhibits cut include 2.2 – An A-A of council services; 3.2 – Local government's contribution to a joined-up drugs policy; 3.3 – How local authorities try to get us to participate; 6.3 – Mayoral referendums, 2001–06; 8.3 – The labyrinthine world of zones and partnerships; 9.1 – The power of well-being; and 11.8 – Split voting, 1997 and 2001. We have also largely done away with the previous practice of dividing illustrative and boxed material into Exhibits and Figures, which confused even us. In this edition all illustrations are Exhibits, except the cartoons (plus the map of English local authorities), which are Figures.

Having introduced the companion website, we should give it a further plug. A principal purpose of the site is to enable readers to keep up with the major changes and developments in UK local government without having to wait for the book's next edition. It contains, therefore, periodic updating briefings – covering, for example, White Papers and other ministerial initiatives, legislation, official and academic publications, local elections, and key changes in post-holders. Then, as mentioned above, there are the guides to further reading and the Exhibits transferred from earlier editions.

Still on the topic of websites, one unchanged practice in this edition is that relating to website references. Unlike some introductory texts, this one does not provide strings of often lengthy website references to all mentioned institutions – partly because these can nowadays be Googled easily, and partly because we feel that readers are likely to learn more about the topic by searching for it themselves. Generally, therefore, we have restricted references to sites that are not obvious, or where we have drawn material from a specific page.

All of which brings us to the final and most pleasurable part of a Preface – the recording of debts of gratitude incurred in producing a volume of this attempted type and range. First come our academic colleagues, headed, as ever, by Emeritus Professors John Stewart and George Jones – possibly the most incisive readers of each new edition and certainly its friendliest critics. A great many others have made important and appreciated contributions, too numerous to mention individually, apart from Professors Gerry Stoker and Steve Leach, who were prominently involved in the book's conception and have remained so ever since.

Then, in an entirely merited paragraph of her own, there is Margaret Spence, whose administrative and secretarial assistance has again been – to use literally for once one of the most abused words in today's popular vocabulary – incredible. Previously, we described her commitment to and enthusiasm for this project as being almost eerie – and it is. She even wakes up thinking about the book! Unbelievable, and – no pun on her name intended – indispensable.

We gratefully acknowledged our publishers in the opening paragraph, but now they should be individually 'outed' and thanked: Steven Kennedy, still keenly involved, but no doubt relieved to have handed over 'chasing' responsibilities to Stephen Wenham and Helen Caunce, who mercifully have inherited, among Steven's many estimable qualities, his almost boundless patience. Thanks once again also to our editorial consultant, Keith Povey, for all his help in making the book as user-friendly as we always hope it will be.

Lastly, though anything but least, we must express our admiration and gratitude to our under-rewarded artists and their respective publications for permission to reproduce their cartoons and caricatures: Malcolm Willett for Figures 2.1, 10.1, 12.2, and 14.1; Patrick Blower for Figure 5.1; Adrian

Teal and CartoonStock for Figure 11.1 – all of which first appeared in the *Local Government Chronicle*; Brick for Figure 12.1, and Harry Venning and *The Guardian* for Figure 15.1.

We trust these and the other illustrations contribute both to the book's merit and our readers' interest. For whatever defects and errors you detect and for the views expressed, we, of course, alone are responsible.

DAVID WILSON
CHRIS GAME

List of Abbreviations

AC	Audit Commission
A&E	Hospital Accident and Emergency Dept
ALDC	Association of Liberal Democrat Councillors
ALMO	Arm's Length Management Organisation
AM	Assembly Member (Wales)
AMS	Additional Member System
ANPR	Automatic Number Plate Recognition
ATC	administrative, technical and clerical
AV	Alternative Vote
BBC	British Broadcasting Corporation
BC	Borough Council
BAME	Black, Asian and Minority Ethnic
BME	Black and Minority Ethnic
BNP	British National Party
BSI	British Standards Institute
BV	Best Value
BVPI	Best Value Performance Indicator
BVPP	Best Value Performance Plan
CAA	Comprehensive Area Assessment
CC	County/City Council
CCfA	Councillor Call for Action
CCT	Compulsory Competitive Tendering
CCTV	closed-circuit television
CE	Chief Executive
CIPFA	Chartered Institute of Public Finance and Accountancy
CLA	Commission for Local Administration
CLG	see DCLG
CORE	Co-ordinated Online Register of Electors
CPA	Comprehensive Performance Assessment
CPS	Centre for Policy Studies
CVS	Community and Voluntary Services
DC	District Council
DCLG	Department for Communities and Local Government (2006–), aka CLG
DCMS	Department for Culture, Media and Sport
DEFRA	Department for Environment, Food and Rural Affairs
DETR	Department of the Environment, Transport and the Regions (1997–2001)

DfES	Department for Education and Skills (1997–2010)
DfT	Department for Transport
DH	Department of Health
DSG	Dedicated Schools Grant
DSO	Direct Service Organisation
DTLR	Department for Transport, Local Government and the Regions (2001–02)
DUP	Democratic Unionist Party (N. Ireland)
DWP	Department for Work and Pensions
ELG	Evaluating Local Governance project (Manchester University)
EMAS	Eco-Management and Audit Scheme
ERDF	European Regional Development Fund
ESF	European Social Fund
ESPO	Eastern Shires Purchasing Organisation
EU	European Union
FoI	Freedom of Information
FPTP	first-past-the-post electoral system
FTE	full-time equivalent
FTSE	Financial Times Stock Exchange
GDP	gross domestic product
GLA	Greater London Authority (2000–)
GLC	Greater London Council (1963–86)
GM	grant maintained (schools)
GO	Government Offices (for the English Regions)
GOL	Government Office for London
GONCS	Government Office Network Centre and Services
HAT	Housing Action Trust
HR	human resources
ICT	Information and communications technology
IDeA/I&DeA	Improvement and Development Agency (from 2010, LG Improvement and Development)
IEA	Institute of Economic Affairs
ILEA	Inner London Education Authority
INLOGOV	Institute of Local Government Studies
IPC	Infrastructure Planning Commission
LAA	Local Area Agreement
LCC	London County Council
LD	Liberal Democrat Party
LDA	London Development Agency
LDF	Local Development Framework
LEA	Local Education Authority
LEP	Local Enterprise Partnership
LFEPA	London Fire and Emergency Planning Authority

LGA	Local Government Association
LGAMS	Local Government Additional Member System
LGIU	Local Government Information Unit
LGMA	Local Government Modernisation Agenda
LIA	Local Innovation Award
LMS	local management of schools
LPSA	Local Public Service Agreement
LSC	Learning and Skills Council
LSCB	Local Safeguarding Children Board
LSP	Local Strategic Partnership
LTP	Local Transport Plan
LVSC	London Voluntary Service Council
MAA	Multi-Area Agreement
MD	Managing Director
MLA	Member of the Legislative Assembly (N. Ireland)
MP	Member of Parliament
MPA	Metropolitan Police Authority
MSP	Member of the Scottish Parliament
MWC	minimum winning coalition
NAVCA	National Association for Voluntary and Community Action
NCVO	National Council for Voluntary Organisations
NDC	New Deal for Communities
NDPB	non-departmental public body
NEC	National Executive Committee
NFER	National Foundation for Educational Research
NGO	non-governmental organisation
NHS	National Health Service
NIS	National Indicator Set
NJC	National Joint Council for Local Government Services
NLGN	New Local Government Network
NNDR	National Non-Domestic Rate (also UBR)
NPS	National Policy Statement
ODPM	Office of the Deputy Prime Minister (2002–6)
OECD	Organisation for Economic Co-operation and Development
OFSTED	Office for Standards in Education (from 2007, Office for Standards in Education, Children's Services and Skills)
O&S	Overview and Scrutiny
ONS	Office for National Statistics
PA	performance appraisal
PB	Participatory Budgeting
PCS	Public and Commercial Services Union
PCSO	police community support officer

PCT	Primary Care Trust
PFI	Private Finance Initiative
PI	Performance Indicator
PLP	Parliamentary Labour Party
PM	Prime Minister; also performance management
PPP	public–private partnership
PR	proportional representation; also performance review
PRG	Performance Reward Grant
PRP	performance-related pay
PSO	public service orientation
PTA	Passenger Transport Authority
QA	quality assurance
QC	quality control
RDA	Regional Development Agency
RSG	Revenue Support Grant
RSS	Regional Spatial Strategy
SATs	Standard Attainment Tests
SCA	Sustainable Communities Act 2007
SCS	Sustainable Community Strategy
SEU	Standards and Effectiveness Unit
SI	Statutory Instrument
SNEN	Single Non-Emergency Number project
SNP	Scottish National Party
SOCITM	Society of Information Technology Management
SOLACE	Society of Local Authority Chief Executives
SRA	Special Responsibility Allowance
SRE	Sex and Relationship Education
STV	Single Transferable Vote
TEC	Training and Enterprise Council
TfL	Transport for London
TPA	The TaxPayers' Alliance
TQM	total quality management
UBR	Uniform Business Rate (also NNDR)
UDC	Urban Development Corporation
UKIP	UK Independence Party
UU	Ulster Unionists
VAT	Value Added Tax
VCS	Voluntary and Community Sector
VCG	Voluntary and Community Group
VFM	value for money

Part 1

Local Government:
The Basics

Chapter 1

Introduction: Our Aims and Approach

You learn, if you look

Seeking a perceptive insight into the diversity of British culture, you would not necessarily turn first to a professional cricketer. But then Ed Smith was not your typical professional sportsman. He also wrote, during his playing career, books, articles, and even some literary criticism, and subsequently became a leader writer on *The Times*. He was a good enough batsman to represent England – three times in 2003, following a once-in-a-lifetime month in which he hit an astonishing six centuries in eight innings. It was an exceptional story that he turned into a fascinating book, in which he notes that:

> One of the best things about being a professional cricketer is the opportunity to experience the rest of the country. You learn, if you look, that *things change quickly from county to county*. You notice smiles come more easily in some grounds and cities than in others. You learn that some counties harbour more hatred of government, or London, or flashiness. You hear different attitudes to money, to drink, to sport. (Smith, 2005, p. 78 – our emphasis)

What a contrast to Raymond Seitz, a former US Ambassador to Britain, whose observations opened this book's previous two editions. Seitz bemoaned Britain's unimaginative vehicle licence plates compared to the American plates he recalled from his childhood, each displaying some slogan relating to its home state: 'New York: The Empire State', 'Tennessee: The Volunteer State', and, more disconcertingly, 'New Hampshire: Live Free or Die'. Through this 'licence plate view of local government', the young Seitz learned early that every state had its own character and identity. State, even local, governments had real authority, and their residents were fiercely proud of being different from their neighbours across a shared boundary. American states had their own constitutions – and legislatures that could raise investment capital and tax their citizens, with taxes that varied from state to state. America was a federal and genuinely pluralist country. Britain, by comparison, was both unitary and uniform.

3

So, who was the more acute observer: Seitz or Smith? Seitz, we suggest, was both right and wrong – constitutionally right, observationally wrong. The UK is indeed a *unitary state,* governed constitutionally as a single unit, through the national Parliament at Westminster. Parliament is sovereign (even without a separate UK Sovereignty Act), and any sub-central governments – the Scottish Parliament, the Welsh and Northern Ireland Assemblies, and Britain's 430-odd local authorities – are necessarily subordinate. All are literally creatures – or creations – of Parliament. Britain differs fundamentally, therefore, from the USA, Canada, Australia, India, Germany and Belgium, which are *federal states*: associations of largely self-governing regions united by a central or federal government.

Where Seitz went too far, in our view, was in equating Britain's unitary form of government with uniformity of practice – though we would not dispute some of his assertions. UK local government, he noted, was under almost constant reorganisation, with boundaries changing and new councils being created without anyone apparently caring very much. Services, benefits, taxes – like licence plates – are basically the same everywhere: 'Central government divvies up the public purse and distributes the funds evenly across a homogeneous society. Who gets what is a national responsibility and a national preoccupation' (Seitz, 1998, p. 270). The egalitarianism, concludes Seitz, may be admirable, but the cost is a 'feebleness' of local government and a 'super-centralism' of policy-making in which 'local government is directed from London in a semi-colonial fashion' (p. 274).

If you've been to one town...

Which is where Ed Smith's call to 'look and learn' comes in. Get out of London more, and get real, we would respectfully have advised the ambassador. Of course, there are not the same extremes of government in the UK as in the USA, which is nearly 40 times its size, as well as being a federation. Seitz was right too – as we show in Chapters 5 and 10 – about our councils regularly being reorganised and subject to greater central government control and direction than most of their European counterparts. But look more carefully and, like Smith, you will quickly see forces of diversity as well as those of uniformity: differing sizes, locations, histories, cultures, economies, social class structures, politics – all militating against even neighbouring councils being the undistinguishable 'administrative units' that Seitz thought he saw (1998, p. 271).

Councils, even of the same type – counties, metropolitan boroughs – 'do' local government in different and distinctive ways, and always have done. This book's first message, therefore, is the importance of getting the balance right. Don't understate the real and pervasive centralism that characterises the British system of government, but don't ignore the equally real local variations that stubbornly remain. As the saying ought to go: 'If you've been to one town ... you've been to one town.'

Local government boring – you mean like cricket?

It was playwright Harold Pinter's belief that 'cricket is the greatest thing God ever created ... certainly greater than sex, although sex isn't too bad either'. There are, however, those who claim to find cricket downright boring: indeed, surpassed in its boringness only by local government – or 'sewage without tears', as the textbook by an illustrious predecessor of ours, John Redcliffe-Maud (1932), was apparently known to his students. For such readers, linking the two subjects as we have must seem what the 8th Amendment to the US Constitution terms a cruel and unusual punishment. Our explanation is simple. Anything complex can seem boring if you know next to nothing about it. Find out about it, preferably guided by someone who knows and can enthuse about it, and with luck it will come to seem more interesting. That's the theory, anyway. This book's aim is to be the equivalent of taking a cricketphobe to an attractive county ground, preferably in warm, midsummer weather, and guiding them through a complete first-class match. We can't promise a local government proxy of an extended Kevin Pietersen innings, but if, at the end, the thing still seems a bore, we're sorry – we'll have done our best.

On the face of it, the boring image ought to be easy to demolish. Check 'boring' in a thesaurus, and it is surrounded by words like 'narrow', 'unvarying', 'monotonous'. Yet, while there are plenty of critical things that can be said – and will be said by us – about contemporary UK local government, being narrow, unvarying and monotonous are not among them. The truth, if anything, is the reverse.

Narrow is something local government has never been. That local authorities 'look after you from the cradle to the grave' – or from sperm to worm – is both a cliché and an outdatedly paternalistic view of councils' wide-ranging responsibilities. But it is also literally true, in that they will register your birth, death, any intervening marriage or civil partnership, and then finally dispose of you, in a cemetery or crematorium, according to taste. Both relevant occupations – registrar (supporting – administration, legal) and gravedigger (protecting – environmental care) – are among the 80 listed in Exhibit 1.1.

Though only a fraction of possible thousands, the 80 job titles and the service areas into which they are grouped provide both an insight into what local government is about and a demonstration of its scale and diversity. They also raise a couple of points on which we shall expand in later chapters. First, only a small minority of the jobs fit the desk-based, back-office, paper-shuffling stereotype that 'local government' seems often to conjure up

Exhibit 1.1 Six major service areas of local government

The 6 areas + key careers	Examples of job titles
BUILDING YOUR COMMUNITY	
Architecture, surveying	Architect, quantity surveyor, estates surveyor
Building, construction	Builder, building control officer, electrician, plumber
Housing	Homeless persons officer, hostel manager
Facilities maintenance	Caretaker, cleaning supervisor, CCTV operator
Finance	Benefits officer, council tax officer
CARING FOR YOUR COMMUNITY	
Care of children and young people	Substance misuse worker, outdoor education worker
Care of elderly people	Day care officer, elderly people's warden
Health	Mental health worker, occupational therapist
Social work	Residential social worker, adoption fostering manager
Other social care	Disability care manager, employment adviser
EDUCATING YOUR COMMUNITY	
School and pre-school teaching	Nursery worker, consultant, teacher of deaf children
School – non-teaching	School secretary, cook, caretaker, lunchtime assistant
Advice and support	Classroom assistant, speech therapist, special needs officer
Information	Archivist, librarian, outreach information officer
ENTERTAINING YOUR COMMUNITY	
Facilities/operations	Sports facility manager, parks officer, catering manager
Front-line staff	Pool attendant, fitness instructor, museum assistant

→

in the public mind. Most involve the provision of a myriad of services, individually and collectively, to residents in the local community – services, moreover, that have a much more immediate and continuous impact on our lives than many so-called 'bigger' issues that make the national political headlines, as indeed we recognise. Rank ordering institutions that have the most impact on our daily lives, we put media at the top (63%), followed by local councils (50%), far ahead of the Westminster Parliament (19%) and the Cabinet (5%) (Hansard Society, 2010, p. 97).

Second, just below the line in Exhibit 1.1 that would include many of

Exhibit 1.1 continued

The 6 areas + key careers	Examples of job titles
ENTERTAINING YOUR COMMUNITY *continued*	
Leisure/sports development	Archaeologist, sports development officer, tourism officer
PROTECTING YOUR COMMUNITY	
Environmental care and conservation	Dog warden, gravedigger, tree officer
Environmental health	Pest control officer, port health officer
Trading standards	Markets officer, trading standards officer
Highways and maintenance	Traffic engineer, street lighting inspector
Waste management	Waste management officer, recycling officer
Planning and licensing	Development control officer, transport planner
Emergency services	Firefighter, scenes of crime officer
SUPPORTING YOUR COMMUNITY	
Administration, legal	Committee administrator, registrar, solicitor
Democratic services	Elections manager, scrutiny adviser
Development	Regeneration officer, inward investment officer
Finance	Revenues officer, fraud investigation officer
Front-line staff	Receptionist, interpreter, customer service adviser
Human resources	Equalities officer, industrial relations officer
IT	Graphic designer, web technician
Marketing	Internal communications officer, press and PR officer
Policy, research and review	Best Value officer, partnerships development officer

Main source: Improvement and Development Agency (IDeA); *career descriptions* from www.lgcareers.com/career-descriptions.

those much-maligned administrative jobs, there is an even more important line: democratic services. For, while the diversity of their service provision makes local authorities exceptional organisations, their uniqueness comes from being run and having their policies set by councillors who are elected by and democratically answerable to the users and beneficiaries of those services.

Nor, returning to Ambassador Seitz's critique, have these local authorities ever been uniform – except in the sense that our planet's whole land mass looks uniform if viewed from far enough away. 'Africa', we have had to learn, is not an undifferentiated continent of wars, starvation, disease and misery, but rather 53 countries, each with its particular blend of natural resources, terrain, history, economy, languages and form of government. Similarly, UK local government is the government of some 430 localities, and an institutionalised recognition of their widely varying characteristics – geographic, demographic, social, economic and, by no means least, political. Throughout this book we shall illustrate the differences that exist even among councils of the same type and of a similar size, and encourage you to discover the uniquenesses of your own councils, or what we term the microcosmos of local government.

As for being monotonous, the very suggestion is likely to raise a pitying, and self-pitying, smile from most of those working in or with local government in recent years. What area of the private sector, they would ask, has had to come to terms with as much change and upheaval on every front: privatisation and the outsourcing of services; Best Value, Comprehensive Performance Assessment (CPA) and Comprehensive Area Assessment (CAA); the introduction and almost instant abandonment of a 'poll tax', followed by a council tax and tax-capping; neighbourhood offices, one-stop shops, enabling councils, beacon councils, private finance initiatives, area-based initiatives, partnerships of every size and shape, inspectorates, e-government, performance indicators and league tables ... all against a backdrop of continuous financial constraint and the actual or threatened rearrangement of the country's whole local government structure.

'A hub of all information relating to local democracy'

If, notwithstanding its manifest importance to all our lives, local government has conveyed an image more insipid than inspiring, two principal offenders suggest themselves. First, we have seen a succession of national governments, of both main parties, 'enfeebling' local government – to use Seitz's phrase – through 'super-centralist' policies of control, direction and undue intervention. Local government itself, though, must take some responsibility for any paleness of its image. Partly out of an excessive nervousness of being accused of 'wasting local taxes', councils have too often failed to project themselves in such a way as to stimulate the awareness – let alone the interest or political support – of those they supposedly represent and serve. In fairness, this criticism is one that many of them have acknowledged and, in their differing ways, endeavoured to rectify. However, it is a regrettable commentary on their comparatively limited impact that central government has felt it necessary to try to impose on them a statutory duty to promote democracy and an understanding of the local government system.

The opening clauses of the all-embracing Local Democracy, Economic

Development and Construction Act 2009 required local authorities to publicise and explain their functions, their democratic arrangements and the various ways in which the public might be encouraged to participate more than they do at present. In short, local authorities should become 'a hub of all information available locally relating to local democracy', which you might suppose should have been a fairly central function all along.

As it happens, while modesty would prevent us claiming a 'hub' role, we would express the aims for the successive editions of this book in somewhat similar terms: to increase public understanding of our local government system by conveying, as directly as possible, a sense of its 'feel' and atmosphere. So who are our public?

We assume that most of our readers will not themselves have worked for any length of time in local government, and therefore that people's main local government experience will generally have been as customers, consumers, clients and citizens; perhaps also, to add a fifth C – as complainants. You may have had various more or less memorable contacts over the years with council officers and employees, and perhaps also with your local councillors. You will certainly be one, and probably several, of the following: council tax payers, education grant recipients, state school or college students, council house tenants, social services clients, library borrowers, sports and leisure centre users, pedestrians, bus travellers, car drivers, taxi riders, planning applicants or protesters, domestic refuse producers and so on. You are probably registered local electors, and possibly actual voters. Yet oddly, given this degree of personal involvement, you are likely to consider yourselves 'outsiders' in relation to the world of local government.

If so, then in this sense we also are outsiders. We are not employed in local government either; but we do work closely *with* local government. In various ways – through teaching and lecturing, research and consultancy – we are in virtually daily contact with local councils, their members and staff. A key part of our jobs involves trying to link together, or narrow the gap between, the 'academic' and 'practitioner' worlds of local government, and that is another facet of the task we have set ourselves in this book.

The classic 'problem' of UK local government is described, by Ben Page, Chief Executive of polling company Ipsos MORI, as people seeing politicians they don't quite trust, doing things they don't quite understand, and getting a direct bill for it. This book addresses Page's problem head-on. It will provide a factual grounding by introducing you to the most important 'things' about Britain's local government and, we hope, increasing your understanding of them. It will, particularly in Chapter 12, explain and set in context the 'bill' that all council tax payers receive each year. And, while we can't promise to increase your trust in local politicians, we will examine the kinds of people they are and some of the not always appreciated difficulties of the job they seek to do.

Exhibit 1.2 Local government's 'movers and shakers', 2008–10

(As judged by a panel convened in 2008 by the weekly journal, *Local Government Chronicle*.)

1 John HEALEY	Minister of State for Local Government (2007–9); succeeded by Rosie Winterton (Lab), then Grant Shapps (2010–).
2 Boris JOHNSON	Mayor of London (2008); MP for Henley-on-Thames (2001–8).
3 Sir Robert KERSLAKE	CE, Homes and Communities Agency – co-ordinating body for housing and regeneration in England ('Bob the Builder'); Formerly CE, Sheffield City Council (1997–2008); Permanent Secretary, DCLG (2010–).
4 Hazel BLEARS	Secretary of State for Communities and Local Government (2007–9); succeeded by John Denham, then Eric Pickles (13) (2010–).
5 Irene LUCAS	CE, Tyneside Metropolitan Borough Council (MBC) (2002–9) – introduced novel management techniques, including Japanese 'continuous improvement' *kaizen* philosophy to previously unfashionable local authority.
6 Sir Richard LEESE	Leader (Labour), Manchester City Council (1996–) – lost congestion charge referendum (December 2008), but oversaw city's extensive regeneration following 1996 IRA bomb devastation of central shopping area.
7 Sir Merrick COCKELL	Leader (Con), Kensington & Chelsea Royal Borough Council (RBC) (2000–) and Chair of London Councils – the co-ordinating body for London's local authorities.

$\rightarrow$

This reference to local politicians touches on a recent bet we had: whether, in a reputational ranking of the most significant or powerful people in this country's local government, those actually from the world of local government would be outnumbered by those on the national stage. In what we have already described as a highly centralised system, it was bound to be close, but, as shown in Exhibit 1.2, in 2008 local government edged it: seven current or former council leaders and two council chief executives, against three ministers, a shadow minister, and two national 'quangocrats' (see Ch. 9). As with all such listings, there are numerous qualifications to be made. Yes, it is date-specific, wholly subjective – including our own counting – and Anglocentric, a limitation that will be addressed particularly

Exhibit 1.2 continued

8 Rob WHITEMAN	CE, Barking & Dagenham London Borough Council – 'Most Improved Council, 2008'; former opera singer (and accountant), writer on public service modernisation; seen as local government visionary. Managing Director, LG Improvement and Development (formerly IDeA), (2010–).
9 Sir Simon MILTON	Deputy London Mayor for Policy and Planning (2008–); Formerly Leader (Con), Westminster City Council, and Chairman, Local Government Association (LGA) (2007–8).
10 Baroness Margaret EATON	Milton's successor as Conservative LGA Chairman (her preferred title); Formerly Leader, Bradford MBC (2000–6).
11 Beverley HUGHES	Minister of State for Children, Young People and Families (2005–10); Formerly Leader, Trafford MBC.
12 Steve BUNDRED	CE, Audit Commission body responsible for improving efficiency of local government in England and Wales (2003–10); Formerly Director, IDeA; Greater London Councillor (Lab).
13 Eric PICKLES	Shadow (Con) Secretary of State for Communities and Local Government (2007–9); Chairman of Conservative Party (2009–10), then Secretary of State, DCLG (2010–).
14 Sir Jeremy BEECHAM	Vice-Chairman (Lab), LGA, and former Chairman (1997–2004); Formerly Leader, Newcastle City Council (1977–94).
15 Lord HANNINGFIELD	Leader (Con), Essex County Council (2001–10); preceded Beecham as Chairman, LGA.

Notes: All serving Ministers were Labour; CE = Chief Executive.

in Chapter 6. But it usefully identifies some of the key institutions you will encounter in the book, and some of the names to look out for.

Your own microcosmos

We referred above to the microcosmos of local government: that, while understanding the 'big picture' is clearly important, appreciating how it works in the 'little world' of your own locality is no less so. A strong recommendation, therefore, is to make good use of the fact that you yourselves will, depending on where you live, be residents of at least one local council,

Exhibit 1.3 Test your own council's website

Two contrasting website monitors:

- Sitemorse – www.sitemorse.com
  Instantly accessible; produces monthly league tables of the technical
  performance of all councils plus other public and commercial sector
  organisations. Wholly automated monitoring is both good – the league
  tables can be fun, especially as councils change position dramatically
  (Birmingham up 409 places in September 2009!) – and bad, in that no
  specifically local government content is tested.

- SOCITM – Society of Information Technology Management
  The professionals – and they know it. Have assessed council websites since
  1999, present annual 'Better Connected' awards, and produce useful
  reports – sadly, member-restricted. Their assessment criteria are local-
  government-relevant and comprehensive, which means that their best
  (Excellent and Transactional) sites don't suddenly become bad; also that
  sites rated Excellent in 2009 are worth listing – and checking out:

  Allerdale BC   Barking and Dagenham LBC   Bristol City C
  East Sussex CC   North East Derbyshire DC   Salford City C
  South Tyneside MBC   Surrey CC.

A dozen test questions for any council site:

1 Is the site genuinely *transactional*, offering a wide range of easily accessible services, or still predominantly *promotional* – a souped-up, online
  brochure-cum-telephone directory?
2 Is there stuff clearly past its sell-by date?
3 Could you find your own councillor(s), using only your address or postcode – that is, if you didn't know the name of your ward?
4 Can you find any account of how your councillors spent their time on
  different aspects of council work over the past couple of months?
5 Is there a clear statement of which political party or parties control the
  council?
6 Is there a 'Where's the nearest?' facility covering a wide range of services,
  including those provided by other local bodies?
7 Does the A–Z of services list 'wheelie bins' or only 'refuse collection'?
  Could you find out which day your wheelie bin would be emptied simply
  by typing in your street name?
8 What information is available in what languages other than English?
9 Could you download useful maps of the council area?
10 Are committee papers – agendas, reports, minutes – available online?
11 Could you find details of how to complain to, or compliment, the council?
12 Could you find out who is the largest employer in the area, and what the
  current unemployment rate is in your ward?

and possibly two or three. These councils produce a mass of information about their services and activities. They may produce and circulate their own council newspaper or magazine, which, contrary to the assertions of the Newspaper Society's fierce campaign against them, are by no means all 'propaganda sheets'. Having criticised some councils for not communicating enough with their residents, we are not about to criticise them when they attempt to do so. Then, of course, there is one council communication you can be sure of receiving: your council tax demand and an accompanying summary of the budgets that produced it. More generally, there should be plenty of leaflets, brochures, pamphlets and other goodies available from your local town or county hall, and, if there aren't, why not ask: 'I understand you're the hub of all information relating to local democracy around here, so can I have some, please?'

Better still, all principal councils have their own websites, and there is no more effective way of finding out about both your own council and local government in general than by comparing these hugely assorted council sites (see Exhibit 1.3). There has been a steady overall improvement in these sites in recent years, but it is disappointing that the 2009 Society of Information Technology Management (SOCITM) survey still found a majority of councils failing to meet their criteria of acceptable transactional capabilities. There are also sites that seem – to us, anyway – more concerned with the latest technological widgets and gadgets than with the site's usability for the average resident. By contrast, Allerdale's site, rated by SOCITM the best district council site of 2009, was 'a joy to use' – with its visual clarity, user-friendly signposting, good range of interactive services, 'Allerdalecompare.com' homepage video, interesting news items, links to Facebook, Twitter and YouTube, and so much more. Test it, and see how your council's site compares.

Our guess is that, after no more than 30 minutes' browsing through one or more council websites in this way, even if you started with no previous knowledge at all about local government, you would be able to piece together a reasonable preliminary impression of what kind of institution a local council is (see Exhibit 1.4). It is far from a comprehensive definition,

Exhibit 1.4 Your local council

Your local council is:

- a large, geographically-defined, multi-functional organisation,
- pursuing a variety of social, political, economic and environmental objectives,
- either through the direct provision
- or the commissioning, indirect funding, regulation or monitoring of
- a very extensive range of services to its local community.

but it is a useful jumping-off point for the more extended discussion of these matters in Chapter 3.

Organisation of the book

Which brings us to the way that this book is organised. It is divided into three parts. Part 1 is concerned with the *basics* of local government, the aim being to provide you with a good foundation knowledge of the purposes and origins of local – and regional – government, its structures, functions and finances, and the context in which it operates.

Part 2 looks at the *dynamics* that drive the system. What makes local government 'tick'? The focus shifts to the people and institutions that make decisions, provide services, and seek to influence the conditions and quality of life of their locality. We become concerned more directly with politics, in order to understand how various local government players perceive their situation and attempt to realise their objectives.

Part 3 turns to the agenda of *change*. The party talk – from all sides – in the run-up to the 2010 election was, on the one hand, of 'localism' and 'decentralising power to local communities', and, on the other, of the severity of the cuts in public services, employment and investment that would be inevitable, whatever government was voted in. Put the two themes together, and it looked certain that the scale and pace of change to which local government has accustomed itself in recent decades would be at least maintained in the new one. Confirmation came with a vengeance in the October 2010 Comprehensive Spending Review, with the Coalition Government's announcement that councils could face a 27% cut in grant funding in the period to 2014–15 and job losses of 250,000. The book's final chapter therefore looks both at the Coalition's immediate plans for local government – financial and otherwise – and at some of the more radical and longer-term ideas being floated in other quarters. One last thing: remember our dedicated website (**www.palgrave.com/politics/wilson**). As noted in the Preface, this is where you will find 'Guides to further reading' for each chapter as well as relevant updating information.

Chapter 2

Themes and Issues in Local Government

Introduction – follow those headlines!

This chapter introduces some of the main current themes and issues in UK local government and the key defining characteristics of the local government system. The latter, not surprisingly, are essentially unchanged from the book's previous edition. Some of the themes and issues, however, have changed significantly, and the same will happen during the lifetime of this edition. We start, therefore, by emphasising the benefit of following local government stories and developments in the national and local media. If, for example, you had been on media watch during the autumn of 2009, the headlines that might have caught your eye would almost certainly have included some of those shown in Exhibit 2.1.

Constant change – with more to come

Our headlines illustrate several key themes of contemporary local government in the UK, starting with its state of apparently perpetual motion. In almost every aspect it continued in the 'noughties', as during the 1980s and 1990s, to be subject to change, much of it of the most fundamental kind. As we describe in Chapters 4 and 5, even the total number of councils has changed – or, more specifically, fallen – in every decade since the 1960s, and this trend continued into the new millennium.

The county, district, unitary, metropolitan and London borough councils that form the statutory structure of UK local government are officially termed *principal councils*, to distinguish them from the usually very much smaller *local councils* – the parish, town and community councils that are to be found only in certain parts of the country. This book is largely about the former group, and, when it first appeared in 1994, there were 540 of them – already a very small number by international standards (see Exhibit 14.3). By the second edition in 1998 the number had fallen to 468. One in every seven had disappeared, in the Conservative Government's transformation of the two-tier, county and district council structures in Scotland, Wales and parts of England into single-tier or unitary systems.

Exhibit 2.1 Selected news headlines, Autumn 2009

1 CIVIL SERVANTS PUSH FOR FURTHER REORGANISATION
Department for Communities and Local Government (DCLG) civil servants tell a private meeting of council leaders that, on efficiency grounds, 'two-tier local government is unsustainable' and further unitary reorganisation is likely to prove necessary.

2 LEEDS TROLLEY BUSES DEPEND ON MINISTERIAL APPROVAL
Funding for Leeds City Council's plan to bring electric trolley buses back to Britain's streets after forty years' absence is fully covered by the Council and the Regional Transport Board, but cannot go ahead without ministerial approval. [Approval received March 2010.]

3 BARNET ADOPTS easyJet MODEL
The London Conservative council plans to provide only minimum levels of service, handing half its budget to residents to choose, as with budget airlines, which 'additional' services they wish to pay for.

4 NOTTINGHAM REFUSED OWN DRINK BAN
The City Council's proposed by-law to impose a total ban on drinking alcohol in the city's parks and public places is squashed by DCLG civil servants on the grounds that public consumption of alcohol is controlled through national legislation.

5 SNP TO SCRAP THATCHER'S 'RIGHT TO BUY'
Facing a severe shortage of affordable rented housing, the Scottish National Party Government in Edinburgh plans to abolish Mrs Thatcher's 'Right to Buy' policy for new council tenants, who will no longer be able to buy their homes at discounted rates.

6 COUNCILS TAKE GOVERNMENT TO COURT ON HOUSING U-TURN
A consortium of councils applies for Judicial Review of the government's decision to withdraw funding from their Decent Homes programmes, after it had already been allocated to housing authorities and promised to selected tenants.

→

The Labour Government, apparently equally convinced that bigger necessarily means more efficient and therefore better, continued the trend towards large-scale unitaries. From 2009, nine new English unitary councils replaced seven counties and 37 districts, reducing the UK total to 434 – but only temporarily. Plans to streamline Northern Ireland's already single-tier structure from 26 to 11 district councils were abandoned in 2010 because of disagreement within the NI Executive, but there was early talk by Coalition Government ministers of further mergers of Welsh councils by 2016. In England too, even if, with a General Election approaching, politicians were

Exhibit 2.1 continued

7 BRIGHTON'S BRA APPEAL
In the first four months of Brighton and Hove Council's recycling initiative of bright-pink bra collection banks, 13,000 bras were donated. The bras are sent to developing countries by a recycling company, which also gives a donation to the town's Breast Care Centre.

8 COUNCILS LOSE PLANNING POWERS TO QUANGO
To streamline the planning process, a ministerially-appointed quango, the Infrastructure Planning Commission, takes over councils' decision powers on major commercial development proposals, as well as national projects such as wind farms and power stations. [Abolished 2010 – see p. 142.]

9 UP TO 95% OF LOCAL SPENDING OUTSIDE DEMOCRATIC CONTROL
First results from the government's Total Place efficiency programme reveal that, of the £7,000 per person spent annually on local public services such as health, education and social care, as little as 5% is controlled by local councillors in some areas.

10 COUNCILS TAKE OVER 16–19 COMMISSIONING
From 2010, local authorities take over the Learning and Skills Council's responsibility for commissioning and funding 16–19 education and training. The change involves a transfer of £7 billion of public money and nearly 1,000 LSC staff.

11 COUNCILLORS SET UP BANK
Using its power to promote local economic well-being, Essex County Council goes into partnership with Spanish Santander Bank to set up 'Banking on Essex', to enable small and medium-sized businesses to access loans of up to £50,000 during the recession.

12 TAXPAYERS' CHRISTMAS CASHBACK
Ealing council tax payers receive £50 cashback from the Council, timed to coincide with the Christmas shopping period. If they spend it locally, there is also free parking in council car parks and a council-backed 'SP£ND LOCAL' discount scheme in shops.

reluctant to address the unitary elephant in the room and risk committing themselves to anything potentially controversial (see Figure 2.1), civil servants were clear that they didn't see the push towards ever fewer and larger councils having ended (see Exhibit 2.1, Item 1). They were right: with the election hardly over, Babergh and Mid-Suffolk DCs announced their intention to merge by 2013, subject to a local referendum.

If, as a reader, you think all this structural tinkering might make for confusion, uncertainty and low morale, just imagine yourself as a council worker, not knowing whether your employing authority will still be in

Figure 2.1 Cartoon – *The unitary elephant in the room*

Source: Local Government Chronicle, 21 August 2008.

existence in a couple of years' time, let alone what powers and service responsibilities it might or might not have. Generally, the picture since the Second World War has been one of local government losing services either to central government or to non-elected special-purpose bodies. In the 1940s, it was gas, electricity and hospitals; in the 1970s, upper-tier criminal courts, water and sewerage, ambulance and other health services; in the 1980s, bus services, polytechnics and higher education colleges; and, more recently, sixth-form education (2002) and magistrates' courts (2005). But the traffic hasn't been entirely one-way. Since the 1990s, for example, local government has been responsible for implementing the growing tranche of community care legislation, and, as we compiled this book's previous selection of news headlines in 2005, councils were taking over liquor licensing powers from magistrates and youth advice from the government's Connexions service (Wilson and Game, 2006, p. 12). This time we see that, while councillors' longstanding involvement in major planning decisions was lost to one new quasi-governmental organisation – itself axed within a year by the Coalition Government – they took back most of those from another, the Learning and Skills Council (see Exhibit 2.1, Items 8 and 10). Then, in the little-forecast but most momentous changes of all, the new government's first NHS White Paper (Department of Health, 2010) announced the abolition of Primary Care Trusts by 2013 and the transfer of their public health improvement functions to local councils, who would employ Directors of Public Health and establish 'health and wellbeing boards' to join up the commissioning of local NHS services, social care and health improvement functions.

Non-elected local government and 'local governance'

There is a trend in much of this functional change to which we have already alluded: the spread of non-elected or indirectly elected local government. It is not in itself a new phenomenon. The original National Health Service (NHS) structure was non-elected; similarly the post-1974 self-governing primary care, foundation, ambulance and other NHS trusts. So too were the New Town Development Corporations and the Scottish and Welsh development agencies, on which the English regional development agencies are modelled.

However, the scale of non-elected government has increased enormously since the 1970s, frequently at the *direct expense* of elected local councils. Under national governments of both major parties, service responsibilities were removed from local authorities and given mainly to single-purpose government-appointed agencies. Inner city development went to Urban Development Corporations (UDCs). Regeneration of particularly deprived estates was taken over by Housing Action Trusts (HATs). Youth training passed to Training and Enterprise Councils (TECs), then, as noted above, to Learning and Skills Councils (LSCs), before completing its journey back to local government. The funding of polytechnics, colleges and Grant Maintained Schools all went to independent bodies, even though some of their actual funding still came from local authorities.

These single- or special-purpose bodies are conventionally known as *local quangos* – quasi-autonomous non-governmental organisations – although purists will argue that *quasi-governmental* is in most cases probably a more accurate description of their function. In fact, as we shall see in Chapter 9, the term 'quango' has long since ceased to have any precise or widely agreed meaning. But it does offer a useful shorthand way of referring to an important and undisputed phenomenon: the radical transformation of the state, nationally and locally, into an increasingly fragmented network of single-purpose bodies, boards, agencies, voluntary and even private sector organisations mixed in with more traditional elected governments. In the local government world, depending on exactly how they are counted, there are perhaps some 5,000 of these local quangos, run by a 'quangocracy' of over 70,000 board members – in both cases, several times the numbers of elected councils and councillors.

The measurable dimensions of this transformed local state were becoming evident as the Labour Government's Total Place initiative unfolded (in Exhibit 2.1, Item 9). A new name, if hardly a revolutionary idea, Total Place was launched by the Department for Communities and Local Government

(DCLG), with the aim first of mapping how – by which bodies and on which services – all the public money coming into an area is spent. Then, by working together more co-ordinatedly, these various spending bodies should be able to achieve their often complex policy goals – better-integrated services for under-5s, children or older people; more affordable housing; tackling alcohol and drug abuse or obesity – more efficiently (see Exhibit 9.4).

Even the earliest pilot study results, unrepresentative though they may have been, were undeniably interesting. In Cumbria, for example, just over £7 billion of public money was spent in 2006–7, or £14,200 per person (Leadership Centre for Local Government, 2009). Nearly three-quarters of this sum was spent by central government departments, greatest spending areas being economic development, 'social protection' – pensions, benefits, allowances – and health. A quarter was spent by Cumbria-based bodies, including 11% by the County Council and 4% by the then six district councils: somewhat higher proportions than suggested in News Item 9, but still distinctly modest. The County Council was the highest local spender, but between them the Primary Care Trust, two NHS Hospital Trusts and the Ambulance Service Trust followed quite close behind. Taxation was even more unbalanced, with 94% of the tax paid by Cumbrian residents going straight to the Treasury, and just 6% to elected local authorities.

So fundamental have these changes been, and so fragmented has public service provision become, that political scientists claim that local government has evolved into something termed *local 'governance'*. This concept is felt to describe more effectively the extensive network of public, voluntary and private sector bodies that are nowadays involved in local policy-making and service delivery (see, for example, Rhodes, 1997; Stoker, 2000, 2004a; Goss, 2001; John, 2001; Leach and Percy-Smith, 2001; Denters and Rose, 2005; Flinders, 2008).

With one of us working in a 'Local Governance Research Unit', it would be perverse to take issue seriously with this analysis, and we don't. Indeed, we use it. But we have not been tempted to re-title or fundamentally re-focus the book. While giving plenty of attention to so-called non-governmental organisations – particularly but not exclusively in Chapter 9 – this particular book's focus remains *elected local government*, which itself remains, as democratically accountable service provider and major resource holder, at the very heart of any network or process of local governance.

Breaking up and making up: partnership working

Long ago, when we were young, there was a tear-jerking Neil Sedaka song, 'Breaking up Is Hard to Do'. It wasn't, of course, and it certainly isn't if you're a national government with a healthy parliamentary majority at your disposal. You can easily pass legislation to break up – or, in public management jargon, disaggregate – parts of multi-purpose local authorities into semi-independent, single-purpose bodies in the way we have just described.

Having disaggregated, though, you soon find that there are complex policy problems – neighbourhood regeneration, crime and disorder, integrated care for children or older people, local sustainable development – which require the people, skills, knowledge and experience that are no longer located within the same organisation, but in a whole range of now disconnected ones. So they have to be brought together again – in the jargon, 'reconfigured' or 'joined up' – in *partnerships*. Partnership working (see Exhibit 2.1, Items 7 and 11; also Chapter 9) has become a central feature of today's local government, and councils may well find themselves working *with* and *through* external organisations that now deliver the services for which they themselves were once responsible.

Like motherhood and apple pie, the partnership principle seems unfaultable. For the government department responsible for local government it has become almost literally an article of faith and in 2009 headed its web page on Local Strategic Partnerships:

> Communities and Local Government believes more gets done if people in an area work together. They could be community and faith groups, the council, police, fire and rescue services, charity groups, businesses, schools, health bodies and more. Pooling experience and expertise, they can understand local people, places and problems. And make sure the right actions are taken and right services delivered.

In this ideal world, 2 + 2 generally equals at least 5, if not 6 or 7; never 3. In practice, bringing together people from bodies representing this breadth of interests, able to speak authoritatively on behalf of those interests and ensure the delivery of any decisions agreed, is exceedingly difficult, and inevitably costly. When it works well, it's like the Ronettes, the great girl group also from the early 1960s, sang: 'The best part of breaking up is making up.' But if partnerships and relationships are tough for a couple of teenagers, they can be a whole lot tougher for a couple of dozen, often competing, organisations.

Diminished, but not eliminated, discretion

As some powers have been removed from local government, those retained have been subject to greater national direction, oversight and control. Switchback changes in local government finance, particularly during the 1980s and early 1990s, were accompanied by the imposition of tighter conditions – government ministers and civil servants becoming more

22

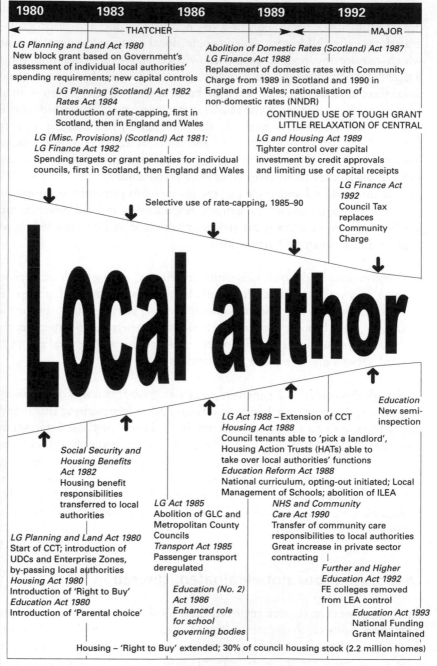

Exhibit 2.2 The funnel of local authority discretion

| 1980 | 1983 | 1986 | 1989 | 1992 |

◄──────────────THATCHER──────────────►◄──────MAJOR──────

LG Planning and Land Act 1980
New block grant based on Government's
assessment of individual local authorities'
spending requirements; new capital controls

Abolition of Domestic Rates (Scotland) Act 1987
LG Finance Act 1988
Replacement of domestic rates with Community
Charge from 1989 in Scotland and 1990 in
England and Wales; nationalisation of
non-domestic rates (NNDR)

LG Planning (Scotland) Act 1982
Rates Act 1984
Introduction of rate-capping, first in
Scotland, then in England and Wales

CONTINUED USE OF TOUGH GRANT
LITTLE RELAXATION OF CENTRAL

LG (Misc. Provisions) (Scotland) Act 1981:
LG Finance Act 1982
Spending targets or grant penalties for individual
councils, first in Scotland, then England and Wales

LG and Housing Act 1989
Tighter control over capital
investment by credit approvals
and limiting use of capital receipts

LG Finance Act 1992
Council Tax
replaces
Community
Charge

Selective use of rate-capping, 1985–90

*Social Security and
Housing Benefits
Act 1982*
Housing benefit
responsibilities
transferred to local
authorities

LG Act 1988 – Extension of CCT
Housing Act 1988
Council tenants able to 'pick a landlord',
Housing Action Trusts (HATs) able to
take over local authorities' functions
Education Reform Act 1988
National curriculum, opting-out initiated; Local
Management of Schools; abolition of ILEA

Education
New semi-
inspection

LG Act 1985
Abolition of GLC and
Metropolitan County
Councils
Transport Act 1985
Passenger transport
deregulated

*NHS and Community
Care Act 1990*
Transfer of community care
responsibilities to local authorities
Great increase in private sector
contracting

LG Planning and Land Act 1980
Start of CCT; introduction of
UDCs and Enterprise Zones,
by-passing local authorities
Housing Act 1980
Introduction of 'Right to Buy'
Education Act 1980
Introduction of 'Parental choice'

*Education (No. 2)
Act 1986*
Enhanced role
for school
governing bodies

*Further and Higher
Education Act 1992*
FE colleges removed
from LEA control

Education Act 1993
National Funding
Grant Maintained

Housing – 'Right to Buy' extended; 30% of council housing stock (2.2 million homes)

Source: Adapted from Hollis *et al.* (1990), p. 22.

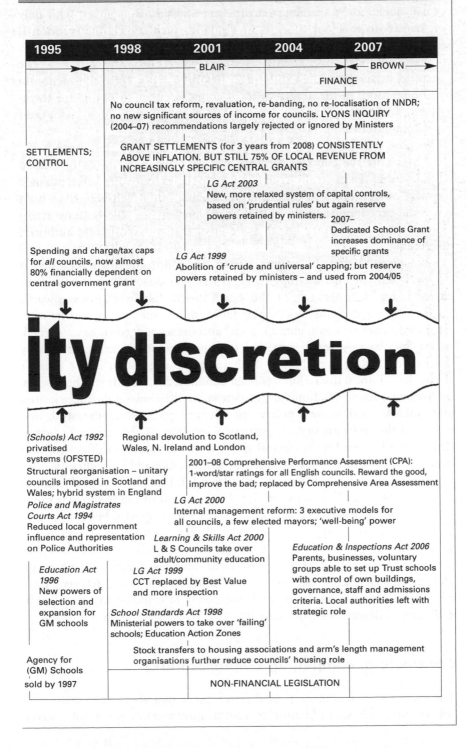

1995	1998	2001	2004	2007

BLAIR — ►◄— BROWN ►

FINANCE

No council tax reform, revaluation, re-banding, no re-localisation of NNDR; no new significant sources of income for councils. LYONS INQUIRY (2004–07) recommendations largely rejected or ignored by Ministers

SETTLEMENTS; CONTROL

GRANT SETTLEMENTS (for 3 years from 2008) CONSISTENTLY ABOVE INFLATION. BUT STILL 75% OF LOCAL REVENUE FROM INCREASINGLY SPECIFIC CENTRAL GRANTS

LG Act 2003
New, more relaxed system of capital controls, based on 'prudential rules' but again reserve powers retained by ministers. 2007–
Dedicated Schools Grant increases dominance of specific grants

Spending and charge/tax caps for *all* councils, now almost 80% financially dependent on central government grant

LG Act 1999
Abolition of 'crude and universal' capping; but reserve powers retained by ministers – and used from 2004/05

ity discretion

(Schools) Act 1992
privatised systems (OFSTED)
Structural reorganisation – unitary councils imposed in Scotland and Wales; hybrid system in England

Police and Magistrates Courts Act 1994
Reduced local government influence and representation on Police Authorities

Education Act 1996
New powers of selection and expansion for GM schools

Agency for (GM) Schools sold by 1997

Regional devolution to Scotland, Wales, N. Ireland and London

2001–08 Comprehensive Performance Assessment (CPA): 1-word/star ratings for all English councils. Reward the good, improve the bad; replaced by Comprehensive Area Assessment

LG Act 2000
Internal management reform: 3 executive models for all councils, a few elected mayors; 'well-being' power

Learning & Skills Act 2000
L & S Councils take over adult/community education

LG Act 1999
CCT replaced by Best Value and more inspection

School Standards Act 1998
Ministerial powers to take over 'failing' schools; Education Action Zones

Education & Inspections Act 2006
Parents, businesses, voluntary groups able to set up Trust schools with control of own buildings, governance, staff and admissions criteria. Local authorities left with strategic role

Stock transfers to housing associations and arm's length management organisations further reduce councils' housing role

NON-FINANCIAL LEGISLATION

directly involved in declaring what *they* calculate each individual local council ought to be spending on different services. Remember, with only just over 350 principal councils in England, such central intervention is feasible in a way that would simply be technically impossible in the much smaller-scale local government systems of other European countries. The outcome, as suggested in Exhibit 2.2, has been a perceptible reduction in local discretion, in the ability of local councils either to decide for them-selves or to finance effectively services they would wish to provide for their local communities.

We shall encounter later many of the specific entries in Exhibit 2.2. We shall also note the contrast between this centralising trend in the United Kingdom and the generally decentralising policies that were being pursued by most other European central governments, but which here have been more the exception than the rule. For the present we merely draw atten-tion to the general shape of what we label the 'funnel of local authority discretion'.

Like a funnel, there is a tapering from one end to the other, modified at the neck end by our attempt to represent the deliberately dualistic, or carrot-and-stick, approach of the Blair/Brown Administrations towards local government. Some modest relaxation of central control and ministe-rial interference was available for local authorities judged to have 'earned' it, but increasingly tough remedial treatment could be expected by any 'backsliders'. Note that there is deliberately no suggestion in the funnel's shape that all local discretion has been eliminated. Councils still have some opportunity, Exhibit 2.2 implies, to determine their own political priorities and embark on their own policy initiatives in response to the needs and wishes of the residents in their particular localities. They may, with justifi-cation, feel hemmed in by central government dictates and directives, but they have by no means been robbed of all initiative and individuality.

Proof of the latter assertion may be found in just about any selection of news headlines, and ours, in Exhibit 2.1, is no exception. Examples range from the momentous and contentious to the almost quirky, but Leeds' trol-ley buses, Barnet's easyJet service model, Brighton's bra appeal, banking in Essex, and Ealing residents' Christmas cashback all have one thing in common. They are all examples of local councils deciding freely to do something differently from how it was being done before, different from what other councils are doing, and *not* merely in response to some central government demand or requirement.

Contracting, competing, commissioning

The picture of contemporary local government that should be emerging is one of inevitable subordination to central government, but hardly craven subservience: councils with perhaps less freedom of action than previously, but far from emasculated.

As for the future, the goal that the Conservative Governments of the 1980s sometimes appeared to have in mind was expressible as a pun. The combination of the government's removal of some functions from the control of local authorities and its encouragement of the contracting out of others to the private sector led to the coining of the term: the *Contracting Authority*. Both in size and in the nature of its work, the local authority of the future, it was suggested, would be a contracting one! Humour, suggested poet and dramatist, T. S. Eliot, is a way of saying something serious, and so it is here. The terminology has changed – 'contracting out' having largely been displaced by 'outsourcing' and 'commissioning' – but the credo of competition ushered in by the Thatcher Government's Compulsory Competitive Tendering (CCT) has long since become part of the day-to-day life of local government.

Both Cs were defining features of CCT, which required councils to put out to tender, or competitive bidding, increasing numbers of the services that most of them had previously provided themselves, using their own employees, equipment and facilities. The compulsion, therefore, was to compete – not necessarily to contract out, which would only happen if the most competitive bid (defined quite simply as the lowest) came from some outside company or organisation, rather than from the council's own workforce.

CCT and similar competition-driven measures of the Thatcher/Major Governments were opposed at the time by Labour, both in Parliament and in local government, where, by the 1990s, it was by far the strongest party political force. When a New Labour Government was elected in 1997, therefore, there had to be changes – but of policy, more than of philosophy. CCT went, but in its place came Best Value service provision – the legal requirement placed on councils to deliver a continuous improvement in the standard and efficiency of their services, bringing in outside contractors as appropriate. The process was driven by the four Cs, with councils expected to *Challenge* the way in which their services were currently being provided; *Compare* their performance with that of others; *Consult* extensively on a plan to deliver continuous service improvements; and *Compete,* wherever practicable, with other potential service providers in implementing that plan. With only a slight adjustment of political emphasis, the Contracting Authority had become the *Competitive Authority* – or, to express what was happening in another way, the *Enabling Authority.*

Traditionally, UK local authorities, in addition to being the elected governments of their localities, were – and were seen as being – large-scale providers and representative of quality services. From the late nineteenth century through most of the twentieth, national governments passed legislation requiring or permitting the provision of all kinds of public services, mainly through the auspices of *other* bodies – and most significant by far of these other bodies were local authorities. Now, however, with some of those services already lost to the private sector or varying single-purpose institutions, and most of the remainder exposed to the force of competition, local authorities' future role, it was argued, would be less as service *providers* and much more as service *enablers*. They might retain the ulti-mate responsibility for service provision, but, rather than do everything themselves with their own directly employed workforces, they would stim-ulate, facilitate, support, regulate, influence and thereby *enable* other agen-cies and organisations to act on their behalf (see, for example, Leach *et al.*, 1996).

As will already have become apparent, the language of local government changes at least as fast as the phenomena it describes. The discipline of working with the '4 Cs' prompted the recognition that there was a great deal more to local government procurement than the cross-departmental purchase of paperclips, and a great deal more to be gained from a seriously strategic approach to the procurement of services as well as commodities. At which point the passive-sounding 'enabling authority' began to be supplanted, terminologically, by the more pro-active, market-challenging *Commissioning Authority*.

The Commissioning Authority

The importance of local government realising, in all senses, the full poten-tial of its commissioning function is hard to overstate at a time when the whole public sector faces the harshest of foreseeable futures. The arithmetic is compelling. The revenue expenditure of English local authorities in 2009 was roughly £120 billion, of which just over half went on employees' pay and just under half on the procurement of goods and services. Local govern-ment employees are demonstrably the 'poor relations' of the public sector, with nearly 60% in 2008 earning below £17,000 p.a., or barely two-thirds of the national average full-time salary. If major 'efficiency savings' are to be found, it would seem to be in everyone's interests if they came wherever possible from the procurement, rather than the employee, chunk of the budget.

Traditionally, as we shall see in Chapter 7, local government has organ-ised itself in ways that undoubtedly have merits, but optimising procure-ment efficiency has not been one of them. Structures vary from one authority to another, and were organised functionally – education, social services, housing, environmental services. Joint-working across these substantially self-contained service areas did not come naturally, even when more of them were provided metaphorically under the same roof. These functional units – the demand side of the procurement relationship – each had its own procurement practices, largely unrelated one to another, and all largely unrelated to the *modi operandi* of private sector suppliers. Almost all service departments require managed services, professional services, ICT services, and products such as office supplies. Yet, until quite recently, little of this purchasing was even co-ordinated, let alone strategically planned to achieve defined policy outcomes. Enormous amounts of money were paid to suppliers, markets were created, but, in the carefully understated phrasing of management consultants, PricewaterhouseCoopers, many of these markets operated in 'a sub-optimal way' (DCLG, 2006a, p. 21).

The Labour Government's conception of the future role of local government had been outlined in 2004 in its so-called *local:vision* document (ODPM, 2004a). Local authorities would remain democratically accountable providers of high quality services. But in future they should provide a more explicit strategic leadership for their localities, establishing partnership arrangements for the delivery of integrated, outcome-defined services in which the local authority would act 'as broker, facilitator and commissioner, as well as provider' (DCLG, 2006, p. 65). The commissioning role in particular would require the development of almost entirely new skills and mindsets: re-focusing from the delivery of 'bricks and mortar' services to how collectively to secure improved community outcomes; investing in the development of strategic commissioning skills of both officers and councillors; negotiating with partners and suppliers with the aim of shaping and leading markets, rather than responding to them (DCLG, 2006, pp. 65–7).

More private sector jargon, more emphasis on service provision rather than local democracy, more elevation of management over politics. As even this brief account has shown, local government has indeed been transformed since the 1970s, and in ways that many of the most fervent supporters of local democracy, including councillors, find unappealing. Elsewhere in this book they are likely to find some support for their instincts. There is nothing democratically admirable, though, in tradition for its own sake, in poor quality management, in inefficient service provision, or in an organisation not using its economic clout to its best advantage.

Choice and quality – 'Customer First'

While the concept of the commissioning authority certainly emanated from central government, that is far from true of all recent change in local government. In recent years councils have examined their performance record more self-critically, looking for ways of improving it and enhancing their public image. They have sought to develop – to quote two now rather dated 'buzz' phrases – a public service orientation, or customer service culture.

Exhibit 2.3 101 – the (temporarily?) sad saga of a SNEN

What is 101?

Nothing to do with George Orwell, *1984*, or even the BBC. It's a SNEN – a Single Non-Emergency Number provided by your local council and police service, available 24/7 to deal with non-emergency crime, policing and community safety issues. It is modelled on the 311 number that operates in many US and Canadian cities and gives non-emergency access to all municipal services – from 'dead animal pick-up' to 'emergency food' (yes, same number, but different services!). (For an example, Google 'City of Chicago 311'.)

And we've followed America's lead?

Not exactly. The Home Office was interested and ran some pilot projects in five areas of England and Wales. After the pilots, a national 101 service would, according to the Civil Service, be 'rolled out across England and Wales by 2008'. Calls would be free from public call boxes; otherwise they would cost a flat-rate 10p. Citizens' confidence in non-emergency public services would be increased and the burden of unnecessary 999 calls reduced.

The pilots were deemed successful. The Home Office reckoned they improved public access to and confidence in local community safety services, and helped local police and councils to target their resources more effectively (*Hansard*, 19 February 2008, Col. 580W). (Google '101, the Single Non-Emergency Number' for a pretty PowerPoint presentation showing what might have been.)

So something happened?

Yes, the government changed its mind and, while temporarily maintaining the 101 telephony infrastructure, withdrew its local funding support. The Northumberland/Tyne and Wear and Leicester services were withdrawn, leaving in 2009 only Hampshire/Isle of Wight and Sheffield, though, thanks to the Assembly for Wales, the Cardiff pilot was extended to the whole of Wales.

Is it one more good idea lost?

Difficult to say. If it's to be really effective, it has to cover more than policing services and be a genuinely Single Number – 101 across the whole country, so that it's easy to publicise and remember and doesn't run alongside other non-emergency numbers for individual councils and constabularies. There are far worse ideas around for an incoming government to consider.

Too often in the past, councils will now concede, they acted as what essentially they were: unchallenged local monopolies providing services *to* – rather than *for* or *with* – a largely captive public. Rarely would service recipients be asked about the type, quantity or quality of service they required, or were prepared, through their own local taxes, to finance. Rarely, in short, were they treated as customers: people able to make choices, with the right to the information on which to base those choices, the right of redress if dissatisfied with the service received, and the right to go to other providers.

Local council services generally were managed professionally, delivered competently, and tolerably efficient. But the emphasis tended to be on quantity rather than quality, with relatively little consideration being given to issues of flexibility, variety and consumer choice. Nowadays, the pendulum has swung almost to the other extreme, with anybody using any kind of council service being referred to as a 'customer', as if they were making the choice to purchase it at an economic price from *their* local authority shop, rather than any of the others to which they might have taken their business. It has undoubtedly led to far greater communication with and responsiveness to users, but it does risk blurring the many very different relationships that most people have with the range of local services they use. Some services are 'universal' (street cleaning, refuse collection), some demand-led (information, advice), some defined by eligibility or assessed need (council housing, day nursery places, most social services), and some imposed through legislation (education, trading standards, mental health services). A local resident may be a consumer of all of these, but in relatively few cases are they in fact a 'customer' in the traditional, choice-exercising sense of the word.

Notwithstanding the linguistic imprecision, most councils today deploy a wide range of 'Customer First' initiatives to improve the quality of their services and communications: neighbourhood offices, 'one-stop shops', call centres (sometimes 24-hour), transactional websites, Facebook fan pages, blogs, 'Twitterings', podcasts, YouTube videos, e-newsletters, public internet kiosks, complaints hotlines, council newspapers, public attitude surveys, discussion forums, public question times. But regrettably, no SNEN (see Exhibit 2.3). As we suggested in Chapter 1 in relation to council websites, it's worth looking out for what your own councils are doing. In doing so, you might ask yourself whether, in putting the 'Customer First', they might not, at least subconsciously, be putting the 'Citizen Second': overlooking the fact their residents are also members of a local political community, with rights and duties relating to political participation and choice as well to service consumption. It is a rhetorical question to which we shall return.

The present system – defining characteristics

Having identified some of the principal themes of modern-day local government, we now pause for some stocktaking. If the world of local government is changing as fundamentally as we suggest, what is it changing *from*? What, in broad introductory terms, does the present system look like? What are its main features and rationale? In the remainder of this chapter we introduce some of the key defining characteristics of the UK's local government system.

Local government, not local administration

We should start with a vital distinction, and explain why we have so far been using, unquestioningly, the term 'local government', rather than 'local administration'. It will serve too as a further introduction: to why the university department for which one of us works is called the Institute of Local *Government* Studies (INLOGOV), and not Local *Administrative* Studies.

All countries of any significant size find it necessary to decentralise some of the basic functions of government. Some do so much more extensively and more enthusiastically than others. Switzerland, for example – albeit an exceptional one – has never had a national Ministry of Education or a Ministry of Health. The Swiss decentralise these services entirely to the control of local authorities, and these are very much smaller authorities than those in Britain.

When central governments decentralise, they may choose to do so in different ways and to different degrees:

- *Administrative decentralisation, or delegation*
  They may delegate purely administrative decision-making to dependent field offices of a central ministry. All major policy decisions will continue to be made centrally, but the service will be delivered and routine administrative decisions made by locally based but centrally employed civil servants. The most obvious example in Britain is the Department for Work and Pensions' (DWP) Jobcentre Plus, whose *cash payments* to the sick, disabled and unemployed are made from local offices of the DWP, or in Northern Ireland the Social Security Agency. They are thus largely separated – unlike the practice in many countries – from the local authority social *services* provided to many of the same people.
- *Functional decentralisation*
  Second, central government can create semi-independent agencies to run specific services. Here, the most obvious example is the NHS, with its current structure of strategic health authorities and trusts, overseen by boards of appointed and nominated members. It may look a little like the structure of local councils, and in many countries the health service is a fully integrated part of the local government system. But, though they work closely with and are scrutinised by local authorities, Britain's health authorities and trusts are quite separate: funded by and ultimately accountable to central government, and thus part of the growing 'quangocracy' referred to earlier, though a greater role for local government in

public health, adult care and health scrutiny was promised in the Coalition Government's early Health White Paper *Equity and Excellence: Liberating the NHS.*

- *Political decentralisation, or devolution*

Third, central government can devolve policy-making responsibilities in a wide range of service areas to relatively autonomous and directly elected regional, provincial or local governments. In this sense, the Scottish Parliament, the Welsh and Northern Ireland Assemblies, and the UK's 400+ local authorities are all examples of political decentralisation – where a constitutionally superior body has chosen to hand over certain powers to constitutionally dependent ones. It is clearly distinguishable from *federalism,* in which *both* the national (or federal) and the local bodies are assigned their powers equally and separately by the constitution. But it is just as clearly distinguishable from administrative decentralisation.

Local authorities, then, are far more than simply outposts or agents of central government, delivering services in ways and to standards laid down in detail at national ministerial level. Their role, as representative bodies elected by their fellow citizens, is to take such decisions themselves, in accordance with their own policy priorities: to govern their locality. If this were not so, there would not be the often dramatic variations in service costs and performance measures revealed in the increasingly popular league tables of local council statistics. Nor would we have seen in several of the Items in Exhibit 2.1 examples of ways in which councils can, to a certain extent at least, determine and pursue their own initiatives.

Local self-government?

So, does the British system of local government – councils of elected politicians making policy decisions on behalf of their local communities – amount to local *self-government?* Do localities and communities have the rights and resources genuinely to manage their own public affairs in what they see as their own best interests? Some writers appear to think so, and use the terms 'local government' and 'local self-government' almost interchangeably.

Others are more hesitant. Local government *ought* to mean local or community self-government, they seem to suggest. It ought to be about democratically elected representatives collectively deciding how best to respond to all the differing needs and wishes of the residents of their area. In practice, though, that is not how it has worked in the UK.

Many countries do have something legitimately describable as local self-government, especially those formed historically by the coming together of several small communities, for mutual help and support – for example, Switzerland, the Netherlands, Italy and the Scandinavian countries. Local councils or municipalities in such countries have, on average, much smaller populations than do UK local authorities. Yet they have something that British councils historically have not had: a *power of general competence* – a general right to undertake any activities that they feel to be in the interests of their citizens, unless such activities are expressly forbidden or assigned to other bodies. Like private citizens, they can do anything they are not expressly forbidden from doing. In these countries, as Allen puts it (1990, p. 23):

> Local government is not looked upon as just a mechanism. Rather, it is seen as the organic self-expression of the people themselves, whose powers are not yielded to the centre, but retained by the citizens of each community in the country to provide necessary local services for themselves.

In the UK, with its long monarchical history, the formal constitutional position is almost precisely the reverse: local councils have been able to do *only* what they are statutorily permitted to do. Their rights and competencies are not general, but specific. To quote Allen again (1990, p. 22), almost echoing Ambassador Seitz from Chapter 1:

> Local government is looked upon essentially as a subordinate mechanism created by the state for its own convenience. It is no more than one of several alternative agencies through which the paternalist central government can arrange the provision of services for the state's citizen-subjects.

Underlining their subordinate status, the common law doctrine under which councils operate is known as *ultra vires,* a Latin term which translates as 'beyond the powers'. If a local council does something or spends money it is not statutorily authorised to, it will be deemed to have acted *ultra vires*: beyond its powers, and therefore illegally. Moreover, until the practice was finally abolished in the Local Government Act 2000, the elected councillors who collectively agreed to the action became individually punishable and personally liable to refund any money spent illegally.

It seemed likely that the Coalition Government's Localism Bill 2010 would bring local authorities into line, in this sense, with their European counterparts and give them a full-scale power of general competence – or at least a vaguer-sounding 'general power of competence' as the Conservatives preferred to label it. Until then, they had to make what they could of a kind of half-way measure introduced in the 2000 Act mentioned above – the so-called *power of well-being.* Local authorities were given a new discretionary power, enabling them 'to promote the economic, social and environmental well-being of their areas'. It was not, *per se,* a power of general competence, and did not at a stroke make councils truly self-governing entities, as there were important qualifications concerning the power's use. It could not be used, for example, to raise money, and it had to be exercised with regard to any guidance issued by the government. But, for enterprising local authorities, it genuinely loosened one of the legal constraints under which they had operated historically – enabling them to think more of the policy outcomes they wished to achieve and the innovations they might make, rather than focusing exclusively on the delivery of existing services (see Exhibit 2.1, Item 11; also Chapter 10).

Creatures of statute

Like all local councils' more specific powers and competencies, though, the well-being power was derived from legislation, and in this sense it reinforced, rather than qualified, local government's necessarily subordinate position in Britain's constitution. The doctrine of parliamentary supremacy derives from the fact that the United Kingdom, like more than 85% of the world's nations, is a *unitary* state, not a federal one – as noted in Chapter 1. There is a single source of constitutional power and authority: the Westminster Parliament, in which usually one party has an overall majority of members and thus forms the government of the day. Parliament, processing legislation introduced by the government, can make or unmake law on any subject whatever – including local government.

In federal systems, constitutional power is divided between the federal government at the centre and the governments of decentralised states or regions. No such division exists in Britain, which is why, as noted above, local authorities are in the same constitutionally subordinate position as the Scottish Parliament and the Welsh and Northern Ireland Assemblies. They are literally the creatures, the creations, of parliamentary statute. Their boundaries, duties, powers, memberships and modes of operation are laid down by Acts of Parliament. Naturally, therefore, they can be abolished by Parliament and, as we have seen, restructured and reorganised at Parliament's will.

Partial autonomy

To summarise: the United Kingdom has a constitutionally subordinate system of local government, without, historically, the wide-ranging competence of many European continental systems. Yet it is far more than a network of field agencies of central government. It could be described as semi-autonomous.

There are semantic purists who will insist that a body can no more be partially autonomous than partially pregnant. We find it useful, however, to be able to describe one governmental institution as having relatively less autonomy than another, or less than it possessed at some time in the past. Indeed, such imprecise terminology fits our uncodified and convention-based constitution appropriately. Most European countries have formal, written constitutions, which usually include some provision for, and protection of, the principle of local self-government. In the United Kingdom, with no similar single constitutional document, there is in theory no limit to the sovereignty of Parliament. There is correspondingly no constitutional protection for local government: neither for the rights of individual councils nor for the system as a whole.

In practice, however, as we shall see in Chapter 4, much of the history of UK local government, particularly during the early decades of the twentieth century, was about governments determining and Parliaments legislating to devolve powers and responsibilities to local authorities. Local councils have been seen, in Allen's (1990) phrase, as a usefully democratic and effective 'subordinate mechanism' for the delivery of all kinds of services that central government has decided should be provided publicly.

Statutory powers can assume various forms. At one extreme they may be *detailed* and *compulsory*, requiring local councils to undertake certain activities according to tightly defined standards and rules – such as those giving tenants the right to buy their council houses at prescribed discounts (News Item 5). Alternatively, they may be *permissive* or *discretionary*, leaving councils to decide for themselves whether – or, were Barnet Council ever able to implement its easyJet service model (News Item 3), whether not – to provide a particular service, and to what standard. Very frequently – like the planning and commissioning powers in News Items 8 and 10 – they are mixed. In fact, much of the legislation affecting local government has traditionally had what might be termed a high 'discretion factor'. Local councils have had a considerable say in how they deliver their services and, sometimes, whether or not they do so. But discretion has no guarantee. It can be curtailed and ultimately withdrawn: hence the aptness of the label 'partial autonomy'.

Directly elected

The characteristic responsible above all others for whatever degree of autonomy local authorities do possess is that of their direct election. They are not composed of locally based civil servants or central government appointees. They consist of local people, chosen at regular and regulated elections to represent the interests and inhabitants of the communities in which they themselves also live and work.

These representatives – known as *councillors* or *elected members*, and sometimes just *members* for short – constitute collectively the local council and are the embodiment of its legal authority. On the basis of that authority, they recruit and employ a wide range of staff – professionally qualified 'officers', other administrative, technical and clerical 'white-collar' staff, and various categories of manual or 'blue-collar' workers – to carry out the policies and deliver the services that they, as democratically elected representatives, determine.

Direct election does not, in the UK's unitary system of government, make councillors the constitutional equals or rivals of Members of Parliament. Councillors may have to face their electorates more frequently than do MPs, and there were, even in 2010, nearly 35 times as many of them. But elections can always be suspended, just as councils can be abolished, at any time that the government, through Parliament, decrees. Until that happens, though, councillors' elected status accords them a legitimacy quite different from that of, say, the appointed members of health authorities or any other local quango.

Councillors have had to present themselves and their policy proposals for consideration and approval by the electorate. That local democratic approval represents a uniquely potent bargaining counter in any subsequent negotiations, whether with ministers, Whitehall civil servants or their own local officers. Their critics may, perhaps with some cause, question voters' genuine understanding of the complex issues involved and their relatively low turnout rates in local elections. But the very fact of electoral backing in any even aspiring democratic society has a force of its own.

Multi-service organisations

If electoral accountability is the prime distinguishing feature of local authorities, the second is their range of responsibilities. They are involved *in some way or other*, it can seem, with an almost infinite variety of different services.

We referred earlier to councils looking after people from womb to tomb. Another way of illustrating the same point is through the A–Z service directories accessible nowadays on almost all councils' websites. The directories are designed for the councils' own sometimes understandably confused residents: to publicise the services that may be available to them and, even more importantly, where to go to access them, and whom to contact. It has been estimated that a typical unitary authority has at least 700 'lines of business', which is far more than most multinational companies, and, it could be argued, make it correspondingly far more demanding to manage.

Multi-functional organisations

Note the phrase emphasised in the previous section: in some way or other. Only a fraction of the services in councils' A–Z directories are provided directly by the council itself. Historically, as noted above, it is true that councils' principal function has been that of *direct service provider*. They purchased the land, provided the buildings and equipment, and employed all the staff necessary to deliver their services.

Councils have always, though, had other functions and roles as well, and it is these roles that are becoming relatively more important. In many cases, the local authority is the *regulator* or *monitor* of the activities of other agencies and organisations. The liquor licensing powers over pubs, clubs, restaurants, takeaways and the like, transferred to councils from local magistrates in 2005, were additional to existing licensing responsibilities for public entertainments, theatres, cinemas, sex establishments, street trading, taxi drivers, animal boarding establishments, hairdressers, late night cafés, performing animals, pet shops, caravan sites and acupuncturists. 'Council plans "fact-finding" mission to lap-dancing club' was no salacious snippet from *Private Eye*'s 'Rotten Boroughs' column, but a proper headline, and doubtless an entirely proper mission, undertaken in furtherance of their licensing duties by fact-hungry Cornwall councillors (*The Guardian*, 7 May 2010, p. 17). Similar responsibilities include the *registration* of private residential homes, and the *certification* of sports ground safety, as the public became acutely aware following the Bradford and Hillsborough football ground disasters.

A further role is as a *facilitator,* providing advice, assistance and possibly finance to individuals or organisations undertaking activities consistent with the policy of the council. Thus a Local Action Team of council officers will provide help in setting up credit unions as part of the council's work in alleviating poverty and debt. Start-up grants and loans are available for the establishment of new businesses and workers' co-operatives, and grants are given also to an extensive range of arts, recreation, social and community groups. Finally, moving a further step away from direct service provision, there is that continuously developing role to which we have already alluded: that of *service contractor.*

Power of taxation

Fundamental as we argued that it is, electoral authority is essentially a moral force. To be effective, it needs something more tangible: the right to tax. A further essential characteristic of local authorities – one that stems directly from the fact that, as multi-purpose organisations, they have choices and priorities to determine, with financial implications – is therefore that they have the power to tax local residents. Other local agencies are funded by government grants and from their own trading income. Local authorities also receive much – too much, we shall suggest in Chapter 12 – of their income from these sources, but for almost 400 years they were also able set the levels of, as well as to collect, their own taxes.

Since 1980, however, the local tax system has undergone an unprecedented series of reforms. Part of the outcome has been that local authorities' taxation power is no longer, as lawyers might say, an unfettered one. As recorded on our funnel of local authority discretion (Exhibit 2.2), Conservative ministers in the 1980s used statutory powers to cap or limit councils' levels of spending and their right to tax their own residents, thereby effectively controlling their budgets. The 1997 Labour Government abolished what it called the 'crude and universal capping' system it inherited, but it retained and in 2004 resurrected the use of a reserve power to intervene and selectively cap the budget and council tax levels of any council proposing to spend in a way that ministers decided was 'excessive'. So, while the power to tax still distinguishes local councils from other public bodies, it is a power exercised nowadays with central government constantly looking over its shoulder.

Conclusion

We have identified in this chapter a set of characteristics that, individually and collectively, serve as a definition of UK local government (see Exhibit 2.4). This is a slightly more elaborate definition than the one we arrived at in Chapter 1, and it will serve as a reference point for several of the remaining chapters in Part 1 of the book.

Exhibit 2.4 UK local government defined

Local government is:

- a form of geographical and political decentralisation,
- in which directly elected councils,
- created by and subordinate to Parliament,
- have partial autonomy
- to provide a wide variety of services
- through various direct and indirect means,
- funded in part by local taxation.

Chapter 3

Why Elected Local Government?

Introduction – ethics and expediency

The local government historian, Jim Chandler, recalled recently the observation of an earlier distinguished academic, W. J. M. Mackenzie – deliverer,
as it happens, of the first university lecture one of us ever attended: ' "There
is no theory of local government," Mackenzie contended (1961, p. 5), "no
normative general theory from which we can deduce what local government ought to be" ' (Chandler, 2008, p. 355).

A major reason is that UK local government's situation is one of inherent tension. On the one hand, local authorities are at the heart of local
democracy, striving to shape the development of their localities and
provide services responsive to local needs. At the same time, they are arms
of the government, delivering a wide range of services on behalf of the
centre, where administrative efficiency is the key criterion. Theories about
the role of local government, Chandler argues, have relied mainly on justifications based on efficiency and expediency, rather than on ethics and
local integrity.

An expediential justification values an institution only to the extent that
it serves the purposes of another. Thus local government would be valued
only for its efficiency as a service deliverer for central government, and for
its expediency in contributing to national political stability. By contrast, an
ethical justification would value local government because it fulfils morally
desirable purposes in its own right. This theoretical distinction also has
important political implications. If local government is valued solely as an
efficient service deliverer for the nation state, it could be seen as legitimate
for the government of the state to control and order the way in which local
authorities undertake their business. If, however, there are independent ethical justifications for local government's existence, irrespective of the needs
of the state, the government would have much less legitimacy in interfering
in local government's affairs and undermining its integrity (Chandler, 2008,
p. 256).

This chapter, we hardly need to emphasise, does not provide Mackenzie's
missing normative general theory. Its more modest aim is to examine some
of Chandler's ethical justifications for local government.

The 'problems' of local government and decentralisation

To central government, it can seem, the commonest 'problem' of local government is when it refuses to do what central government wishes: when local councils pursue different goals from those of the party in power nationally. An alternative interpretation of such a battle of wills is that it demonstrates the robustness of a governmental system. Far from constituting a problem, it is an affirmation of precisely what local government should be about: locally elected and accountable representatives developing policies embodying *their* judgements of the best interests of *their* local communities, not the judgement of the centre.

The 'problems' of local government we have in mind are rather more subtle and complex: the potential costs and considerations involved in any decision to devolve administrative responsibility, let alone political power. Some of these potential costs are merely the obverse of possible benefits. But it is still worth addressing some of what Allen (1990, ch. 1) terms the 'disadvantages of decentralisation'.

The first argument deployed against decentralisation is its *financial cost*. Indeed, it is almost the only argument audible in the ongoing debate about the merits of all-unitary local government in England. Decentralisation duplicates scarce financial resources and staff. Things could be run more cheaply from the centre, critics suggest, whether the centre in question is London or, when considering the case for area or neighbourhood offices, from a council's own headquarters.

To which the response must be: not necessarily, and not in Birmingham's experience. That city's council, ever conscious of being the country's largest local authority, has devolved much of its service delivery and policy-making to, respectively, neighbourhood offices and district committees of local councillors. Residents apparently liked the localised arrangements, but councillors wanted, through one of the council's all-party Overview and Scrutiny Committees, to undertake a systematic study of the devolution, including its financial cost. They were surprised:

> The conventional wisdom is that decentralised systems are inherently more costly than centralised ones, even though they may well bring benefits. We therefore asked officers to advise us on the costs of moving from the current district structure back to one that was more centralised ... We would certainly not have been averse to a conclusion that operating the Birmingham localised system involved a small net additional cost ... [But] to our surprise, the advice was that, more likely than not, a more centralised model would entail higher operating costs than the current devolved structure ... Savings only arose if functions were dropped. (Birmingham City Council, 2006, pp. 7, 43).

But was it so surprising? Anyone taking the most basic Economics course will have encountered diseconomies of scale. There are also, as a Birmingham officer put it, 'economies of smallness, that can be enormous when you get more local engagement and volunteering.' (Smulian, 2007, p. 16).

Closely linked to finance is *efficiency*. It might be difficult to attract experienced staff and enterprising management, especially if the decentralised units are small and poorly resourced. The argument loses some force, however, when there is a national government responsible for, among other embarrassments, the Millennium Dome; a Child Support Agency writing off a third of the revenue it should have collected; the poll tax; non-firing army rifles, non-flying Chinook helicopters, non-transmitting Clansmen radios; and a Home Office, parts of which even a Home Secretary (John Reid) described as 'unfit for purpose'. In Britain at least, inefficiency is not confined to any single level of government.

A different kind of argument is that of *inequality*. The more decentralised a service, the greater will be the resulting disparities across geographical areas and social groups. These disparities are condemned as products of a 'postcode lottery', rather than as the outcomes of decisions made by local representative bodies responding to their assessment of local needs and priorities – or 'managed difference', to use the less emotive phrase adopted in the Lyons Inquiry report. The 'postcode lottery' cry sets off a public, media and electoral demand for greater 'fairness' and minimum national standards, followed by central government's intervention, with resource distribution formulae bringing greater territorial equity but at the cost of local political and financial discretion.

Sir Michael Lyons, author of his Inquiry's report, felt Britain and its media in particular are uniquely and damagingly 'preoccupied with the "postcode lottery" in a way which can lead us to value uniformity far above the need to find the right solution for each area' (Lyons, 2007, p. 79). He believed, however, that his Inquiry's research had shown public opinion to be rather more nuanced than is often supposed. Most people do favour government-set national standards for 'core' services – health, education, social services, the emergency services – though even here 'there was a recognition that they needed to be able to reflect local circumstances' (p. 100). But for most services there was 'a clear view that ... local government should have a greater role in setting priorities than central government', and a readiness to accept a 'managed difference' in levels of service delivery, *provided* people felt they had been consulted and were happy with the services they received (pp. 101–2).

Finally, there is the charge of potential *corruption*, levelled in most governmental systems more frequently at local politicians and officials than their national counterparts – and hardly surprisingly. There are many more of them; they are more likely to be directly involved in allocation decisions of serious financial value affecting people personally known to them; and they may will be both less experienced in public administration and less well paid. In the circumstances, the noteworthiness may be that there have been so few, rather than so many, major cases of local government corruption since the 1970s: the 'Poulson affair' in 1974, 'Donnygate' in the 1990s, and, between them, the rather different Shirley Porter 'Homes for Votes' case in the 1980s.

In 1974 the West Yorkshire architect, John Poulson, was found guilty and imprisoned for bribing several leading politicians and senior public sector employees into helping him corruptly secure building contracts. 'Poulson's cadre' (Doig, 1984, p. 142) embraced a Cabinet minister, MPs of two parties, civil servants, health service and nationalised industry employees, as well as councillors and officers. But the MPs all avoided prison, and the case led to the formulation of a National Code of Conduct for the guidance of both councillors and officers, which may explain the case being remembered primarily as an example of *local* government corruption.

'Donnygate' had striking similarities to the Poulson case, but was unambiguously a local government scandal, and big enough to earn the '-gate' suffix deriving from the Nixon/Watergate scandal of the 1970s. Big enough too for its negative resonances still to be perceptible to the Audit Commission as it made its recommendation for ministerial intervention more than a decade later (Audit Commission, 2010a, p. 11). The South Yorkshire borough of Doncaster was effectively a one-party (Labour) state, and abuse of power was systemic:

> Half the serving councillors were prosecuted for expense fraud; an officer [was] involved in contract illegalities; revelations about the sexual antics of a Deputy Leader of the Council added spice to the story; and finally there was corruption in the planning service. Other abuses ... involved malpractice in recruitment and selection and widespread bullying of both councillors and officers. (Burley, 2005, p. 526)

The planning corruption involved the manipulation of the borough's unitary development plan, the designation by bribed councillors of unneeded residential development sites, and the allocation of planning permissions to developer Alan Hughes – Doncaster's Poulson – who similarly was imprisoned for five years.

'Homes for Votes' also concerned an alleged abuse of political power, but for partisan advantage rather than personal financial gain. Dame Shirley Porter was the assertive, controversial Conservative Leader of Westminster City Council. She and five councillor and officer associates were found by a local government auditor to have operated an illegal housing sales policy, devised specifically for the electoral benefit of the Conservative Party, and which deprived the council of many millions of pounds. Properties were sold in politically marginal wards at sub-market prices to tenants judged likely to vote Conservative, while probable Labour-voting tenants were moved into poorer quality accommodation in less marginal areas. The Court of Appeal found in favour of Dame Shirley, but its decision was reversed in the House of Lords and she was surcharged ultimately nearly £49 million. However, as Jones correctly notes in a strenuous defence of Dame Shirley, she was never charged with a criminal offence, never went to jail, and her surcharge was imposed under archaic legislation that has since been abolished (Jones, 2009, p. 144).

These cases, then, are both different and complex. Our point, though, is simple: no set of politicians – local or national, Party A or Party B – is intrinsically more virtuous or more corruptible than any other. We should retain a sense of perspective and keep in mind Allen's warning (1990, p. 12) that, despite all the evidence showing that 'central agencies are often at least as incompetent, inefficient or corrupt as local bodies, one or two notorious cases can suffice to keep the whole concept of local government in disrepute'.

The values of local government

These supposed 'problems' of decentralisation should not be dismissed lightly. Our contention, though, is that they are more than balanced by its positive features: justifications of local government based on ethical values. As Chandler demonstrates, there has been a resilient strand of such thought stemming back to at least the mid-nineteenth century that provides a corrective to the dominant expediency theme. There is room here for only the briefest of snatches, but Joshua Toulmin Smith, for one, merits a quote. A political theorist and lawyer, Smith was a passionate advocate of 'Local Self-Government' – always in capital letters: 'Centralisation deadens every feeling of generous emulation; destroys every incentive to effort at improvement; and damps every ardour for the progressive development of resources' (Smith, 1851, p .60 – cited in Chandler, 2008, pp. 357–8).

Smith's contemporary, the philosopher-politician, John Stuart Mill, is far better-known today, but they shared the conviction that Liberty is as important a principle for communities as it is for individuals. Moving into the twentieth century, even the generally centralist Fabian socialists, Sydney and Beatrice Webb, advocated a measure of independence for local government based on 'the principle of neighbourhood' (1920) – a theme taken up in the 1930s by their London School of Economics colleague, Harold Laski, in his espousal of the 'genius of place' (Laski, 1934, p. 412). Neither the Webbs nor Laski were among the sources quoted by Sir Michael Lyons when he first proposed the term 'place-shaping' for the strategic role of local government (Lyons, 2005, p. 30), but they might well have been, for

Exhibit 3.1 The values or justifications of elected local government

Elected local government is likely to be better than a combination of central government and local administration at:

1 Building and articulating community identity;
2 Emphasising diversity;
3 Fostering innovation and learning;
4 Responding swiftly, appropriately, corporately;
5 Promoting citizenship and participation;
6 Providing political education and training; and
7 Dispersing power.

it is in a direct line of descent from these earlier localists. In the remainder of this chapter we have tried to group the ideas both of these 'great names' and of more recent writers (for example, Sharpe, 1970; Jones and Stewart, 1983; Young, 1986b; Clarke and Stewart, 1991; Lyons, 2007) into a set of what are mainly 'ethical' justifications for local government under the seven headings shown in Exhibit 3.1.

Building and articulating community identity

Chapter 2 concentrated particularly on local *government* and its contrast with local administration. We now focus on *local* government: the government of a particular geographical area and, if the relevant boundaries have been drawn appropriately, the government of a community. The institutions of local government ought both to reflect the importance of locality and place and to reinforce people's sense of community: 'A local authority has the capacity to shape an area, to preserve it, to develop it, to change it, and in doing so to give it a new identity' (Clarke and Stewart, 1991, p. 29). Lyons puts it even more forcefully. Local government's place-shaping role is about much more than physical development and regeneration. Its ultimate purpose: 'should not be solely to manage a collection of services, but rather to pursue the well-being of a place and the people who live there by whatever means are necessary and available' (Lyons, 2007, p. 61).

But this identity-building and place-shaping take time and need encouragement, and both of these have been at a premium in recent years. Chapter 2 contrasted the kind of 'bottom-up' local self-government found in some European countries, which grew out of local communities coming together for mutual help and support, with the UK's more 'top-down' version, deriving from parliamentary statute and national drawing of boundary lines on maps. The inevitable danger of over-frequent 'top-down' restructuring is the severing of links between a local authority and community identity, a

visible sign of which is the imposition of alien council names that at best
bewilder and at worst infuriate.

The reorganisation of the early 1970s produced countless examples of
these 'artificial' names, initially as unfamiliar to their own residents as they
still are to many outsiders. We have the metropolitan districts of Calderdale
and Kirklees (respectively, the areas around Halifax and Huddersfield),
Knowsley (east of Liverpool) and Sandwell (mainly West Bromwich). And,
among the many non-metropolitan district candidates, Adur, West Sussex
(the name of a river – who lives in a river?); Bassetlaw, Notts (an Anglo-
Saxon name for an area around Worksop, today not even a village); Three
Rivers, Herts (see Adur); and the doubly confusing Wyre, Lancashire (yet
another river) and Wyre Forest (Worcestershire).

Then there are the dozens of 'compass point' councils – where real towns
and places considered too small to govern themselves have been lumped
together and anonymised into meaningless geographical mongrels – North
Hertfordshire, South Somerset, East Northamptonshire, West Lancashire.
Each of these four contains a town of at least 30,000 – Letchworth, Yeovil,
Rushden and Skelmersdale – that would qualify for self-governing status in
almost any other European country. In Britain, however, they and their like
can be seen as testaments to a national political culture that is inclined to
build and restructure its local government system 'more on bureaucratic
and professional principles than upon local needs and community identities' (Lowndes, 1996, p. 71).

The government of difference and diversity

A sense of place and past implies *distinctiveness*: of an area's unique geography, history, economy, social and political culture, and of its consequently
distinctive preferences and priorities. It is the recognition that even local
authorities of the same type, with identical statutory powers and responsibilities, can be utterly different from each other and have different governmental needs.

In a federal system like that in the USA, where the states can pass their
own legislation, the diversity of local demands and circumstances can
appear extreme, even bizarre. In Alaska, it is illegal to take a pet flamingo
into a barber's shop; in California, to grow oleander plants; in Delaware, to
whisper in church; and in Georgia either to possess a sex toy or to wear a
hat in a cinema (see www.dumblaws.com). But UK local authorities can
differ so greatly in character that it is possible to imagine them enacting
equally singular legislation, given the chance.

Test it out yourself. Take any two councils of the same type and spend a
few minutes finding out – through Google, Wikipedia, oneplace.direct.
gov.uk, or their own websites – whatever you can about them and the areas
they serve. We picked Ashford and Ashfield, two non-metropolitan district

councils that are probably sometimes confused with each other – although, as we shall see, they certainly shouldn't be.

Ashford Borough Council in Kent has a population of 114,000, though only half live in Ashford itself, a rapidly expanding market town, but old enough to have featured in the Domesday Book. Historically, though, the small town of Tenterden was more important, and its 1449 Royal Charter enabled Ashford, created out of a merger of smaller authorities in 1974, to inherit the courtesy status of a borough council. Only 5% of residents are from black and minority ethnic (BME) communities, though, following the change in immigration laws, these include a growing settlement of Nepalese Gurkha veterans. The 43-member council is strongly Conservative and, even in the depths of the party's unpopularity in the mid-1990s, it remained the largest party group. Second-largest in the 2010 elections were the Liberal Democrats, and there is a small but lively group of three Ashford Independents, who believe councillors' first loyalty should be to local residents, not a national party.

Already on the M20 corridor, Ashford, with its new international rail station, is now just 37 minutes from London on the High Speed 1 line which carries passengers to Paris and Brussels. The government has designated Ashford a growth area, and the urban population is set to double over the next 25 years, with 11,000 new homes due to be built by 2016 – a commitment that, as a result of the recession, the Council is finding it difficult to meet.

Ashfield District Council in Nottinghamshire would be relieved if a stuttering housing programme was the most serious problem it faced from the recession. Its population is almost identical to Ashford's, and it too was created from a 1974 amalgamation of smaller councils. But the similarities end there. There is no town of Ashfield, and most residents live in one of three towns – Sutton-in-Ashfield, Hucknall and Kirkby-in-Ashfield – that lost their independent civic identities in 1974 along with their long-standing councils. Kirkby, the smallest, was chosen for the council's new civic centre, but all have populations of over 25,000 and their size, histories and municipal integrity would have ensured them their own councils in other local government systems. All, like Ashford, are mentioned in the Domesday Book, but their heyday came with the nineteenth century expansion of the mining industry. The pit closures in the 1980s and 1990s brought a huge slump in the local economy, the effects of which are still evident today. As in many mining areas, the council was for decades overwhelmingly Labour-dominated, and from 1995 to 1999 the party held every single seat. That position has since changed dramatically. The rise of a strong Independent group and then the Liberal Democrats resulted in Labour losing control of the council in 2007 to a minority Lib Dem administration, which itself was later displaced by a minority Labour administration holding just 8 of the 33 seats, but with Conservative and Independent support.

Local disaffection with Labour was doubtless a reflection of the national government's unpopularity, but Ashfield, with its three potentially competing urban centres and relatively high levels of deprivation in employment, income, health, education and skills levels, is a challenging authority to manage. There are signs of economic regeneration, with coalfield areas being reclaimed for development and recreational use, new employers arriving, and good levels of investment. But the recession has and will continue to hit the area hard and, while house prices are among the lowest in the country, Ashfield's housing problem is that many low-income residents still cannot afford to buy.

Our guess is that any pairing of two authorities would produce just as great a contrast. Yet central government's instinct is to focus on the authorities' relatively few similarities and overlook their obvious differences and uniquenesses. Ministers and civil servants struggle to devise formulae enabling all such councils to be treated as a single group. A thriving local government does the reverse. It emphasises and gives voice to the distinctiveness of local communities. It is the *government of difference or diversity*.

Fostering innovation and learning

One of Professor John Stewart's many local government aphorisms is that, if you impose a single uniform practice, you may learn only that you have made a mistake everywhere. Even if it appears successful, you will never know if it might have been done better. By responding to diverse local circumstances and acting as the government of difference, local authorities enhance government's learning capacity. They develop their own solutions and initiatives, some of which may prove unsuccessful or applicable only to their specific locality, but some of which may be adaptable – either by other local authorities or even by central government.

Local authorities are constantly learning from each other – through official bodies such as the Audit Commission and the Improvement and Development Agency (now LG Improvement and Development); through initiatives such as the Beacon Council programme and Local Innovation Awards, publicising examples of 'best practice' (see Chapter 19); through conferences, seminars, the many local government professional magazines and journals; and by simple word of mouth. Refer back to our news items in Exhibit 2.1. Other councils will have needed no ministerial encouragement to investigate Essex's banking ideas, Ealing's council tax-payers' cashback, and perhaps even Brighton and Hove's foundation garment initiative.

Almost every local authority has developed some new service that has subsequently been adopted or adapted for use elsewhere. North Kesteven built council homes out of tightly packed straw to save on heating bills. Dudley installed Gummy Bins® for chewing gum disposal and recycling.

Liverpool offers its under-5s free membership to leisure centres and dance classes. Waltham Forest had young people train police in conducting 'stop and search' procedures without causing offence. Brighton and Hove used a lottery to allocate places at over-subscribed secondary schools. Dartford funded the town football club's ultra-ecological stadium, including a sedum roof blanket providing natural air filtration and a sunken pitch to reduce noise and sound pollution. Tameside piloted a hydration-based health programme, installing 'pee charts' in toilets to enable staff to gauge their hydration from the colour of their urine. The list is endless, and we defy you to find a council that cannot claim some service innovation to boast about.

Necessity, they say, is the mother of invention, and the economic recession and its ensuing spending cuts have presented local authorities with necessity in abundance – to which in 2009 they were already responding with a wide range of inventive, but particularly locally-tailored, initiatives. Different areas, with different local economies, employment patterns and degrees of social deprivation, faced widely varying problems. As an Audit Commission report acknowledged, even the best-conceived national policies cannot 'utilise the local knowledge and targeting that councils can provide' (2009, p. 7). Among the council policies that impressed the Commission were:

- Northumberland's funding of a management buy-out of a local food company, to secure local jobs;
- Medway's easing of the criteria for its business loans, no longer requiring bank backing;
- Wakefield's interest-free loans for homeowners with mortgage arrears to prevent homelessness;
- Gateshead's doubling of its apprenticeship programme for 16–18-year-olds;
- North Yorkshire's funding of a credit union, to be operated from libraries and district council offices, with staff taking deposits;
- Harrow's X-cite outreach employment project, bringing Jobcentre vacancies and training opportunities to residents at their housing estates and at children's centres; and
- Essex's investment through its Crime and Disorder Reduction Partnership to deal with an anticipated increase in domestic violence.

Responding swiftly, appropriately, corporately

Distance delays. It can distort perception. Being multi-service, multi-functional organisations, local authorities should be able to identify better and faster than central government the most appropriate response to any local event or issue. They should be able to organise that response themselves, quickly, in a co-ordinated manner, and possibly more economically.

Sharpe (1970, pp. 155, 165) terms this ability the 'knowledge value' of local government:

> central government is not equipped to grasp the inimitable conditions of each locality. Local government is preferable precisely because locally elected institutions employing their own specialist staff are better placed to understand and interpret both the conditions and the needs of local communities ... out-stationed field agencies could not ... co-ordinate their activities with each other.

A vivid and vital example of such co-ordination was provided by Cumbria County Council's emergency support operation following the devastating flooding in and around Cockermouth in November 2009. The regular Flood Bulletins are probably no longer on the Council's website, which is unfortunate in a way, as they recorded both the extensive range of the Council's own services that were called upon, as well as the strategic co-ordination of numerous other public, voluntary and private sector bodies that it is hard to imagine being led by any organisation other than the County Council.

Almost all Council departments and services were mobilised: the highways and bridge engineers in Transport and Roads; emergency planning and debris disposal in Environment and Planning; libraries from Community and Living as flood support and free internet access centres; organisation of school closures and reopening by Children's Services; social work support, housing and benefit advice from Adult Social Care; advice to prevent householders being exploited by rogue traders and builders from Trading Standards. The list of other agencies is even longer: district councils, the NHS, local hospitals, the Highways Agency, Citizens Advice, WRVS, Age Concern, the Chamber of Commerce, the Samaritans. The body responsible for the Flood Recovery Fund, though, and whose website was listed alone at the foot of each Flood Bulletin, was the County Council.

'Holistic' or 'joined-up' government (Perri 6 *et al.*, 2002; Bogdanor, 2005) are contemporary terms for this kind of co-ordinated operation, the contrast being 'silo' organisations: long, vertical towers making policy pronouncements and attempting to deliver services independently of one another. Those in multi-functional local authorities can find it disconcerting to be lectured about the virtues of joined-up government by ministers in their less effectively integrated Whitehall departmental silos. Many of our most intractable policy problems – crime, community safety, social exclusion, job creation, drugs (see Wilson and Game, 2006, Exhibit 3.2) – require cross-cutting, multi-service intervention that local authorities, with their wide range of duties, powers and services, are ideally placed both to provide and to co-ordinate.

Promoting citizenship and participation

Local *administration* is about acceptance: local officials' acceptance of nationally determined policy, and service recipients' acceptance of those officials' implementation of that policy. Local *government* is about choice and challenge. It actively encourages citizen involvement and participation. Obviously, elected local government involves citizens as voters and elected representatives. Regular local elections mean we generally have the chance to vote for our councillors more frequently than for our MPs, even if only a minority of us do so. Compared with many countries, the UK has an exceptionally small number of councillors (roughly 21,000) – who are therefore unknown personally to most electors – and an exceptionally large number of MPs (650). Even so, for every MP there are more than 30 councillors in our principal councils.

These figures, moreover, exclude the 90,000 or so elected members of the country's 'local' – that is, parish, town and community – councils. There are about 8,700 parish and town councils in England, and some 2,000 community councils in Wales and Scotland, with an average of nine councillors each, though some also double as members of principal authorities. Some of these councils are larger than smaller district councils, representing communities of over 30,000 people. In many countries they would be the basic institutions of local government with a full set of powers and responsibilities, equivalent to French *communes* and German *Gemeinden*. In Britain, though, their powers are limited mainly to the discretionary provision of minor services, and to representing their residents' views to principal councils and other agencies. Not surprisingly in these circumstances, many elections go uncontested, but these councils remain democratically constituted and accountable bodies, and offer citizens the means of participating directly in the government of their localities.

Anyway, elections are only the tip of the participation iceberg. There are numerous other methods that councils use nowadays to encourage people to get involved in local decision-making – from traditional public meetings and committee co-options to service-user forums, citizens' juries, and tenant management committees (Lowndes *et al.*, 2001; Wilson and Game, 2006, Exhibit 3.3). But despite the abundant opportunities to participate, many, even most, simply prefer not to – feeling that their interests are already adequately represented, and they have better things to do. Understandably in the circumstances, councils can become irritated at being constantly challenged by ministers to find new ways to 'engage' their local communities. You cannot, in a democracy, force people to engage.

Governments of all parties, however, will continue to try. Hazel Blears, the most enthusiastic participationist of Labour's local government ministers, set out her personal vision for empowerment in a 2008 White Paper, *Communities in Control: Real Power, Real People*. Going substantially beyond merely encouraging more extensive consultation, the paper's proposals included statutory duties requiring councils actively to promote democratic understanding and participation, and to respond to public petitions, including e-petitions, relating to local authority responsibilities. Councils should also seek to introduce participatory budgeting opportunities, enabling citizens to help set local spending priorities, and consider transferring assets into community ownership, empowering people to run their own local services. The new statutory duties were included in the 2009 Local Democracy, Economic Development and Construction Act, but opposed by the Conservatives as 'a textbook example of prescriptive overdrive' (Caroline Spelman, *House of Commons Debates*, 1 June 2009, col. 41) – ministers intervening unnecessarily and probably unenforceably to dictate how councils should act, rather than trusting them to decide for themselves.

Meanwhile, the Conservatives, in their own Policy Green Paper, *Control Shift: Returning Power to Local Communities*, proposed more direct democracy. Residents should be able to veto, through local referendums, proposed council tax increases they consider to be too high, and to instigate referendums on other local issues. Residents in England's major cities should also have referendum votes on whether their councils should be run by directly elected mayors, rather than, as at present, mainly by indirectly elected leaders (see Chapter 7). The police too should become more publicly accountable, with each force being headed by a directly elected Police Commissioner. These Conservative policies on elected mayors and police were incorporated into the 2010 Coalition Agreement (HM Government, 2010).

Providing political education and training

Participation is itself a form of political education. In the UK, political education was traditionally a neglected field of study in schools and colleges. Not before time, this situation was remedied in 2002, with Citizenship Education becoming a compulsory component of the secondary school curriculum. In Key Stages 3 and 4 students are now expected to develop a broad knowledge of their rights and responsibilities as citizens, and of the functioning of government, and to be actively involved in school and community activities. In time these developments should raise levels of political literacy and community involvement. Even then, though, governmental institutions themselves – particularly locally – will continue to have a role as stimuli of political learning.

Local elections are especially important for their educative role. Even non-voters may have their political awareness increased through the heightened media attention given to local issues and candidates during the campaign period. Most UK local elections take place in May, shortly after councils have set their annual budgets and sent out their council tax demands. Councillors and candidates, through their election addresses and manifestos, have to defend their actions or propose alternative policies. Statistics are produced, challenged and debated. People may still remain unaware of who their councillors are and what their councils do, but without elections that ignorance would be even greater.

For its most active participants, local government provides not just education, but also training and an apprenticeship for a professional political career. In recent General Elections there has been no more important recruiting ground than local government – for all political parties. In the 2001 and 2005 Parliaments, over half of all MPs had previously served as local councillors – comprising some two-thirds of Labour MPs, 60% of Liberal Democrats, and more than 30% of Conservatives. The Conservative figure in particular almost certainly rose in 2010, with at least 66 (45%) of the party's 147-strong new intake being former councillors, including 8 former council leaders. Striking as such statistics are, the key term is 'had previously served', for, having become MPs, almost all of them will have resigned from their councils at the earliest opportunity. There is in Britain much less career overlap between national and local politics – with local government having a correspondingly less powerful voice nationally – than in many countries.

Dispersing power

Finally, we come to arguably the most fundamental value or justification of local government: that of pluralism. To quote the Widdicombe Report on the Conduct of Local Authority Business: 'the case for pluralism is that power should not be concentrated in one organisation of state, but should be dispersed, thereby providing political checks and balances, and a restraint on arbitrary government and absolutism' (Widdicombe, 1986a, p. 48). This same idea is to be found on the opening page of any dictionary of quotations: Lord Acton's famous aphorism that 'power tends to corrupt, and absolute power corrupts absolutely'. Like many supposedly well-known sayings, it is frequently misquoted, but for our purposes the placement of the emphasis is insightful. The dispersal of power may lead to corruption, but Acton's certainty is reserved for its concentration.

Conclusion

This chapter is not putting forward an idealised and uncritical case for decentralised government. UK local authorities can easily be shown to exhibit the various disadvantages of decentralisation that we enumerated, as well as finding it difficult to live up to its claimed values. As instruments of pluralism, platforms for increased participation, champions of their communities, their deficiencies are manifest and will not be glossed over elsewhere in this book. They can be inefficient, bureaucratic and sometimes plain daft. Camden Council, to protect a fine piece of public sculpture near Hampstead Theatre, placed it behind glass – including the Braille inscription designed especially for the visually impaired. Hampshire County Council's website, urging people to turn out to vote, used a picture of a ballot paper marked with a large black tick – which technically would lead to the vote being counted as spoiled. Such idiocies are part of the inherent price – and delights – of a decentralised democracy.

Nor are we challenging the ideas expressed in Chapter 2 about a unitary state, parliamentary sovereignty, and the constitutional subordination of local government in such a state. We are, however, suggesting that a significant dispersal of power away from the centre, by extending choice, encouraging initiative and innovation, and enhancing active participation, is likely to do more for the quality of government and the health of democracy than will centralisation and concentration. The problems associated with democratic decentralisation are relatively minor compared with those stemming from the centralisation of power.

Chapter 4

The Way It Was

History – shaper of the present

Why include a historical chapter in a book on contemporary local government? Why not just focus on the present system, its structure and operation? Two reasons. First, and most fundamentally, because in all sorts of ways that present system is shaped by its history, as Professors Jones and Stewart explain:

> History can be seen in the *buildings* of local authorities; in particular, in the Victorian and Edwardian town halls built to express the pride of civic government ... The *law* about local government has been built over time ... *Legal precedents* deriving from past cases are important in present-day local government ... The history of *particular local authorities* is important in moulding their distinctive cultures. (2009, p. 22 – emphases ours)

The present cannot be properly understood without some appreciation of how it developed and differs from the past – especially in Britain, where local government has evolved gradually over the centuries, without any codified constitution defining its rights, responsibilities and relationship to central government. Second, if ever we were inclined to drop the history chapter, it would seem particularly wrong to pick a time when the Children's Secretary in the Brown Government, Ed Balls, was trying to abolish primary school 'history' and subsume it into an 'area of learning' – the totalitarian-sounding 'historical, geographical and social understanding'. It might be construed as supportive.

So the chapter stays, albeit as a brisk overview – a thousand years in about half that number of lines. In fact, the story starts properly in the twelfth century, and our account ends around 1990, before the nationwide, and easily comprehensible, two-tier structure introduced in the early 1970s began to fragment into its present hybrid state under successive governments' enthusiasm for single-tier or unitary local government.

Anglo-Saxon origins and traces

Two main struggles dominate even the briefest histories of UK local government. The first is that of localities seeking freedom from the centre

53

– historically the monarch, nowadays central government – to raise their own revenues in order to govern themselves. The second is that of towns, seeing their interests as being significantly different from those of more rural surrounding areas, and again seeking freedom to govern themselves in their own preferred ways. David King, with an economist's instinct for numerical precision, reckons the earliest success in the first of these struggles was in 1130, which therefore becomes the year from which 'local government in the United Kingdom really dates' (King, 2006, p. 267). The precision may be Wikipedian, but the big picture is spot on.

Elements of our modern-day local government originated in at least Anglo-Saxon, if not Roman, times (see Chandler, 2007, pp. 1–2). It was the Anglo-Saxons who divided England into provinces, which they called *shires*. The Normans renamed them *counties*, after their own word *comté*, and both names have survived. England's non-metropolitan counties are known unofficially (and tautologically) as 'shire counties', and the fact that many can trace their history back to pre-Norman times must be one reason why people today become concerned when they when their counties are threatened with abolition. Anglo-Saxon shires were divided for administrative, military and judicial purposes into *hundreds* – the land area sufficient to sustain roughly 100 households – and were presided over by shire-reeves or *sheriffs*, supplemented by a group of assistants as a kind of early, unelected town council. Across the central and southern English counties there were also burhs – early *boroughs* – though some were more like overgrown forts than the fortified towns they were intended to be. Some larger burhs were divided into *wards*, though for policing purposes, rather than the political and electoral units they are today.

UK High Sheriffs today (except in Scotland, where Sheriff Courts provide the local court service) are theoretically the sovereign's judicial representatives in their respective counties, while Lord Lieutenants are their personal representatives. Both positions are largely ceremonial and unpaid. By contrast, under the Norman kings, sheriffs were extremely powerful – the king's first officers – and appropriately rewarded. They looked after his properties, collected his tolls and revenues, and – sitting in the county court, assisted from the fourteenth century by *Justices of the Peace (JPs)* – were responsible for conserving the King's Peace (Chandler, 2007, pp. 2–10).

Not surprisingly, the larger towns resented the sheriff's extensive authority, and, starting with Lincoln in 1130, they started to negotiate 'opt-outs'. They paid revenues directly to the king, were in exchange granted Royal Charters, and became in effect the first local authorities: islands of municipal self-government, with the title and status of *boroughs*, within otherwise sheriff-controlled counties (King, 2006, p. 267). Many of our most historic cities, therefore, had behind them up to eight centuries of local self-government, when, in the 1970s, they were 'reorganised' into new two-tier counties (regions in Scotland) in which they were suddenly junior partners. It is not hard to imagine their sentiments.

Parishes, as units of ecclesiastical administration, also date back to the Anglo-Saxons, who founded regional churches or minsters, staffed by teams of priests serving areas covering a number of what later became parishes. Gradually, with the spread of local churches, there developed a network of church parishes, which came to double as units of civil administration, diminishing further the authority of the king's county sheriffs. From 1555, parishes became responsible for road maintenance, every parishioner being required to work several days a year on the roads, under the direction of a local Surveyor of Highways. More important still, under the 1601 Poor Law Act, parishes assumed the dissolved monasteries' role of caring for the poor. They appointed overseers, who could charge a *rate* – the first local property tax – to support the poor of the parish.

Nineteenth-century ad hocery

It took a violent revolution, but the French entered the nineteenth century with a rational and uniform system of local government by elected councils that still exists today:

- a municipality or *commune* in each urban or rural community, and all 36,000+ *communes*, from the smallest hamlet to Paris itself, with the same constitutional status; and
- each *commune* with its own elected assembly and a mayor responsible to central government as well as to the *commune*.

In Britain there was nothing approaching a 'system'; nor would there be for most of the nineteenth century. Rather, there was what Patricia Hollis has graphically labelled 'a tangle' (Hollis, 1987, pp. 2–3), comprising principally – but very far from exclusively – the three historical units of British local government described above: the parish, the county and the borough.

Parishes, of which there were over 15,000 by the 1830s, appointed various unpaid officers – constables, highway surveyors, overseers of the poor – to take responsibility respectively for law and order, road maintenance and the provision of work or financial relief for the poor. *Counties* were administered by Crown-appointed JPs, who by now had both a judicial role, exercised through the county quarter sessions, and increasing administrative responsibilities, for highways and bridges, weights and measures, and general oversight of the parishes. The 200 or so *boroughs* that had opted out of this jurisdiction of JPs effectively governed themselves through Corporations established by Royal Charter. They determined their own systems of government – sometimes elected, sometimes self-appointed – to

Exhibit 4.1 The structural evolution of UK local government

1835   **Municipal Corporations Act** – an initial 178 directly-elected municipal borough councils in England and Wales replace self-electing and frequently corrupt medieval corporations. In Scotland, the 1833 Burgh Reform Act had introduced similar reforms.

1888   **Local Government Act** – established 62 elected county councils and 61 all-purpose county borough councils in England and Wales. Paralleled by Local Government (Scotland) Act 1889.

1894   **Local Government Act** – established within county council areas a network of 1,270+ urban and rural district and non-county borough councils. Town Councils (Scotland) Act 1900 established equivalent Scottish structure.

1899   **London Government Act** – 28 metropolitan borough councils complete the 'modern' structure of local government.

1929   **Local Government** and **Local Government (Scotland) Acts** – abolished Boards of Poor Law Guardians and transferred their responsibilities to local authorities.

1963   **London Government Act** – extended, from 1965, London's two-tier structure to the conurbation: strategic Greater London Council (GLC), 33 boroughs (including unchanged City Corporation), plus Inner London Education Authority (ILEA).

1972   **Local Government Act** – abolished county boroughs and established, from 1974, a two-tier structure in England and Wales: 47 counties incorporating 333 non-metropolitan districts, plus, in 6 metropolitan areas, 6 counties and 36 districts.

1972   **Local Government (Northern Ireland) Act** – replaced 73 local authorities with 26 single-tier district councils elected by proportional representation.

1973   **Local Government (Scotland) Act** – established, from May 1975, a largely two-tier structure: 9 regional and 53 district councils, plus 3 unitary island councils, to replace over 400 authorities that had existed since 1929.

1985   **Local Government Act** – abolished the GLC and the 6 English metropolitan county councils. ILEA abolished from April 1990.

1994   **Local Government (Scotland)** and **(Wales) Acts** – replaced, from 1996, Scottish and Welsh two-tier systems with, respectively, 32 and 22 unitary councils. In parallel, 46 new English unitary councils created by Statutory Orders, in place of 5 county and 58 district councils.

1999   **Greater London Authority Act** – created UK's first directly-elected executive mayor and a 25-member Assembly, both first elected in May 2000.

2009   **Local Government and Public Involvement in Health Act** – created a further 9 English unitary councils, in place of 7 county and 37 district councils.

decide how to raise the money due to the king, and how to run their own courts. This same principle of local self-rule was being developed and extended in Scotland through a considerably larger number of *burghs,* with their councils of burgesses.

Then in addition there were hundreds of *ad hoc authorities,* established by local Acts of Parliament, each providing a specific service within a particular area whose boundaries rarely coincided with those of any other authorities. Thus Turnpike Trustees levied tolls on road users to build and maintain roads, while Improvement Commissioners provided rate-funded services such as lighting, street cleansing, and later fire engines and gas and water supplies.

Pressures brought about by the Industrial Revolution – urban poverty and unemployment, overcrowding and poor sanitation, disease and crime – showed up this 'tangle' for what it was and demonstrated the urgent need for reform. The existing patchwork of institutions could not cope effectively with the demands of a developing urban industrial society.

Central government's response took two contrasting forms, reflected in two major reform acts of the 1830s. First, the Poor Law Amendment Act 1834 heralded the creation of still more *single-purpose ad hoc authorities.* The Act replaced the parishes for the administration of workhouse-based poor relief with some 700 unions, or groupings of parishes, under ratepayer-elected Boards of Guardians. These Boards were subject to strong central direction from national Poor Law Commissioners, but the very fact of their election and resulting electoral accountability distinguishes them from most of the single-purpose authorities created more recently. Plenty of other ad hoc bodies followed – local health boards, highways boards, elementary school boards, sanitary districts – partly a consequence of the delay in any more comprehensive reform of sub-national government.

The nearest the early nineteenth century came to such reform was the second of the two 1830s statutes: the Municipal Corporations Act 1835 (Chandler, 2007, pp. 42–5). By establishing 178 reformed, multi-purpose, elected local authorities not concerned with the administration of justice, this Act can be seen as the foundation of present-day local government and earns the first entry in our summary of structural legislation in Exhibit 4.1. The powers of these new councils were limited and their franchise even more so – restricted to male ratepayers of over three years' residence – but the principle of elected multi-functional local self-government was established.

A dual urban–rural system emerges

Despite these 1830s reforms, there was nothing until almost the end of the nineteenth century that qualified as a *system* of local government. There still remained the chaos of literally thousands of appointed and elected bodies, of both single- and multi-purpose authorities.

Rationalisation was overdue, and it took the form of a group of Acts passed in the last dozen years of the century, the collective endeavour of which was to try to square a circle: to create a two-tier structure of elected local government, without destroying the independence of the boroughs (see Chandler, 2007, ch. 5). The inevitable compromise unfolded in stages:

1. 62 *county councils*, including the London County Council (LCC), took over the administrative responsibilities of the JPs/magistrates, became genuine elected local authorities for the first time, and formed the upper tier of the two-tier system in England and Wales. They varied enormously in size and initially had only limited powers – responsibility for highways and bridges, asylums, weights and measures, and partial control of the police – but these functions grew steadily as the twentieth century progressed.

2. The hundreds of urban and rural sanitary districts – responsible since the 1870s for the vital public health issues of clean drinking water, sewers, street cleaning and slum housing clearance – became *urban and rural district councils* and formed the lower tier.

3. Initially, 61 of the larger boroughs were allowed to retain their independence and became all-purpose *county borough councils* – in effect, holes in their surrounding counties.

4. Those boroughs not becoming county boroughs were a further part of the compromise. These *non-county boroughs* retained some of their independent status, sharing powers – notably education – with their respective county councils.

5. In London, 28 *metropolitan boroughs* provided the second tier of local government under the London County Council (LCC). The unique City of London Corporation, with its centuries of history, its Lord Mayor, Courts of Aldermen and Common Council, remained unreformed.

6. Scottish legislation established a similar, though less complex, two-tier county-district structure, with the four largest burghs – Glasgow, Edinburgh, Dundee and Aberdeen – becoming all-purpose *counties of cities*, equivalent to English county boroughs.

Between them, these Acts achieved a constitutional mini-revolution. There was now a *dual system* of elected local government throughout the country: all-purpose county boroughs/burghs in the largest towns (outside London), and a two- or three-tier system elsewhere, with powers shared between county, district/burgh and parish councils. It was not the neatest of systems; nor, with each tier protective of its own responsibilities and self-sufficiency, the most harmonious. It was to last, though, for three-quarters of a century – almost an eternity by today's tinkering standards.

The 'golden age'

This chapter is chiefly about the structural evolution of UK local government, but to jump straight from the 1890s to the structural reform of the 1960s would bypass what was arguably local government's 'golden age' – a brief period peaking perhaps in the early 1930s. During these years a system of multi-functional, elected and genuinely local authorities was the provider of more major services to its citizens than at any time before or since. Raising much more of their revenue from their own local rates than from central government grants, these authorities were substantially free from detailed central direction and intervention. A thriving local government was even valued as part of the democratic defence against fascism (Griffith, 1985, p. xii). The period was a high water mark and warrants a mention.

Almost immediately after their establishment in 1889, the new elected county councils had begun to add to their initially modest service portfolios: further and technical education, road maintenance, elementary education, vehicle and driver registration, school meals, maternity and child welfare, careers advice, mental health services, secondary education, 'home help' schemes, libraries, planning and development control and civil defence. Similarly, the county boroughs spearheaded the 1920s' council housing drive and acquired control of the public utilities – water, gas, electricity and public transport – as well as, in some cases, docks, airports, telephone systems, theatres, crematoria and slaughterhouses.

The authors of the book, *Half a Century of Municipal Decline* (Loughlin *et al.*, 1985), picked 1935 as their start date – mainly because it was a sequel to a previous volume (Laski *et al.*, 1935), commemorating *A Century of Municipal Progress* since the 1835 Municipal Corporations Act. They could well, though, have picked 1935 in any case, as the preceding five years can be seen as a kind of prelude to the decline, starting with the 1929 Local Government Act, rightly famous for its overdue dismantling of the poor law system with its infamous workhouses. The Act was partly structural, and it established a process whereby boundary reviews could recommend the abolition through a merger of urban and rural district councils judged to be too small to be able to manage their growing service responsibilities effectively. But the Act's more historic abolition was of what by then were the last remaining ad hoc authorities, the Boards of Poor Law Guardians, whose functions – poor law administration and the payment of unemployment relief, civil registration, hospitals and infirmaries – were transferred to the county and county borough councils. Local government's inheritance, however, was short-lived, because, responding to the impact of the Great Depression, the 1934 Unemployment Act established the national Unemployment Assistance Board (Chandler, 2007, pp.146–7). It was a preview of the real decline in powers and responsibilities that followed the Second World War, with the Labour Government's massive legislative programme of health, welfare and nationalisation all taking services away from local government.

Serious structural reform at last

By the 1960s, the structural problems already evident in the inter-war years had come to seem acute. There were major disparities of size between local authorities of the same type. The sheer number of authorities – though far smaller than in other similar-sized European countries – was said to cause public confusion; equally, the fragmentation of responsibility for service provision. Pressure for change mounted, and it came first in London.

London becomes Greater London

Following a Royal Commission review, the London Government Act 1963 created a new two-tier structure based on the previously vague concept of a Greater London conurbation, covering the former counties of London and Middlesex, parts of Essex, Kent, Surrey and Hertfordshire, plus the three former county boroughs of Croydon, East Ham and West Ham. The LCC was succeeded by a much larger Greater London Council (GLC), and 32 London boroughs – 12 in Inner London, 20 in Outer London – replaced 82 former boroughs and urban districts. As in the 1890s, the City of London Corporation survived unscathed and became effectively a 33rd borough. The boroughs were allocated the bulk of services – housing, social services, non-metropolitan roads, libraries, leisure and recreation and refuse collection – leaving the GLC with the more 'strategic' functions of fire, the ambulance service, main roads and refuse disposal. The maverick was education, there being a widespread wish to retain intact the LCC's high-reputation service. So, while the outer boroughs took responsibility for education, Inner London had its separate service administered by the Inner London Education Authority (ILEA), a special committee of the GLC comprising elected councillors from the 12 boroughs.

Reaction to the new structures was mixed. Some argued that reform was unnecessary; others that it did not go far enough, that the GLC boundaries had been too tightly drawn, and that it did nothing to alleviate the problems caused by the division of services between two tiers of councils. But, whatever its merits or defects, the reform had demonstrated that wholesale change was possible without services being totally dislocated. It also established the principle that an entire conurbation – in this case, the biggest of them all – should be governed as a single unit. Reform of the rest of the system would surely follow – eventually.

England and Wales

In 1966, two separate reforming Royal Commissions were established: England's chaired by Lord Redcliffe-Maud and Scotland's by Lord Wheatley. Both reported in 1969. Wales, as in the 1990s reorganisation, was treated differently from England. A Commission was not deemed necessary; a White Paper from the Secretary of State for Wales would suffice.

The Redcliffe-Maud Commission produced two reports. The majority of the Commissioners favoured a structure based predominantly on all-purpose unitary authorities embracing both town and country. But a powerful Memorandum of Dissent by Derek Senior advocated a multi-tier system of provincial councils, city regions, district and local councils. At the time, both reports were kicked into the proverbial long grass. Unitary authorities fell, along with the government, in Labour's June 1970 election defeat – only to be rediscovered by John Major's Conservative Government in the 1990s.

Rejecting the Redcliffe-Maud Commission's unitary authorities, the Heath Conservative Government opted to extend to the whole of England and Wales a two-tier system based mainly on existing counties – partly on philosophical grounds, but partly also because most county councils were dominated by the government's own party members and sympathisers.

The Local Government Act 1972 abolished, from 1974, all county boroughs and reduced the 58 *county councils* in England and Wales to 47, with populations ranging at that time from 100,000 (Powys) to 1.5 million (Hampshire). Within these counties, over a thousand municipal boroughs, urban and rural districts were merged into 333 *district councils,* also with hugely varying populations: from 19,000 (Radnor) to 422,000 (Bristol). In the major conurbations, six *metropolitan county councils* were established – Greater Manchester, Merseyside, West Midlands, Tyne and Wear, South Yorkshire and West Yorkshire – and 36 *metropolitan districts/boroughs* with populations ranging from 172,000 (South Tyneside) to almost 1.1 million (Birmingham). Ever the exception, the Isles of Scilly had their substantial independence even of Cornwall confirmed, and, with their population of 2,000, became effectively England's first, and incomparably smallest, unitary authority.

The former county boroughs, many with centuries of experience of independent self-government and mainly now Labour strongholds, were thus reduced to the lower-tier status of districts or boroughs in the new two-tier system. The loss, outside the metropolitan counties, of education and social services to generally more Conservative county councils was felt especially bitterly. But even without inter-tier partisan differences, the retention of a two-tier structure could continue to make co-ordination of policy and administration potentially difficult, especially in those services, such as

planning and leisure, where counties and districts had concurrent powers –
though, again, other countries seemed able to cope with two- and even
three-tier systems.

Parish councils were, and still are, rare in the metropolitan counties, and
Londoners did not until 2007 have the right even to petition for a parish
council. But outside the major cities, at the third, or sub-principal, tier in
England – confusingly, also referred to as the first or most local tier, especially by these local councils themselves – civil parishes were retained in
1974. Of the more than 10,000 parishes, about 8,700 have elected councils, the more urban of which are known as town councils. Small parishes,
with fewer than 200 electors, can instead hold parish meetings that all local
electors can attend. In Wales, parishes were replaced by *communities*,
which had either elected councils or community meetings, like their English
counterparts.

Scotland

In contrast to its English counterpart, the Wheatley Commission proposed a
two-tier system, which was largely adopted by the Conservative Government
in the Local Government (Scotland) Act 1973 and implemented in 1975.
Here too the large number of small authorities was seen as the fundamental
weakness of the existing system, and their numbers were reduced proportionately by even more than in England and Wales: 431 counties, cities,
burghs and districts were amalgamated into 9 *regions,* ranging from a population of 100,000 (Borders) to almost 2.5 million (Strathclyde); 53 *districts,*
with population from 9,000 (Badenoch and Strathspey) to 850,000
(Glasgow); and 3 *'most-purpose' island authorities* for Orkney, Shetland and
the Western Isles. Additionally, some 1,350 communities set up their own
optional *community councils* as a kind of third tier, though they had no
statutory powers and a lower status than even parish councils.

Wheatley's network of regional and district councils fitted with the
Conservative Government's preference for two-tier local government, but
now it was the large size and remoteness of the regional tiers that came in
for criticism. The huge Strathclyde Region in particular comprised almost
half of Scotland's total population and eventually had to establish non-
elected sub-regional councils for administrative convenience.

Northern Ireland

Exhibit 4.1 shows that Northern Ireland's local government was reformed
at the same time as that in the rest of the UK. That reform, though, and the
significantly different structures it produced, needs to be set in the context
of the political conflicts between the province's Unionist and Republican
communities, which had intensified during the 1960s.

Since the Local Government (Ireland) Act 1898, Northern Ireland had had a structure similar to that on the mainland. There were two all-purpose county boroughs – Belfast and Londonderry – and a two-tier system of 6 counties *(not* the nine counties of the historic Ulster province) and 55 urban and rural district councils. The majority Unionist population had ensured that boundaries were drawn so as to give them control of most councils and exclude the Republican parties from any significant influence.

The resulting inequalities of service provision, particularly discriminatory housing allocations, were among the principal grievances of civil rights protesters in the 1960s, and eventually in 1969 a Review Body was set up, chaired by Patrick Macrory. Influenced by the Wheatley Commission, the Macrory Report proposed a scaled-down two-tier model, with most services being provided by regional councils and a greatly reduced number of districts.

The Local Government (Northern Ireland) Act 1972 implemented some of these recommendations, but, with the suspension of the Stormont government in the same year and the introduction of direct rule from Westminster, the proposed elected regional tier did not materialise. In an attempt to remove sectarian bias, most local authority powers in housing, personal social services, health, education and planning were placed in the hands of various non-elected boards, agencies and departments of the Northern Ireland Office.

Local democracy in Northern Ireland was therefore limited to 26 *district councils* elected by the single transferable vote (STV) system of proportional representation, but, compared with their mainland counterparts, their responsibilities were restricted – if not wholly to the 'bins, bogs and burials' that is sometimes suggested. In addition to refuse collection and disposal, public conveniences, cemeteries and crematoria, there were leisure, recreational and cultural facilities, consumer protection, environmental health and safety, and, increasingly, tourism. But, added together, the 26 districts' annual spending amounted to less than 4% of Northern Ireland's total public expenditure, and the list of functions for which their responsibility extends only to rights of consultation includes education, social services, housing, roads, transport, fire, police, libraries, and even street lighting. Filling the democratic deficit, or the 'Macrory gap', were area boards and various other quangos. Policy power effectively remained at Westminster.

The Conservative years – politics turns to spite?

By the mid-1970s, then, the dual town/country structure of local government, fundamentally unchanged since the end of the nineteenth century, had been comprehensively restructured. A two-tier system was in place across almost the whole country. It had its tensions – competing mandates, resource jealousies, the blurring of lines of responsibility and accountability for service provision – but it would, surely, see us through to the next millennium? Hardly, as you will already have gathered from Exhibit 4.1: parts of this new structure were to be dismantled almost before they had had a chance to establish themselves.

The Conservative Government that took office in 1979, despite having far more councillors and controlling far more councils than any other party, was not well disposed towards local government. The prime minister, Margaret Thatcher, 'did not have much time for local councils, which she expected to be the agents of central government' (Baker, 1993, p. 111). Other ministers saw it as 'wasteful, profligate, irresponsible, unaccountable, luxurious and out of control' (Newton and Karran, 1985, p. 116). The result was a barrage of legislation aimed at remodelling the finances of local authorities, but not initially their structure.

Then in 1983 the Conservative Party introduced into its General Election manifesto a pledge to abolish the six English metropolitan county authorities and the GLC. As Elcock notes (1991, p. 39), the

> official reason given for this hasty proposal was that these authorities had few functions and were therefore redundant: but in 1981 all seven had fallen under Labour control and the GLC Leader, Ken Livingstone, had emerged as a colourful and effective antagonist with his headquarters just across the Thames from Mrs Thatcher's.

There was a clear party-political dimension to this structural reform, just as there had been to the reforms of the 1970s, and as there will be in any reorganisation of sub-central government in a unitary state. This abolition of a tier of elected local government, 'very much a personal decision of Mrs Thatcher, [was] widely regarded as an act of political spite ... right off the normal political agenda and in almost any other European country ... unconstitutional' (Hebbert, 1998, quoted in Travers, 2004, p. 30).

The Government's case was encapsulated in the title of its post-election White Paper, *Streamlining the Cities* (DoE, 1983). Abolition of these councils would reduce bureaucracy, duplication and waste, and generally 'roll back the frontiers of the state'. In transferring most of their already limited range of functions to borough and district councils, government would be brought closer to the people, making it more comprehensible and accessible, and thereby enhancing local democracy. In doing so, the Government would also be removing the irritation of the policy conflicts between the top-tier metropolitan authorities and central government whenever, as at the time, the two were controlled by different political parties.

Despite cross-party Parliamentary opposition, the Local Government Act 1985 was eventually passed, and from 31 March 1986 the GLC and the six metropolitan county councils ceased to exist, London having no city-wide government for the first time since the 1850s. Many of the abolished councils' responsibilities were taken over by the London boroughs and metropolitan district/borough councils, but some continued to be run on the same metropolis-wide scale, by a range of joint boards and committees, ad hoc agencies and central government departments. The result was a degree of complexity and fragmentation that could seem not so much a 'streamlining' of our cities as a return to the administrative 'tangle' of the nineteenth century.

In the metropolitan areas the picture was less perplexing than in London. Ceremonially and statistically, the metropolitan counties continued to exist. It was their councils that were abolished, and most of their functions were taken over by the districts/boroughs, which became effectively unitary authorities (see Exhibit 5.1). Fewer functions than in London went to quasi-governmental agencies, but those that did were among the biggest-spending and highest-profile services. In all six metropolitan areas there were *joint boards* for passenger transport, police, fire and civil defence, and in Greater Manchester and Merseyside also for waste disposal. In addition, *joint committees* were established dealing with recreation, arts and economic development. None of these joint bodies was *directly elected*, most being controlled by councillors *nominated* from the constituent metropolitan districts. In the terminology introduced in Chapter 2, the abolition of these councils constituted a step along the road from directly elected local government towards the world of local governance.

One of the 1986 reforms, however, was exceptionally short-lived. The *Inner London Education Authority* had been a sub-committee of the GLC, covering the former LCC area. With the GLC's abolition, a new arrangement was needed, and the ILEA became, unusually for this country in the twentieth century, a *directly elected unifunctional* council, similar to the elected school boards in parts of the USA. But its almost inevitable Labour domination, allied to its high expenditure levels and perceived enthusiasm for 'progressive' education, led to its almost instant abolition in the Education Reform Act 1988. From April 1990, responsibility for education services passed to the individual Inner London boroughs.

Summary – into the 1990s

Later that year, in November, Mrs Thatcher was replaced as prime minister by John Major, whose biggest inherited local government headache was the hugely unpopular poll tax, or community charge, and how to get rid of it. In comparison, the structure of the system might have seemed reasonably straightforward and unproblematic.

A similar structure of elected local government existed throughout the *non-metropolitan areas* of England, and the whole of Wales and mainland Scotland. There were two principal tiers of local authorities, each tier providing a range of services judged appropriate to its scale. In England and Wales, the upper-tier authorities, with most of the big-spending and labour-intensive services, were known as *counties*; in Scotland they were designated *regions*. The lower-tier authorities were known as *districts,* some of which were entitled, for historic reasons, to call themselves *cities* or *boroughs*. The dramatic contrast between counties and districts in size, employment and overall contribution to the local government economy can be seen in Exhibit 15.2. In much of non-metropolitan Britain there was also a 'sub-principal' tier of authorities, known as parish councils in England and community councils in both Wales and Scotland.

In *metropolitan* England and London there was only one elected tier of local government – *metropolitan* and *London boroughs* – describable as *unitary* or *most-purpose* local authorities. Instead of sharing responsibility for service provision with other elected councils, they now operated alongside other indirectly elected or nominated bodies. In practice, single-tier local government – even more so today than in the 1980s – is far from as simple as it sounds; so, even in this book, when you read 'unitary', think 'most-purpose', rather than 'all-purpose'.

In Northern Ireland there was a single-tier structure of 26 district councils with a more limited range of service responsibilities than even their non-metropolitan district counterparts on the mainland. The major functions of health and social services, education and libraries were organised through *area boards* made up of approximately one-third district councillors and two-thirds ministerial appointees.

None of these UK local authorities had been in existence for more than 25 years, and most for barely 15. The system had been restructured fundamentally in the 1960s and 1970s, and substantially tinkered with in the 1980s. Time, you might have thought, for a period of stability, in which they could settle down and establish a presence and identity in their communities, while people became familiar with who their local governors were, and what they did. If so, as will be seen in Chapter 5, you could hardly have been more wrong!

The Way It Is: External Structures

Mapping change and changing maps

The next three chapters outline the present-day arrangements of UK sub-central government – that is, both local and regional. The Office for National Statistics (ONS), who produce the most authoritative maps of these things, used to suggest that the UK saw more administrative boundary changes each year than the rest of the European Union (EU) put together. The EU is now larger, so it may not be literally true, but the underlying point is – to the extent that, to cover recent developments satisfactorily, two chapters in this book's previous edition have become three. Chapter 7 deals with the *internal* structures of local authorities: the varying ways they manage themselves and conduct their business. Before that, we look at *external* structures: in Chapter 6 at the devolved institutions in Scotland, Wales, Northern Ireland and the English regions, and first at local authorities, updating the evolution of our local government system, which was left hanging at the end of Chapter 4.

England – hybridity, or a dog's breakfast?

We saw in Chapter 4 how structural reform, once it enters the agenda of national political debate, can acquire its own momentum. That may explain why, following the bouts of reorganisation in the 1960s, 1970s, and 1980s, there was further GB-wide structural reform during the 1990s. For, unlike thirty years previously, there were no longer large numbers of small authorities struggling to cope with the problems of urban and suburban growth and geographical mobility, and few in the local government world were keen to uproot a structure less than a generation old.

The reform impetus came predominantly from a single individual, Michael Heseltine, a Conservative leadership contender following Margaret Thatcher's resignation in 1990, who became instead Secretary of State for the Environment. Keen both to make a late-career impact and to deflect electoral attention away from the massively unpopular poll tax, Heseltine ensured that local government reorganisation featured prominently in the 1992 Conservative manifesto: 'We will set up a commission to examine, area by area, the appropriate local government arrangements in England',

Figure 5.1 *Cartoon – A confusing solution*

Source: *Local Government Chronicle*, 16 September 1994.

the manifesto proclaimed, the main objective being to decide 'whether in any area a *single tier* of local government could provide better accountability and greater efficiency' (emphasis ours).

That phrasing was interesting. It clearly signalled a *structure-led* or *cartographic* remedy for any perceived deficiencies of local government: a keenness to draw revised boundary lines on maps, rather than respect the integrity of localities. It seemed also rather a topsy-turvy approach to reform: deciding the structure of local government before addressing its future role. It didn't in itself, though, signal anything about the scale or localness of the envisaged authorities. Single-tier authorities could in principle be any size. We already had some examples: Birmingham – over a million; Liverpool, Manchester, Sheffield – over half a million; Orkney and Shetland – around 18,000; Isles of Scilly – 2,000. At the very least, a unitary structure could be based on either existing districts or a required merger of districts. But the heavy hint was contained in that final manifesto phrase: 'greater efficiency'. Even then, that was central government shorthand for 'bigger', and in succeeding years it has come to be an almost unchallenged precept: bigger equals more efficient. The result Michael Heseltine envisaged was a structure whose population scale was much closer to the metropolitan districts' 325,000 than the non-metropolitan districts' 100,000.

The government's intention was that its Local Government Commission's county-by-county structural reviews would produce unitary local government across most of non-metropolitan England, bringing it into line with the all-unitary systems that, as we shall see later in this chapter, were being imposed on Scotland and Wales through ministerial diktat.

Figure 5.2 *The local authority map of England, 2009/10*

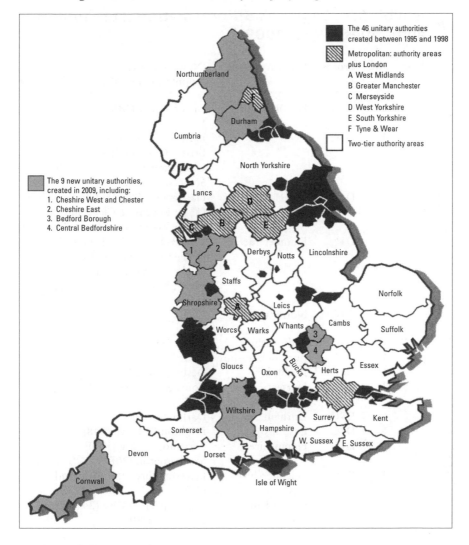

Initially, that looked to be a likely outcome. But the public, when consulted, were unconvinced. Though many liked the *idea* of unitary local government, far more, when asked, were opposed to the Commission's detailed plans for their own counties, and to their likely upheaval and cost. In most counties the weight of opinion favoured the status quo.

The almost inevitable outcome – given the Major Government's national unpopularity and minimal parliamentary majority – was a policy retreat. Instead of unitary local government becoming the norm in England, there emerged 'hybridity', to use the technical expression for a mix of single- and two-tier local authorities, or a dog's breakfast – the latter obviously being

Exhibit 5.1 England's 55 non-metropolitan unitary authorities, 1995–2009

Year	No.	Process	Former county	'New' unitaries (population in 000s)
1995	1	C+D	Isle of Wight	Isle of Wight (133)
1996 (13)	4	D+C	Avon	Bath & NE Somerset (169); Bristol City (381); South Gloucestershire (246); North Somerset (188)
	4	D+C	Cleveland	Hartlepool (89); Middlesbrough (135); Redcar & Cleveland (139); Stockton-on-Tees (179).
	4	D+C	Humberside	East Riding of Yorkshire (314); (Kingston upon) Hull City (244); North Lincolnshire (153); North East Lincolnshire (158).
	1	D+C	North Yorkshire	York (181)
1997 (13)	1	D+C	Bedfordshire	Luton (184)
	1	D+C	Buckinghamshire	Milton Keynes (207)
	1	D+C	Derbyshire	Derby City (222)
	2	D+C	Dorset	Bournemouth (163); Poole (138)
	1	D+C	Durham	Darlington (98)
	1	D+C	East Sussex	Brighton & Hove (248)
	2	D+C	Hampshire	Portsmouth City (187); Southampton (208)
	2	D+C	Leicestershire	Leicester City (280); Rutland (34)
	1	D+C	Staffordshire	Stoke-on-Trent City (241)
	1	D+C	Wiltshire	Swindon (180)

the view presented in Figure 5.1, showing Sir John Banham, the Commission's chairman, hammering a final piece of the reorganisation puzzle into place.

To be fair, the true picture, presented in Exhibit 5.1 and Figure 5.2, was less chaotic than the cartoon suggests. Between 1995 and 1998, 46 new unitary authorities were created, covering just over a quarter of the population of non-metropolitan England. Only 4 of the 39 former county councils disappeared entirely, 14 counties stayed unchanged, and the remaining 19 became hybrid structures: one or two unitary authorities – mainly cities

Exhibit 5.1 continued

Year	No.	Process	Former county	'New' unitaries (population in 000s)
1998 (19)	6	D+C	Berkshire	Bracknell Forest (110); Reading (143); Slough (119); West Berkshire (145); Windsor & Maidenhead (134); Wokingham (150)
	1	D+C	Cambridgeshire	Peterborough City (156)
	2	D+C	Cheshire	Halton (118); Warrington (191)
	2	D+C	Devon	Plymouth City (240); Torbay (130)
	2	D+C	Essex	Southend-on-Sea (161); Thurrock (143)
	1	D+C	Hereford & Worcester	Herefordshire (175)
	1	D+C	Kent	Medway (250)
	2	D+C	Lancashire	Blackburn with Darwen (137); Blackpool (142)
	1	D+C	Nottinghamshire	Nottingham City (267)
	1	D+C	Shropshire	Telford & Wrekin (158)
2009 (5)	1	C+D	Cornwall	Cornwall (524)
	1	C+D	Durham	Durham County (492)
	1	C+D	Northumberland	Northumberland County (307)
	1	C+D	Shropshire	Shropshire (289)
	1	C+D	Wiltshire	Wiltshire (450)
(4)	1	D+C	Bedfordshire	Bedford Borough (153); Central Bedfordshire (241)
	1	D+C	Cheshire	Cheshire East (356); Cheshire West & Chester (324)

Note: C+D = County taking over district functions; D+C = District(s) taking over county functions.

or large towns, including many former county boroughs – in otherwise unchanged two-tier counties (see Exhibits on linked website). With most of the Commission's merger recommendations failing to materialise, the average population of the new unitaries was around 180,000: huge by any other than UK standards, but modest in comparison with what was to come.

There was thus a second generation of largely urban unitaries to add to the 36 metropolitan districts and 32 London boroughs that became unitary in 1986. And, if that arrangement sounds vaguely familiar, it is: an at least partial return to the pre-1974 structure described in Chapter 4, when county boroughs were the 'independent islands' within two-tier counties. As for the Local Government Commission, its review functions were absorbed into the Electoral Commission – an independent body, established in 2000, with a remit to keep under review all UK electoral law and practice. It is now the Boundary Committee for England, to distinguish it from the Boundary Commission, which deals with parliamentary boundaries.

The end of English 'local' government?

The relatively small total of 46 new English unitaries was no measure of the demands this restructuring episode had made on local government. All 39 counties were reviewed, and the Commission's draft recommendations had been for 99 new unitaries in 35 of them (Game, 1997). Virtually every county and district council, therefore, prepared its submission, demonstrating its capacity to be a stand-alone unitary, part of some multi-district unitary, or indeed anything other than completely abolished. It was divisive, setting district against district, and all districts against their respective counties, which tended to have both the resources and arguments to make the strongest case for unitary status. Such experiences are not easily forgotten, and few local government 'insiders' imagined that, even with a change of government, they had heard the last of restructuring. They were right.

After a brief hiatus, unitary authorities reappeared in the Labour Government's plans for the directly elected regional assemblies that it hoped would constitute the English dimension of the devolution programme already in place in Scotland, Wales and Northern Ireland. Local people would have a referendum vote on whether they wanted an elected assembly, but the *quid pro quo* was that they would also have to choose a form of unitary local government, if they didn't already have one. No region would be allowed more than one tier of sub-central government, lest ministers be accused of 'increasing bureaucracy'. In the event, as we shall see in Chapter 6, only one referendum took place, in the North East in 2004, where voters decisively rejected an elected regional assembly, which made their accompanying views on alternative structures of unitary local government in Northumberland and Durham irrelevant – for a couple of years, anyway.

Both Conservative and Labour Governments had now failed to restructure England's sub-central government from the top down in ways they had wished. Which perhaps explains why the Labour Government's 2006 White Paper, *Strong and Prosperous Communities*, adopted a different, 'invitational' approach. The document's analysis started promisingly:

Ideally, local government structures and boundaries would reflect people's natural sense of place. But achieving this objective is not always easy – particularly in shire areas where economy of scale has in some cases led to services being organised over areas with little connection to recognised communities ... Many district boundaries reflect artificial communities with little significance for local people. This lack of community identity is reflected in the artificial names of some district councils. In other areas the boundary does not reflect the natural economic boundaries of a city or town, making it harder to plan for growth. (paras 3.50–3.52)

Absolutely; we could hardly have put it better ourselves – though we did try in Chapter 3. It read like a prospectus for a structure based on a single or lower tier of 'recognisable' town- and community-based local authorities. But then the White Paper authors revealed their antipathy to two-tier structures and their certainty of the virtues of size. Two-tier systems – like those of all other Western European countries with populations of over 10 million (apart from those with three-tiers) – were apparently, in Britain, recipes for confusion, duplication and inefficiency. Turning to size, it should be noted that England's smallest district at this time had a population of over 25,000, or nearly five times that of the *average* municipality elsewhere in the EU, while the average district area was about ten times that of the average EU municipality. Yet our 'small' authorities – presumably those between 25,000 and, say, 75,000 – in some way lacked the 'capacity to secure efficiency, drive change and provide strong leadership' (para. 3.52), and would have to fight to justify their continued existence.

The White Paper detected 'a widely held view that moving to unitary structures would be the best way [to] improve accountability and leadership, increase efficiency, and improve outcomes for local people' (para. 3.55). This time, though, the government would not try to prescribe or impose. Rather, it would invite local authorities in shire areas to make proposals themselves for unitary local government that would enhance strategic leadership, empower local neighbourhoods, command broad support, and be affordable, in the sense of representing value for money and meeting the costs of change from councils' existing resources (para. 3.55). These criteria were defined imprecisely and consequently were open to questionable interpretation by ministers (Chisholm and Leach, 2008), but they were undeniably demanding, and the White Paper indicated that only a handful of proposals were expected by the three-month deadline specified (January 2007). However, even in two-tier areas not moving towards unitary structures, there would still have to be new and more effective 'governance arrangements' between county and district councils, in order to achieve similar efficiency gains to those expected of the new unitaries (para. 3.59).

Perhaps ministers overlooked how much preparatory work on unitary status had been done a decade earlier and was still gathering dust on councils' shelves, for they were almost deluged by a total of 26 bids that they had barely two months to evaluate. In March the 26 were reduced to 16, which then went out to consultation. In July, the Minister for Local Government, John Healey (No.1 'Mover and Shaker' listed in Exhibit 1.2), announced a supposedly final list of nine successful bids – except that that success depended on the little matter of parliamentary approval of the 2007 Local Government and Public Involvement in Health Act, which was still some months from becoming law. On these grounds, two councils involved in unsuccessful bids challenged the legality of the whole review, but the Court of Appeal declared it had been legalised retrospectively. It was ministers who had taken Parliament for granted, but the chief losers in the delay were Exeter City and Ipswich Borough Councils, both of whose approved bids for unitary status were suspended, while the Boundary Committee undertook further reviews. Finally, an additional 'last minute' Central Bedfordshire unitary was created from a merger of Mid and South Bedfordshire districts, despite having previously fallen at the first hurdle, back in March.

It was a quicker process than in the 1990s, but, as an exercise in rational, evidence-based policy-making, hardly more satisfactory. The outcome was the nine new authorities listed at the end of Exhibit 5.1: five whole-county and four split-county unitaries, some of whose first councils were elected in May 2008 with the remainder in June 2009, over two months after their authorities had come into official existence, on 1 April 2009. Councillors, therefore, as well as MPs, were taken for granted in this unitary stampede – not that there were all that many of them left.

Residents in the nine new unitaries had 1,321 (or 64 per cent fewer) councillors in 2009 than they had previously, each councillor having to attempt to represent an average of more than 4,200 residents. Which is one reason why 'local' in the title of this section is given so-called ironic quotation marks, because, if it wasn't already a dubious description for the scale of this country's local government, these most recent arrivals – particularly the whole-county unitaries – have surely made it so now. These five 'local' authorities have average populations of over 400,000, compared to the 180,000 average of the 1990s' unitaries. In area they range from Durham (860 square miles) to Northumberland (1,942 square miles) – each larger than at least a fifth of the countries of the world, in what is itself only about the 79th largest. Of course, there are bigger lower tier units of local government in countries like Australia, Canada and the USA, but our reference point is Europe, and Northumberland is twice the size of Luxembourg.

Luxembourg – albeit with a larger population – has 118 *communes* with over a thousand councillors. Forty years ago, local democracy in Northumberland was not that different: 22 councils with about 620 councillors (Game, 2009b, p. 21). The reorganisation of the 1970s cut numbers of councils by two-thirds and councillors by over a half. Today, to

Luxembourgers and many other Europeans, it is probably unrecognisable as local government at all: one council with 67 councillors, each attempting to represent about 4,600 residents.

Bedrock loses out to buck bang

The startling drop in councillor numbers seems strange, given the 2006 White Paper's acclaim of councillors as 'the bedrock of local democracy ... [with] a key role in ensuring local services are responsive to the needs of the needs of their constituents and enabling local people's voices to be heard' (para. 3.10). Indeed, it went much further: 'We need to reaffirm the importance of councillors' role as democratic champions' (para. 3.11). They should be given new powers, their role as community champions more clearly defined, and they should be recruited from more diverse socio-economic backgrounds, making them more representative of their communities (para. 3.11). The White Paper did not explain, and neither did ministers, how all this boosting of councillors' roles and making the (still part-time) job more appealing to a wider cross-section of the electorate would be achieved by cutting their numbers by two-thirds. It seemed more like a deliberate undermining of that local democratic bedrock.

Minister John Healey, in his press conference on 1 April 2009, celebrating 'the biggest shake-up of local democracy in one single day since the seventies', didn't actually mention the big shake-out of councillors. He did, though, make it unmistakably clear what this 'stripping out a layer of local government' was all about: efficiency savings. The new unitaries would ultimately, between them, make annual savings of a suspiciously round £100 million; senior positions would be slashed by 300 posts – nine chief executives instead of 44. Local democracy, in short, came in a poor second to, in the Minister's expressive phrase, 'more bang for taxpayers' buck' (DCLG, 2009a).

Scotland and Wales – fewer councils increase democratic deficit

John Major's Conservative Government in the early 1990s was as keen on bringing unitary local government to Scotland and Wales as to England. Politically, though, there was one big difference. While the government's narrow parliamentary majority rested entirely on its having more than 60 per cent of the 524 English MPs, in Scotland the party held just 11 out of 72 Commons seats and in Wales 6 out of 38. It might look inequitable, even cynical, but Ministers could afford to treat Scotland and Wales differently, and they did. There were no independent commission reviews to examine options and make recommendations area by area. Instead, the Scottish and Welsh Secretaries of State simply proposed single-tier structures of authorities that would, it was claimed, have greater local identity, be more efficient and more accountable. There were a few parliamentary amendments, but what resulted – thanks substantially to the votes of English Conservative MPs – were the nationwide unitary systems the Government sought: 32 unitary or 'all-purpose' authorities in Scotland and 22 in Wales.

In both Scotland and Wales, these ministerially driven reorganisations halved the numbers of councils, which inevitably cover larger areas than the former districts and, as in England, have far fewer councillors (see Exhibits on linked website). The outcome of the successive bouts of reorganisation is that Great Britain has, on average, the largest local authorities and the highest ratios of citizens to elected councillors of any country in Western Europe (see Exhibit 14.3). The term 'democratic deficit', often applied to the alleged deficiencies of the European Union, seems more than justified here as well.

It doesn't have to be this way

To be honest, neither of us are great fans of the Blow Monkeys, in either their original or more recent incarnations, but the title of their best known hit does have a direct relevance here. For the obvious question raised by Britain's insistent drive, in the name of efficiency, towards ever-larger, single-tier 'local' government is: why aren't all other countries doing the same? Do they want to be inefficient?

First, as we see in Exhibit 5.2, Britain is not entirely alone. Other European countries have sought to merge their smaller local authorities and enlarge the scale of their local government systems to a proportionally similar (or, in Denmark's case, greater) extent. Where we stand out is obviously that our mergers and enlargements started from a much larger base than did these other countries, and today therefore our 'most local' local authorities have an average population size of between 2.6 and 87 times the size of theirs.

Second, it is also evident from Exhibit 5.2 that some countries – France, Italy and Spain, for example – have not seen the merger process as being inevitable. It doesn't have to be this way, and their governments have either chosen or been forced to adopt alternative strategies. In France, the most extreme example, it has been a mixture of both. A proposal for even the smallest communes to merge and thereby lose their governmental identity and independence is likely to meet fierce local opposition, and the outcome has been a proliferation of *communautés* – inter-municipal co-operatives. There are over 33,000 of these, covering most communes, many with their own tax-raising powers. Spain has a similar network of *mancomunidades*

Exhibit 5.2 Mergers and scale of local government in Europe

	No. of municipalities (most local tier)			Population	
	1950	2009	% change	Average	Smallest
Denmark	1,390	98	−93	56,000	2,058
UK	2,060	407	−81	150,000	35,000
Belgium	2,670	589	−78	18,000	84
Netherlands	1,010	443	−56	37,000	113
Germany	24,150	12,340	−49	6,600	5
Spain	9,210	8,111	−12	5,500	6
France	38,000	36,783	−3	1,730	0
Italy	7,780	8,101	+4	7,320	33

Main source: CLRD, 2008.

or municipal associations. In both cases, the aim is to achieve the economies and efficiencies of co-operation, but without losing the institutions and democratic benefits of real and established local communities governing themselves.

Thirdly, such countries would seriously question – as would many in the UK – whether there is any general correlation at all between organisational size and the quality or efficiency of service provision in the way our governments seem to take for granted. Both common sense and economic theory suggest that economies of scale will operate in different ways for different services, and there are few deliverers of more diverse ranges of services than local authorities. Moreover, the government knows this too, because it commissioned the research that demonstrates it, and published it on the same day (26 October 2006) as its White Paper.

The main conclusion of the Cardiff University research team was that the relationship between local authority population size and service performance is a highly complex one, varying across services and between different performance measures of the same service. If the balance of evidence suggested that performance tends to be better in large than in small authorities (Andrews *et al.*, 2006, p. 5), it must be remembered that 'large' referred to existing authorities, not the huge whole-county unitaries the White Paper was encouraging. But even that modest conclusion emerged only through a welter of completely cross-cutting statistical relationships, as illustrated in Exhibit 5.3.

Simply crunching the numbers produced statistically significant population size effects for approaching half of the 520 performance measures

Exhibit 5.3 Varying effects of council size on service performance

Positive linear: ↗ Bigger = better	Negative linear: ↘ Bigger = worse	U-shape Bigger = worse, up to a point	Inverted U-shape Bigger = better, up to a point
17 of 47 statistically significant results, including:	7	12	11
Percentage of household waste recycled	Speed, accuracy of processing benefit claims	Percentage of council tax collected	Percentage absence in secondary schools
Percentage of unfit private sector dwellings made fit for habitation	Reviews of child protection cases	Percentage of pupils achieving 5 or more A*–C GCSEs	Percentage of council housing repair appointments kept
No. of museum visits per 1,000 population	Percentage of footpaths easy to use by the public	Percentage of buildings accessible for disabled people	Educational qualifications of looked-after children

Source: Andrews *et al.* (2006), table 4, pp. 18–25.

tested. But those effects were of the four differing types shown in Exhibit 5.3: positive linear – the bigger the authority, the better the performance; negative linear – the reverse; non-linear U-shaped – performance falls initially but improves after a certain size; and non-linear inverted U-shaped – the reverse. Exhibit 5.3 shows only a handful of the size effects from one type of performance measure, but even these demonstrate the near-impossibility of identifying a single 'best' size for a local authority with even this small selection of service responsibilities. If anything, it might appear to make the case for a two-tier or multi-tier system, with different sizes of local authority providing different types of service – such as the one established back in 1974.

The Greater London Authority – strategic local government

The creation during the 1990s of the second generation of English unitary authorities did not quite complete the sequence of local government restructurings during the last decades of the twentieth century. There was still London: since 1986, the only major Western capital without a democratic voice of its own. The Labour Party, in control of the GLC at the time of its abolition, had pledged consistently to restore some form of directly elected government to Greater London, and in 1997 its chance arrived. The party's manifesto (p. 34) promised:

> a new deal for London, with a strategic authority and a mayor, each directly elected. Both will speak up for the needs of the city and plan its future. They will not duplicate the work of the boroughs, but take responsibility for London-wide issues – economic regeneration, planning, policing, transport and environmental protection.

The intention was to produce a novel and unique set of institutions: a mix of strategic local government and embryonic regional government. The Greater London Authority (GLA) would be quite different from the mayoral town and city councils that the Government was planning for the rest of England. But neither would it be permitted the self-governing powers of the devolved administrations in Scotland, Wales and Northern Ireland.

Every local government structural reform, we emphasised in Chapter 4, has its party political dimension. The GLC was abolished because of the Thatcher Government's detestation of 'Red Ken' Livingstone's 'municipal socialist' administration. The new GLA owed just as much to party and personality politics – only this time it was the *internal* politics of New Labour and, extraordinarily, the personality of the same Ken Livingstone. Following the GLC's abolition, Livingstone had become a broadly left-wing, iconoclastic Labour MP, regularly attacking the direction in which his party was being led and those doing the leading. They in turn still held him, his GLC, and other like-minded 1980s' Labour councils, heavily responsible for the party's unpopularity and successive general election defeats.

Justified or not, Tony Blair and his ministers were determined that, under no circumstances, would they permit the creation of a GLC Mark II – a democratically legitimate body with the powers and tax base to enable it to challenge seriously the policies of their own national government. First, unlike the proposed elected mayors of other cities and towns, who would be taking over councils with wide-ranging services and correspondingly large budgets, London's mayor would have direct control of none of these services and limited tax-raising opportunities. Most day-to-day services – education, social services, housing, environmental health and consumer protection, leisure, recreation, the arts – would still be provided by the 32 London boroughs, several perhaps with mayors of their own. The London mayor's importance would be as a figurehead and spokesperson for the nation's capital, with considerable patronage and influence in making appointments to the new executive agencies through which the GLA would exercise its responsibilities, but limited direct powers. Second, continued this prime ministerial line of reasoning, the party leadership's control of its own party machine would prevent the reviled Livingstone from even winning the Labour candidacy for mayor, let alone getting elected.

As obviously should happen for a government with a huge parliamentary majority, things went to plan – to begin with; 72 per cent of Londoners approved the government's White Paper proposals in a referendum, and Labour's massed MPs passed the Greater London Authority Act. With nearly half of London's general election votes, and three-quarters of its MPs, Labour was confident of winning the mayoralty, whether against the Conservatives' initial candidate, the soon-to-be-disgraced Lord (Jeffrey) Archer, or his replacement, the former Minister for Transport in London, Steven Norris. So the ministers' main concern was to secure the selection of a 'politically acceptable' party candidate. A bitter and cynically manipulated selection process ensued, in which the unconcealed objective of the prime minister and his colleagues was to 'Stop Livingstone' at all costs. He was stopped, being narrowly defeated for Labour's candidacy by former Cabinet minister, Frank Dobson, but at the cost of the party's integrity and the scapegoat Dobson's own electability.

The ministerially victimised Livingstone was never more popular and, in a two-stage (Supplementary Vote) election in May 2000, he was elected as an Independent to be London's first executive Mayor, with more than 776,000 votes against Norris's 564,000 – Dobson having been eliminated after the first round of counting. Ken was back, in the remarkable position of being able to say: 'Before I was so rudely interrupted 14 years ago ...'. His vote, moreover, even on a disappointing 34 per cent turnout, was still the highest ever won by a British politician – a significant mandate for an office with deliberately limited direct powers (D'Arcy and MacLean, 2000; Travers, 2004, ch. 3).

Those limited powers – outlined in Exhibit 5.4 – are, however, a real, if utterly predictable, problem. Even in relation to the 'functional bodies' through which most of the GLA's work is done, the Mayor's authority is shared with or constrained by central government departments. As Travers notes (2004, p. 184):

> Any mayor would be rendered largely powerless by the arrangements [of] the Greater London Authority Act ... Expenditure in London on the National Health Service, higher education, further education, training, the arts, housing and social security are all determined by central government. On the other hand, schools, social care, local transport, environmental services and some social housing are responsibilities of the boroughs. The mayor is squeezed between these two blocs of established financial and political power.

Exhibit 5.4 The Greater London Authority (GLA)

What is it?
A unique form of strategic city-wide government for London. It comprises:

- **A directly elected executive Mayor** – the first in the UK. The first Mayor of London, elected in 2000, and re-elected in 2004, was Ken Livingstone (Independent/Labour). He was defeated in 2008 by Boris Johnson (Conservative).
- **A separately elected 25-member Assembly.** Membership following 2008 elections was: 11 Conservatives, 8 Labour, 3 Liberal Democrats, 2 Green Party, 1 British National Party.

The Mayor and Assembly are advised and assisted by a permanent staff of about 600, cut since the election of Mayor Johnson.

What does it do, and how?
Its main responsibilities are *strategic* – principally transport, policing, fire and emergency planning, economic development, planning; secondarily culture, the environment, health. The London boroughs retain responsibility for education, housing, social services, local roads, libraries and museums, refuse collection and environmental health.

The GLA's main responsibilities are exercised through 'The GLA Group' of four *functional boards*, whose members are appointed mainly by and accountable to the Mayor:

- **Transport for London** (TfL) – responsible for most public transport in London, including fare structures and future investment.
- **Metropolitan Police Authority** (MPA) – previously accountable to the Home Secretary.
- **London Fire and Emergency Planning Authority** (LFEPA).
- **London Development Agency** (LDA) – a new body to promote employment, investment, economic development and regeneration in London. Similar to the other eight English Regional Development Agencies.

Who's in charge – the Mayor or the Assembly?
The Mayor decides policy – prepares plans on transport, land use, the environment, culture and so on; appoints and sets the budgets for the functional bodies.

The Assembly works through committees, scrutinising the Mayor's activities and the budget – which it can overturn with a two-thirds majority. Johnson's budgets are therefore effectively safe. It investigates other issues of relevance to Londoners, and makes policy recommendations to the Mayor.

How much does it spend?
The GLA's total (gross) budget for 2010/11 was £14 billion: TfL – £9.6 bn; MPA – £3.6 bn; LFEPA – £0.5 bn. The cost of the GLA itself was about £140 million; 50% of the budget comes from central government grants plus business rates; almost 40% from fares and charges; 7% from London taxpayers – or £310 on a Band D Council Tax bill.

Where is it?
'City Hall' occupies one of London's most spectacular new buildings: Lord Foster's award-winning, glass fog-lamp-resembling construction alongside Tower Bridge – sometimes known as the Mayor's 'glass testicle'. It featured, along with the original 'wobbly' Millennium Bridge, in the Hugh Grant film, *Love Actually*.

The argument is indisputable, though 'largely powerless' is perhaps a little exaggerated, not least because Livingstone was a skilful enough politician to make it so. Even in his first term, Livingstone had some significant policy achievements. Bus usage increased to its highest total in forty years, there were cuts in fares, the Oyster smartcard public transport ticketing system, the Docklands Light Railway extension, the redevelopment of Trafalgar Square, and the recruitment of additional police officers. Above all, road user or congestion charging – on this scale, a completely untested approach to traffic management – was introduced successfully in 2003 in the face of massive user and media opposition and ministers' expectation, if not hope, that it would fail spectacularly (Glaister, 2005, p. 226). Its success, and the international interest it created, meant the time had arrived for an embarrassed prime ministerial climb-down, and, in time for the 2004 mayoral election, Livingstone was grudgingly readmitted to the Labour Party and adopted as its candidate. Whereupon, still campaigning largely under his previously Independent colour of mauve, rather than Labour's red, he was comfortably re-elected until 2008, again defeating the Conservatives' Steven Norris, this time by 828,000 votes to 667,000.

The Million Vote Mandate

Livingstone, now an asset to the government, particularly following his leading role in the successful 2012 Olympics bid, pushed hard for increased powers, and appeared to be rewarded with the 2007 Greater London Authority Act. The Act increased the Mayor's strategic role in relation to housing, health inequalities, planning, culture, climate change, waste and the environment. It gave him the right to appoint – or be – Chair of the Metropolitan Police Authority. It did not, however, drastically reduce the number of boroughs; or give the mayor significant powers to check on their performance; and it certainly did not scrap the Assembly and replace it with a borough leaders' committee – all key Livingstone projects. The irony is that a Conservative-led government, committed to strong mayoral leadership and to maximising efficiency savings through mergers and joint working arrangements, could conceivably deliver all three.

Livingstone, however, will not be in City Hall to press the case, because in the 2008 election he was defeated by Boris Johnson, the well-known Conservative MP and journalist, whose candidacy he had perhaps ill-advisedly dismissed as a joke. In truth, his defeat probably surprised onlookers more than Livingstone himself. The Labour Party nationally was desperately unpopular, and he had long doubted his ability to persuade enough electors to give him their second preference votes, rather than effectively waste them on candidates never realistically likely to be in the Supplementary Vote run-off between the leading two. He was right.

However, the high profile contest had raised turnout by 10 per cent, enabling Johnson to become the first UK politician able to claim a 'Million Vote Mandate', winning 1,169,000 votes to Livingstone's 1,029,000. He was also No. 2 'Mover and Shaker' in Exhibit 1.2, and at that point arguably the most powerful Conservative in the country.

Johnson's candidacy was secured in a novel 'primary' election open to all London voters, but his successful campaign focused on the Conservative-inclined boroughs of Outer London that he claimed were neglected under Livingstone's 'Zone 1' mayoralty. His manifesto was light on policy specifics, but immediately on taking office he began to follow his predecessor's example in making the most of his office's limited powers, while capitalising on his evidently appealing personal style. His early initiatives included banning alcohol consumption on London Transport; taking the Chair of the Metropolitan Police Authority and forcing the resignation of Police Commissioner Ian Blair; producing plans for ending long-term 'rough-sleeping', the world's second-largest (after Paris) urban cycle hire scheme, the replacement of Livingstone's controversial 'bendy buses' with fuel-efficient, open-platform Routemaster IIs, and making London the electric-vehicle capital of Europe. He also froze council tax in each of his first two budgets and cut staffing in City Hall – making it difficult for anyone to claim that, in London at least, local elections don't change anything.

One element of continuity, however, has been the campaign by mayoral incumbents to increase the limited formal powers given to them in the initial legislation. Johnson was quick to use the arrival of a new Conservative-headed government to bid for more powers over health provision, traffic control and the awarding of rail franchises, for the executive and scrutiny functions of the Metropolitan Police Authority to be split between the Mayor and the Assembly, and for the Olympic Park Legacy Company to become a more democratically accountable Mayoral Development Corporation. Interestingly, though, the Mayor's early shopping list omitted any reference to tax-raising powers – for a city that, thanks partly to the unrebanded council tax, now raises well under 10 per cent of its expenditure from its own taxation, compared to New York's 50 per cent.

Joint arrangements

One obvious difference between the London reorganisation and most of the other recent restructurings is that in London an additional, supposedly co-ordinating, body was being created, whereas the other cases were about merging existing authorities into smaller numbers of unitaries. In London, therefore, one might expect there to have been an institutional streamlining and sharpening of accountability. But, with borough functions remaining largely untouched, and the GLA's powers being so constrained, the extent to which this has occurred is distinctly limited. Travers maps what he calls 'a rococo layering of government departments, regional offices, appointed boards ... joint committees' (2004, pp. 185–7), in addition to, and often competing with, the institutions of elected government.

If this is the picture in London, it is hardly surprising to find something similar in areas of England where in the 1980s and 1990s the metropolitan and 'newcomer' county councils were broken up, and in Scotland and Wales where districts were merged into new unitaries. Not all of the service responsibilities of abolished local authorities can be divided up easily and handed over to new or different elected councils. Across much of the UK nowadays, therefore, alongside the directly elected structures – as part of an area's local governance (see Chapter 2) – there are frequently fretworks of *nominated or indirectly elected joint bodies* and other joint arrangements between councils.

There are three main forms of joint arrangement through which councils work together to provide services:

- *Joint boards.* These are legal bodies, set up by two or more local authorities to provide statutorily required services. Their membership and management require ministerial approval, but they have independent financial powers, enabling them to raise money by 'precept' from their constituent authorities. In Scotland and the English metropolitan areas there are joint boards for police, fire, public transport and waste disposal. In Wales and parts of non-metropolitan England – for example, Thames Valley, West Mercia – there are also joint police boards, where counties are judged to be too small to justify their own force.
- *Joint committees.* Similar to joint boards, these are *voluntarily* created bodies, where two or more smaller authorities establish joint committees of councillors to carry out specific council functions, such as the provision of specialist schools or residential homes, more effectively than they could on their own.
- *Contracting or agency arrangements.* Local authorities have long made contracts with each other for the provision of services. Commonest were probably highways agency arrangements between county councils, the highways authorities, and their district, town and parish councils, with the latter carrying out minor functions such as grass-cutting and vegetation clearance. In the past few years, prompted by the government's drive for more partnership working and efficiency savings, such joint service delivery agreements have increased exponentially, between authorities as well as with other bodies.

As noted at the end of Chapter 4, it is the proliferation of these different kinds of joint arrangement that leads critics to question the labelling of this country's single-tier or unitary councils as 'all-purpose' authorities. They may be the only *directly* elected local authorities in their area, but 'most-purpose' would be a more accurate label. Joint boards, committees and other working arrangements may often offer efficient and effective services, but they do inevitably add to the *fragmentation* of local government, to the potential confusion and uncertainty of the public, and to the dilution of electoral accountability. Those concerned about such developments will point out that in this, as in many other respects, Britain is unusual: Luxembourg, Finland, Cyprus and Malta are the only other Western European countries to have unitary local government systems.

Sub-principal authorities

As emphasised in Chapter 3, this book focuses chiefly on the activities of the country's 'principal' local authorities, and the account of the 2009 reorganisation enables us to summarise diagrammatically how the structure of principal authorities in Great Britain has evolved since the 1970s (see Exhibit 5.5). The Exhibit also includes the multitude of 'non-principal' authorities: parish councils in England, and community councils in Scotland and Wales. Often ancient in origin, they are by no means anachronistic. They have survived the traumas of recent structural reorganisations and, indeed, have increased in number and seen their roles and powers enhanced.

In England, there are approximately 10,200 parishes, of which about 8,700 – predominantly in more rural areas – have parish or town councils, on which serve some 75,000 elected councillors. These 'civil' parishes – to distinguish them from the entirely separate Anglican parochial church councils of 'ecclesiastical' parishes – are, for about a third of the population, a vital part of the British system of local government: independent democratic bodies elected by and accountable to their villages, smaller towns and suburbs. 'Town council', incidentally and confusingly, is synonymous with 'parish council', and any parish council is able to style itself a town council, often entirely appropriately, as some of these parishes are larger than some smaller district councils, with the largest – Weston-super-Mare Town Council – serving a population of over 70,000. Most, however, are far smaller – nearly two-thirds had populations of under a thousand when last surveyed systematically (Ellwood *et al.*, 1992). In Wales, there are some 900 'communities', about 750 of which have established community councils, comparable to English parishes. Scotland is also divided into some 1,200 communities, but Scottish community councils are not local authorities in the same sense, as they have no statutory basis, and neither the power to tax nor any access as of right to public funds.

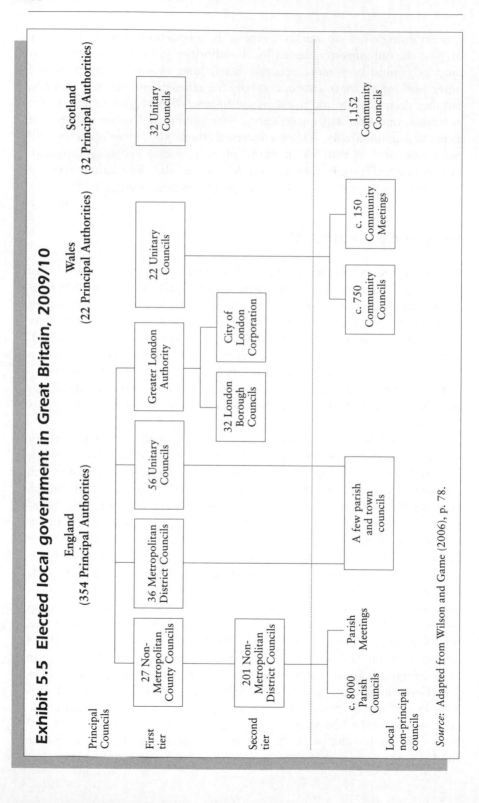

Exhibit 5.5 Elected local government in Great Britain, 2009/10

	England (354 Principal Authorities)	Wales (22 Principal Authorities)	Scotland (32 Principal Authorities)

Principal Councils

First tier
27 Non-Metropolitan County Councils
36 Metropolitan District Councils
56 Unitary Councils
Greater London Authority
22 Unitary Councils
32 Unitary Councils

Second tier
201 Non-Metropolitan District Councils
32 London Borough Councils
City of London Corporation

Local non-principal councils
c. 8000 Parish Councils
Parish Meetings
A few parish and town councils
c. 750 Community Councils
c. 150 Community Meetings
1,152 Community Councils

Source: Adapted from Wilson and Game (2006), p. 78.

The principal functions of Scottish community councils, therefore, are not in the provision of services, but rather in consultation and representation: ascertaining and articulating the views of their local residents. These roles are obviously just as important for any parish, town or Welsh community council. These latter councils, however, have certain rights – to be consulted, for example, by their district and county councils about local planning applications and footpath surveys. They also have potentially wide service-providing powers, acting either on their own initiative or as agents of their county and district councils. The services that tend to be listed most frequently are the provision and maintenance of village halls and community centres, allotments, playing fields, gymnasiums and public baths, footpaths, parks and open spaces, shelters and war memorials, street lighting, car parks, churchyards and burial grounds.

This permitted list was extended in the final days of the Major Conservative Government to include a range of transport and crime prevention powers. Nowadays, therefore, parishes are as likely to be involved in helping with the provision of meals on wheels, providing recycling facilities, organising community buses, setting up car-sharing schemes, installing CCTV cameras to prevent crime, enabling local post offices and stores to remain open, or arranging local GP clinics. A parish council may in addition spend money on any purpose it considers to be of direct benefit to its area or its inhabitants – up to £5 per local elector.

All these powers, however, are *discretionary*: there is no requirement that the services be provided. Where they *are* provided, they are financed partly by fees and charges and partly through a 'precept' added to the council tax collected by their district council from the area's tax-payers. These precepts vary greatly across the country, from under £10 in some places to £100 per council tax Band D property in others, reflecting the equally great variation in the councils' activities. It is this wholly discretionary nature of parish and town councils' work, and not primarily their size, which accounts for the limited attention they receive in this book. They are *not universal* – encompassing less than a third of the population of England and Wales – and they have no *specific duties* to provide services or facilities. They are not to be compared, therefore, with the similarly sized French *communes*, German *Gemeinden*, or Spanish *municipios* that, with their extensive range of powers and competencies, form the basic constitutional tier of their local government systems.

Our local councils, though, are about far more than delivering services:

> they are about a form of democracy close to the people. They derive their legitimacy from elections, and their power comes through reflecting, mobilising and using public opinion as well as from what they can deliver directly, either on their own or in partnership with larger local authorities. (Coulson, 1998, p. 248)

Most counties and districts work seriously these days at developing relations with their parish and town councils, not least because the growing scale of local government forces them to acknowledge the importance of these genuinely *local* councillors as spokespersons for communities that have only a diluted representation in their own memberships. A linked development has been the creation of parish and town councils in metropolitan areas – Leeds, Bradford, Barnsley, Doncaster, Wakefield, St. Helens, Newcastle – and the backing of figures such as Ken Livingstone and Sir Robin Wales, Mayor of Newham, for parish councils in London. The Labour Government's establishment in 2003 of its Quality Parish and Town Council scheme has provided a further boost. A Quality Council has to prove itself both able and efficient – through, for example, having contested elections, regular meetings, training programmes for key personnel, and effective consultation procedures. Having passed this 'quality test', it can seek, particularly by working in partnership with its principal authorities, community and voluntary organisations, to extend the range of services it provides. By 2010, the number of Quality Status parish and town councils was approaching 700.

All this sounds commendable, but there is a real concern that, at the same time and sometimes driven by the same ministers, there have been numerous other *non-elected* 'localist' initiatives – area committees, neighbourhood forums, Local Strategic Partnerships, Local Area Agreements – that have the capacity to compete as well as confuse. It is a theme to which we shall return.

Chapter 6

Devolution for the Nations and Regions

The road to quasi-federalism

For an administration led by a prime minister with no evident interest in the subject, the 1997 Labour Government's record of constitutional reform was remarkable. Within four years it reformed the House of Lords, introduced the Human Rights and Freedom of Information Acts, codified the financing of political parties and election campaigns, introduced an avalanche of new electoral systems, and, as we have seen, continued the structural reform of local government. But, arguably more far-reaching than any of these – and with obvious consequences for a book on UK local government – was its devolution programme. The new devolved institutions in Scotland, Wales and Northern Ireland have changed not just the content of the British constitution but also its very nature. Britain has become an asymmetrical union: effectively a quasi-federal state.

Some will contest 'quasi-federal', so let us briefly justify the use of the term. In a federal state, central and sub-central levels of government are relatively autonomous. Each possesses constitutionally defined powers that the other level cannot encroach upon, and each has a voice in the central policy-making of the state (Deacon and Sandry, 2007, pp. 198–9). Clearly, in these terms, the UK has not suddenly 'gone federal'. There has been no transfer of sovereignty from Westminster; we have no written constitution and no constitution-guarding Supreme Court; devolved institutions have minimal tax-raising powers and no institutionalised role in central policy-making. The Westminster Parliament, then, remains constitutionally supreme, but in practice that supremacy now means different things in the four parts of the UK. In Scotland, Wales and Northern Ireland 'large powers have been removed from the purview of ministers and Members of Parliament' (Bogdanor, 2001, p. 149). The UK has changed and now, without becoming a federal state, resembles one in certain respects; hence 'quasi-federal'.

Devolution to Scotland and Wales

As with the Greater London Authority, the Government's intentions for devolution to Scotland and Wales were outlined in its 1997 manifesto (pp. 33–4):

As soon as possible, we will allow the people of Scotland and Wales to vote in separate referendums on our proposals, which will be set out in white papers. For Scotland we propose a parliament with law-making powers, including limited financial powers to vary revenue, and elected by an additional member system. The Scottish parliament will extend democratic control over responsibilities currently exercised administratively by the Scottish Office. The Welsh assembly will provide democratic control of existing Welsh Office functions. It will have secondary legislative powers, and will be elected by an additional member system. Following majorities in the referendums, we will introduce in the first year of the Parliament legislation on the substantive devolution proposals.

Party manifestos are often dismissed with contempt. This manifesto pledge, however, was implemented to the letter. White Papers were published within two months of the Labour Government taking office, and referendums held in September 1997. The Scottish referendum included two questions, with 74% of Scots voting for a Parliament and 64% for one with limited tax-varying powers. The Welsh Assembly, in contrast, was approved by only the narrowest of majorities: just 50.3% on a 50% turnout.

Legislation followed, as did the first elections in May 1999. Both devolved bodies sought consciously to 'do politics' differently from the traditional and publicly unappealing Westminster model, and they also differed from one another (see Exhibits 6.1 and 6.2). While the Scottish Parliament was from the outset a legislative body, the Welsh Assembly had to wait until 2006 to receive even a limited version of the equivalent powers that it felt it merited. Both institutions have attracted, predictably, their share of criticism. Nationalists and radical devolutionists were almost bound to be dissatisfied, while unionists saw even comparatively modest devolution as an inevitable first step towards an eventual break-up of the UK.

What cannot be disputed is that, long before the 2007 transformation of the SNP and Plaid Cymru from parties of nationalist protest into parties of government, the new institutions had made their presence felt. Though both devolved administrations were Labour-dominated, they pursued from the start policy agendas that diverged openly from those of Labour ministers in London. Michael Keating, summarising key results of a major academic study of Devolution and Constitutional Change, described significant differences in both policy style and substance that are as applicable to Wales as to Scotland (ESRC, 2005, p. 6):

The greatest policy divergence concerns modes of public service delivery. Labour in England has moved away from uniform, publicly provided services towards differentiation, internal markets and mixed models of delivery. This is a matter of belief ... [but] Scotland has not reintroduced internal market elements, and there are no star ratings or foundation hospitals. The Sutherland proposals on free personal care for the elderly, rejected in England, were taken up north of the border.

Scotland has placed more emphasis on local government as a service provider and less on the voluntary sector. There is an explicit commitment to comprehensive education, largely abandoned in England, and there are no school league tables. All parties in the Scottish Parliament have rejected top-up fees for universities, and there is no move to create elite universities or concentrate all the research funding in a few institutions.

It was the early replacement of 'up-front' tuition fees for Scottish students with a (later abolished) graduate endowment – a direct reversal of the Blair Government's policy – that prompted the prime minister's revealing outburst that 'you can't have Scotland doing something different from the rest of Britain ... I am beginning to see the defects in all this devolution stuff' (Ashdown, 2001). He really seemed not to 'get' that, with devolution, policy divergence is precisely what you can have – and, as shown in Exhibit 6.3, *do* have. The last item on the Scottish list is of particular interest. Having already gone their own way on political management and local finance reform, Scottish councils since 2007 have been elected by the single transferable vote (STV) system of proportional representation, eliminating almost all 'one-party monopolistic' or 'one-party dominant' councils (see Exhibit 13.2).

Both Scottish and Welsh devolution have received a kind of independent seal of approval. In Wales the (Lord) Richard Commission that led to the extension of the Assembly's powers in the 2006 Act made recommendations that went considerably further than did the government. Encouraged by the 'growing consensus in favour of devolution' (Richard, 2004, p. 254), the Commissioners proposed a primary legislative Parliament of at least eighty Members, less beholden to Westminster, and elected by STV. The Coalition Government made early arrangements for a referendum on extending the Assembly's law-making powers to be held on 3 March 2011, and indications were that, while support for independence remained limited to about 15% of voters, a plurality of around 40% would favour extending the Assembly's powers, including the power to raise taxes (Constitution Unit, 2009, pp. 45–6).

The 2009 Commission on Scottish Devolution chaired by Professor Sir Kenneth Calman was even more positive. Devolution had been 'a real success' (Calman, 2009, para. 14), and the Commission's recommendations were generally for more devolved powers all round: more tax-raising and borrowing powers; more policy responsibilities – for elections, drink-driving and national speed limits, airgun regulation; and more ministerial involvement in matters relating to UK-wide bodies such as the BBC. As in Wales, there were no consistent signs that nationalist involvement in

Exhibit 6.1 Devolved government in Scotland

What is it?
Unicameral (single-chamber) legislative devolution: the UK Parliament's constitutional sovereignty is unchanged, but it will not, by convention, legislate on devolved matters in Scotland: health, education, local government, economic development, transport, law and home affairs, the environment, agriculture, fisheries and forestry, sport and the arts.

The Scottish Parliament
There are 129 members (MSPs) elected by Additional Member System (AMS) form of proportional representation (see p. 249). 73 members (56.5%) represent individual constituencies; 56 represent 8 electoral regions. The 1999 and 2003 elections produced Labour-dominated 'hung' parliaments and Labour–Liberal Democrat coalition administrations. In 2007, the Scottish Nationalists gained a narrow plurality of seats over Labour: SNP 47 (+20 from 2003), Labour 46 (–4), Conservatives 17 (–1), Liberal Democrats 16 (–1), Greens 2 (–5), Independent 1 (–2). 43 MSPs (33%) were women, compared with 19.6% of MPs.

The Scottish Government
The government of Scotland for all devolved matters. It comprises:

- The First Minister – elected by the whole Parliament; effectively Scotland's prime minister. From 2007, Alex Salmond (SNP).
- A Cabinet of 6 ministers (12 in previous Labour–Lib Dem administrations), appointed by the First Minister and approved by Parliament.
- An advisory Civil Service of about 15,000, organised into 7 Directorates – including Finance and Corporate Services, responsible for relations with local government.

Westminster's reserved responsibilities
These are exercised through the **Secretary of State for Scotland**, and include: the UK constitution, foreign policy, Europe, defence, fiscal and economic policy, employment, benefits and pensions, transport safety, broadcasting policy, the National Lottery.

Financial arrangements
Total 2010/11 budget was £33 billion, only 13% of which was funded by taxation powers devolved to Scotland; almost all the rest was by 'Barnett formula' grant from Westminster. The Scottish Parliament can choose to vary the basic rate of income tax for Scottish residents (the 'tartan tax') by up to 3p – equivalent to £1.3 billion (2008) – but so far has not done so.

Parliamentary committees
Much of the Parliament's work is done through its committees, which are both more powerful – combining both legislative and scrutiny/investigative functions – and more proactive than Westminster's. Significantly, they can also initiate legislation. Committee chairs/convenerships are distributed according to the parties' shares of MSPs.

How is local government handled?
It is part of the large portfolio of the Cabinet Secretary for Finance and Sustainable Growth (John Swinney in 2010). A parliamentary committee for Local Government and Communities can question the minister and scrutinise legislation.

Where is it?
The Parliament Building is a splendid, award-winning structure adjacent to the Palace of Holyroodhouse, Edinburgh. Though wildly over budget and less futuristic than London's City Hall, it is a modern, innovative showcase for many indigenous materials – Kemnay granite, Caithness flagstones, Scottish oak – and companies.

Exhibit 6.2 Devolved government in Wales

What is it?
Initially, a form of executive and administrative devolution, with the UK Parliament retaining control over all primary legislation, but devolving to the National Assembly the power to make secondary legislation on certain matters – similar to the Scottish list. The 2006 Government of Wales Act gave the Assembly limited legislative powers through Assembly Measures, but still subject to Westminster approval.

The National Assembly for Wales
There are 60 Assembly Members (AMs) elected by the Additional Member System: 40 (67%) representing individual constituencies, and 20 representing 5 electoral regions. None of the first three elections gave any party an overall majority of seats, so Labour governed mostly as a minority administration until 2007. In 2007, Labour won 26 seats (–4 from 2003), Plaid Cymru (Welsh Nationalist) 14 (+2), Conservatives 13 (+2), Liberal Democrats 6 (=), Independent 1, and a Labour–Plaid Cymru coalition was formed: a kind of inverse prototype for Westminster in 2010. The 50% of women AMs elected in 2003 (47% in 2007) was the highest in the world for a national legislature, achieved by Labour's 'pairing' of constituencies, and local activists sorting out the allocation of male and female candidates.

Welsh Assembly Government
Initially, unlike the UK Government and Parliament, the Assembly Cabinet was *part of* the Assembly, not separate from it. The 2006 Act introduced a clear separation of powers, with the Welsh Assembly Government answerable to the Assembly. The Government comprises:

- The First Minister – elected by the whole Assembly and therefore usually the leader of the largest party. Labour's Rhodri Morgan (2000–9) was succeeded by Carwyn Jones.
- A Cabinet of 9 Assembly ministers, appointed by the First Minister: 6 Labour, 3 Plaid Cymru since 2007. Exceptionally open, with publication of Cabinet minutes and advice papers to subject committees.
- A Civil Service of 5,700 (2009), divided into 7 directorates – including Local Government and Public Service Delivery.

Financial arrangements
Westminster allocates a formula-based grant to the Assembly for all devolved services (£15 billion in 2010). The Assembly has no income-tax-varying power, but can influence council tax levels and key service charges – for NHS prescriptions, residential care, university tuition.

Assembly committees
Since 2007, three types of committee – Legislative, Scrutiny, Other – all designed to examine the Government's policies, actions and spending, including proposals for new legislation. Deputy ministers may be members (but *not* chairs) of committees, and AMs have more involvement with policy than Westminster MPs. All Assembly business is conducted bilingually, with most being broadcast on a dedicated Assembly digital channel, S4C2.

How is local government handled?
A Minister for Social Justice and Local Government (Carl Sargeant, Labour, from 2009) is scrutinised by the Health, Wellbeing and Local Government Committee. The Assembly works collectively with local government through a Partnership Council, comprising AMs and local government representatives.

Where is it?
A state-of-the-art Senedd/Senate building on Cardiff Bay waterfront, designed by Richard Rogers – of Pompidou Centre and Millennium Dome fame – to reflect principles of openness, transparency and environmental sustainability.

Exhibit 6.3 Innovative or distinctive policies in Scotland and Wales

The Scottish Parliament

- Free long-term personal care for the elderly
- Abolition of 'up-front' student tuition fees
- Public health – early public smoking ban, alcohol licensing regulations
- Less restrictive Freedom of Information legislation
- Abolition of ban on 'promoting homosexuality in schools'
- Improved nutritional standards of school meals
- 'One-stop-shop' Public Services Ombudsman
- Proportional representation in local government elections.

The Assembly for Wales

- UK's first Children's Commissioner and world's first Commissioner for Older People
- Free medical prescriptions for under-25s and over-60s, and free hospital car parking
- A Homelessness Commission, and the UK's first homelessness strategy
- Abolition of Key Stage 1 testing and of secondary school 'league tables'
- Introduction of Welsh Baccalaureate
- Free breakfast for all primary school children
- Free swimming for children and over-60s
- Free bus travel for over-60s and concessionary fares for the disabled.

government had increased support for independence, which has tended to fluctuate between 30% and 40%. There was, though, strong backing for a referendum on constitutional change, but, unlike in Wales, the Coalition Government proposed moving straight to a Scottish Bill to start the process of implementing some of the Calman proposals.

Northern Ireland – interrupted devolution, postponed restructuring

There was no restructuring of local government in Northern Ireland corresponding to the spread of unitary councils in Scotland, Wales and parts of England. The position remained essentially as outlined in Chapter 4, with elected local government confined to 26 district councils, relatively small in British terms, and responsible for far fewer services than their counterparts elsewhere in the UK. Most services affecting people's daily lives continued to be administered by appointed Area Boards and numerous other public bodies – one of which, the Rate Collection Agency, even collects the 'rates' or residential property taxes which the province retains.

It is true that the more proactive councils and councillors have optimised their limited powers. In the years when there was no provincial elected assembly, they acted as an important debating forum for any key issue affecting Northern Ireland. They developed an important advocacy role, both for their own local areas and to help individual residents, whose voting turnout in local elections invariably exceeds that on the mainland. Some also worked closely with councils on the other side of the Irish border, and were highly effective in negotiating European development funding. It had long been clear, though, that devolution of further significant powers was totally dependent on there being substantial and consolidated progress in the so-called peace process.

The uncertainty of such progress meant that Labour's 1997 manifesto pledge with respect to Northern Ireland devolution was much more vague than for Scotland and Wales. Yet it proved to be the Northern Ireland Assembly, following the famous Belfast 'Good Friday' Agreement in April 1998, that was the first of the three devolved regional bodies to be elected. Within weeks, the Agreement was endorsed in simultaneous referendums in both parts of Ireland, and a month later the Assembly was elected. Notwithstanding its title, the Assembly is an example of full executive and legislative devolution. Constitutionally, therefore, it resembles the Scottish Parliament more than the Welsh Assembly, and its 108 Members are known as Members of the Legislative Assembly (MLAs). It has authority over those matters previously within the remit of the Northern Ireland Office, including agriculture, economic development, education, environment, health and social services. The most obvious omissions, compared to the Scottish Parliament, are security functions, policing and the courts.

Six MLAs are elected from each of Northern Ireland's 18 parliamentary constituencies by STV – the electoral system used in all non-Westminster elections in Northern Ireland since 1973, specifically because it facilitates representation of the full range of opinions across the Catholic/Republican and Protestant/Unionist communities, and hence prevents any single faction gaining an overall Assembly majority. This inclusive principle is continued in the formation of the Executive Committee of Ministers, an example of power-sharing (technically, 'consociationalist') government, based on the guaranteed representation of key political groupings. The Executive is headed by a joint (or diarchic) leadership of a First Minister and Deputy First Minister – the leaders of the two largest parties – who must be elected together by MLAs, while ministers are elected in proportion to party strengths in the Assembly.

Not surprisingly, the Good Friday Agreement's aspiration to create a 'new politics' in Northern Ireland has proved difficult to realise. Distrust and disagreements between the main unionist parties – the traditionalist Ulster Unionists (UU) and the Rev. Ian Paisley's Democratic Unionists (DUP) – and Sinn Fein, the largest nationalist party, led to the Assembly and

Executive spending half of their first decade suspended, the Executive's functions reverting to the UK Secretary of State for Northern Ireland. Both the 2003 and March 2007 elections in fact took place while the Assembly was under suspension, the latter being essentially a referendum on the 2006 St Andrews Agreement – a formula for the restoration of devolution. The two leading parties were the DUP (36 seats) and Sinn Fein (28), and a few weeks later an incredulous world was treated to extraordinary pictures of Paisley, the demagogic Protestant preacher, and Martin McGuinness, former Irish Republican Army chief, behaving like the Chuckle Brothers comedy act as they assumed the offices of First and Deputy First Minister, respectively.

Paisley stood down in 2008, shortly before his 82nd birthday, and was succeeded as DUP leader and First Minister by Peter Robinson. The Executive in 2009–10 comprised 10 departmental ministers – 4 DUP, 3 Sinn Fein, 2 Ulster Unionist, and 1 Social Democratic and Labour – almost all of whom are also Westminster MPs, something 'unthinkable in Wales or Scotland' (Constitution Unit, 2008, p. 22). Local government is part of the brief of the Minister for the Department of the Environment, and was to have been the next part of the UK system to undergo a major restructuring.

A comprehensive Review of Public Administration was launched by the Executive in 2002, but was soon, and throughout the Assembly's 2002–7 suspension, taken over by the Northern Ireland Office, and it was thus the Northern Ireland Secretary, Peter Hain, who in 2005 announced radical proposals to reduce the province's 26 councils to 7 'super-councils' with several significant new powers, including planning, local roads, regeneration and community relations. Apart from Sinn Fein, however, the reaction of all major parties was hostile, and, following the restoration of devolution, there was a kind of review of the Review, and eventually in 2008 an arithmetical compromise was reached. Instead of the 7 councils favoured by Sinn Fein or the 15 favoured by most other parties, there would be 11. Councillor numbers would be reduced by 'only' a fifth, from 582 to 460, and the new, far less 'local', councils would have almost no new powers of any substance. The delayed first elections to these new authorities were scheduled for 2011, but, before they could be planned in detail, further disagreement within the Executive led to the abandonment of all structural reform.

English regional government – agencies and assemblies

If the 1997 Labour Government delivered promptly on most of its devolution commitments, the one area on which it under-delivered was English regional government. The 1997 manifesto promised to: 'establish one-stop

Regional Development Agencies (RDAs) to co-ordinate regional economic development, help small business and encourage inward investment' (p. 16). These RDAs would be linked to appointed regional chambers, following which, if and where popular consent was established, arrangements would 'be made for elected regional assemblies' (pp. 34–5).

Eight *Regional Development Agencies* (RDAs) and associated Regional Chambers were duly set up in 1998, with an equivalent in London arriving in 2000 with the Greater London Authority and Assembly (see Exhibit 5.4). The RDAs were headed by ministerially appointed boards of up to 15 members, including four from local government. Some were known simply as Development Agencies; others opted for more macho names – Yorkshire Forward, Advantage West Midlands, for example – reflecting their predominantly male, business-led board memberships. They were required to produce a Regional Economic Strategy, defining the region's economic priorities and the means by which they would deliver long-term sustainable economic growth. They spent and invested £2.3 billion on these activities in 2007/8, channelled from six central government departments, and, with the exception of the London Development Agency – run by the Mayor – they reported to what in 2009/10 was the Department for Business, Innovation and Skills.

Regional Chambers, later known as *Regional Assemblies*, were nominated bodies of local councillors plus representatives of business, trade unions and other regional interests. Their original role was to input regional views to the preparation of regional economic strategies, and scrutinise their RDAs' activities – though, significantly, it was not to the Assemblies that the RDAs were ultimately accountable, but to ministers and Parliament. In 2004, with the abolition of local-authority-prepared structure plans, the Assemblies also became regional planning authorities, responsible for developing a Regional Spatial Strategy (RSS) – a 15–20-year vision and strategy for the region, identifying areas for development and regeneration and the issues arising.

Together with the *Government Offices for the Regions* – the combined regional presence of domestic central government departments (see also pp. 198–9) – each spending on average over £1 billion p.a., the RDAs and Assemblies formed a not inexpensive tripartite structure, but with limited powers and confused accountabilities. To extend these powers and unravel accountabilities was to be the function of directly elected regional assemblies.

These assemblies or mini-Parliaments would have considerably less power than the Scottish Parliament or Welsh Assembly, but would be similar in some ways to the Greater London Authority, with responsibility for strategic planning, economic development, skills and employment, transport and housing strategy, public health, culture and tourism. They would also be able to levy a charge on residents' council tax bills – in what the

Conservatives, opposed to the whole scheme, labelled a 'devolution tax'. No region would be forced to have an elected assembly, but, where there was evidence of public support for one, people should be able to demonstrate it in a referendum – in which they would also vote for their preferred structure of unitary local government. No region should have more than one tier of sub-central government, lest ministers be accused of 'increasing bureaucracy'.

The government's staunchest regionalist by far was the Deputy Prime Minister, John Prescott. His initial hope was for three referendums – in the North East; Yorkshire and the Humber; and the North West. In the event, faced with the scepticism of Cabinet and party colleagues and widespread public indifference, he had to settle for one, held in the North East in November 2004, which produced a respectable postal vote turnout of 48%, but a humiliating 78% 'No' vote. The exercise cost an estimated £10 million and, almost needless to say, is unlikely be repeated (see the conference paper – Game, 2005 – on the linked website). The government, however, had no Plan B, so the unsatisfactory tripartite structure staggered on for a time in a kind of policy vacuum.

Regions, sub-regions, city-regions

The first serious concepts to emerge to fill this vacuum were those of *city-regions* and *Multi-Area Agreements*. City-regions were not a new idea. They featured in Derek Senior's Memorandum of Dissent to the Redcliffe-Maud Commission (see Chapter 4), and the short-lived Metropolitan County Councils (1973–86) amounted to a partial city-region system. But the public rejection of elected regional assemblies prompted a more general questioning of whether our very large, arbitrarily defined regions were appropriately sized units for strategic policy development and delivery. City-regions – the enlarged areas from which cities and major towns draw people for work and services such as shopping, education, health, leisure and entertainment – seemed to reflect rather better than our 'official' regions the geography of everyday urban life. In addition, cities themselves were increasingly seen as being the principal engines of the economic growth the country was experiencing in the new millennium. For some, the solution that suggested itself, and that would feature in Labour's 2010 manifesto (p. 9:4), was the creation of large city-regional authorities headed by powerful directly-elected mayors. Before that, though, the Labour Government, in its 2006 White Paper, *Strong and Prosperous Communities*, and 2007 Treasury *Review of Sub-national Economic Development and Regeneration*, linked its new enthusiasm for city-regions to what was a new concept: Multi-Area Agreements (MAAs).

MAAs were based on the recognition that some major policies – transport, land use planning, tackling unemployment, infrastructure provision – need to be managed on a scale even larger than that of our exceptionally large local authorities. They require the co-ordinated collaboration of several authorities, in a similar way that Local Area Agreements (LAAs – see p. 161) involved inter-organisational collaboration within individual local authority areas. LAAs were three-year agreements between a local authority and central government, detailing the area's policy priorities and how various public, private and third sector bodies would work together to improve service provision for local citizens. MAAs would operate at a broader, sub-regional level, and be much more bottom-up, voluntary partnerships than the more top-down, prescriptive LAAs.

The *Sub-national Review* also recognised, however, that some sub-regions might in fact want something that went beyond voluntary and limited MAA-style partnerships – like the metropolitan Passenger Transport Authorities (PTAs) that had survived the abolition of their respective metropolitan county councils. It would require legislation, but the Labour Government indicated its readiness to consider groups of councils establishing statutory sub-regional authorities that pooled economic and other responsibilities on a permanent basis (HM Treasury, 2007, p. 91). In his 2009 Budget Speech, Chancellor of the Exchequer Alistair Darling announced that the Manchester and Leeds City Regions would pilot a form of devolved strategic government with powers comparable with those of the GLA, and in March 2010, Greater Manchester was selected provisionally as the country's first 'Combined Authority'. With an executive composed of a nominated councillor from each of the conurbation's ten metropolitan boroughs, the new strategic authority, if approved, would have powers over public transport, skills, housing, regeneration, waste management, carbon neutrality and planning permissions.

Fifteen MAAs had also been signed by the end of 2009, involving more than a hundred English councils. Most were based, like Greater Manchester, Leeds, and Tyne and Wear, on city regions; but others covered sub-regions in which several smaller cities and towns were identified as engines of growth: PUSH (Partnership for Urban South Hampshire) (11), Regional Cities East (6), Pennine Lancashire (7) and Gatwick Diamond (9) (see Hopes, 2009).

Meanwhile, with the 2010 election approaching, the future of the Regional Assemblies and RDAs became, respectively, more and less clear. The Assemblies would go. Even with their added planning role, their public profile was virtually non-existent, and in 2007 the government announced that they would disappear – their executive responsibility for developing the RSS transferred to the RDAs, and local authorities given an increased scrutiny role over RDAs through participation in new *Local Authority Leaders' Boards*.

RDAs, however, were altogether weightier bodies, as well as politically controversial ones. Labour ministers, particularly the Secretary of State for Business, Lord Mandelson, saw them as performing an important role that would become more vital still as the economy strove to recover from recession: 'The role of Regional Development Agencies will be crucial ... led by business, working in partnership with local authorities, universities and others, they are the key economic co-ordination body in each region. Not just for the North, but for the country as a whole' (quoted in Marshall, 2008, p. 1). For many Conservatives – like Mover and Shaker No.13, Eric Pickles (see Exhibit 1.2), the 2010 Coalition Government's first Secretary of State at DCLG – they were wasteful, unaccountable quangos, and candidates for axing: 'RDAs are a terrible unit for economic development. In terms of our plans for quangos, you could say we were looking toward restructuring them – in a similar fashion to Anne Boleyn' (quoted in Marshall, 2008, p. 1).

Official Conservative policy was only marginally less drastic. The Party's 2009 local government Green Paper, *Control Shift*, in its section on 'Removing Regional Government', proposed a two-strand localisation of both the economic and non-economic functions of RDAs (p. 30):

> We will immediately remove from RDAs all the powers they have been given as part of the present Government's attempt to turn them into unelected regional governments – including powers over housing, planning and 'regional spatial strategies'. These powers will immediately be given to elected local governments.
>
> We will also give elected local authorities the power to come together to establish new enterprise partnerships that truly reflect natural economic divisions, and to take over from their RDAs the responsibility for economic development within those areas.

Despite some brief uncertainty about the future of the RDAs in the north and the West Midlands, the Coalition Government announced within its first three months its intention to abolish this regional tripartite structure almost completely, in furtherance of its commitment to localism and decentralisation, and of its conviction that these 'arbitrary government regions' were neither efficient nor popular. RDAs would be abolished, along with RSSs; funding for regional Leaders' Boards would stop; all Government Offices, including London's, would be closed. In place of RDAs, there would be a £1 billion Regional Growth Fund to support economic growth in parts of England particularly hard hit by public spending cuts, and institutionally they would be replaced by joint council- and business-led *Local Enterprise Partnerships* (*LEPs*). These LEPs would effectively supercede MAAs and would be created around major cities and other 'real functional economic and travel-to-work areas', to enable, as the government's Budget document put it, 'improved co-ordination of public and private investment in transport, housing, skills, regeneration and other areas of economic development'.

How many LEPs would be approved by ministers – from an unexpectedly large number of 56 bids, how they would be funded, and how they would differ in practice from RDAs were all unclear prior to the publication of the Localism Bill 2010. The Conservative Green Paper critique of RDAs, however, was acknowledged to have its validity – in particular the two 'contradictory agendas' they had been given (p. 30):

> Firstly, they must promote the economic development of their own region; secondly, they must 'narrow economic disparities between regions'. The latter objective indicates that RDAs should work together towards a national purpose; but the former implies that they must compete against each other for investment.

There is little authoritative evidence of regional economic disparities having been significantly eroded through RDA action, and for this reason other critics questioned not the existence of RDAs *per se*, but the need for all regions to have essentially the same institutional machinery.

The implications for local government of these and other possible regional developments are obviously huge. England may be unique in Western Europe as a country of 50 million inhabitants without an electorally accountable tier of regional government, but that doesn't mean there isn't a vast amount of regional *governance* being undertaken by a whole forest of non-elected bodies. Decisions hitherto made in the RDAs and regional Government Offices constitute only a modest part of the total picture, which must also include all those other agencies – Benefits, Child Support, Highways, Countryside, the Environment – and regional bodies for employment, the arts, sport, tourism, plus the health service, the prison service, and many more.

A few years ago, an attempt to map 'the structure of governance in the West Midlands' identified some 50 public bodies responsible for a total annual expenditure of nearly £23 billion. Of this figure, the then 1,935 elected councillors in the region, or their 38 local authorities, were responsible for a combined budget of under £6 billion, some three-quarters of which was itself controlled by central government in the form of grants. Local government's judgement, then, of any regional reforms is going to focus on the extent to which they redress this democratically unhealthy imbalance. A full transfer of RDA functions to the relevant local council bodies would have been preferred; by comparison, council leaders negotiating the geography of LEPs with local business organisations is a modest step, but not a negligible one.

Chapter 7

The Way It Is: Internal Structures

A political management 'revolution'

The radical external structural reforms to the British local governmental system outlined in Chapters 4 and 5 have been at least matched by changes taking place within it – in particular, the advent of 'executive local government'. Indeed, 'reform' is too moderate a term for the transformation in their day-to-day working practices that many councils have experienced in recent years. In overthrowing almost two centuries of committee-based decision-making, the new mayoral and cabinet executives discussed in this chapter have amounted to a small revolution. Some elements of this revolution are already being reversed or modified under the Coalition Government, while the relentless search for efficiency savings is prompting additional momentous developments in councils' structures and organisation. It makes for a rapidly changing scene, which this chapter will attempt to capture in the equivalent of a long-exposure snapshot.

To appreciate the scale and significance of the new executive-based systems and institutions it is important to understand what they replaced. This chapter opens, therefore, with a brief account of councils' traditional institutions and operations, before moving on to the changes arising from the Local Government Act 2000 and subsequent legislation.

Some basic terminology

We have already referred in passing to several terms that should now be clarified. First, *local authorities* and *councils* – frequently used interchangeably (including in this book). Strictly speaking, though, the council is the legal embodiment of the local authority: the body of *elected councillors* who collectively determine and are ultimately responsible for the policy and actions of the authority. In recognition of this legal responsibility, councillors are often referred to as the elected *members* of the authority, which distinguishes them from its paid employees, the *officers* (not 'civil servants', a term reserved in the UK for central government administrators) and other professional, clerical and manual staff.

As already noted, British local authorities are large organisations and, with the spread of unitary authorities, becoming even larger: in 2010, 434 for the UK's 61 million population, or one for every 146,000 people. Several have more than 80 councillors, and the largest county and metropolitan councils have tens of thousands of full-time and part-time staff: Birmingham 52,000, Essex 44,000, Hampshire 39,000, for example, though all employee numbers are likely to fall in the next few years. The councillors and staff comprise the 'two worlds' of local government. Decisions and policies emerge from the formal and informal interaction of these two worlds. In most authorities it would be neither possible nor desirable for councillors to take all necessary policy decisions in full council meetings, or for officers to manage and oversee delivery of the hundreds of local government services, without some kind of internal structural divisions. The way in which local authorities traditionally organised themselves, before the post-2000 advent of political executives, was through *committees* of councillors and professionally based *departments*.

Councillors and committees

The committee system was a key feature of 'the inherited world' of multifunctional authorities (Stewart, 2000, ch. 4) that enabled them to work both effectively and democratically, without elected councillors handing over all policy-making to unelected officials. Committees were a council's workshops, where councillors' local knowledge and their political assessment of local needs came together with officers' professional and expert advice to produce, it was hoped, democratically responsive and implementable policy. For speed and efficiency, councils would *delegate* to committees much of their work and specified decision-making powers, but the full council remained the ultimate decision-making body, and neither committee members nor even the chairperson had the executive authority *as of right* to take decisions.

Council committees, then, were composed of (and chaired by) elected councillors, and advised by officers. A few, such as education and social services, were *statutory* for councils with these responsibilities. Most, though, were *permissive*, enabling councillors themselves to decide how to arrange and divide up their council's work. Councils with identical service responsibilities might well have very different committee and sub-committee structures – frequently, dozens of each, with correspondingly formidable numbers of meetings. The sense that such systems could duplicate discussion, slow down decision-making, and be altogether too time-consuming, was one of the driving forces behind the recent reforms.

Committees make easy targets for criticism: groups of people, so the joke goes, who individually can do nothing, and as a group decide that nothing can be done. But in their rush towards 'modernisation', reformers possibly underrated the committee system's many positive features that had served local government well for most of its history. Committees enabled councillors to acquire specialist knowledge, as well as developing their public speaking, chairing and other potential leadership skills. Decisions were taken, debated and scrutinised in public meetings, where opposition parties could put forward alternative proposals, and, it is hoped, the quality of decisions was thereby enhanced.

On the other hand, it is true that councillors could over-specialise and become almost duplicate officers, defending 'their' service and failing to appreciate the interests of the council as a whole. Committee discussions were often dominated by operational detail at the expense of major policy issues, strategy and the monitoring of service performance. Committees could be excessively party political, creating a 'scrutiny shortfall' (Leach, 1999, p. 82): with majority party members being reluctant to criticise their own leadership publicly, and opposition members being in too small a minority to scrutinise effectively.

Most important of all for a multi-functional authority trying to present a coherent corporate image to the world, service-based or department-linked committees could become 'compartmentalised' and difficult to co-ordinate. This is why almost all councils ultimately developed some kind of *central co-ordinating committee*, known generally as 'Policy and Resources'. This committee, usually chaired by the Leader of the Council and containing its most senior members, sought to co-ordinate the work of the committees and provide the council with overall policy leadership. Some critics argued, however, that, without any *directly elected* individual leader, even the most coherent policy leadership was unable to impress itself on local residents, service users and voters – which was part of the case for elected executive mayors put forward by both the 1997 Labour Government and the 2010 Coalition.

Officers, departments and directorates

The second of our complementary and interacting local government worlds is that of the council employees, and in particular the 'white-collar' officers in their town hall and county hall departments. Traditionally, the arrangement and even the names of local authorities' *departments* would mirror closely their committees. There would be similarly large numbers, some providing services direct to the public – Education, Housing, Social Services, Libraries; some a servicing role for other departments – Finance (or Treasurer's), Personnel, Construction and Design. Each department was headed by a *chief officer*, who was a qualified *professional* and specialist in a relevant functional area.

Today, those 'matching' corporate management structures are history. Most policy committees have gone, and, with local government's more strategic approach to service organisation, and councils becoming 'commissioners' of services, rather than direct providers, departmental arrangements are unrecognisably different. Terminology has changed – sometimes usefully and imaginatively, sometimes not: Personnel is Human Resources Management; Museums (and sometimes zoos) are part of Heritage; Housing may or may not be the Built Environment; and Community is a near-universal default prefix. Westminster in 2009 was planning to abolish departments completely and replace them with 9 Delivery Units and 10 Service and Strategic Support Units (Westminster City Council, 2009).

Every council, it seems, wants its own unique management structure, increasingly headed by a slimmed-down number of directorates, combining several departments with linked interests. Today's typical county council might have no more than five directorates – Children's Services; Adult Social Care; Transport and Environment; Corporate Resources; and Communities – each comprising a number of previously separate departments. So Transport and Environment, for example, might include Engineering, Highways, Waste Management, Environmental Health and Trading Standards. Our own current favourite, for its almost complete opacity, is the metropolitan borough with three directorates: for People, Community and Society; Economy, Place and Skills; and Performance, Capacity and Services. We struggle to think of any service that couldn't fit into all three.

Those heading directorates – usually Executive/Strategic/Corporate Directors, all of which titles, we suspect, signify much the same thing – will have been appointed primarily for their *managerial* skills and experience. But they, like the *Principal* or *Chief Officers* who head the various services in their directorates, will still most probably be trained and qualified in one of the professions within their policy remit, as will many of the staff employed at lower levels in their respective departments.

As noted with committee structures, local authorities have considerable discretion in the departmental arrangements they adopt and the officers they appoint, but there are exceptions. All authorities must have a *Head of Paid Service* – the senior leader of the council's staff – to advise the council on the staffing numbers and organisation required for the discharge of its various functions. In most authorities the role is undertaken by the *Chief Executive* (CE), but this latter is not a statutorily required post. Several councils nowadays, presumably keen to publicise their business-like culture, prefer *Managing Director* (MD) or *Borough Director*. One such is Newport City Council in Wales, who in 2009 appointed Tracey Lee as MD, thereby adding to the slowly but steadily growing number of just over a fifth of CEs and MDs who are women.

A second statutory post is the *Section 151 Officer*, who (under Section 151 of the 1972 Local Government Act) is responsible for the legal and financially prudent administration of the council's affairs. The holder must be a qualified accountant, which usually rules out the CE, who, if Head of

Paid Service, is also barred from holding the third required post of *Monitoring Officer* – responsible for ensuring that the council's decisions are within the law, and for maintaining standards of conduct among its members. Finally, and thankfully only rarely, there is the exceptional statutory intervention – such as that following the Laming Report into the ill-treatment and death of 8-year-old Victoria Climbié (Laffin, 2008, p. 120). The 2004 Children's Act required educational and social services for children to be integrated under a Director and a lead councillor for Children's Services, who are, respectively, professionally and politically accountable for the local authority's delivery of these services.

As Head of Paid Service, the CE has an explicit co-ordinating responsibility, and will generally chair a directors/chief officers' management team. Arrangements vary, but almost all authorities have some such mechanism for ensuring effective liaison and policy co-ordination across departments.

Directors and chief officers have overall responsibility for implementing council policies. Though professionally trained and qualified, and, by most standards, very well paid, they are as much employees and 'servants' of *the council* as the most recently recruited manual worker. Unlike councillors – often much less formally educated and trained, and less handsomely remunerated – officers have not been elected and do not have democratic legitimacy and authority. The role, therefore, of those officers who work with councillors is to provide the various types of advice the councillors may need to make their decisions – specialist, professional, technical, legal, financial, managerial – and then to ensure that the decisions made are implemented. In the traditional system, where policy was formally the responsibility of the whole council, officers' responsibility was to the *whole* council, and *not* to any particular party, whether it happened to be in majority control or not. We discuss later in this chapter how these long-cherished principles of political neutrality and a unified officer structure are challenged by the arrival of executive government, when the councillors who scrutinise policy, as well as those who make it, require officer advice.

Early approaches to internal management reform

The internal management reforms we shall describe shortly are about the institutions and processes of *executive local government* – Cabinets, elected mayors, Overview and Scrutiny Committees – introduced in the 2000 Local Government Act. But this Act and the consultation papers preceding it were not the first attempts at reform. There were earlier governmental reports and inquiries, the most important of which are summarised below.

Maud 1967 – chief executives in, management boards out

The Committee on the Management of Local Government, chaired by Sir John Maud (later Lord Redcliffe-Maud), was an example of premature radicalism. Acknowledging the tendency of committees to spend their time on day-to-day administration rather than on broad policy and strategy, Maud proposed that all major local authorities should have a *Management Board* of between five and nine senior councillors, with wide delegated powers. The numbers of committees and departments should be radically pruned, and each authority should appoint a *chief executive officer* – not necessarily a lawyer, like the traditional town clerk – who would be undisputed head of the authority's paid staff.

As with the more recent proposals for executive-based local government, Maud's prescription was rejected as elitist, with many councillors being instinctively fearful of becoming second-class members of their authority, excluded from the management board and with no policy influence. Nevertheless, Maud was a stimulus for change: councils did start to rationalise their committee systems and some appointed chief executives, especially as similar analyses emerged a few years later from the Bains and Paterson Reports.

Bains 1972 and Paterson 1973 – corporate icing, traditional cake

These two committees advised on internal management structures for the new authorities being established under the Local Government Acts of 1972 in England and Wales, and 1973 in Scotland. Change was occurring in any case; even so, management boards were left in the long grass, and the reports' main recommendations were that the traditional departmental attitude that permeated much of local government needed to give way to a broader corporate, or authority-wide, outlook. Following Bains/Paterson, the vast majority of the new authorities appointed *chief executives* and set up *policy and resources committees* and *senior officer management teams*. There were visible signs of internal structural change, but redrawing organisation charts does not itself transform an organisation's working culture. New and apparently more corporate *forms* of management emerged, but Bains' strong, co-ordinating chief executive remained the exception, with ingrained departmentalism continuing to hold sway in most authorities.

Widdicombe 1986 – overdue recognition of party politics

The Widdicombe Committee on the Conduct of Local Authority Business was the Thatcher Government's reaction to the policies and campaigning activities of a number of New Urban Left authorities, or, as the tabloid press labelled them, the 'loony left'. A mainly younger generation of Labour councillors in London and some other cities came into office committed to using local councils as testing grounds for radical interventionist policies in economic development, housing, transport and planning, and to defending their communities against central government spending cuts.

Maud, Bains and Paterson had focused mainly on organisational structures, paying only secondary attention, if any, to the roles of elected members and the increasingly prominent party political dimension of the country's local government. Widdicombe addressed these issues head-on. But, instead of criticising the spread of party politics, the Committee studied it and welcomed many of its positive features: more contested elections, clearer democratic choice, greater policy consistency, and more direct accountability. At the same time, the Committee was concerned to safeguard the position of councillors from minority parties and of individual and non-party councillors.

The Widdicombe recommendations led, in the Local Government and Housing Act 1989, to the effective banning of one-party committees and sub-committees, and to senior officers being barred from all public political activity. Overall, the Committee's impact was to introduce a number of 'checks and balances', without seriously challenging the right of a majority party to determine and see implemented its policy proposals. It injected a new air of realism into discussions about local authority management.

New Labour's 'modernisation' – separate executives

The New Labour government elected in May 1997 published its thinking about local government in a set of consultation papers early in 1998, the first of which – *Modernising Local Government: Local Democracy and Community Leadership* (DETR, 1998b) – subsequently evolved into the Local Government Act 2000. New Labour wanted to emphasise its commitment to democratic local government – in contrast, it claimed, to its Conservative predecessors. But it saw the existing system 'falling short of its great potential':

> Turnout at local elections is on average around 40 per cent and sometimes much less. There is a culture of apathy about local democracy. The evidence is that councillors – hard-working and dedicated as they are – are overburdened, often unproductively, by committee meetings which focus on detailed issues rather than concentrating on essentials. The opportunity for councillors to have a stronger voice on behalf of local communities is being missed. (DETR, 1998b, para. 1.3)

The consultation paper detailed the shortcomings of a system 'designed over a century ago for a bygone age' – inefficiency, secrecy, opacity and lack of accountability. Councillors spent too little time on what should be their most important role – representing their communities. They spent too much time inefficiently – preparing for, travelling to, and often contributing little to, council committee meetings, while the 'real' decisions in most councils were being made in party group meetings, behind closed doors, beyond the reach of either public or opposition party scrutiny. Council committees, in any case, were a poor vehicle for developing and demonstrating community leadership and accountability, because they confused the executive (policy-making) and representational roles of councillors. It was often unclear who had in fact taken a decision, and who therefore could be held to account.

The consultation paper acknowledged that progressive councils had already developed innovative ways of rethinking their committee practices and involving the public in their decision-making, but far more fundamental change was needed. There had, in the government's view, to be a *separation* of councillors' executive and representative roles – a contentious departure from the long-established culture that saw all councillors, formally at least, as equal. Legally, under the committee system, no councillor had decision-making power as an individual – not even committee chairs. Even the slightly questionable practice of 'chairman's action' – enabling officers to take urgent decisions between committee meetings – was 'legalised' by having the action confirmed at the first available meeting. The envisaged role separation would produce greater clarity about where decisions are taken, by whom, and who is to be held accountable. It would also enable a sharper scrutiny of those decisions. In fact, the greater the separation, the better:

> The Government is very attracted to the model of a strong executive directly elected mayor. Such a mayor would be a highly visible figure ... elected by the people, rather than by the council or party, [who] would therefore focus attention outwards rather than inwards towards fellow councillors. The mayor would be a strong political and community leader with whom the electorate could identify. Mayors will have to become well known to their electorate, which could help increase interest in and understanding of local government. (para. 5.14)

The choice is yours – but from our models

There were hints in the 1998 consultation paper that councils might be allowed to pilot a variety of managerial arrangements: cabinet systems, lead member systems, directly-and indirectly-elected mayors. The eventual legislation, however, was both narrower and more prescriptive. The Local

Government Act 2000 required all major local authorities in England and Wales to choose one of just three specified forms of executive, or propose some other ministerially acceptable arrangements, as summarised in Exhibit 7.1.

This restricted choice, plus its predisposition towards the controversial directly elected mayor, led to fierce parliamentary opposition, and the government was forced to make some concessions. One was that so-called 'smaller' shire districts – the approximately one-third with populations under 85,000 population – were allowed to make 'alternative arrangements' in the form of a 'streamlined' committee system, provided they had local community backing. All other authorities were required to prepare plans for new structures based on one of the three executive models, to be submitted for ministerial approval in 2001 and in operation by 2002.

Scotland by then had its own Parliament and went its own way, steered partly by recommendations from the 1999 McIntosh Commission, set up to study the implications that the Scottish Parliament would have for Scottish local government. The Commission's most publicised proposal was for proportional representation for local government elections – eventually introduced in 2007. But it looked also at how councils organised their political decision-making, proposing that the 32 councils should review their own management arrangements against stated criteria of openness and accountability. Thus, while the UK ministers were prescribing just three executive models for all but the smallest English and Welsh councils, the Scottish Executive explicitly rejected any 'central blueprint', preferring to encourage the emergence of a 'rich diversity of different models'. As a result, there are no directly elected Provosts (Scottish mayors). Only a handful of the 32 councils opted for a Leader/Cabinet model, while the remainder preferred streamlined, or sometimes not so streamlined, committee systems.

As noted in Exhibit 7.1, the government's set menu of executive models was modified in the 2007 Local Government and Public Involvement in Health Act – because, as the 2006 White Paper, *Strong and Prosperous Communities*, made clear, ministers were frankly irritated that most councils hadn't previously made the choices they were required to. Far too many had taken an overly 'cautious approach to change' (p. 55):

> Only 12 local authorities have introduced the strongest leadership model, an elected mayor. Four out of five councils have opted for the leader and cabinet model ... Of these councils, only a relatively small number give the leader authority to act alone. Rather, they act collectively with other cabinet members, whom the leader often does not have the power to select ... Moreover, in most authorities leaders face election every year. This can make it hard to take and see through essential but difficult decisions that may in the short term be unpopular.

Exhibit 7.1 Executive-based political management

The traditional committee-based structure

Council decisions could be delegated to officers, but *not* to individual councillors – not even to council leaders or committee chairs. Decisions not delegated had to be taken either in full council or by committees or sub-committees of councillors. *All* councillors, therefore, were legally part of the decision-making process.

The Local Government Act 2000 introduced, for the first time, a clear separation between the *making and execution* of council decisions and the *scrutiny* of those decisions. The council's policy framework and budget are agreed by the full council, following proposals from the executive. The executive then implements the agreed policy framework.

Possible forms of executive arrangement

In the 2000 Act, all councils in England and Wales – apart from shire districts with populations of less than 85,000 – were required, after consulting their local residents, to choose one of three specified forms of executive, or to propose some other ministerially acceptable arrangement:

1 **Mayor and Cabinet executive** – a mayor elected by the whole electorate, who appoints an executive/cabinet of between 2 and 9 councillors.
2 **Leader and Cabinet executive** – an executive leader, elected by the full council (therefore usually the leader of the largest party), plus between 2 and 9 councillors, either appointed by the leader or elected by the council.
3 **Mayor and Council manager** – a mayor elected by the whole electorate, providing the broad policy direction, with a day-to-day manager appointed by the council. Eliminated in the 2007 Act.

Smaller shire districts had an additional option:

4 **Substitute arrangements (not involving a separate executive)** – retention of the committee system, subject to ministerial approval that decisions would be taken in an efficient, transparent and accountable way, with acceptable provisions for overview and scrutiny.

Mayoral options could be introduced only after approval in an authority-wide referendum – triggered by the council itself, by a petition signed by 5% of local electors, or by direction of the Secretary of State. Also removed in the 2007 Act.

Overview and scrutiny committees

All councils operating executive arrangements must set up overview and scrutiny committees of non-executive members (and possibly non-member co-optees), to hold the executive to account. These committees may make reports and recommendations, either to the executive or the authority, on any aspect of council business or other matters that affect the authority's area or its inhabitants.

Stronger, more stable – some would say more macho – leadership was required, if councils were to deal with the 'constantly changing economic, social and cohesion challenges' facing them (p. 54). Initially, therefore, three revised 'strong leadership' models were proposed: a directly elected mayor, a directly elected executive slate or team, and an indirectly elected leader. All should be elected for four-year terms, and all executive powers vested in the individual mayor or leader, who would decide how these powers should be discharged.

Little serious thought appeared to have gone into either the practicability or potential appeal of these proposals. One example is the 'guaranteed' four-year term of office for a council-elected leader, who remains removable, as ever, by a council vote of no confidence, but not – the legislation intends – following a loss of the confidence of their own party or a change in the council's party make-up (Leach and Wilson, 2008, pp. 315–6). The elected executive slate option was dropped almost as soon as it was introduced – during the Bill's Committee Stage – following the government's own removal of the earlier, equally unpopular, Mayor/Council manager model. The outcome, therefore, of this part of the 2006 White Paper and 2007 Act is one less executive model than the government started with, and otherwise little change: something of a damp squib.

Where New Labour's aim throughout was to push as many authorities as possible into adopting its definition of a strong leadership model, the Coalition Government is about authorities being able to choose for themselves how they should govern their own areas. Communities and Local Government Secretary, Eric Pickles, acknowledged that the Cabinet system had failed to win universal popularity. Initially, about two-thirds of the sub-85,000 authorities opted to retain and streamline their committee systems, and, while some had since introduced separate executives, some larger authorities would have liked to make the reverse switch. There would be provision, Pickles indicated, in the 2010 Localism Bill for such authorities to revert to the committee system, if they wished, but, as to the choice they made, like Clark Gable's Rhett Butler in *Gone with the Wind*: 'Frankly, my dear, I don't give a damn' – though Pickles chose his own characteristic metaphor (Dale, 2010):

> I don't care how things are organised. They can have it on the basis of a committee system, on a cabinet basis, on the mayoral system. If they want to introduce it on a choral system with various members of the council singing sea shanties, I don't mind, providing it's accountable, transparent and open. That's all I need to know.

It sounded, at least, a very different approach.

Where are the mayors?

The government's intention in the 2000 Act had been to do everything possible to persuade local authorities to adopt elected mayors. The public – albeit in opinion polls asking them something that most had never even thought about – seemed broadly supportive of the principle. But, within local government, support was minimal and opposition fierce. Councillors were both critical and understandably concerned: critical of the concentration of power in the hands of a single individual, and concerned that, if they were not among the minority of executive councillors, they could find themselves excluded from the policy-making process. Much safer, surely, to go for the Leader/Cabinet model that, while still involving an executive/ non-executive split, would be closer to that with which they were familiar.

The Mayor/Council manager model suffered the double handicap of being based partly on an elected mayor and partly on another complete novelty in British local government, the council manager. Council or city manager systems are popular forms of urban government in the USA, and are also found in Ireland, Finland and New Zealand. Their appeal is the apparent combination of the strong political and policy leadership of an elected mayor with the managerial expertise and experience of a professional manager, appointed by the council and responsible for day-to-day decision-making. In practice, giving substantial power to an appointed official was, if anything, even more distasteful to serving councillors than giving it to an elected mayor.

Ministers did little to explain how a council manager system might work, and only one authority – Stoke-on-Trent City Council – opted for it, following a successful campaign for a referendum masterminded by the eventually elected Independent mayor, Mike Wolfe. It proved hard, however, for a politically inexperienced mayor, with no party organisation behind him, to get to grips with a wholly untested management model in a 60-member council opposed politically both to him personally and to the system. Wolfe lost his re-election bid to Labour's Mark Meredith, who campaigned on the pledge to call a further referendum on the mayoral issue as soon as legislation permitted – which proved to be in 2008. Less than 20% of a disenchanted electorate turned out, a clear majority voting to replace the mayor with a Leader/Cabinet system. Stoke thereby wrote itself a second footnote in the record books, as the first authority to abolish an elected mayor. In 2010, the formerly wholly Labour council was being run by a cabinet comprising Labour, Conservative, City Independent and Liberal Democrat councillors. Whatever Westminster can do, somewhere in local government it will already have been done, and more extremely.

The 2000 Act required all major authorities in England and Wales, following supposedly full and fair consultations with their electorates, to select one of the three specified models. If they chose one of the two elected mayoral models, they had to get voters' backing in a referendum. They could also be *required* to hold a referendum, if (a) there was a petition in favour of an elected mayor, signed by 5% of local electors; or (b) the Secretary of State concluded that, in opting for a non-mayoral system – the Leader/Cabinet model – a council was misrepresenting the views of local people.

There was apparent misrepresentation, as defined in the government's guidance notes to councils, but ministers were reluctant to intervene, particularly with large councils run by their own Labour comrades. Yet it was these councils that might have proved powerful mayoral role models – such as Birmingham and Bradford, both of which found that, while a clear majority of their consulted electors were in favour of *one or the other* of the mayoral systems, the *single* most popular option, despite being supported by a minority, was the Leader/Cabinet model. This preference, reflecting their own views, was the one councillors reported to the Secretary of State, who might have investigated, intervened and ordered a referendum, but chose instead to decline the challenge (Game, 2003, p. 20 – see the full article on the linked website).

To ministers' disappointment, in the initial selection of executive systems in 2001–2, just 30 mayoral referendums were held and only 11 produced 'Yes' votes for an elected mayor. As was later noted in the 2006 White Paper, the overwhelming majority of councils (316, or 81%) opted for the Leader/Cabinet model, and a further 69 (15%) took advantage of the 'smaller council' concession of 'alternative arrangements'.

Who are the mayors?

Elections for the historic first generation of English executive mayors were held in 2002, and they produced some remarkable results. Of the 11 contests, five were won by Independents, which, when Ken Livingstone was included, meant that half the popularly elected mayors in Britain's highly party politicised system of local government had won by *defeating* candidates of all the established national parties. As two years earlier in London, the party most damaged in this carnage was Labour. In Middlesbrough, their candidate lost to a populist former policeman, Ray Mallon. In North Tyneside, where Labour had controlled the council for 28 years, voters elected a Conservative. In Watford, the council's Labour leader lost to a Liberal Democrat schoolteacher, Dorothy Thornhill. In Stoke, Mike Wolfe, having organised the petition that had triggered the election, became the country's first openly gay mayor. 'Who's Afraid of the Big Bad Wolf?' taunted his campaign slogan; Labour was – especially the defeated candidate, George Stevenson, one of Stoke's MPs.

Then there were the 'monkey hangers', as Hartlepudlians have been known since, as the story goes, they hanged a monkey dressed in French military uniform during the Napoleonic Wars, the only survivor of a ship-wreck, on the assumption that it was a spy. This time, to the delight of cartoonists everywhere, they *elected* a monkey – or, rather, Hartlepool Football Club's mascot, H'Angus the Monkey, aka Stuart Drummond, who campaigned in full monkey costume under the slogan 'Vote H'Angus – he gives a monkey's'.

The message, not just from Hartlepool, could hardly have been more shrill: voters wanted a change – almost any change – from the established coteries of local politicos who had been running their councils, worthily or otherwise, for what seemed too long. Even some of the successful Labour candidates – Martin Winter in corruption-ridden Doncaster (see p. 41), Jules Pipe in Hackney, a council financially so mismanaged that it was threatened with a central government takeover – were elected in the hope that they would be 'change agents', rather than 'consolidators' (Stoker, 2004b).

But, while the message itself may have been emphatic, its democratic delivery was feeble. Despite an average of nearly seven candidates per contest, turnouts in the 2002 elections averaged less than 30% – and, as shown in Exhibit 7.2, they have scarcely improved since. In 2002, only Middlesbrough's Ray Mallon could claim the support of even a quarter of his *potential* electorate, while Mike Wolfe was returned by under 7% of his (Game, 2003, pp. 25–6). In the elections summarised in Exhibit 7.2, Mallon's support had fallen to 18%, slightly behind Dorothy Thornhill's 20%, while a later recruit to the mayoral ranks, Nicholas Bye, won with barely 5% of his 100,000 Torbay electorate. Electoral legitimacy becomes hard to claim when support falls this low, and there is no reason to suppose that, without the boost of a coinciding General Election, the 2010 figures would have been any better. Indeed, when later in the year Tower Hamlets became the latest council to opt for a directly elected mayor, Luftur Rahman – a former Labour leader of the council, though standing as an Independent – was elected decisively with 52% of first preference votes, but on a turnout of less than 26%.

It is also clear – as it was in the 2008 London mayoral election (see pp. 82–3) – that many voters in these elections simply fail to realise that the Supplementary Vote system gives them the opportunity to express a second preference, if they wish, and know what to do with it. Their incomprehension is symbolic of the tepid reception of New Labour's intended flagship of local government reform, which might have been expected to disappear quietly along with its ministerial creators. Instead, it is likely to receive a hefty jump-start. David Cameron, encouraged by or perhaps notwithstanding the achievements of his fellow Old Etonian, Boris Johnson, is a mayoral enthusiast, and the Conservative manifesto reflected his commitment:

In our biggest cities, there is a strong case for new powers being placed in the hands of a single accountable individual – an elected mayor who

Exhibit 7.2 England's directly elected mayors, 2010 – excluding the GLA

Council	Mayor (first elected)	Mayor's party	Council control	Most recent Mayoral elections				Comment
				Date	1st count Mayor's %	2nd count Mayor's %	% turnout	
Bedford BC (U)	Dave Hodgson (2009)	LD	NOC (LD)	2009	26	54 vs. Con	31	By-election, following death of Frank Branston, Ind. Mayor 2002–9
Doncaster MBC	Peter Davies (2009)	ED	NOC (Lab)	2009	25	50.4 vs. Ind	38	Ex-Lab, Con, UKIP and teacher; succeeded previous Labour Mayor
Hackney LBC	Jules Pipe (2002)	Lab	Lab	2006	47	73 vs. Con	34	Journalist; Council leader to 2002
				2010	54 vs. LD		58*	
Hartlepool BC (U)	Stuart Drummond (2002)	Ind	NOC (Lab)	2005	42	72 vs. Lab	51*	Hartlepool Utd football mascot turned first 3-term Mayor
				2009	25	53 vs. Ind	32	
Lewisham LBC	Steve Bullock (2002)	Lab	NOC (Lab)	2006	38	57 vs. LD	33	Council leader, 1988–93
				2010	45	59 vs. LD	61*	
Mansfield DC	Tony Egginton (2002)	Ind	Ind	2007	46	61 vs. Lab	40	Ex-President, Newsagents' Federation
Middlesbrough (U)	Ray Mallon (2002)	Ind	Lab	2007	59 vs. LD		31	Ex-Det. Supt ('Robocop'), Cleveland Police
Newham LBC	Sir Robin Wales (2002)	Lab	Lab	2006	48	62 vs. Resp	35	Council leader to 2002
				2010	68 vs. Con		51*	
N. Tyneside MBC	Linda Arkley (2003–05)	Con	Con	2009	45	54 vs. Lab	38	Health visitor; regained mayoralty from Labour in 2009
Torbay (U)	Nicholas Bye (2005)	Con	Con	2005	22	58 vs. LD	24	Estate agent; ex-LD Parliamentary candidate
Watford DC	Dorothy Thornhill (2002)	LD	LD	2006	51 vs. Con		39	Ex-assistant headteacher and councillor
				2010	46	67 vs. Con	65*	

Notes: U = Unitary council; * = mayoral election held on same day as General Election; NOC (LD) = No Overall Control council, in which Liberal Democrats are the largest party, but with less than 50% of the seats; ED = English Democrat, Resp = Respect can provide the city with strong leadership ... We will legislate to hold a referendum in England's twelve largest cities on having an elected mayor. In these cities – Birmingham, Leeds, Sheffield, Bradford, Manchester, Liverpool, Bristol, Wakefield, Coventry, Leicester, Nottingham, Newcastle upon Tyne – a mayoral system will be established unless voters reject that change.

That pledge went straight into the Coalition's *Programme for Government*, but without hinting what the 'new powers' might be. Obvious possibilities might include the right to appoint the authority's chief executive, to raise and lower Council Tax, to introduce a supplementary business rate, and to have the equivalent of the London Mayor's control over transport policy (Hope and Wanduragala, 2010). But there were also signs that Pickles had in mind place-based or community budgets, with mayoral councils being offered financial incentives to pool public sector budgets – in, for example, social care, education, housing and health improvement – across their respective areas.

Obviously, if there were more of them – as we suggested there might well have been – the mayors' impact on the local government world as a whole would have been greater. Even so, few as they were, all could claim, in their own council areas, to have 'made a difference'. All but two of the initial 11 were re-elected, which is not a bad start, and by 2010 five were into their third term of office, including the most contentious of them all, Hartlepool's Stuart Drummond. They are generally far better known than were their predecessor council leaders. They have raised their councils' profiles, and, as even a sceptic acknowledged (Kemp, 2009, p. 4): 'mayoralties in places like Watford, Newham and Hackney have radically transformed their local councils for the better ... [They] have taken a clear internal role by working with their senior staff to cut out waste, improve decision making and improve outcomes for residents'.

In other cases – Mansfield, Middlesbrough, North Tyneside, Watford again – it was the council's political complexion and culture that were transformed. All mayors have had their personal policy initiatives and campaigns, and all their authorities – apart from the already 'Excellent' Hartlepool – improved their Comprehensive Performance Assessment (CPA) rankings: the independent measures by which the government judged councils' efficiency (see p. 179). The record, in summary, seems sufficiently encouraging to view the prospect of super-powered 'big city' mayors with positive anticipation.

Leaders and cabinets

As noted above, elected mayors were intended to be the flagship admirals of New Labour's political management reforms. But flagships lead fleets,

Exhibit 7.3 Leicestershire County Council's Leader/Cabinet system, 2009/10

The full County Council (55 members – 36 Con, 14 LD, 4 Lab, 1 BNP)

- The Council's ultimate policy-making body; therefore the only body able change the Council's **Constitution**.
- Appoints the Leader and members of the Cabinet.
- Approves the Council's **Policy Framework** – a series of major plans – and its budget.
- Approves or rejects any Cabinet proposals outside the policy framework or the budget.
- Receives reports from scrutiny bodies on activities of the Executive/Cabinet.

The Council's executive role

- Is carried out under **delegated powers**, primarily through the 9-member **Cabinet**, acting individually and collectively, and chief officers.
- The **Executive** comprises the Leader of the Council – elected by the Council, and therefore usually the leader of the largest party – and the (all-Conservative) **Cabinet**. It is responsible for the more important executive decisions needed to implement the Council's policy framework and budget.
- Cabinet members take **lead roles** on specific services; and exercise individual powers, as delegated to them through the full Council and its Constitution.
- Cabinet **support members** (3 in 2009) may be appointed by the Council to assist specific Cabinet members in their duties, but do not form part of the Cabinet.
- The Cabinet will refer to the full Council any proposal departing significantly from the policy framework or the budget.
- Any meeting of the Executive at which an executive decision is taken is held in public.

The Council's overview and scrutiny role

- Is directed and co-ordinated by a cross-party, 13-member **Scrutiny Commission** of non-executive members, chaired by the leader of the largest minority (LD) group.
- Is undertaken by 3 standing **Overview and Scrutiny Committees** also comprising only non-executive members, covering Adult Social Care and Health Services; Children and Young People's Services; Budget and Performance Monitoring.

→

Exhibit 7.3 continued

- These committees have roles in policy development and review, as well as scrutiny:
  - o reviewing and scrutinising decisions made by the Executive and chief officers;
  - o questioning Cabinet members and chief officers about specific decisions, their views on issues and proposals, and their general performance;
  - o researching policy issues and proposing possible options; and
  - o liaising with and scrutinising the performance of other public bodies in the area.
- The Scrutiny Commission also appoints small, time-limited, task-and-finish **review panels** to study and report on matters of particular concern – for example, concessionary travel, road safety, sex and relationships education.
- A **Joint Health Scrutiny Committee,** including councillors from Leicester City and Rutland Councils, scrutinises the activities of the major county and East Midlands health bodies.

The Council's regulatory role

Bodies responsible for 'regulatory', non-executive functions include:

- **Development Control and Regulatory Board** – development control (planning), licensing.
- **Standards Committee** of at least 2 councillors and a voting member independent of the Council – to monitor standards of conduct of all elected members and officers.
- **Employment Committee** – to deal with conditions of service, disciplinary issues.
- **Constitution Committee** – to advise the Council on constitutional and electoral matters and members' allowances.
- **Pension Fund Management Board** – management of the Leicestershire Pension Fund, covering council staff, plus staff of Loughborough and De Montfort Universities.

Representational role of individual councillors

- To work to ensure the well-being of the community they represent.
- To bring constituents' views and concerns to the attention of the relevant bodies.
- To contribute to the overview and scrutiny of the Council's policy and performance.
- To contribute to the development of corporate policies and local initiatives.

Exhibit 7.4 Leicestershire County Council's Leader/Cabinet executive structure, 2009/10

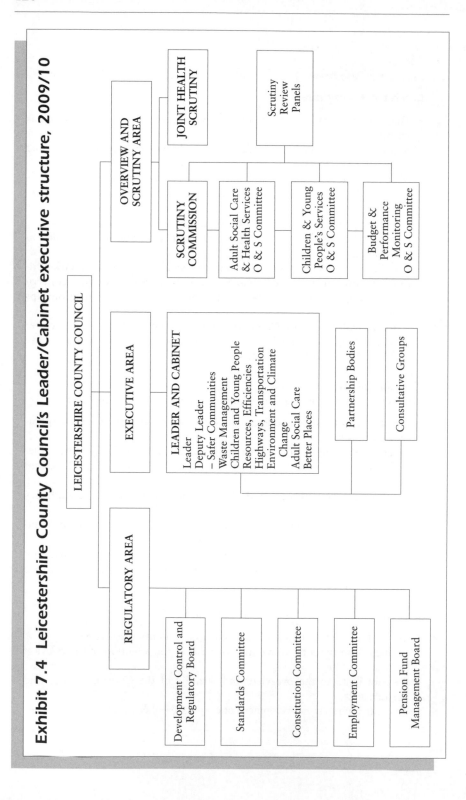

and executive local government was always about changing the working of *all* English and Welsh authorities, including the majority who would never seriously consider having an elected mayor. As set out in Exhibit 7.1, the key objectives of the Local Government Act 2000 were the separation of the *making* of policy from its *scrutiny*, and the requirement that councillors become *either* executive *or* non-executive members. They could no longer be both. The Leader/Cabinet systems adopted by the great majority of authorities have therefore meant almost as fundamental a role change for councillors and officers as have mayoral systems. Moreover, just as mayoral leadership styles differ, so too do Leader/Cabinet systems in the subtle differences in powers that may be available to leaders – as was critically observed in the earlier quote from the 2006 White Paper. A 'strong' leader could appoint the cabinet, allocate their portfolios, and take significant executive decisions personally; but a 'weak' leader would have none of these powers (Gains *et al.*, 2009, p. 79).

All authorities – apart from exempted 'smaller districts' – now have a fairly small cabinet or executive of, on average, nine members with personal policy portfolios, who individually and collectively are the policy-makers for the authority. They operate within policy and budget frameworks approved by the whole council, but, in contrast with the previous committee system, this minority of executive members are clearly identifiable as the ones to hold to account for any particular decision. They are identifiable because all councils must publish, usually on their websites, a *forward plan or decision list*, giving advance notice of key decisions to be made, when, and by which executive member(s), and a similar list of executive decisions taken. These lists serve as a small but eloquent indicator of the extent to which councils have had to change since the turn of the millennium, and of the increased transparency and accountability the changes were designed to bring.

There is, of course, one inherent difference between the Mayor/Cabinet and Leader/Cabinet models. Mayors owe their position to the voters; leaders owe theirs to the fellow councillors who elected them – principally their party colleagues. It is their support that leaders must retain, whereas mayors need the support of the electorate, because the councillors alone cannot remove them. The 2007 Local Government and Public Involvement in Health Act sought to alter these dynamics by requiring council-elected leaders as well as mayors to serve four-year terms of office. As noted above, these provisions appear hard to square with the realities of council politics, and time will tell how they work in practice.

Leicestershire County Council offers an example of the Leader/Cabinet system. An additional requirement of the 2000 Local Government Act was that councils must have, and make publicly available, a *formal constitution*, detailing their management structures and working arrangements, roles and responsibilities of members and officers, and much more besides. Some authorities adopted almost wholesale the standard 'modular' constitutions that the government made available. There are several signs here, though, in Exhibit 7.3 of an attempt to institutionalise something of a 'Leicestershire culture': the delegation of powers to individual Cabinet members; the Cabinet support members; the absence of any sub-authority network of area or neighbourhood committees; the Scrutiny Commission and task-and-finish groups. Other councils – even other county councils – will arrange things differently, as a quick website visit will confirm.

Regrettably, relatively few councils produce downloadable diagrams of their political management structures with which Exhibit 7.4 can be compared, though Birmingham, Essex and Redbridge are all worth checking out. It can, however, usefully be contrasted with Leicestershire's very different 'pre-modernisation' committee structure (Wilson and Game, 1998, p. 72; see also the Exhibit on the linked website), with its Policy and Resources Committee, six main service committees, plus sub-committees and working groups too numerous to list.

Overview and scrutiny

Executive-based policy-making involves two sets of bodies – executive and non-executive. The overview and scrutiny (O&S) provisions in the Local Government Act 2000, which would hold executives to account, were as important as the choice of executive models. Some went further still: 'Overview and scrutiny is potentially the most exciting and powerful element of the entire local government modernisation process. It places members at the heart of policy-making and ... is the mechanism by which councillors can become powerful and influential politicians' (Snape *et al.*, 2002, Executive Summary).

That was the theory. Practice has proved rather different. Councils and councillors have found it the hardest part of the executive package to operate effectively. It involves ideas and ways of working that were novel to those who had become used to decision-making by committee. Many non-executive councillors, told they were no longer policy *makers,* tended to assume they were being cut off from the policy process completely, whereas potentially the reverse was true: they could have more influence on *shaping* policy or on evaluating its impact than many of them would ever have had under the committee system (see Exhibit 7.5). If non-executive members in some authorities saw O&S as 'just a talking shop' which left them 'out of the loop' of real decision-making (Fenwick *et al.*, 2003, pp. 29, 35), others were discovering that this need not necessarily be the case.

The main reason, however, that the scrutiny role has proved so difficult is the entrenched nature of the political party system in modern-day local government and, within the council, the traditionally all-powerful party

Exhibit 7.5 Overview and Scrutiny – what it is and how it's done

The key non-executive role
Non-executive councillors have many roles. But effective Overview and Scrutiny (O&S) is an essential part of the checks and balances necessary to hold the executive and other decision-makers to account.

It's not 'Overview'n'scrutiny'!
It was originally going to be just 'Scrutiny'. Its revised form changed and extended the function. The two parts involve different skills and processes and should be distinguished.

Scrutiny – the critical friend
Means holding the executive to account, by:

- scrutinising decisions *before* they are made or implemented – ideally through consultation with the executive, but if necessary through use of *'call-in'* powers, requiring the executive to reconsider its decision; and
- scrutinising decisions *after* implementation.

The aim is to be a 'critical friend' to the executive, but it's tricky. Be too adversarial, and executive members will be reluctant to co-operate; but too cosy and the whole purpose of the exercise is undermined.

Overview – you name it!
Can include:

- Policy development and review – for example, examining whether a policy's implementation is achieving its intended outcomes; undertaking 'big picture' reviews of broad policy areas;
- External scrutiny – investigating the work of outside bodies: such as health service bodies, transport providers, utility providers, police, fire and rescue services; and
- Performance management and review – assessing the council's performance against corporate priorities and targets.

How it's organised
However the individual authority chooses. Different models include:

- Several O&S committees/panels, with or without a co-ordinating Scrutiny Commission or Management Board.
- Single standing Scrutiny Committee, undertaking both Overview and Scrutiny work; somewhat similar to House of Commons Select Committees.
- Different structures for different roles – for example, a separate Scrutiny Committee and various policy review panels.

What can O&S members do?
Just about anything, preferably behaving as unlike a traditional committee as possible:

- interview and cross-examine executive members, officers, expert witnesses, service users – possibly at their workplace.
- undertake/commission research.
- visit sites, other authorities and organisations.
- co-opt representatives of partner organisations, user groups, outside bodies.
- hold public meetings, organise workshops.
- organise press releases and media launches.
- act as 'mystery shoppers' to test out council services.

political group. As Copus vividly explains: 'The defining characteristic of the political party group is that it demands the loyalty of the councillors that constitute its members *to the exclusion of* all other potential sources of loyalty ... including the wider local party' (2004, p. 92 – our emphasis). Councillors who worked for years under that guiding principle – you challenge your party colleagues in closed party group meetings, but in public you support them loyally – are bound to be reluctant to criticise, in a public setting and in front of their political opponents, senior members of their own party. It goes against every political and personal instinct and, quite possibly, party group rules (Copus, 2004, pp. 220–8). Government guidance may have pronounced 'whipping' – requiring all group members to follow the pre-determined party 'line' – incompatible with properly conducted scrutiny. The best that many authorities can manage is to get the parties' whipping arrangements recorded in the committee minutes.

There is also the problem of adequate and appropriate officer support for the O&S role. Nearly 10 years passed before the 2009 Local Democracy, Economic Development and Construction Act required authorities to designate even a single scrutiny officer. So it is not surprising that many councils were initially slow to appreciate that, if a scrutiny committee is to investigate and question executive policy effectively, it will need something approaching the same quality of advice and support available to the executive members themselves. Over half of all councils and two-thirds of larger ones now provide *specialist* support in the form of a dedicated Scrutiny Support Unit of officers working only to O&S committees. Most others (including Leicestershire) attempt a form of *integrated* support, with officers from several departments working partly for O&S and partly for the executive (CfPS, 2010, p. 6). Both systems have their defendants; what is indefensible is the *minimal* support still offered by some councils for this vital role.

The issue of officer support for O&S serves as an overdue reminder that these political management changes have had major implications for officers, as well as for councillors. The long-standing principle in local government is that officers serve the whole council. With separate mayoral and Cabinet executives, local government has become more like central government, where senior civil servants' first duty is to their minister, not to Parliament as a whole or equally to all parties. Local government officers now have to try to do both: in effect to wear two hats. They must serve *both* executive and non-executive members, both the policy-making process and the critical scrutiny of that process, with all the potential for role conflict that entails.

Shared services and managers

When we wrote that last sentence in the previous edition of this book (p. 116), we had not anticipated the speed at which a very different – and, on the face of it, even more testing – form of role conflict was approaching: chief executives and senior managers splitting themselves not between different sets of councillors, but between different councils. It has been a remarkable development. Executive-based political management, as we saw, was essentially a central government idea imposed on local government through legislation. Shared chief executives, shared management teams, shared services have all been driven much more by local authorities themselves – albeit prompted by an increasingly tough Treasury efficiency drive and a savage economic recession.

The efficiency drive was officially launched in 2004 by Sir Peter Gershon's Treasury-commissioned Review of Public Service Efficiency, with its business roots and private sector title: *Releasing Resources to the Front Line*. Improved public services, asserted Gershon, depended on increasing efficiency and redirecting a proportion of the savings to the delivery of 'front-line' services direct to users – education, social services, refuse collection, environmental services and road maintenance. The separate parts of the public sector were therefore set escalating year-on-year targets for the efficiency gains that would be expected of them – targets that for local government were cascaded down to individual local authorities. Cutting already over-stretched budgets or 'reducing headcounts' (business-speak for redundancies) are almost always politically unpalatable, so many authorities opted for the streamlining of business processes, mainly through information and communications technology (ICT), and/or the sharing of primarily 'back-office' services – finance, payroll, procurement (purchasing), legal, human resources (HR), asset management, marketing, communications.

There was nothing intrinsically novel about local authorities sharing aspects of service provision, and there were plenty of pre-Gershon examples, particularly involving procurement – like the Eastern Shires Purchasing Organisation (ESPO), set up in the 1980s as a purchasing agent for its member authorities, and today buying energy on the spot market by the hour, to reduce the cost of street lighting and transport fleets. There were also, as part of the growing integration of health and social services, partnerships between local authorities and NHS Primary Care Trusts to improve the quality and accessibility of services to patients. Moreover, it is unlikely that our inter-authority co-operative working will ever reach the scale of that in France and Spain (see pp. 76–7). However, the particular stimulus of Gershon should not be understated, and different forms of shared service provision are already transforming the UK local government landscape and will do so in the future even more radically.

Initially, these arrangements were generally modest, both in scale and geography – pairs or triads of usually neighbouring councils sharing a limited range of services. But councils quickly became more creative, developing partnerships involving all imaginable permutations of bodies and working arrangements: local authorities, other public and voluntary sector agencies, private sector companies, insourcing, outsourcing, even the contemplation of off-shoring. In 2008, the Local Government Association (LGA) itself transferred its back-office functions to Liberata, one of the growing number of outsourced business process providers with what presumably are seen as dynamic, rather than meaningless, names: Accenture, Oracle, Steria, Vertex and Xansa.

Possible models for the future, therefore, range from the small, specialist, purely local authority partnership to the massive, multi-sector business enterprise. In the first group would be the Wales Penalty Processing Partnership, which processes all parking penalty notices across a group of North Wales Councils; and the licensing partnership between Maidstone, Sevenoaks and Tunbridge Wells Councils in Kent, whose joint licensing team issues licenses for everything from taxis and street trading to gambling premises and alcohol sales. At the other end of the scale is Southwest One, a 10-year public–private project involving Somerset County and Taunton Deane Borough Councils, Avon and Somerset Police, and IBM, and, in 2009, 1,400 of their seconded staff. Initially projected savings were huge – up to £200 million a year through joint procurement, HR, ICT and finance services. These projections, however, have since been scaled down – understandably, following pre-tax losses of £19 million in the first two years of operation.

Sharing services in the quest for efficiency savings inevitably leads to consideration of the additional potential savings obtainable through sharing staff, particularly higher paid, senior managerial staff. Again, the idea was not a complete novelty, as chief executives (CEs) had often doubled up in an interim capacity – either while an authority waited for a vacancy to be filled or, at the minister's behest, to help turn round an authority judged to be 'failing'. But the drive for efficiency savings and the shared services agenda led to it becoming a regular practice – to the extent that the Improvement and Development Agency was able in 2009 to report on the experience of 10 of these pairing arrangements (IDeA, 2009), while as many as a quarter of the districts in a 2010 *Local Government Chronicle* survey were at least actively considering them.

With one exception – Essex County and Brentwood Borough Councils – the IDeA cases were 'first generational' pairings of neighbouring district councils, with combined populations of well under 200,000: in UK terms, not large at all. This, though, was clearly just the start. In 2010, the Conservative leaders of three contiguous London councils – Hammersmith and Fulham, Kensington and Chelsea, and Westminster – announced that they were looking to save up to £100 million a year through merging their boroughs' environmental, family and corporate services into a unit serving a population of almost 600,000. The news met with the warmest approval of Communities Secretary Pickles, who was also challenging the local government world with his ideas of combining the role of council leader with that of chief executive – thereby, alleged critics, politicising the role of senior managers and undermining local accountability.

To many of those understanding the traditions but also the practice of British local government, these kinds of developments are questionable as permanent solutions to the substantial and certainly not decreasing demands of local authority management, as – to pick another example – is the also growing practice of councils appointing a single director to oversee both children's services and adult social care, with responsibility for up to three-quarters of those councils' total budgets. Merging the services of even two councils is by no means always straightforward and financially beneficial, and redesigning a service to fit the requirements of a single council's own users may well produce greater efficiencies. Our guess is that, as arguments about the merits of executive local government dominated the first decade of the millennium, those about shared services and managements may well come to dominate the second decade.

Chapter 8

Functions and Services

Knickers and haircuts

Chapter 7 ended on a note of scepticism: the suggestion that achieving major efficiency savings through service-sharing might prove harder in practice than it appears. The sceptics here are chiefly people in local government who – to steal an analogy from Lewisham Council's chief executive, Barry Quirk – are most aware of the differences between knickers and haircuts. Statistically, the chances are that your knickers were made in China, but would you go to China for a haircut? Probably no – because, while products are nowadays global commodities, services are local, or should be.

Some local authority activities – some of the 'back-office' functions referred to in Chapter 7 – do have certain of the characteristics of products and could therefore be suitable for sharing and/or outsourcing to the private sector, or even off-shoring to China. But for local authorities these functions are secondary to their main purpose, which is providing or organising the provision of so-called 'front-line' services to their residents in ways that, like haircuts, meet as closely as possible their individual wishes and needs. Shared services may have their place, but treating services as products and putting them at the head of the efficiency savings drive risks distracting local government from its central function.

Local government's principal front-line services are what this chapter is about. It will be looking therefore at the fundamental distinction between local government and either the private sector or central government. To risk a crude but valid generalisation, the private sector is mainly about products, local government mainly about services, and central government mainly about policy. The fact that there are only about half a million central government civil servants, compared to nearly 3 million local government employees, is because UK central government is not, on the whole, a large-scale provider of services. There are important exceptions – most obviously the Department for Work and Pensions, and the Home Office – but generally, ministers and their London-based departments produce *policy, not services*. They decide, through legislation, what services to provide for citizens, by whom, and how they are to be financed. Others, in the main, do the providing, and throughout the twentieth century by far the biggest providers of services were local councils.

This basic role distinction continues today, though, as Chapter 2 noted, local politics and service delivery have been significantly 'transformed' – to use the title of Stoker's interpretative book (Stoker, 2004a, p. 3): 'from a system dominated by elected local government to a system of local governance in which a wider range of institutions and actors are involved'. Councils have lost some of their service responsibilities. Those retained are exposed to more central regulation, more private sector competition, or both. The key future role of local government is seen as being the *commissioning*, rather than the direct provision, of services. Already – sometimes out of choice, sometimes not – councils are working alongside a wide range of other service-providing agencies in their localities, as we shall see particularly in Chapter 9. First, however – and we feel the order is important – it must be recorded that, while service provision at local level is certainly more complex and diffuse than it used to be, it remains a major role for local authorities, albeit not necessarily through direct employment and in-house management.

Still big business

Local government in Britain, even after all the constraining legislation of recent years, the transfers of services to other agencies, the property sales and the enforced competition, is still very big business. On one estimate, local councils undertake, on their own or in partnership, over 800 different functions (LGA, 2009c). In 2010 they spent £173 billion – over a quarter of total government spending and 12% of the UK's gross domestic product (GDP) (see ukpublicspending.co.uk). Their 2.9 million employees constituted a tenth of the British workforce. If individual local authorities were listed by expenditure, almost a hundred would rank alongside the top 500 British companies. Kent County Council's 1.4 million population makes it larger than a quarter of the states in the United Nations, and its £2.3 billion revenue budget (2009–10), even with a weak pound, was higher than that of a fifth of them.

County councils are among the biggest of local government 'businesses', together with metropolitan districts, London boroughs and the larger unitaries. As can be seen from Exhibit 8.1, these authorities are responsible for most of the council-provided services in their areas, or at least for the most labour-intensive and biggest-spending ones, particularly education and social services.

The county/district division in non-metropolitan England is not a hierarchical relationship. While in Exhibit 5.1 the counties and former Scottish regions appear above their respective districts, the two tiers should properly be seen as having equal legal status, each responsible for the services felt to be provided most appropriately on either a relatively larger or a more localised scale. There is, however, a large imbalance in size between the

Exhibit 8.1 Who does what? Main service responsibilities of UK local authorities

	Metropolitan/London authorities				Shire/Unitary authorities		
	Metropolitan districts	Joint authorities	London boroughs	GLA	County councils	District councils	Unitary authorities
Education including schools, youth service, adult education, under-5s	*		*		*		*
Housing including renovation, redevelopment, homeless persons	*		*			*	*
Social services including residential and community care	*		*		*		*
Highways including traffic regulation, road safety, on-street parking	*		*	*	*		*
Passenger transport	*	*	*	*	*		*
Strategic/structure planning	*		*	*	*		*
Local planning/development control	*		*			*	*
Fire and rescue including road accidents, safety inspection and certification		*		*	*		*
Libraries	*		*		*		*
Museums, galleries	*		*		*	*	*
Leisure/recreation including arts, leisure centres, playing fields, parks	*		*			*	*
Waste collection	*		*			*	*
Waste disposal	*	*	*	*	*		*
Consumer protection	*		*		*		*
Environmental health including food safety, pollution control, Agenda 21	*		*			*	*
Council tax collection	*		*			*	*

Cautionary note: This table is presented as a guide to usual practice. We have deliberately not complicated it with a string of detailed and technical footnotes. For details of how any particular service is provided in your area, go to the website(s) of your own council(s).

tiers, with the cost of county-provided services being four or five times that of district-provided services in any particular district area. Unitary authorities in principle have responsibility for all those services in the parts of England that are not split into counties and districts. In practice, as described in Chapter 5, there is a complex network of joint boards, committees and other agencies – captured only partially in our simplified Exhibit 8.1 – that contribute to service provision: bodies composed of councillors not directly elected to them but nominated by their respective councils.

In addition, there is the jigsaw of other 'local public spending bodies' that are involved in the governance of a locality: none directly elected, and many with no elective element at all. They too are big business and, though their precise numbers are not easy to determine, their total spending on local service provision in any given area may well be several times that spent directly by elected councils – as shown by one of the early Total Place pilot studies (see Exhibit 2.1, Item 9). These non- or quasi-governmental bodies have changed the way in which local government services are managed and delivered, as we shall see in more detail in Chapter 9. First, though, we look at the services themselves.

A classification of services – Britain's particularity

Britain's local authorities cover exceptionally large population numbers and, as we have just seen, are diverse organisations with big budgets and workforces, responsible for hundreds of different services. But their *range* of services is neither as extensive as it once was, nor as extensive as in many other European countries. Our local authorities are unusual in *not* having direct responsibility for hospitals and preventive health services, which are provided through the entirely separate institutions of the National Health Service (NHS). In this respect they keep company only with some of the smaller EU countries – Ireland, Greece and Portugal (John, 2001, p. 36). Most social assistance benefits are administered centrally in Britain through the Department for Work and Pensions and Her Majesty's Revenue and Customs (Tax Credits and Child Benefit), rather than through local councils, as is common European practice. Councils' involvement has been limited to housing and council tax benefits, though from 2013 they will take on the new and controversial responsibility for administering the Coalition Government's proposed weekly benefits cap, by assessing claimants' total benefit income and adjusting their housing benefit accordingly.

While our health and social services are less institutionally integrated than in much of continental Europe, our education system has been more so. Education has been by far the biggest spender in British local government, because an education-administering local authority – known traditionally as a Local Education Authority (LEA) – has provided almost all

Exhibit 8.2 A categorisation of local services

1 **Need services** – for example, education, personal social services, housing benefit. Services provided for all, regardless of means, and which therefore contribute to the redistribution of resources within the community.

2 **Protective services** – for example policing and community safety, fire and rescue, emergency planning. Services provided for the security of people, to national guidelines. Access to them cannot be restricted, and use by one person does not affect their availability to others.

3 **Amenity services** – for example highways, street cleansing, planning, parks and open spaces, environmental health, refuse disposal, consumer protection, economic development. Services provided largely to locally determined standards to meet the needs of each local community.

4 **Facility services** – for example housing, libraries, museums and art galleries, recreational centres, refuse collection, cemeteries and crematoria. Services for people to draw on if they wish, sometimes in competition with private sector provision.

education services: from building schools and employing teachers to providing books, pencils and computers. In much of Europe, local authorities provide and maintain school premises, but the national government employs the teachers. Frequently too, responsibility for primary and secondary schools is split between different tiers of local authorities. In the USA and Canada, many schools are run by elected special authorities or boards.

In 'public utilities' Britain is also the exception. In almost all other European countries, municipalities still provide one or more of the utilities – water, electricity, gas – that were mainly local government services in Britain until their nationalisation in the 1940s and privatisation in the 1980s. British policing, by contrast, historically has been, and remains, more localised than in many countries. In Scandinavia, the Netherlands, Australia and New Zealand it is not a local function, whereas, even in the UK's post-1995 independent police authorities, there is still majority councillor representation.

These cross-national differences are worth keeping in mind as we deal briefly with the major local government services. We follow the fourfold classification summarised in Exhibit 8.2, starting with 'need services', which account in Britain for well over half of total net local government spending, reflecting the role of councils' role as deliverers of major parts of our welfare state. In other countries 'amenity services', for example, might feature more prominently.

Need services – for all of us, regardless of means

Education – the LEA's transition from provider to commissioner

Education covers much more than compulsory schooling: early years development and nursery provision, youth and community education, adult and further education. But it was their responsibility for schools that gave an education committee and department their once unique position as literally a Local Education Authority within a local authority; and it is this responsibility that has been challenged and reduced to the point where in many respects school education today has become a national function.

The basis of our modern school system was the 1944 Education Act, which set up the functional split described at the start of this chapter. Central government legislated and set the national policy framework – free compulsory schooling from the ages of 5 to 15 (later 16), every LEA to appoint a chief education officer, 'aided' or 'controlled' status for voluntary/church schools, and the free school milk. But the provision, staffing and running of schools were in the hands of local authorities. LEAs decided how they organised their schools: selective or non-selective, primary/secondary or first/middle/junior high, grammar schools or sixth-form colleges.

Since the 1980s, that central–local balance has changed fundamentally. There was an average of at least one Education Act each year during the 1980s and 1990s, some of which are included in the 'funnel of local authority discretion' (see Exhibit 2.2). Some Acts removed LEAs' responsibilities completely for polytechnics, colleges and institutes of higher education, sixth-form and FE colleges. Others reduced their role in schools management. The keynote legislation was the 1988 Education Reform Act. It brought in the national curriculum and 'key stage' or Standard Attainment Tests (SATs), with results published in school performance league tables. It introduced Local Management of Schools (LMS), requiring LEAs to pass on at least 85% of their education budget to school governing bodies, who thus became responsible for overseeing the running of their own school and its financial operation. Even more provocatively, it enabled schools, through parental ballots, to 'opt out' of the control of their LEA and be funded instead, as 'grant-maintained' (GM) schools, directly by central government, which then recharged the cost to the LEA.

Though it would soon introduce its own essentially similar academies, the New Labour Government abolished GM status in 1998, at which time only about 5% of state schools had actually opted out. LEAs continued to maintain the other 95%, but their involvement in day-to-day school management, already much reduced through LMS, was further eroded under Labour. A national Standards and Effectiveness Unit was set up, and literacy and numeracy targets for 11-year-olds introduced immediately. The inspection regime under OFSTED (the Office for Standards in Education) was strengthened, and ministerially directed intervention in under-performing schools increased. Ring-fencing of schools' funding – putting it outside the LEA's control – was first extended and, with the 2007 introduction of the Dedicated Schools Grant (DSG), completed. Now, instead of the local authority acting as a local government and deciding how much of its general 'formula' grant should go to schools, taking into account all its other services, it simply receives the DSG as a large, hitherto ring-fenced, specific grant that central government has decreed *must* be used to fund the authority's schools and for no other purpose.

New Labour's keynote legislation was the 2006 Education and Inspections Act, a wide-ranging and controversial Act that implemented, thanks to Conservative support and several enforced concessions, the 2005 White Paper, *Higher Standards, Better Schools for All*. The strategy was clear: to make secondary schools in particular more appealing to and controllable by middle-class parents, so that their children would stay part of the 93% in the state system and they themselves would support the government's public investment programmes, rather than demand tax cuts. The government would therefore build on its introduction of academies: self-governing secondary schools, independent of local authority control, and funded directly by central government with additional support from corporate or personal sponsors. All new schools, and eventually LEA-run community schools, should be publicly funded and independent. But they would take different forms and have differing degrees of separation from their LEA, to increase parental choice: academies, part-privately sponsored specialist schools, trust and foundation schools, church and other faith schools. The 2010 Conservative manifesto pledged swiftly and substantially to increase academies: by enabling all schools – primary as well as secondary – to apply for academy freedoms, and 'any good education provider' (undefined) to set up a new academy school.

The corollary of having a diverse range of promoters providing schools is that the traditional local authority providers become instead *commissioners* of school provision – within what, for other reasons, are usually comprehensive Children's Services Directorates. Their strategic commissioning role – until the Coalition Government made it likely that almost all schools would in future be academy or free schools – was to establish the demand for school places, identify children's needs and parents' preferences, and champion their interests in finding new and appropriately diverse providers – but excluding, except in exceptional circumstances, themselves. They remained responsible also for the management of admissions, appeals, parental advice, home-to-school transport, assessment of educational needs and free school meals eligibility. In support, they offered educational welfare, catering, security, grounds maintenance, ICT support and cleaning services, but schools could, and were encouraged to, look for alternative cost-effective providers.

The Coalition Government's early Academies Act 2010, inspired supposedly by the Swedish free school system, aimed to enable all publicly-funded schools in England to become academies, with a greatly increased discretion over matters such as the curriculum and teachers' pay. All local authority secondary and primary schools could apply immediately for academy status, and any with an OFSTED 'outstanding' rating would be automatically pre-approved, regardless of the view of the local authority. In September 2010, 121 new academies opened, adding to the 203 created before the General Election. The number was far short of some of the wilder predictions, but the trend was unmistakably set. Much, however, remained unclear – including how academies' additional funding would not leave the schools remaining under local authorities relatively disadvantaged, and what the future educational role of those authorities would be.

Personal social services

The emphasis here is on *services,* because, as noted above, most benefit and allowance payments are made not by local government but through Jobcentre Plus and other local offices of the Department for Work and Pensions. Local authorities, frequently working through voluntary and private organisations, provide for a range of client groups services that include residential care, day care, help (such as meals, laundry, home modifications, practical aids) to enable people to remain in their own homes, counselling, fostering and adoption, and child protection.

The scale of activity is massive, and frequently sensitive. Like teachers, social workers really do provide a 'front-line' service, living with the continuous pressure both of new legislative demands and public expectations. Both groups too have become used to the exceptional case that propels one or two unfortunate individuals, a single institution or department, and indirectly the whole profession, into the glare of national media headlines. For social workers, it can be a tragic case involving the failure of child protection and the ensuing investigations into either inadequate or misguidedly zealous professional behaviour. Such cases are atypical, which is why they attract the attention they do. But the depth of their coverage, especially if they provoke an official inquiry report, can reveal much about the day-to-day operations of the responsible council departments.

It was a particularly shocking inquiry report – by Lord Laming into the death of Victoria Climbié – that, as noted in Chapter 7, led to the Children Act 2004 and in effect the overthrow of the concept of generic social services that had dominated the profession since the 1970s. The 1968 Seebohm Report had heralded the 1970 Local Authority Social Services Act, which merged the traditional health and welfare and children's departments into a single social services department, headed by a new chief officer – the Director of Social Services. The 2004 Act ended that structure, requiring the integration of what was usually the Children and Families branch of Social Services with the LEA to form a new Children's Department, organisationally separate from Adult Social Services.

Councils also had to promote co-operation to protect children's safety by establishing Local Safeguarding Children Boards (LSCBs), comprising all agencies with responsibilities towards children, including strategic health authorities and primary care trusts, the police, probation service, youth offending teams, and governors of prisons or secure training centres. These bodies, however, have brought their own controversy – particularly in Haringey, the London borough whose child care services were found to have failed Victoria Climbié and that seven years later were also involved in the death of 17-month-old Peter Connelly (Baby P), again from repeated abuse and ill-treatment. It is LSCBs who in such circumstances undertake serious case reviews, that in Baby P's case prompted questions about their independence – the original Board having been chaired by the Director of Children's Services – and the practice of publishing only executive summaries of their reports. The Director's precipitate sacking – live on television – by Children's Minister, Ed Balls, also, hardly surprisingly, raised acute questions about relations between local and central government – the subject of Chapter 10 – as well as about the manipulation of information that underpinned it.

If the key developments in children's services seem to have been driven by legislation and public outcry, those in adult care have emerged rather more peaceably, from a historic concordat – *Putting People First: A Shared Vision and Commitment to the Transformation of Adult Social Care* (2007) – and an earlier Department of Health White Paper, *Our Health, Our Care, Our Say: A New Approach to Community Services* (2006). The concordat signatories were six government ministers, the Local Government Association, and representatives from the NHS and public and private social care providers, and their vision was a complete transformation and personalisation of social care provision. Instead of care professionals allocating services and controlling budgets for social care customers, users were to become the centre of the system – people with all levels of need taking control of their own care and support. Personalisation and individual budgets were not themselves innovations; for some years a small minority of those eligible for adult social care had been able to tailor services according to their specific needs and receive support through a direct payment. *Putting People First* was about making this choice of treatment and payment available to almost all recipients: a personal budget, some or all of which can be taken as a direct payment, enabling them to make informed choices about how best to meet their treatment needs.

For care providers, the implications of personalisation are equally radical. It means collaborative working across sectors and service boundaries – involving housing, benefits, leisure, transport and health – and a strategic shift of emphasis towards earlier intervention, prevention and assistive technology, to enable as many as possible of those with support needs to continue living independently at home. The role changes for social workers and care managers in particular are obviously profound, but far from straightforward. Delivered effectively, personalised support and earlier intervention should produce a more efficient use of resources, but initially the funding implications, not least the cost of staff training, would be substantial. Existing services would have to be redesigned, and local authority budgets redirected, but, as with schools, the government helped to ensure the implementation of its policy with a new ring-fenced Social Care Reform Grant to councils, which had escalated to £240 million in 2010/11.

Protective services – for our security

Community safety and crime reduction

Until the 1990s, policing in the UK was a local authority service. Apart from London – where the Metropolitan Police reported directly to the Home Secretary before, in 2000, becoming the responsibility of the new Greater London Authority (GLA) – chief constables were accountable to the police committees of county councils: in a similar way to other council committees, apart from their memberships, which comprised two-thirds councillors and one-third local magistrates.

The Police and Magistrates Courts Act 1994 changed the composition and role of police authorities by making them independent authorities, with enhanced powers over their own service provision, and more independent of their respective councils. Their membership comprises nominated councillors, magistrates and co-opted Home Office nominees – with a bare councillor majority – and the local government interest has generally become the weakest link in the tripartite structure of central government, local government and Chief Constable. Police authorities still depend on local government for about a third of their income, and we shall see in Chapter 12 how they levy a 'precept', which councils must include in the council tax bills they send out to their residents. When determining their local policing objectives, however, they are likely to be concerned to adhere first to the Home Secretary's national objectives, rather than the policies of their local councils.

The Conservative manifesto proposal for directly elected police commissioners, with the power to hire and fire Chief Constables and set force budgets, was included in the Coalition's *Programme for Government*. It was inevitably controversial, but its aim is to hold more effectively to account perhaps the least accountable leaders of any public service in the country. The first of the new commissioners is likely to be elected in 2012. The commissioners will have strong personal mandates, and Coalition Liberal Democrats – who favoured the direct election of existing police authorities – will be particularly keen to ensure that they are subject to the 'strict checks and balances by locally elected representatives', that the Coalition Government promised.

The structure of 43 county-based police forces in England and Wales (with eight in Scotland and the Northern Ireland Policing Board) could, like local authorities, come under pressure to merge into larger, even regional, units. For most citizens, though, the striking visible development of recent years must have been more localised neighbourhood policing. Based partly on the success in Chicago and other US cities of community policing – the term also used in Scotland – neighbourhood policing seeks to increase public confidence and community engagement and thereby reduce crime, through the presence on our streets of visible, accessible and locally known police and community support officers. Since 2008, every neighbourhood in England and Wales has had its dedicated policing team – as can be checked through either individual police websites or on the UK Government website: www.directgov.co.uk. Taking one of our own areas as an example, the West Midlands force is divided into 248 neighbourhoods each with an average population of around 10,000. Each neighbourhood is policed by a team of around 15 people – police officers, uniformed police community support officers (PCSOs), special constables – generally supported by local authority street wardens.

Fire, rescue and emergency planning

Not until the late 1930s were all local authorities outside London required to maintain fire services, and then these local brigades were amalgamated almost immediately into a National Fire Service during the Second World War. The Fire Services Act 1947 returned them to local control, and today's structure is not dissimilar from that of the police: 50 county-based or combined authorities in England and Wales (including the London Fire and Emergency Planning Authority), eight in Scotland, plus the single Northern Ireland Fire Brigade. The most notable difference is that fire authorities continue to consist entirely of councillors.

In contrast to the education world with its almost annual legislation, it took nearly 50 years for the 1947 Act to be updated in the Fire and Rescue Services Act 2004. The title extension reflects how the service's work has evolved, from fire-fighting to prevention and rescue. The Act introduced an explicit duty to promote fire safety and help to create safer communities. More generally, it set a legislative framework in which fire authorities could be more proactive, work more closely with other bodies, and focus on responsibilities scarcely envisaged in 1947: rescue from road traffic accidents, train and aircraft crashes, and dealing with chemical spillages, and environmental and terrorist emergencies.

In addition to London's incorporation of 'Emergency Planning', six other authorities – those in the areas of the metropolitan county councils that were abolished in 1986 – are officially entitled Fire and Civil Defence Authorities, reminding us of another local government function that has changed dramatically in recent years. The Civil Defence Act 1948 gave certain local authorities powers – though little financial assistance – to organise and protect their civilian populations from an emergency that was expected to take the form of either industrial and civil unrest or a nuclear attack from a hostile foreign nation.

The 9/11 attacks and subsequent events promoted emergency planning and what is now termed 'building resilience' from a backwater of local government to a primary policy concern. Nationally, responsibility shifted from the Home Office to the Civil Contingencies Secretariat in the Cabinet Office, and the contentious Civil Contingencies Act 2004 was passed: 'Blair's Enabling Act', as it became known. It gave the government wide powers to declare a 'state of emergency', and imposed new emergency planning duties on 'Category 1 contingency response bodies' such as major local authorities. These duties included contingency planning, risk assessment, warning the public, and strengthening co-operation between response bodies: local resilience forums, based on police force areas. With far more centralised direction of planning and response than previously, this is a more subsidiary role than formerly, but one that is defined more explicitly.

Amenity services – for our community needs

Highways, transportation and traffic management

These functions are the most shared of all public services, covering motorways to bridleways, and involving all levels of government from the Department for Transport (DfT) to parish councils. The Secretary of State is responsible for trunk roads and motorways, with decisions often being taken in regional offices and most maintenance contracted out by the Highways Agency, an executive agency acting on the minister's behalf. Counties, unitaries and metropolitan districts, and in London the boroughs and GLA, have responsibility for other primary and secondary roads. 'Responsibility' here includes the design of routes, taking into account the cost, environmental impact, safety, residential and industrial needs; road building and maintenance; highway management, including parking restrictions, speed limits, street lighting, traffic signs, and street cleaning; and winter maintenance and road safety. In practice, however, 'agency agreements' are common, and several of these functions are likely in two-tier areas to be undertaken by district councils. Local authorities also work with bus and rail companies to improve their local public transport networks, for the 14% minority of us who travel to work via this mode.

In its 1997 manifesto, Labour committed itself to developing 'an effective and integrated transport policy at national, regional and local level' and particularly to increasing the use of public transport (Labour Party, 1997, p. 29). To this end, as in other policy areas, councils produce plans: comprehensive 5-year Local Transport Plans (LTPs) that are submitted to the DfT, whose ministers and civil servants assess proposed schemes against value-for-money criteria before deciding whether to approve them for funding – as with Leeds trolley buses (Exhibit 2.1, Item 2). The two most discussed issues in the first (2001) set of LTPs were how to reduce traffic congestion and improve passenger transport (particularly buses), and the most interesting transport initiatives of the early 2000s were pioneering authorities' efforts to implement the more radical of these measures.

First, in 2002, came Durham City Council's rising bollards, restricting vehicle access to the city's historic centre through the country's first road-user charge. Between them, the bollards and the charge increased pedestrian and bus usage and greatly reduced traffic. In 2003, London's Mayor, Ken Livingstone, introduced an electronic army of Automatic Number Plate Recognition (ANPR) cameras and the Central London congestion charge – and again bus usage increased and congestion was reduced. Encouraged by London's success, the government's 2004 Transport White Paper – and the prime minister in a personal foreword – endorsed the idea of road-user charging: a radical policy, but seen by many as the most feasible long-term solution to traffic management. Local authorities were encouraged to bid for grants to develop pilot schemes.

City centre congestion charging is obviously a form of road pricing, but they are not the same thing, and the government's envisaged road pricing would have been instead of additional road taxes and therefore, it was claimed, tax-revenue-neutral. The distinction, however, was not well explained, and was largely lost in the public mind. So when the prime minister's official No.10 website presented the opportunity, over 1.8 million signed an e-petition demanding that 'the planned vehicle tracking and road pricing policy' be scrapped – which it promptly was, for the foreseeable future.

Public hostility to any form of road pricing also affected the next major referendum vote on congestion charging – in Manchester in 2008. The Greater Manchester Council had taken up the government's invitation to bid for funding to develop the area's public transport and enable the introduction of a congestion charge covering what would have been a large proportion of the Manchester conurbation. The benefits in government funding and job creation could have been substantial, but voters were unconvinced, and in a high turnout postal referendum rejected the proposed scheme by a majority of 4 to 1 – and in doing so probably also sealed the fate of several other cities' charging plans.

Planning and development

There are two principal planning functions: development control; and strategic or land use planning. *Development control* is exercised by unitary, metropolitan and district councils, who respond, mainly on the basis of local development plans, to applications for planning consent to construct, demolish or adapt the use of buildings. Planning authorities process these applications, uncontentious cases normally being delegated to officers, with more controversial and complex developments being determined by the council's planning committee – one of the 'regulatory' committees that have continued to exist even after councils' adoption of executive arrangements. Various responses are available to councils – from unconditional consent through to refusal of an application clearly incompatible with the local plan – and a disappointed applicant has the right of appeal to a planning inspector appointed by the Secretary of State, and ultimately to the High Court. The whole process was excellently portrayed in the BBC's 2008–9 documentary series, *The Planners Are Coming* (still downloadable at the time of writing).

If all politics is about the allocation of necessarily limited resources, land-use planning is about the allocation of arguably the most precious resource of all. Sir Simon Jenkins sees it as 'the defining activity of politics. Through it, people express how and at what pace they want their communities to change' (Jenkins, 2006a) – and, it goes almost without saying, that expression should be through democratic channels. *Strategic planning* is the process of producing the development plans with which planning applications should conform. Planning authorities decide how they want their area as a whole to develop over, say, the coming fifteen years or so. In the past, after extensive consultations, *structure plans* were drawn up by county councils, and local plans by district councils, while in unitary authorities the two were combined in a unitary plan. These plans would allocate areas of land for future housing, industrial, commercial and leisure developments, taking into account national and local policies for protecting the environment. Housing allocations tended to be especially contentious, with developers wanting more generous provision of greenfield sites, and councils, backed by local residential and environmental pressure groups, usually preferring 'brownfield' redevelopment. Governments have their own, not always consistent, views, and the Secretary of State had the power to 'call-in' a structure plan for modification or rejection.

The Planning and Compulsory Purchase Act 2004 changed this system – into what Jenkins (2006a) labelled 'the most centralised planning system in the free world'. County councils' statutory planning powers were regionalised, and the non-elected assemblies became – for the few years until they were abolished – the new regional planning bodies, responsible for preparing *Regional Spatial Strategies* (RSSs). In practice, this meant that, while local authorities were consulted and the draft RSS underwent a public examination, the final say on, for example, the balance between housing, factories and amenities was the minister's, in line with central government's priorities. These strategy documents then became the framework within which unitary and local councils produced their local plans, known as Local Development Frameworks (LDFs). The 2004 Act contained several commendable measures, aimed at speeding up the planning process and introducing sustainable development as an explicit objective of the planning system, but for the actual planning process it seemed another move away from local democratic accountability.

Keen to be seen restoring that local accountability, Communities and Local Government Secretary, Eric Pickles, made a precipitate announcement of the Coalition's intention to abolish this regional planning framework, RSSs, housing targets – and thereby the whole process through which local authorities granted permission for new housing. The result, in the short-term at least, was more anarchy than accountability. Housing projects were abandoned or postponed, construction workers were laid off, and waiting lists lengthened.

The Coalition Government's other early planning intervention also had its costs. The purpose of the 2008 Planning Act, noted in Exhibit 2.1, Item 8, was to streamline the process, acknowledged as inefficient, for approving the construction of nationally significant infrastructure projects. Costly and protracted public inquiries would be abolished and location decisions on, for example, airports, power stations, major roads, railways and hazardous waste facilities would be made not by the Secretary of State but by a new and unaccountable quango: the Infrastructure Planning Commission (IPC). However, after costing some £16 million and without signing off a single planning decision, the IPC was abolished by the Coalition and its responsibilities transferred to a unit within the Planning Inspectorate – that is, back to democratically answerable ministers, who will be required to consult local communities and 'take account' of their objections. Lest it be thought, though, that taxpayers seem not to have done terribly well out of these events, it should be noted that in future, if local residents do agree to new building, they should benefit by seeing their council tax cut.

Environmental and public health

This set of functions is one of the oldest local government services. Victorian local government pioneered the provision of clean water, decent public housing, food inspection, and the treatment of infectious diseases, and today's borough and district councils grew out of the local boards of health and sanitary authorities set up under the Public Health Acts of the 1870s. Yet, in creating a National Health Service in the 1940s, the Labour Government opted for what in effect was a free-standing 'national sickness service', controlled by and answerable to ministers – rather than a comprehensive *health care* service, integrated with linked functions such as social care, housing, education and the environment, both responsive and accountable to elected local councils. Local government lost most of its curative health functions in 1948 and 1974, leaving it with 'only' environmental health, though this responsibility still gives councils – as employers, service providers, regulators and community leaders – greater health promotion and disease prevention potential than any other institution, including the NHS itself.

So extensive are councils' environmental health and consumer protection responsibilities that in this book's second edition we produced an A–Z of these services – from abandoned vehicles via dog fouling and tree preservation to zoo licensing (Wilson and Game, 1998, p. 26, plus an Exhibit on the linked website). The full list involves all those functions of inspection, regulation, registration, licensing and certification that tend to be relatively unnoticed until there is a food contamination crisis, a dangerous dogs scare, a massage parlour scandal, or a threatened flu pandemic.

The Labour Government gave huge funding priority to the NHS, but at the same time there was growing acknowledgement that health should be seen as a public, as well as a private, good. The result, as already noted, is that institutional links and joint working arrangements between local authorities and health bodies are closer today than at any time in the history of the NHS. Some of these developments – pooled budgets and joint investment plans, councils' health scrutiny role – pre-dated the Labour Government's development of its health inequalities and improvement agenda. But it was that agenda, set out in the 2004 public health White Paper, *Choosing Health: Making Healthy Choices Easier* – reducing smoking, increasing exercise, reducing obesity and improving diet, encouraging sensible drinking, and improving sexual and mental health – and the Communities for Health programme that followed it that really ratcheted up local government's health improvement role. Launched in 2005, the Communities for Health programme sought, through partnerships between local authorities, primary care trusts, community and voluntary organisations, to develop innovative projects that would 'engage communities in their own health' and in turn lead to individual behavioural change for healthier lifestyles. Managed by the Department of Health, the initial 25 pilots were judged sufficiently successful for the programme to be extended in 2007 to a further 56 areas (see Department of Health, 2009; also Baggott, 2007).

If Communities for Health represented a boost for local government's public health role, the Coalition Government's NHS reform White Paper, *Equity and Excellence* (DH, 2010) promised several completely new roles.

The headlines of the radical reform programme were that all Primary Care Trusts (PCTs) and Strategic Health Authorities would be abolished, along with the Labour Government's performance targets, and commissioning of care services would be devolved to new organisations: consortia of GP practices and an NHS Commissioning Board. Local authorities' new responsibilities would include integrating the commissioning of local NHS services, social care and health improvement; commissioning local HealthWatch organisations to listen and respond to the collective voice of public and patients; and taking over PCT responsibilities for local health improvement by employing a Director of Public Health.

Economic development and regeneration

Look at some councils' websites and you might suppose that – with their business parks and industrial estates, commercial property files, relocation grants, advisory and investment services – economic development and business promotion are their principal activities. The importance of these would seem to be confirmed by the powers acquired by councils in the 2000 Local Government Act to promote the *economic,* social and environmental well-being of their area. In fact, statutory recognition of councils' key role in economic development dates back only to the Local Government and Housing Act 1989, and in another sense too it is a modern role, involving as it does close partnership working with both the private sector and other regional and local bodies. It remained, however, a comparatively low-status function in most local authorities – until given a potential boost in the 2009 Local Democracy, Economic Development and Construction Act.

The Act imposed a statutory Economic Assessment Duty on local authorities, with the aim of increasing their economic development and regeneration work. Upper-tier authorities would be required, following consultations with local organisations, and particularly their lower-tier councils, to produce a Local Economic Assessment identifying their economy's comparative strengths and weaknesses, the opportunities and threats facing it, and the key factors enabling or constraining sustainable economic development. It seemed likely, however, that the statutory requirement would be short-lived, and reduced by a self-consciously localist Coalition Government to merely a discretion.

Facility services – for all of us, if we wish

Housing – reports of its death exaggerated?

A glance at a local authority's Housing Strategy document will show immediately the breadth of the modern-day housing management function. The strategy covers all homes, both privately owned and rented. It records the age and condition of the housing stock, monitors how well it is selling and how many properties are empty, and assesses what type of housing is needed in both the short and the longer term for all categories of residents. It is likely to contain specific strategies for tackling homelessness, for allocations – giving priority to those in greatest housing need, but also offering choice to applicants – for older people's housing, student housing, black and minority ethnic housing, and possibly lesbian, gay, bisexual and transgender housing – at least in Brighton and Hove. These documents are necessarily the product of partnership working with a wide range of organisations, including housing associations and builders, and reflect how, as in relation to other services, the core of local government's housing role has shifted from provider to facilitator.

Just as local authority education was traditionally about running schools, so housing was about building, allocating and managing council houses. Yet, as we noted in this book's previous edition, 'some housing experts predict that the council home – one of the integral features of Britain's post-war welfare state – will have virtually disappeared by 2015 (Wilson and Game, 2006, p. 135). With the number of new council homes completed in 2008/9 being easily the highest this century, and set to rise considerably, those death reports seem, as American writer Mark Twain put it on reading his own obituary, exaggerated. But other figures quickly make clear why the predictions were made.

Council housing tenure peaked in the late 1970s, when there were nearly 7 million homes – a third of the nation's housing stock – and their management was a major local authority activity. By 2009, the number of council homes in England was fewer than 2 million – just 9% of the housing stock (DCLG, 2009b). The decline is attributable largely to two potent government policies: the Conservatives' 'Right to Buy' legislation in the 1980s and the large-scale housing transfers initiated by the Conservatives but accelerated by successive Labour Governments.

In 1980, the Thatcher Government's Housing Act gave council tenants the right to buy their homes at discounts of up to 70 per cent, depending on their length of tenancy. Labour councils sought to resist, concerned at the reduced housing stock that would be left available for people unable to rent privately, but they could be forced to comply. If the Secretary of State believed a council was restricting tenants' rights to buy their homes, a housing commissioner could be sent in – as happened in Clay Cross, Derbyshire – to take over the sales process. In 1997, with nearly 2 million former council properties in private hands, the new Labour Government declined to abolish an obviously popular policy. It clearly exacerbated the incipient housing crisis, and there was evidence of abuse by property developers who would pay tenants to buy their homes so that they could let them out at market rents, but ministers would go no further than to reduce the maximum discounts available. A further 500,000 sales were completed by 2004 and the remaining stock fell below 3 million.

Even a declining housing stock, though, has to be maintained, and, as governments restricted both the revenue spending and capital borrowing of local authorities, large backlogs of repairs built up. Rather than allow councils to borrow against their assets to obtain the funding required to deal with these backlogs themselves, governments preferred the transfer approach. The Conservative Government's 1988 Housing Act introduced 'tenants' choice', allowing new landlords – notably housing associations who were permitted, unlike councils, to raise private finance – to take over council housing following a ballot of tenants. In the decade to 1997, some 250,000 council homes were transferred to housing associations, who quickly overtook local authorities as the main providers of new housing for rent.

The incoming Labour Government in 1997 thus inherited a council housing stock that was both declining and – because 'Right to Buy' had generally taken the better-quality homes – increasingly dilapidated. When the government made the commitment in its 2000 Green Paper, *Quality and Choice: A Decent Home for All*, to bring all social housing up to a 'decent' standard by 2010 – warm, weatherproof, and with reasonably modern facilities – there was a £19 billion backlog of repairs and modernisation work for council housing alone. Still prohibited from borrowing, councils unable to meet their modernisation costs out of existing resources were presented with three options, none very palatable to many of the councillors forced to choose between them:

- Transfer all or some of the stock to a housing association or *Registered Social Landlord*, who could borrow from banks and building societies;
- Enter into a long-term service contract under the *Private Finance Initiative* (PFI) with private sector providers, who would finance, improve, maintain, but also manage the council's housing, being repaid over the contract period with additional money from the government; or
- Set up an *Arm's Length Management Organisation* (ALMO) – a not-for-profit company to whom, if approved by the Audit Commission, the government would make additional funding available.

For councils wanting to keep their housing stock in public ownership, ALMOs proved the least unpopular option, as the Labour Government intended when it set them up for the purpose. As the original 2010 Decent Homes deadline approached, they were managing a million homes in 66 authorities – more than councils owned directly. But, with their primary function nearing completion, ALMOs faced an uncertain future. Their local authorities could take their management function back in-house, or, if that seemed too costly, there was the option of the ALMO transforming itself into a Registered Social Landlord.

A third possibility, however, not available ten years previously, was that they become house builders as well as managers. In another demonstration of New Labour's ambivalence towards council housing, Prime Minister Gordon Brown anticipated in January 2009 'the biggest council house building programme since the 1950s' (Sherman and Gilmore, 2009), and later that year Housing Minister John Healey announced a £500 million public investment programme – half from the government, half from local authorities – to build more than 4,000 new council homes across every region of England. In comparison with the 1970s, when councils were building 100,000 homes annually, it seemed small beer indeed, but it didn't sound like the imminent death of local government's traditional housing role either.

The Coalition Government's social housing policy was initially difficult to identify, as it appeared not to have one: none of the 31 policy headings in the *Programme for Government* addressed housing. A possible explanation, though, was suggested by the October 2010 Comprehensive Spending Review: it was essentially the same as the rest of its policy. Capital spending by local government, most of which goes to social housing, was projected to fall by two-thirds – from £7.4 billion to £2.5 billion – over the 4-year review period, yet 150,000 new affordable homes would be built. Even this number would still leave millions on waiting lists, but the assumption had to be that, as in other areas of the economy, as the public sector withdraws, private investors fill the vacuum, in this case lending to housing associations, unconstrained by the borrowing restrictions imposed on local authorities. Some councils would continue to build, but they could forget any favours.

Libraries – genuine local service or idea store?

Local authorities have been providing libraries for 150 years – though not until 1919 were they permitted to spend significant amounts of money to fill them with books. In the 1964 Public Libraries and Museums Act the provision of a 'comprehensive and efficient' public library service was made a statutory requirement, but during subsequent periods in which budgets, stocks, opening hours and whole libraries were being cut, there has been uncertainty in this essentially discretionary service about what the two key adjectives really meant. In 2009 we were given some idea, as Wirral Council proposed cutting 11 of the borough's 24 libraries in a drastic restructuring of the service. Local outrage ensued – protests, a 55,000-signature petition, plans to form a new political party – and, in the first such action since 1991, Culture Secretary Andy Burnham intervened and ordered an inquiry, whereupon the Council changed its mind.

Even in non-recessionary times, libraries are a vulnerable service. They are regularly described as a service in distress, or even crisis, but recent statistics, until the drastic grant cuts of 2011/12, were not all as distressing as is sometimes supposed or as they were in, say, the 1990s. The number of libraries was gradually falling, and so, hardly surprisingly, were book stocks and issues. But opening hours had risen, audio-visual, electronic and other stocks were increasing, while total library visits had fluctuated around the 330 million mark since the year 2000 (Davies, 2008, p. 22; CIPFA, 2009a) – a figure that is invariably described as higher than the number of British people who attend either football matches or the cinema, though usually without much referenced evidence.

Libraries' popularity is part of their problem. Everyone has views about what they should be like, and most of them tend to be polarised. The 'book-keepers' think libraries should continue to be very largely about books – preferably selected, read and borrowed in near-silence – regardless of what is happening in the outside world. 'Diversifiers' think they should be about books, but should also serve – as best they can and depending on local demand – as free online workstations, DVD rental stores, careers and resource centres, university extra-mural departments, cultural hubs, meeting places, even, as in Tower Hamlets, 'Idea Stores'.

As a public service, libraries have to try to do the impossible and please everyone, which is why the Department for Culture, Media and Sport in its 2003 *Framework for the Future*, presented an extremely catholic vision of what public library services should offer in 2013 (p. 51). Too long to reproduce in full, the list included:

- access for any public library member to materials held in higher and further education libraries;
- the chance for all school-age children to join a homework club or reading group;
- personalised intensive help for any adult struggling with adult basic skills;
- help in creating and managing community content online for community groups; and
- an invitation to all babies and new parents to become library members within the first year of the baby's life.

As 2013 approaches, it might be tempting to suggest testing your own local library against the DCMS 2003 checklist – except that this would defeat the main point of the exercise. In our increasingly large council areas, libraries are among our few genuinely local institutions, with, as Holden and Ezra (2007) put it, 'a real bond between the staff, regular customers and the community at large'. 'Adopting a "one size fits all" approach would be wrong and patronising – it wouldn't give local communities the chance to voice how their local services should be constructed. Put simply, in some places more books will indeed be what people want; in other places, they may prefer to invest in more computer access.'

Leisure, arts and recreation

These last services are the most discretionary of those we have addressed. All the others have discretionary aspects to them – different councils according them differing priorities, providing services in differing ways, with differing standards of efficiency. But most of the legislation concerning leisure and recreation is *empowering* rather than mandatory. Councils *may* provide museums and art galleries; they *may* contribute to provision by other authorities; they *may* establish orchestras, concert halls, promote tourism, and provide all manner of sports and leisure facilities (see Gray, 2002).

Almost all sizeable projects nowadays in culture, recreation and the arts are carried out in partnerships with other agencies – for example, the Regional Development Agency, Arts Council England or Sport England. Your council may have been one of the 300 offering free swimming to over-60s and under-16s as part of the nationwide 'Free Swimming Programme' aimed at securing a long-term legacy from the 2012 Olympics. Though several councils had been running free swimming schemes for some years, this national programme was promoted by the Department for Culture, Media and Sport (DCMS) and was a partnership with the participating councils, Sport England and British Swimming. Those councils that did not bid for their allotted pot of funding may have appeared mean-spirited, but the likelihood is that they calculated that, for them, the scheme was not fully funded and the loss of fee income from existing swimmers would leave their tax-payers out of pocket. As a citizen, this discretionary dimension of recreational services can prove frustrating if you happen to live in an authority with relatively modest standards of provision, or one that imposes high charges for its facilities. As a student of local government, however, you can learn much about a council's political, social and cultural values from the scale and patterns of its leisure expenditure.

Conclusion – more sharing of the local turf

This overview of local authority services rounds off a chapter that began with our emphasising councils' continuing role as large-scale service providers, despite severe economic pressures and increasing collaboration with partners. Almost all the services mentioned have undergone a significant transformation during recent years and, in an increasing number of cases, the council's former, largely exclusive, role is being shared with a range of other providers. But while the balance and much of the detail have changed and will certainly change further, the 'traditional' picture is still recognisable:

> it has never been the case that local authorities have exercised all governmental powers in any particular locality. Others have always been involved but, in the past, local authorities confidently saw themselves as the rightful and undisputed leaders of their communities. Now their position is under challenge as they find themselves sharing the local 'turf' with a whole range of bodies also exercising governmental powers at the local level. (Davis, 1996, p. 1)

Chapter 9

Governance and Partnership

Introduction – a crowded pitch, but it's not all over

Chapter 8 focused specifically on elected local authorities as direct service providers. Yet, even with that focus, numerous other organisations crept in: trust and foundation schools, police and health authorities, primary care trusts, registered social landlords, regional development agencies – plus, almost everywhere it seems, partnerships. It was a telling illustration of how the 'established ways of doing local government are giving way to new ... governance alternatives' (Stoker, 2004a, p. 9). Local government today is just one part of the complex organisational mosaic now widely termed 'local governance' – though unique in being directly elected and thereby electorally accountable. Davis (1996 – quoted on p. 150) used the metaphor of elected local authorities getting used to 'sharing the turf'. Tony Blair's image was more aggressive (Blair, 1998, p. 10): 'There are all sorts of players on the local pitch jostling for position where previously the local council was the main game in town.' Unlike the conclusion of Kenneth Wolstenholme's immortal 1966 World Cup Final commentary, however, this pitch invasion does not signal that 'it's all over' for elected local government – simply that there have been some extensive changes in the rules of engagement. This chapter will map and evaluate these changed rules, the world of partnerships and the ubiquitous quango.

Local governance – less delivery, more steering

Until recently the term 'governance' carried no great theoretical meaning; if used at all, it was as a synonym for government. The 1990s, however, saw an explosion of interest in governance as a concept – initially in Britain (see, for example, Rhodes, 1997, 1999; Stoker, 1999, 2000; Goss, 2001; Leach and Percy-Smith, 2001, Perri 6 *et al.*, 2002), and subsequently across Europe (see, for example, John, 2001; Denters and Rose, 2005). It is particularly valuable as an organising framework that enables us to understand better the processes of governing. Local governance brings together governmental and non-governmental agencies in flexible partnerships to deal with different problems by using different strategies. It is not based on a single authority, the provision of a specialised service, or a new set of structures,

151

Exhibit 9.1 'Government' and 'Governance' – differing emphases

Government	Governance
Concerned primarily with the **institutions** of the **state**	Concerned more with the **processes** of **governing** and with the many **non-state actors** and **agencies** involved
Primarily about what happens in the **public sector**	Much more **inclusive**, recognising that policy-making, service provision and problem-solving nowadays involve **all sectors** of society – private, voluntary, community, as well as public
Focuses mainly on **structures**	Concerned more with **policies**, **outputs** and **outcomes**
Organisations are characterised by **bureaucratic hierarchies, authority relations** and **clear lines of accountability**	About **networks** and **partnerships**, **bargaining** and **exchange relations** between individuals and organisations, and **blurred accountability**
About **providing, directing** and 'rowing' (Osborne and Gaebler, 1992)	About broader, but less involved, roles of government – **enabling, facilitating** and 'steering'

Source: Information from Leach and Percy-Smith (2001, pp. 2–5).

but on a fusion of different styles and different working relationships. Flexibility of approach is central; given that the boundaries between public and private sectors have become increasingly blurred, the traditional hierarchical and bureaucratic styles of governing are no longer appropriate. The key features and emphases that an appreciation of governance brings to the study of government are summarised in Exhibit 9.1.

Those hoping that the New Labour Government, critical in opposition of the 'quango state' being created by the Conservatives, would swiftly restore to councils some of their lost responsibilities, soon realised it was not about to materialise. There would be no return to local authorities being near-monopolistic service providers; provision would continue to be shared with a range of partners. An early indication were the US-style zones – Employment Zones, Health Action Zones, Education Action Zones – all demonstrating the new government's commitment to working through the same mixed economy of local provision that had characterised the previous decade. Similarly, the New Deal for Communities (NDC) programme for the regeneration of the country's poorest housing estates, and Sure Start, designed to support pre-school children and their families. Such initiatives were early evidence of the Labour Government's intention to embrace collaboration between agencies as a way of joining up hitherto fragmented services to meet community needs more effectively. Indeed, the development of 'joined up', more integrated government was a central theme of the 1999 White Paper, *Modernising Government* (Cabinet Office, 1999).

For those of us seeking to make sense of it, the world of local governance is a complicated one. No longer, even in a city such as Birmingham with a so-called unitary council, is the organisation of government straightforward. In addition to the city council, there were in 2010, among numerous others, the separate police authority, several joint boards, eight NHS hospital and health care trusts, four primary care trusts, a Learning and Skills Council, regeneration partnerships and task forces, boards of further education colleges and foundation schools, housing associations, the Housing Corporation, Jobcentre Plus, Connexions, Sure Start, the Regional Development Agency, and a regional Government Office. The city council was involved in or with all these bodies, but it no longer has direct control over, or direct responsibility for, the service delivery it once had. As Leach (2009, p. 5) has observed:

> At one time we elected local councils to provide a wide range of services and functions, and had the opportunity to hold them to account if they performed unsatisfactorily. We now elect them to network and negotiate with 'partners' to do things for which they would previously have had exclusive responsibility.

Robert Hill, an early local government adviser to Prime Minister Blair, is a 'cup half-full', rather than half-empty, man, and emphasises the positive side of these changes. Councils themselves deliver fewer services than previously, but their sphere of influence has increased. They have acquired duties and powers that enable them to steer events and developments in their area – to 'place-shape', in local government's vogue jargon (Hill, 2008, p. 15). They are the democratic leaders of partnership working.

The local quango state – mapping the five thousand

The Conservative years saw not only a reduction in the number of elected local authorities, but also the rapid growth of non-elected or indirectly elected bodies at the expense of directly elected councils. Weir and Beetham (1999), in their *Democratic Audit of Great Britain* outlined the nature of Labour's inheritance in 1997 (pp. 251–2):

The local quango state is now extensive and has taken over or usurped the role of local authorities in providing many services. In social housing, the Housing Corporation has taken control of most new housing investment from local authorities. It also oversees the local housing associations which have become the main channel for investment in new social housing programmes locally ... A handful of housing action trusts have replaced local housing department management on some public housing estates. In education, grant-maintained schools have been removed from local authority control ... all further education colleges, formerly run by local authorities, have been merged and transformed into quangos; polytechnics have moved from local authority control to become universities within the province of the Higher Education Funding Council; the school careers service has been taken out of local government and passed on to private companies. In planning, 12 urban development corporations were created in England to take over planning in inner-city areas ... Local authorities lost their representatives on health authority boards; and their role on the new police authorities was further diminished.

These new associations, councils, companies, corporations, boards and trusts are all structured differently, but they are all appointed directly or indirectly by central government, performing functions and providing services that had previously been provided mainly or exclusively by local authorities. They bypass local authorities and may well come into conflict with them. They add greatly to the complexity of sub-central government, and add to the influence of their respective 'sponsoring' departments at the local level – especially useful if local political control happens to differ from that at the centre. They are agents for the centre, or, as Weir and Beetham (1999) describe them, 'government's flexible friends' (p.196). Collectively, they came to be known as 'the local quango state'.

'Quango' is the acronym for quasi-non-governmental organisation, or quasi-autonomous non-governmental organisation, as it is conventionally known. As even that last sentence suggests, it is a slippery term, definable in a multitude of ways, depending on whether the political objective is to minimise or to maximise the count. Governments are minimisers, especially if they came into power as did New Labour, vacuously promising 'to sweep away the quango state' (Skelcher *et al.*, 2000, p. 13). Auditors of democracy tend to be maximisers. Oddly, the government, having for years run a 'quango website' and offered a definition – a body with a role in the processes of government that operates at arm's length from ministers – suddenly declared pompously that it 'does not use the term'. The Cabinet Office now refers exclusively to non-departmental public bodies (NDPBs), of which in 2007/08 there were 790; a quarter of these were executive NDPBs, which spent £43 billion (Cabinet Office, 2009, pp. 3–5).

Some of these big-spending executive NDPBs relevant to the local government world were investigated by the Local Government Association (LGA), to see whether they delivered value for money, and worked 'with the kind of openness and transparency that taxpayers get from democratically accountable organisations like – for example – local councils?' (LGA, 2009a, p. 4). Obviously, the LGA had its own agenda, but the research was methodologically sound using mainly objective measures – at least six for each of three criteria: value for money; accountability; and openness. Most of the 11 quangos scored 'satisfactory' for openness – meaning that they publish their budget, annual report, board meeting minutes and agendas, and some accountability details on their websites. For accountability itself, however, all were either a 'cause for concern' or a 'serious problem' – with narrowly recruited board members, whose interests are not published and whose meetings are closed to the public. Three were judged to give satisfactory value for money – the Arts Council, the Homes and Communities Agency, and the Museums, Libraries and Archives Council – with the poorest overall performers being the Equalities and Human Rights Commission and the transport watchdog, Passenger Focus (Golding, 2009; LGA, 2009a).

To get an idea of the scale of the *local* 'quango state', no more elaborate a definition is needed than Charter 88's simple 'unelected bodies spending public money'. When counted by the House of Commons Public Administration Select Committee in 2000, the number of such bodies in the UK came close to 5,000 (see Wilson and Game, 2006, Exhibit 8.2 – also on the linked website), and it seems unlikely to have fallen dramatically since then. The largest category, then and now, would be the roughly 2,000 Registered Social Landlords, followed by foundation schools, further education institutions, and over 200 primary care trusts. They are run by more than 60,000 mainly ministerially appointed or self-appointed 'quangocrats', totalling almost three quangocrats for every councillor.

Earlier Democratic Audit reports had expressed concern at the scale of this new 'local quangocracy', at the arbitrary and partisan way in which quango board members were appointed, and at the serious deficiencies in the accountability and openness of many boards. New Labour, as noted above, promised to unleash a 'quango cull', but didn't. Instead, the goal was modified to one of 'keeping the number to the minimum necessary' (Cabinet Office, 1998), and by 2005, at least 111 completely new quangos had apparently proved to be necessary – not least the English Regional Development Agencies and new Welsh and Scottish bodies following devolution (Lewis, 2005). The Coalition Government adopted the reverse approach. In opposition, David Cameron had carefully refrained from talk of quango bonfires, but within six months the government had set light to a pyre of 192 of them – some to be completely cindered, others to have their functions taken over by government departments. A forensic, rather than ideological, approach to reform had been promised, with the object of increasing accountability, rather than saving money – which may explain why ministers were often unable to put a financial cost or saving on a quango's abolition, but raised the question of how groups of Whitehall civil servants suddenly acquired their new accountability.

The local government world produced some interesting examples. Regional Development Agencies (RDAs) were the early and unsurprising high-profile victims. Estimated savings of £1.85 billion were instantly announced – followed several weeks later by a grudging acknowledgement that the costs of abolition, the contractual obligations, redundancy payments and the like would amount to a very similar sum. Much less expected was the complete disbandment of the Audit Commission (AC). Ensconced in its offices in Millbank Tower in Victoria, London, the AC's critics had long seen it as an insatiable sponge: a creature of the Whitehall state, soaking up increasingly and unaccountably vast sums of public money. It had to go, decided Communities and Local Government Secretary Eric Pickles, but, while planning its demise, a coded project name was required within the DCLG – hence the 'Baking of the Victoria Sponge'. There were genuine concerns within local government about the abolition – about the propriety of local authorities appointing their own auditors and the loss of the AC's value-for-money studies and research – and, like the RDAs, its abolition costs, with its hefty pension liabilities, seemed likely to exceed initial forecasts. Finally, no longer will there be any Standards for England, which sounds alarming, were it other than the former Standards Board for England, whose responsibility for promoting ethical standards in local government could, ministers felt, be exercised more effectively in other ways.

There is no question that, both locally and nationally, quangos can perform important functions, and can do so effectively. They can bring valuable experience and expertise into government, including sections of society under-represented through the local electoral system. They may be able to bring objectivity and a nonpartisan perspective to the discussion of sensitive issues. Democrats would argue, however, that taking over whole areas of policy-making and service delivery from elected and accountable local authorities runs the risk of opening up a serious democratic deficit.

In addition to their members being elected, and thereby being knowable by name and readily accessible to their constituents, local authorities conduct their business openly and transparently. They produce annual reports, have their accounts audited annually, advertise their meetings, publish agendas, minutes and background papers, meet in public, report their major decisions, invite complaints, and keep registers of members' interests. They are also subject to extensive central direction, inspection and regulation. Many quangos, as the Commons Public Administration Select Committee found, are required and choose to do none of these things (House of Commons, 2001, table 11).

Partnerships – the new paradigm

Local authorities almost inevitably resent their loss of power and the fragmentation of their previously direct service provision. Even so, many of them – well before the government increasingly required it – were working closely and productively in partnership with some of the new quangos, and with local private sector and voluntary organisations. 'Community leadership' as a key future role for local authorities made its first major appearance in 1998 in the title of the Labour Government's first local government consultation paper (DETR, 1998a). Yet, by that time, many were already assuming, much more proactively than in the past, a broader leadership role in their communities. Economic development, urban regeneration, environmental protection, community safety and anti-crime measures, anti-poverty initiatives, preventative health schemes and anti-domestic violence projects were all areas where local authorities had embraced the vision of community governance. The government's particular contribution was to introduce a series of funding schemes that variously encouraged and required such programmes to be undertaken through formal partnerships – indeed, to promote partnerships as the new 'paradigm' for policy-making and service delivery (Lowndes and Sullivan, 2004, p. 52).

The paradigm was outlined by the prime minister personally in the early days of the new government (Blair, 1998, p. 13):

> The days of the all-purpose [local] authority that planned and delivered everything are gone. They are finished. It is in partnership with others ... that local government's future lies. Local authorities will deliver some services but their distinctive leadership role will be to weave and knit together the contribution of the various local stakeholders.

Partnerships were seen by central government as the most promising vehicle for 'addressing successfully those endemic social ills of society: low educational standards, social exclusion, poor health and poverty. No one agency could tackle such obdurate problems; these "wicked issues" cross organisational boundaries and require collaborative solutions' (Snape and Taylor, 2003, p. 1). For local authorities too, partnership working had obvious attractions. Partnerships can overcome the limitations of separately run services in meeting the needs of some of society's most vulnerable groups – disadvantaged children, older people, the disabled. They could increase citizen participation and community engagement more effectively than democratic local government seemed able to do. The outcome was a sizeable local eruption of partnerships that brought together public bodies, private firms, and community and voluntary groups, with central government funding becoming increasingly contingent on the formation of such multi-agency partnerships.

Exhibit 9:2 One council's partnership working

A selection of the 30+ partnerships in which Hull City Council, its officers and members are involved. For a complete list, see Hull City Council (2009).

	Type of partnership	Description
ONE HULL	City's Local Strategic Partnership (LSP)	Partnership of public, private and voluntary sectors to develop city's Sustainable Community Strategy and delivery plan, the Local Area Agreement
Hull Forward (City Development)	Council-owned limited co. – with RDA, Homes and Communities Agency	Successor to Hull Citibuild, an Urban Regeneration Co. (UDC) formed to lead city's economic and physical regeneration. Built Hull World Trade Centre
Gateway Pathfinder	Regional partnership: councils, LSPs, RDA, Housing Corporation	Regeneration agency to attract public and private funding to revitalise Hull's housing market
City Care (LIFT)	Public–private partnership: NHS Hull, Community Health Partnerships, private firms	NHS Local Improvement Financial Partnership, enabling PCTs to invest in new premises, to improve frontline primary and community care facilities
Hull Valuing People Partnership Board	Learning disability partnership: public and voluntary services, service users, MENCAP, etc.	Government-promoted partnership to implement its *Valuing People Now* programme for people with learning disabilities
Hull Children's Trust	Partnership of all children-related organisations on LSP	Custodian of 'Learning' block of ONE HULL – produces annual Children's and Young People's Plan
Sure Start Children's Centres Partnership	Multi-sector partnership: incl. schools, Jobcentre Plus, NHS, plus private and voluntary sectors	Based on 2006 Childcare Act requirement that local agencies work together to improve health and well-being of especially the most disadvantaged children
Local Safeguarding Children's Board (LCSB)	Statutory partnership: councils, NHS bodies, police, probation, Connexions, and many others	Partnership of representatives from all relevant agencies working together to keep children safe from harm and neglect
Building Schools for the Future	Investment partnership: schools, colleges, churches, trade unions, LSC, local businesses, etc.	Partnership with capacity to use capital investment to transform city's education, through design of quality new buildings, development of e-learning, etc.
Hull Citysafe Crime and Disorder Partnership	Multi-agency partnership: incl. police, fire and rescue, PCTs, probation, community groups	Required partnership to co-ordinate action to tackle crime, disorder and drugs misuse

The phenomenon was documented by Sullivan and Skelcher (2002, p. 26). They identified across the UK some 5,500 partnership bodies at local or regional level *stimulated or created directly by government*, spending £4.3 billion a year (our emphasis). But even then, as the authors speculated to the Commons Public Administration Committee, the total number, including all the partnerships formed without stimulus from government, was probably double, or nearer to 11,000 (House of Commons, 2003; see also Game, 2007a). Actual total expenditure could well have been four times their calculation, and the number of partnership board places around 75,000 – significantly more, that is, than local executive quango members.

These local partnerships vary in every conceivable way – by size, function and service area. They include the statutory and voluntary, executive and non-executive, strategic and operational, limited companies and charitable trusts. This book's previous edition contained a classification of almost 3,000, including most of the more significant ones (Wilson and Game, 2006, Exhibit 8.3 – also on linked website). In contrast, Exhibit 9.2 takes a micro, rather than a macro, approach and focuses on a single unitary authority – Hull City Council, which monitors its partnership working more systematically than most, in dedicated annual reports. Technically, one or two of the bodies listed are not partnerships, but rather, as we shall see later with the Private Finance Initiative, forms of contractual arrangement. Almost all, however, fit comfortably the definition of unelected bodies spending public money, and their hundreds of board members outnumber the 59-member City Council several times over.

Partnership works? Not always

At Grateley railway station near Andover there is, or was, a large sign: 'Welcome to Hampshire, where partnership works' – the apparent implication being that, just across the county border, Wiltshire citizens prefer insularity and apartheid. That is the problem with partnerships: their goodness is taken for granted. They are only occasionally rigorously defined, and very rarely critically questioned. But there are exceptions. Skelcher questioned the local partnership eruption that he had helped to quantify, seeing it as a potential challenge to the 'functional sovereignty' of local authorities, undermining their political authority 'as the democratic voice of the community' (2004, p. 35). The Local Strategic Partnership (LSP), for example, can become a forum for bargaining among the leaderships of the constituent bodies, with the public interest becoming marginalised.

Then there are the costs, as emphasised by the Audit Commission (2005a, p. 25): 'Partnership working incurs costs. If partnerships spend too much time in meetings discussing process issues instead of focusing on achieving their objectives, the costs can outweigh the benefits.' The

Commission felt the government's uncritical enthusiasm for partnerships might have gone too far, too fast: 'Is it possible to manage all these collaborations successfully to produce benefits that public bodies could not achieve by other means?' it asked rhetorically (p. 5), and then made clear its doubts. Few of the organisations in the Commission's study even knew the number of partnerships in which they were involved, and 'almost none ... had tried to calculate the total cost involved in working in partnership'. As one confessed: 'We've never looked in detail at inputs, outputs and outcomes, and would find this damned scary, since it would clock up big numbers' (2005a, p. 25).

If these accounting issues in multi-agency partnerships are difficult and consequently evaded, accountability is necessarily weakened. It is impossible to claim effective management of resources, or to demonstrate quantitatively either benefits achieved or value for money. The Commission's main conclusion was that nothing like the same standards of scrutiny and performance measurement were brought to bear on partnerships as on the non-partnership work of the bodies involved, with the result that partnerships regularly broke down, many others experienced significant problems – sometimes acknowledged, sometimes not – while the effectiveness of the remainder was unassessable. 'Local public bodies,' the Commission advised, 'should be much more constructively critical about this form of working: it may not be the best solution in every case' (2005a, p. 2). Five years on, it must be hoped that this state of affairs has improved somewhat. At least it has in Hull, which is one reason for our focusing on it. Hull City Council has developed a Partnership Toolkit with which it assesses all its partnerships in terms of their cost, staffing, investment delivered, value for money, priority to the Council, and any development needs.

Returning to Exhibit 9.2, heading the partnership list is ONE HULL (their capitals, not ours) – the city's LSP. Despite a possibly odd choice of name – Be Birmingham (Jeremy Clarkson's opinion?), Calderdale Forward (a local footballer?), One Epping Forest (a posh address?) – an area's LSP constitutes the hub and driving force of local partnership working, as outlined in Exhibit 9.3. Equivalent bodies in Scotland and Wales are known respectively as Community Planning Partnerships and Local Service Boards. The importance of the whole LSP/SCS/LAA operation was strengthened in the 2007 Local Government and Public Involvement in Health Act. Breaking with previous practice, the preparation of a Local Area Agreement (LAA) became a duty, and a lengthy list of named partners – police, fire and transport authorities, health service trusts, probation boards, the Highways and Environment Agencies – was required to co-operate in agreeing and implementing LAA targets.

Local government's leadership role was also emphasised, although there is still the resemblance to Kipling's famous description of the harlot's prerogative in reverse: not power without responsibility, but potential

Exhibit 9.3 LSPs, LAAs, SCSs, MAAs

Local Strategic Partnerships (LSPs)

The Big Tent – the partnership of partnerships. They started in 2000 in the 88 most deprived local authority areas, part-financed by the government's Neighbourhood Renewal Fund, to tackle those areas' intractable problems – industrial decline, entrenched poverty, unemployment. Then spread to remaining 280+ areas, without government funding, to increase co-ordination of service provision and generally improve the quality of life. They match council boundaries – so usually two in two-tier areas.

Partners are supposedly senior representatives of bodies working in employment, education, crime reduction, health, housing, the arts – from all sectors, including the main service providers and, where possible, hard-to-reach groups. Chief responsibilities are to produce a **Sustainable Community Strategy (SCS)** and a delivery framework, a **Local Area Agreement (LAA)**.

Sustainable Community Strategies (SCSs)

The visionary plan. The SCS sets the long-term vision and strategic direction for the area's economic, social and environmental well-being over 10–20 years. It tells the story of the place, identifying community needs and aspirations, backed by evidence and analysis, and is thus the obvious platform for the expression of councils' place-shaping role.

Titles can be cringe-worthy – 'Birmingham: global city with a local heart'; 'Proud to be Slough' – but the documents are serious enough. They should fit in with existing regional and local strategies and also demonstrate the SCS's sustainability credentials – enabling today's residents to enjoy a better quality of life without compromising that of future generations.

Local Area Agreements (LAAs)

The central–local deal. LAAs are 3-year targeted action plans to deliver the policies and eventually the vision of the SCS. Since 2007, however, they are statutory documents that must be agreed by central government – through the regional Government Office. They must also incorporate 35 negotiated policy priorities chosen from a set of 188 *national* indicators, covering issues such as health, education, employment and crime.

The 2008–11 LAAs agreed for all 150 upper-tier authorities in England are the most tangible outcome of the working relationship between central and local government. Only upper-tier authorities are required to have them, but district councils are 'statutory consultees' for their county's SCS and, like all LSP partners, should be actively involved in delivery.

Multi-Area Agreements (MAAs)

The Really Big Tent. We encountered these at the end of Chapter 6 (pp. 98–9). Intended to complement LAAs where necessary, they bring together local authorities to tackle issues that are best addressed in partnership at regional or sub-regional level: economic development, transport and infrastructure projects, skills deficits. As with LAAs, targets and also the pooling of funding arrangements are agreed with central government through their regional Government Office.

Exhibit 9.4 Total Place – mapping and diving

What is 'Total Place'? Who started it?

It was a 2009 DCLG initiative to stimulate efficiency savings and partnership working, but significantly as part of the Treasury's wider Operational Efficiency Programme. It first 'maps' how all public money is spent in a local area – the 'total place'. By which bodies, on which services, with what outcomes? Then public, business and voluntary sector organisations work together, as they already do in LSPs, to identify how that spending might be used more efficiently by avoiding overlap and duplication. It started with 13 pilot studies across all English regions, following earlier trials in Cumbria and Birmingham (see Be Birmingham/Ekosgen, 2009).

How does it actually work?

There are two complementary strands to the initial investigative work: (i) the 'counting' process that maps the money spent in the area by all public bodies; and (ii) the thematic/service focus that, through so-called 'deep dives', explores the spending on specific services. The deep dives enable a service to be approached holistically to see how desired outcomes might be achieved more efficiently and perhaps more imaginatively. Topics chosen in the pilots included children's services, aged care, drugs and alcohol, housing, crime and mental health services.

An early taster

The representative body, London Councils, commissioned Pricewaterhouse-Coopers (PWC, 2010) to undertake a Total Place-style study covering all Greater London. The study found London's total public expenditure to be £73.4 billion – 58% by local bodies, including PCTs and NHS trusts; 34% by national government; and 8% by more than 150 NDPBs or quangos. Three key policy themes were selected: chronic medical care, anti-social behaviour and unemployment. PWC estimated that, with more effective cross-agency working, £1.5 billion could be saved annually on these services alone, and £11 billion or 15% on London's total public spending.

Has it got legs?

Sceptics recalled similar exercises in the 1970s and 1980s being thwarted chiefly by central government's reluctance to let go of either programmes or finance. But in the 2010s several things are different: the recession-driven urgency to find public spending cuts, Treasury backing, the commitment to and experience of multi-agency partnership working, and, perhaps above all, its apparent acceptability to the Conservatives. Early Coalition indications were that Local Area Agreements (LAAs) would be abolished and replaced with some form of council-coordinated place-based or community budgeting. Keep up to date through the dedicated Total Place website – available at: www.localleadership.gov.uk/totalplace/about/faqs/.

responsibility without effective power. Councils' democratic legitimacy gives them a natural leadership role in partnership working, which the government expects them to exercise. But it doesn't give them 'a monopoly on leadership' (DCLG, 2006b, p. 98), or the right to chair the LSP, or, for example, to override the local police commander's prime accountability to the Chief Constable and Police Authority, rather than to the LSP. As Leach sees it (2008, p. 187):

> How can such an amorphous collectivity be held accountable, and who will be required to deliver improvements if poor performance is identified? The fact that the principal local authority involved has been designated the 'lead authority' in partnership working, and its capacity to scrutinise the performance of partner agencies has been enhanced, gives the government a convenient reference point (scapegoat?) if poor performance is identified. ('You're the lead authority, you sort it!')

As the 2010 General Election approached, however, it began to seem possible that all LAAs could be not so much sorted as superceded – by yet another partnership initiative: Total Place (see Exhibit 9.4). Though none of the 13 official pilot studies were due to report back until the 2010 Budget, the positive early reception accorded to Total Place suggested that the broad concept might have a future (even if the name changed) – for some of the reasons indicated in the Exhibit.

The Private Finance Initiative (PFI)

Many of the cross-sectoral bodies referred to in this chapter could be described as public–private partnerships (PPPs). The PFI, however, is a particularly important, and controversial, form of partnership in which local authorities can gain access to new or improved capital assets. It originated in the early 1990s, when the Conservative Government was continuing its long-term policy of reducing public spending, but also facing the political consequences of years of under-investment in schools, hospitals, transportation and other parts of the nation's economic and social infrastructure. It was a new way of enabling the public sector to afford capital-intensive projects (such as buildings, roads, plant, apparatus and vehicles) without inflating the government's public expenditure figures, while at the same time extending the 'privatisation' of public services.

Instead of the government borrowing from the private sector to finance these capital projects and then owning and operating them itself, the private sector would be invited not only to finance the construction, but also to provide some or all of the *services* associated with the project. In return, the government would pay for the *use* of the asset and its associated services over a long period of time – often 25 years or more – with these fees to include the costs and compensation of risk associated with the capital investment. There are several varieties of PFI schemes, some in which the entire asset and service provision is undertaken by the private sector, others involving a mix of public and private funding, and still others involving leasing arrangements.

Though slow to take off, PFI gradually spread from large-scale transport projects – such as the Channel Tunnel Rail Link and the Jubilee Line extension – to hospitals, prisons, roads, and new teaching and residential accommodation in further and higher educational institutions. For local government, though, the first PFI projects did not even start until 1996/7 – largely because of the tight legal and financial constraints under which British local government finance has to operate. It was New Labour, therefore, that was responsible for local authorities' extensive use of PFI.

Many PFI projects are 'financially free-standing' in the sense of their not needing central government revenue support – in which case they do not require endorsement by the relevant government department. For most major local authority projects, however, government backing is essential, and between 1997 and 2009 some 370 PFI projects and £21 billion of funding were endorsed by different central government departments (DCLG, 2010a). Schemes have included a wide range of services, as illustrated in Exhibit 9.5, but PFI's biggest impact has been on the school rebuilding programme and housing refurbishment.

PFI has obvious attractions for central government. It shifts the immediate burden of government expenditure from capital spending today to current spending in the future. Proponents would also point out the advantages of transferring the risks involved in the design, building, financing and operation of the asset to the private sector, and of having private sector management skills contributing towards the enhancement of service quality and efficiency. Critics, on the other hand, would argue that these risks are concentrated largely in a project's construction phase, yet are treated as if they were spread evenly over the length of the contract, thereby giving the contractor a greatly exaggerated rate of return.

There are other reasons why PFI projects cost more than if they were built by the public sector. The private sector has to pay higher interest rates to borrow money, and has to make a rate of return for shareholders. Moreover, when things go wrong, it is still the tax-payer who is likely to have to foot the bill: the council tax-payer in the event of a project failure or default, or the national tax-payer if, as in 2009, the government had to come to the rescue because the banks would not lend. A common view in local government, therefore, especially among Labour councillors, has been that, while PFI has enabled projects to go ahead that a resource-strapped public sector could not afford, in practice what is being achieved is an

Exhibit 9.5   A selection of local government PFI projects (with sponsoring department and value of central government support)

Schools in Rochdale – rebuilding, remodelling or refurbishing 11 mainstream secondary schools and two Pupil Referral Units. DCSF; £132 million.

Sheltered housing in North Tyneside – refurbishment and redevelopment of 25 of the borough's sheltered housing schemes. DCLG; £112 million.

Waste facility in Leicestershire – Energy from Waste (EfW) plant with potential to generate Combined Heat and Power (CHP). DEFRA; £87 million.

Gloucestershire fire stations – four new community fire stations plus a new-build community life skills centre. DCLG; £40 million.

Bristol Leisure Centre – multi-sport centre with swimming pool, health and fitness facilities. DCMS; £35 million.

Disabled support centres in Wolverhampton – Hub and Spoke support centres for disabled adults. Department of Health (DH); £29 million.

Source: Data from DCLG Endorsed Project List: January 2010 – www.local. communities.gov.uk/pfi/index.htm.

expensive accountancy trick: simply a delay in the cost to the public purse. Far from being a saving, it is in fact the reverse.

That injection of government cash was both substantively and symbolically significant. It seems likely that PFI has passed its peak, and not only for the obvious reason that there will be less infrastructure investment in the future than previously. Many projects – such as those featured in Exhibit 9.5, are already under way, so PFI will not disappear, but it will probably not be utilised so extensively. Other options will be developed, relying more perhaps on the local authorities themselves to raise funds or underwrite debt – which financially they may not necessarily welcome, but that, as we shall see in Chapter 12, really would represent a break with the past in terms of responsibility.

Chapter 10

Central–Local Government Relations: The Formal Framework

Introduction – ten years on and still hypercentralised?

A good part of this book has already been about aspects of central–local government relations. Chapter 2 noted the statutory and financial constraints that limit local government's operational discretion. Chapter 4 outlined the successive 'top-down' restructurings that have produced its present-day shape and scale. Chapters 8 and 9 described local government's loss of power to quangos and central government's insistence on partnership working, and several of the remaining chapters will also refer to the topic. The fact is that an account of local government in a unitary state such as the UK must necessarily also be an account of its central–local relations. The latter provide the backdrop, the stage, the direction and much of the script for the former, and it is appropriate that, in these pivotal central chapters of the book, we bring the various strands of the subject together.

This section's heading conveys an idea of the direction that Chapters 10 to 12 will take. They will explain, for example, why – ten years after our sub-national government was described as 'hypercentralised' by European standards (Loughlin, 2001, ch. 2) – the House of Commons Communities and Local Government Select Committee still saw England as 'one of the developed world's most centralised democracies' (House of Commons, 2009a, para. 9).

The Select Committee concluded that the central–local government relationship in England deviated from the European norm in three major ways: constitutional protection; central government intervention; and financial autonomy. All three deviations served 'to tilt the balance of power towards the centre' (ibid., para. 38), and they provide the foci of the next three chapters. Chapter 10 outlines the formal framework or architecture of the central–local relationship: local government's constitutional weakness and consequential subordination to, or dependence on, ministers, their legislation and directives. Chapter 11 compares actual practice, first to that formal constitutional position and second to some of the academic literature on the topic. Chapter 12 describes the local government financial system, serving as a special case study of the relationship.

No constitutional protection – we keep the sweetshop

The UK is not unique in not having a codified constitution – New Zealand and Israel don't either – but it is unique in Europe. For local government this means there is no document defining its status, rights, responsibilities and relationship with central government. Ultimately, it has no guaranteed existence and no protection in the way that other countries' local authorities have. Germany's Basic Law, for example, guarantees the right of elected councils not only to exist, but also 'to regulate all local affairs on their own responsibility'. In Sweden, central and local government have equal constitutional weight: public power stems from the people, and is realised 'through a representative and parliamentary polity and through local self-government'. Talk to other Europeans and they see this constitutionally guaranteed status as key to the relative strength and autonomy of their local governments.

Its importance is recognised here too, which is why the Local Government Association (LGA) and others have campaigned for either a full written constitution or at least something to give local government a statutory underpinning. One possibility would be to give the *European Charter of Local Self-Government* a statutory basis. The Charter is a document of the Congress of Local and Regional Authorities of the now 47-member Council of Europe and commits its ratifying members to guaranteeing the political, administrative and financial independence of local authorities. As its title suggests, it endeavours to define and enshrine the principles of local self-government and of subsidiarity – the idea that decisions should be taken by the level of government closest to the citizen. It was opened for signature in 1985, and most European countries signed at the first opportunity – but interestingly not the UK, whose Conservative Government felt unable to accede to some of its Articles. The 1997 Labour Government made a show of signing almost immediately on taking office – since when, as one witness put it to the Select Committee, 'it has hardly been in the thinking of Government since they ratified it. It was put on the shelf' (House of Commons, 2009a, para. 132). More seriously, it was suggested that the government was 'not compliant' with up to four Articles dealing with the statutory recognition of local self-government, administrative intervention and financial autonomy (para. 130). Ministers contested such charges (DCLG, 2009c), besides which the Charter has no significant enforcement mechanisms, so there will be no consequences of note – including any imminent incorporation of the Charter into UK law.

The other possible basis of some constitutional settlement might seem to be the *Central–Local Concordat* signed in 2007 by the then Communities Secretary, Hazel Blears, and the Chairman of the LGA (DCLG, 2007). The DCLG spun it as 'a powerful statement of principles for how central and local government should work together to serve the public' and the LGA seemed keen to agree. Unfortunately, the principles were expressed in terminology so imprecise that even at the time they seemed unlikely to produce any noticeable change even in ministerial behaviour, let alone our centralist culture. Councils, for example, have a right to shape their communities' future 'without unnecessary direction or control'. Central government will only intervene 'as a last resort, to avoid significant underperformance', and will 'progressively remove obstacles' preventing councils from pursuing their role. There was no mention of who would define 'unnecessary', 'last resort', 'significant', 'progressively' and all the other loose phraseology; none was needed. As one sceptical correspondent to *The MJ* magazine put it (10 January 2008, p. 10): 'A more honest Concordat would start with a preamble saying: "We think local government is very nice to work with, but we have no intention of handing over the sweetshop to the kids, thank you very much." '

The formal framework: controls and constraints

In the absence of any constitutional shield, there is a considerable range of instruments available, principally to ministers and their departments, to control and direct local authorities and generally keep local government in its subordinate place.

Legislation

Legislation is the most direct instrument of central control of local authorities, and one used in recent years with unprecedented frequency and impact. The Conservative Governments from 1979 to 1997 produced well over 200 Acts of Parliament affecting local government, and now the Conservatives themselves claim that 'since 1997 nearly 300 pieces of legislation have been enacted with the words "local government" in the title' (Conservative Party, 2009, p. 6). The Coalition Government's Queen's Speech in May 2010 maintained the legislative pace, with at least half of the 22 Bills having direct implications for local government – though ministers would claim that their flagship Localism Bill, with its general power of competence, abolition of Comprehensive Area Assessment (CAA) and RDAs, and greater financial discretion, was about loosening central control, rather than tightening it.

In Chapter 2 we used the term 'partial autonomy' to describe the constitutional status of British local government, and indicated the constraints imposed by the *ultra vires* doctrine. National governments can, through legislation, create, abolish and amend local authorities' powers as and when they determine. Local authorities, for their part, are authorised to provide or secure the provision of certain services, but only within a framework of national legislation. The so-called *'well-being power'*, introduced in the Local Government Act 2000 as an important element of New Labour's modernisation agenda, significantly qualified this traditional position, but did not overturn it. It enabled local authorities 'to promote the economic, social and environmental well-being of their area' in ways that could previously have been *ultra vires*, as was illustrated in this book's fourth edition (Exhibit 9.1, p. 159 – also on the linked website). It genuinely extended local authorities' powers and linked directly into the implementation of their Community Strategies and LAAs, but it was not unlimited and did not change their constitutional position as 'creatures of statute'.

The same applied to another Labour Government innovation, the *Sustainable Communities Act 2007* (SCA), important and interesting though it was. The Act began as a remarkable community campaign organised by the Local Works coalition, was introduced into Parliament as a Private Member's Bill, and was finally backed by the government. It provided a channel for people, through their local authorities, to ask central government to take action, or allow action to be taken, that they believed would improve the economic, social or environmental well-being of their area. This Act seized people's imaginations more quickly than the well-being power had done, and in 2009 over 300 proposals were received by the LGA, who short-listed 199 and passed them on to the government for consideration (see Exhibit 10.1).

The selection in Exhibit 10.1 is almost arbitrary. Yet it is likely to strike readers more familiar with other local governmental systems that several of these proposals appear to be seeking powers and discretions that one might have expected our large authorities to have already. They would probably also note how constrained councils' income sources are, when they cannot, for example, retain revenues they themselves collect in business rates, landfill taxes, and council house rents and sales. While generally welcoming the SCA, like the well-being power, larger local authorities in particular find them clumsy means of acquiring often quite minor powers. Ministers meanwhile claimed that councils now had something very close to a power of general competence, allowing them to do whatever their elected members judged to be in the interests of residents and the locality. In which case, it is difficult to see why, instead of doling out powers and concessions in this grudging, piecemeal fashion, the Labour Government did not simply legislate a power of general competence of the kind that most other European local governments have. It would hardly have amounted to handing over the whole sweetshop.

A similar sweetshop owner mentality can be seen in relation to local

Exhibit 10.1 A selection of Sustainable Communities Act proposals shortlisted for government consideration, 2009

Main theme	Lead Authority	Proposal
Supporting communities during recession	Lambeth LBC	New legal powers for councils to compel a freeholder to make a commercial property available for temporary use by social enterprise after being vacant for 6 months.
Supporting communities during recession	Islington LBC	Amend legislation restricting council's power to require its contractors to pay the London living wage.
Reforming local finance system	Chorley BC	Allow councils to retain a proportion of the revenue from business rates to be spent on local priorities.
Reforming local finance system	Lewes DC	Allow councils to set increased council tax rates for properties kept solely as second homes or holiday lets.
Tackling climate change locally	Brighton & Hove City C	Increase financial incentives to homeowners and landlords to install micro-renewable energy sources.
More effective transport systems	Wiltshire CC	All MOT tests to include statutory recording of mileage.
Waste disposal and minimisation	Warwick DC	Government to return 1% of the landfill tax paid by councils, to be used to increase recycling rates.
Delivering effective local services	Sheffield City C	Council to have responsibility for maintaining and sustaining the post office network in the local area.
Delivering effective local services	East Lindsay DC	Remove mandatory duty to maintain closed churchyards, which should be a matter of local democratic choice, supported if necessary by the council.
Delivering on housing	Cambridge City C	Government to allow Council to keep all revenue collected from council housing rents and all receipts from right-to-buy sales of council homes.

Source: LGA (2009b).

authorities' powers to initiate private legislation and make by-laws. Both powers are important and probably unwarrantedly neglected by commentators (Jones and Stewart, 2004, p. 24). *Private legislation* – giving the promoting body powers *over and above* the existing law – was used extensively during the nineteenth century, not least by local authorities, for the construction of railways and tramways, gas and water systems. Private bills, however, are both procedurally complex and readily blockable, either by government departments or by other interests affected, and have become rarities in modern times.

By-laws, in contrast, are to be seen everywhere – hanging from lamp-posts, displayed inside taxis, pinned on public notice boards. They are a form of delegated legislation, which permits local authorities and other bodies to make regulations *within* existing law that relate to a specified area – regarding, typically, the use of recreation grounds, swimming baths or libraries, control of dogs, public urination (by us, not them!), skateboarding, or ball games. You might suppose that here, surely, is something no minister or civil servant in their right mind would want to get involved in – but you would be wrong. There is a Byelaws Section in the DCLG, and, until the 2007 Local Government and Public Involvement in Health Act, all by-laws had to gain ministerial approval. (For the reasons for our preferred, and etymologically accurate, spelling, see Game, 2008 – also on the linked website.) What is more, this overdue change in practice then featured prominently in the Labour Government's listing of ways in which it had strengthened local democracy – giving up the exercise of powers that in most countries they would never have had in the first place.

Statutory instruments, circulars, advice and guidance

Acts of Parliament are 'primary legislation'. Many Acts, however, require detailed 'secondary legislation' or clarifying regulations before they can be implemented fully. This secondary legislation consists mainly of Statutory Instruments (SIs), which, even though they escape full parliamentary debate, are generally seen as a regrettable but relatively harmless inevitability of modern-day life. Some, though, take the form of so-called 'Henry VIII clauses', allowing ministers – following the Tudor monarch's practice of legislating by proclamation – effectively to amend or even repeal primary legislation.

In 2009, as in most years, there were around 2,000 SIs, a high proportion of which would have impinged on one or more services of one or more local authorities. All are available on the website of the official home of UK legislation (www.legislation.gov) for inspection by those directly affected or merely curious – in either sense of that word. Last listed, SI 3468, fell squarely into the 'harmless inevitability' category: The East Harling Internal Drainage District (Alteration of Boundaries) Order 2009. For the curious,

East Harling is a village in Norfolk. The first 2009 SI listed, though, was altogether more exciting: significantly affecting local government, and a minor embarrassment. For part of The Local Government (Structural Changes) (Further Financial Provisions *and Amendment*) Regulations 2009 (our emphasis) corrected a small but potentially costly mistake in earlier regulations concerning the transitional financial arrangements for the creation of the nine new unitary councils.

A number of these SIs implement regulations and directives from the European Union. Just how many is almost incalculable, and so is inevitably the subject of wild assertions – that 50%, even 75%, of British laws result from our EU membership. But even if, as the House of Commons Library suggests (2008), the true figure is around 10%, that would still amount to 350 SIs a year. As illustrated in Exhibit 10.2, the worthy intent of these directives is usually clear, but – like the Landfill Tax or the Drivers' Hours Directives – they can have extensive and expensive implications. One really big measure, with potentially positive implications for local government and the British economy generally is the EU Services Directive 2006/123/EC, adopted in 2006 but only transposed into UK law in 2009. It opens up the European internal market to cross-border trade in services by making it easier for service providers – such as local authorities – to offer their services or even set up businesses in other EU countries. The Department for Business, Innovation and Skills claims the national economy could benefit by up to £6 billion per annum, and in this case our local authorities' large size and economic weight, as well as the quality of their professional experience, could stand them in good stead.

In addition to SIs, government departments issue circulars to local authorities containing advice and guidance on how they should exercise their various responsibilities. Not all circulars are directive, and some are the product of genuine negotiation and contain useful practical advice. Others, though, openly spice up the advice with instruction – such as the DCLG's Planning Policy Statements. These circulars, the DCLG explains, '*provide guidance* ... on planning policy and the planning system'. However, 'local authorities *must* take their contents into account in preparing their development plan documents' (our emphases). But the DCLG are *laissez-faire-ists* compared with Education. Sir Simon Jenkins (2006b) reckons that, between 1997 and 2006, the Department for Education – by way of confirming the extent to which education had become a national function – issued: '500 regulations, 350 policy targets, 175 efficiency targets, 700 notes of guidance, 17 plans and 26 separate incentive grant schemes. In 2001 Hansard reported an annual average of 3,840 pages of instructions being sent to schools in England (which the government does not even run)'. Those 3,840 pages were two-and-a-half times the total number of regulations, directives and decisions made that year by the EU Commission and Council of Ministers between them – bodies that are reckoned to know

Exhibit 10.2 Examples of European legislation affecting local government

Local impact	EU directive
Delays in public service contracts	**Publication of contracts** – contracts above about £100,000 must be publicised in the EU's Official Journal
	Procurement remedies – period must be set aside before implementation of contract to allow losing bidders to appeal
Less discretion over noise abatement	**Strategic noise maps** – must be produced for major roads, airports, railways and industry, mapping noise levels defined by the EU
Higher waste and recycling costs	**Landfill waste** – councils must reduce landfill waste by half of 1995 levels by 2113, or face fines of up to £180 million p.a., prompting some councils to move to fortnightly bin collections
Higher staff costs	**Temporary staff** with 10 weeks' employment have same entitlement to holidays, pensions and sick pay as permanent staff
Compromised teaching standards	**Professional qualifications** of teachers qualified in other EU countries must be regarded as equal to UK qualifications, regardless of language competence and familiarity with the curriculum
Bus regulation	**Tachographs** must be fitted to buses on routes of 30+ miles.
	Disabled access – all buses must have disabled access. This contributed to the withdrawal of the London Routemaster fleet

Main source: Kamall (n.d.).

a thing or two about bureaucracy (House of Commons, 2008, p. 7). It is, of course, a silly comparison, but it does prompt mention of one further and important EU policy: its Eco-Management and Audit Scheme (EMAS). The environment is the policy area in which the EU has had perhaps its greatest impact on UK local government, and EMAS provides organisations with an independently verified management framework to audit the environmental impact of their activities and services, and continuously improve their performance. The EMAS regulation is voluntary, and it is one of the more demanding environmental management schemes available – requiring, for example, that the compliance of a council's suppliers and contractors is also audited. Even so, it was noticeable that in the 2009/10 EU total of 4,434

EMAS-registered organisations, the UK's 65 – including 15 local authorities – lagged more than a little behind Germany's 1,379, Spain's 1,159 and Italy's 1,037 (European Commission, 2010). Whether these figures reflected our limited interest in eco-management *per se* or simply in EU systems for doing it was unclear.

Judicial review

Ministers have some formidable levers of power at their disposal, but they are not unchallengeable. No major government authority is. Through the procedure of judicial review, any departmental policy or ministerial decision may be challenged and ultimately reviewed by a judge, with a view to having it quashed – on the grounds of it being unreasonable, beyond the powers (*ultra vires*) of the relevant body, or having been taken improperly (see Exhibit 2.1, item 6). The same is true of local authority decisions, which puts councils in a Janus-like position with respect to judicial review: potentially both challengers and challenged.

They have lost high profile cases in recent years – on, for example, school allocation decisions and the payment of full court costs in judicial child-care proceedings, and, as more services are cut and redundancies announced, there seem bound to be more such challenges. At the same time, if a local authority not only disagrees with a government decision, but feels it was unlawfully taken, it can similarly apply for judicial review – something that happens nowadays much more frequently than in the past. The big escalation came in the period of Conservative Government from 1979, when, as Loughlin put it, both Parliament and the courts were brought back into the central–local relationship (1996b, p. 61). We summarised in a previous edition several prominent cases from this period (Wilson and Game, 2002, p. 154, plus Exhibit on linked website). In two cases, the House of Lords, then the highest court in the land, ruled in favour of ministers against local authorities, but in the other cases ministers lost. In such situations they can, of course, try to persuade Parliament quickly to make legal what has just been pronounced illegal, but in the short term an adverse judgment can prove both embarrassing and a policy setback.

Governments, then, have never liked losing, but recently some ministers have questioned whether even challenging them is in the best public interest. Challenges over service inspection ratings and the nine judicial reviews of its 2007–9 unitary proposals seemed particularly to irk the DCLG, whose Minister wondered 'whether we can justify spending taxpayers' money on one part of government taking another part of government to court' for a case that may be, as he put it 'a legal try-on' (Conrad, 2009). Local authorities would see things differently. Judicial review is the last resort for them and those they represent – perhaps as their council teeters on the brink of being abolished – and courts themselves set a high threshold before allowing reviews. Norfolk and Devon County Councils would surely have been remiss *not* to have considered challenging the attempt by Communities Secretary John Denham in February 2010 to create new unitary authorities in Norwich and Exeter for what were interpretable as party political reasons. In rejecting the counties' own unitary claims, the Minister had departed from his department's assessment criteria and overruled his Permanent Secretary, plus the known views of the Treasury, the Boundary Committee for England, and the previous Minister. Similarly, those councils threatened with losing millions of pounds of investment they thought they had been promised for school building projects: should they and their tax-payers be expected to accept placidly Coalition Education Secretary Michael Gove's decision to withhold the funding, despite their reservations about both its substance and process? Other ways of saving tax-payers' money, therefore, might include central government imposing slightly fewer external inspections, drafting legislation that is more review-proof, and ministers following consistent criteria when taking decisions.

The local ombudsman

As noted above, individuals can challenge local authority decisions ultimately through judicial review, but such cases are exceptional – usually because the outcome might affect a whole class of cases beyond the immediate one, or because all other means of redress have been exhausted. Principal among these other means is their local government ombudsman – or, to give the office its official, and thankfully now largely abandoned, title: the Commission for Local Administration (CLA).

The CLA and the separate commissions in Wales and Scotland were established in 1974, following the creation of a national ombudsman, the Parliamentary Commissioner for Administration, in 1967 – just 158 years after Sweden created its first ombudsman or 'agent of the people'. The public sector appointments proved to be trendsetters, and in the following two decades there sprang up private sector 'ombudspersons' for everything from insurance, banks and estate agents to funeral services. It is true that neither parliamentary nor local commissioners have achieved the profile of several of their European, and especially Scandinavian, counterparts. But the three English local ombudsmen alone deal nowadays with some 21,000 complaints and inquiries a year – chiefly concerning housing, planning and building control, education and school admissions (LGO, 2009) – which, in their absence, would constitute a great deal of unhealthily pent-up suspicion of council maladministration.

That is what Britain's local ombudsmen mainly do: they investigate written complaints from the public about injustice caused by *maladministration* on the part of their local councils, police and fire authorities, education appeals panels, and (concerning admissions practices) school governing bodies. They do not initiate their own investigations, though they have in recent years taken up what might be termed 'class actions' arising out of individual cases – as with more than 5,000 mental health patients wrongly charged for aftercare by social services authorities, who have received reimbursements totalling tens of millions of pounds. Nor do they deal with complaints about the actual policy of a council. They are concerned solely with the policy's administration: the speed, efficiency, fairness and propriety with which it was implemented.

The ombudsmen will accept complaints either from citizens themselves or via their local councillor. If the complaint is one of the nearly 50% that qualify for investigation, the ombudsmen will normally require the local authority concerned to respond in detail and, if there seems to have been maladministration, do everything possible to bring about a local settlement – successfully in around a third of the cases they take on. In only a small minority of cases will a much fuller investigation be required, resulting in a final report and published judgment of whether or not maladministration and injustice have been found. If so, the ombudsmen will look to the local authority for some form of satisfactory action: an apology, financial compensation, or a change of procedure in dealing with future cases. Usually acceptable action is forthcoming, but on occasion a council will continue to dispute the ombudsmen's judgment, whereupon the latter is left with little sanction beyond the production of a second critical public report.

Default, engagement and intervention

Legislation sometimes confers default powers on ministers, so that a minister dissatisfied with the way an authority is providing a particular service can, as a final resort, step in and take it over, or transfer responsibility to another local authority or special body. For years, the invariably cited example of default powers being exercised was that of Clay Cross, Derbyshire, when the Labour council refused to increase its council house rents to the 'fair rent' level defined in the Housing Finance Act 1972. The Conservative Government sent in a housing commissioner to take over the council's housing responsibilities, and 11 Clay Cross councillors were disqualified from holding public office and surcharged £63,000 (well over £1 million at today's prices, measured by average earnings) for the money lost through the Act not being implemented.

The sheer practical difficulties involved in government-appointed officials taking over the running of a whole council service, quite apart from the political and personal animosity provoked, meant that such default powers used to be exercised only very rarely. In recent years, though, specific powers of ministerial intervention have been written into all kinds of legislation – from planning and environmental protection to (as was noted in Chapter 8 – p. 147) public libraries and museums. In particular, Comprehensive Performance Assessment (CPA – see Exhibit 10.3) had intervention – in its more cuddly guise as 'engagement' – as a core principle. Some councils, assessed as weak or poor performers, would need outside assistance in order to improve that performance.

As might be expected, the services in respect of which governmental intervention has been most prevalent – indeed, a key policy instrument – in recent years are children's social services and education. Children's Secretary Ed Balls' personal and dramatic intervention in the 'Baby P' case in Haringey – noted in Chapter 8 (p. 136) – received all its presumably intended media attention. But around the same time, his department was engaged in more structured and less nationally publicised interventions in several other authorities – Cornwall, Doncaster and Rotherham – through the establishment of Improvement Boards and the drawing up of improvement plans.

One of Ed Balls' predecessors, David Blunkett, had been an equally 'hands-on' Education Secretary ten years previously. His 1998 School Standards and Framework Act gave him powers to intervene in Local Education Authorities to secure higher standards, and, if necessary, to require them to contract out some or all of their functions. Over the years, though, a more graduated and less confrontational approach evolved than had at first seemed likely, under which, the DCSF's Standards and Effectiveness Unit (SEU) claims, over 1,500 schools have been successfully 'turned around', after being identified by the schools inspectorate, OFSTED, as being in need of the application of 'special measures'.

Monitoring and inspection

If the Thatcher Governments prompted a mushrooming of judicial reviews, the Blair Governments' equivalent contribution was monitoring and inspection (Game, 2009c – also on linked website). External regulation of local service providers, by schools and police inspectors, dates back to the mid-nineteenth century, but today it has become a seriously expensive inspection *industry*. OFSTED, probably the best known national inspectorate, became in 2007 the new OFSTED – the Office for Standards in Education, Children's Services and Skills, bringing together some 1,500 inspectors from four predecessor bodies into a single inspectorate for children and learners of all ages. Schools are now only one of its regulatory responsibilities, which also include child-minding, day care and all children's services, colleges and 14–19 provision, and adult and community learning. There have been other rationalisations too, but there are still several other sets of inspectors – from the Care Quality Commission, the HM Inspectorates of Constabulary, Prisons and Probation – who, especially following the launch of Comprehensive Area Assessment (see below), could descend with their proverbial clipboards on a local authority without much warning.

Then there was the inspector-in-chief – the Audit Commission (AC) – for Local Authorities and the National Health Service in England and Wales, to give it its full title: a big enough beast in the local government jungle – until being metaphorically shot, or baked, in the Coalition Government's quango hunt (see p. 156) – for its CE to be guaranteed 'mover and shaker' status (see Exhibit 1.2, item 12). The traditional part of the AC's role was to provide the auditors for local authorities' annual accounts. Its more recent and massively expanded role, however, was that of inspector and assessor – primarily, until 2008/9, through the *Comprehensive Performance Assessment* (CPA). CPA was a by-product of the exceptional scale of Britain's local government and of its relatively small number of local authorities. It involved an external inspection and scoring of every one of the then 388 principal local authorities in England (see Exhibit 10.3) – a simply inconceivable exercise if Britain had the 9,000-plus authorities putting the country on a par with the rest of the EU.

Any ranking exercise such as CPA is bound to be contentious and to have its critics. It was by no means a zero-sum game, and, as Exhibit 10.3 shows, most became winners. They, like the AC and government ministers, were naturally inclined to judge the system as being successful (Audit Commission, 2009). But there were losers – the poor performers – who might try to protest the unfairness of their ranking through judicial review, before settling down to negotiate their recovery plan with a DCLG-appointed external engagement team.

Even its supporters, though, conceded that CPA and the larger inspection regime of which it was part were a cumbersome and costly imposition on local authorities, who at the same time were being pressed by the Treasury to produce year-on-year efficiency savings. Few in local government would dispute the value of independent inspection of public services: it provides external challenge and assurance, and can be an important stimulus to improvement. That recognition, however, is accompanied by widespread criticism of the scale, overlap, inflexibility, overwhelming centralism, and above all, the phenomenal cost and burden of the regime created by the Labour Government. A 2005/6 study by PricewaterhouseCoopers found that the average local authority was required to make 566 separate performance returns to central government departments – 275 of these to the Departments of Education and Health alone – at a cost of £1.8 million, this 'upwards' reporting representing 80% of its total performance reporting costs (DCLG, 2006c, p. 7). The whole inspection industry was estimated even in 2004 to cost over £600 million (Hetherington, 2004), so that suggestions of it approaching £2 billion by 2010 were probably not wildly inaccurate. It isn't necessary to be rabidly anti-centralist to feel that was a lot to divert from serving the local public to serving national inspectors, particularly when one outcome of all the diverted time and energy was almost inevitably damage to staff morale.

Exhibit 10.3 Comprehensive Performance Assessment (CPA)

What was it?
A core element in the Labour Government's agenda for continuously improving public services. It developed out of the Best Value regime, in which external inspectors assessed individual council services on two 4-point scales: quality of service (3 to 0 stars) and prospects for improvement (yes/probably/unlikely/no). CPA was similar, but assessed the performance of the whole council. Through external inspections and other evidence, all 388 English councils were placed into one of just five categories: initially, these were Excellent, Good, Fair, Weak or Poor; from 2005 to 2008, 4 stars to 0 stars.

Top performing (4- and 3-star) councils were 'rewarded' with various 'freedoms and flexibilities', while 0- and 1-star councils received external 'engagement' – ministerially appointed officials overseeing and assisting the wayward authority in formulating and implementing a recovery plan.

How were the assessments determined?
In a process overseen by the Audit Commission, three main aspects of council activity were assessed and allocated scores:

- **core service performance,** covering six key services: children and young people, adult social care, housing, environment, libraries and leisure, benefits;
- **use of resources** – financial and strategic management, including achievement of value-for-money;
- **ability to improve** – with, from 2005, a 'direction of travel' rating, indicating progress made towards achieving improvement.

Isn't giving a large, multi-service organisation a single adjectival or star rating a bit crude?
Not 'a bit' – extremely! Even a generally excellent organisation has its known weaknesses, and, more important, even under-performing organisations have areas of strength and good practice. Inner city authorities representing areas of multiple deprivation felt – with some justification – that they in particular lost out in this nationwide league table (Game, 2009c).

So how good is English local government really?
Almost too good to be true! Between the first CPA scores for unitary and county councils in 2002 and the last in 2008, and even after toughening up assessment criteria, Excellent and Good authorities rose from 51% to 80%. Weak/1-star councils fell from 14% to 3%, while Poor councils, 9% in 2002, had disappeared completely by 2006 – and that was official! That's the difficulty with a system required to demonstrate 'continuous improvement' to sceptical local authorities and critical local media: in this case, sooner rather than later, almost everyone becomes at least good, with few left, evidently, needing major improvement.

The real stars?
Either the 13 councils who achieved the highest rating every year (too many to list – see Audit Commission, 2009, p. 25), or, better still, those going from Poor to 4-star: namely Coventry, Islington, Wakefield and Waltham Forest.

As it became clear that CPA would be wound up after 2008, something of a consensus emerged on how any successor performance assessment system should work. In particular, it should end the illogicality of subjecting high- and low-performing authorities to equivalent inspection regimes. It should also be much more locally driven, measuring aspects of service provision relevant to the specific locality and with more input from councillors, service users and community representatives. The government seemed to accept this prescription, and the 2006 White Paper promised that Comprehensive Area Assessment would be 'a more proportionate risk-based regime which will cut bureaucracy' (DCLG, 2006b, p. 11).

In fact, *Comprehensive Area Assessment* (CAA) could be seen as a kind of 'Grace Brothers' approach to performance – in tribute to the department store in the long-running TV sitcom, 'Are You Being Served?' Its principal focus was not on councils' delivery of specified services, but on how communities were being served and their quality of life enhanced by the whole, and, it was hoped, co-ordinated package of public services they receive – from health, police, fire and rescue services as well as councils. *Area assessments* were undertaken by six inspectorates, who reported on the effectiveness with which their respective services were tackling major issues in the area and the likelihood of their performance improving in the future. In contrast to CPA, these assessments were not scored – because they were supposedly based on local, rather than national, priorities. Instead, they highlighted – with unmissable green flags – examples of exceptional performance or innovations that others might learn from, and identified – with red flags, naturally – significant concerns, where action was needed.

Ministers were unable to kick their addiction to ranking and league tables completely, though, and the other elements of CAA involved *organisation assessments*. Here the inspectorates did score their organisation's performance management – its contribution to the delivery of the services and outcomes important to local people – and its use of resources in a way that provided value for money. These scores were then combined in precisely CPA style into an overall ranking of whether they were performing excellently, well, adequately or poorly.

One of CAA's most important features was that all of the above and much more became highly accessible, in user-friendly, downloadable 'area assessments', through a single 'Oneplace' website – http://oneplace. direct.gov.uk – the future of which, at the time of writing, was uncertain. CAA itself was near the head of the queue for abolition by the new Coalition Government. Many local authorities had felt that the co-ordination of inspectorates wasn't working, that the cost and burden particularly on 'risk-free' authorities wasn't noticeably reduced, and that the whole thing was pitched too broadly to tell them anything they didn't already know– 'a weapon of mass distraction', as the CE of Brent LBC put it (Daniel, 2009). Besides which, while 60 authorities received top rankings in the last round of CPA, only 15 managed it in the first round of CAA, published in 2009 – hardly a recipe for making friends and influencing people. Its replacement, therefore, by peer reviews – backed up possibly by a system of yellow and red cards, in which councils would step in to help struggling colleagues – was seen as a welcome step towards a regime of responsible self-regulation.

Finance

Chapter 12 is devoted entirely to finance. Here, therefore, we simply note in passing that additional means available to a central government wishing to control local authorities are through, first, regulating the amount of money they can spend locally; and, second, scrutinising the way in which that money is spent. The government – by, for example, capping local budgets effectively and controlling capital investment – can, and does, tightly restrict local spending.

There are countless examples of central government in effect bullying or blackmailing local authorities into doing what it wants – refusing them cash for school repairs, for example, if they refuse to consider establishing city academies. Our concern here, though, is with macro-management, not micro-meddling, and there has been no more macro influence on local authority finances in recent years than 'Gershon' – Sir Peter Gershon's 2004 proposals for *Releasing Resources to the Front Line* (see p. 125). Gershon's initial requirement was for £21 billion of efficiency savings by the public sector by 2007/8, with local government, including police authorities, responsible for delivering £6.45 billion. At least half of these *efficiency savings* were to be 'cashable', releasing resources that could be recycled into frontline service delivery. Several particularly 'promising' areas of potential savings were suggested:

- *back office functions* – for example, finance, human resources, IT support, legal services, asset and estate management, marketing and communications;
- *procurement/purchasing* – of, for example, utilities, ICT systems and services, professional services, construction, social housing, social care, environmental services; and
- *transactional services* – for example, calculation and payment of benefits and pensions, collection of taxes, charges or fees, registration of births and deaths.

Each local authority had to identify its own ways of achieving efficiency gains over three years equivalent to some 2.5% of its revenue budget, and early reactions were that such figures would be exceedingly difficult to achieve – not least because of the apparent inherent unfairness of the

Figure 10.1 *Cartoon – Back office savings*

Source: *Local Government Chronicle*, 18 June 2009.

exercise. Previously inefficient authorities ought to find it easier to meet this kind of blanket target than those already working more efficiently. In the event, however, local government achieved its target a year early, and released cash savings of £3.4 billion between 2004 and 2008. So a new target was promptly produced – of 3% a year efficiency savings by 2010/11 – which, following the country's economic downturn, was raised to 4% a year, or a total of £5.5 billion.

Back office savings contributed an average of 28% of councils' 2004–8 totals (DCLG, 2009d). But in the local government world, 'good' statistics are as exploitable as bad ones, and ministers were quick to note that back office contributions to councils' individual figures ranged from 6% to 91%, which suggested there were plenty more savings to be extracted, not least through greater use of shared services, as described in Chapter 7. Clearly, back offices are set to remain, in this context, right up there in the front line (see Figure 10.1).

Financial scrutiny, as noted above, has been exercised in England in recent years principally through the Audit Commission (AC), and in Scotland, Wales and Northern Ireland through their own audit offices. The AC, a public corporation, was established in 1982/3, initially to appoint auditors to local authorities, but its remit was steadily extended to cover health, housing, fire and rescue, and community safety bodies. The Commission would appoint external auditors for these bodies, either from its own staff of 'district auditors' or from private accounting firms of accountants such as PricewaterhouseCoopers, Deloitte and KPMG.

External auditors traditionally have checked an authority's accounts to satisfy themselves that its (or the tax-payers') money has been spent legally and reasonably. Nowadays they must also audit for value for money (VFM), to confirm that the council is securing the '3Es' – economy, efficiency and effectiveness – in its use of resources. Following this process, the auditors will send an Audit and Inspection Letter to the authority, summarising their views and identifying key issues arising. These letters should be accessible on councils' own websites, and, at least until its disappearance, probably around 2012–13, they are also available on the Audit Commission's site, as are all CPA reports, prepared in the Commission's more recently acquired capacity as inspector of local authority service performance.

Though established by a government anxious to impose a tough scrutiny regime on what it saw as financially irresponsible local authorities, the Audit Commission was never central government's poodle. It could be outspokenly critical of government policy when it deemed it appropriate, and on occasion strongly supportive of individual councils' spending priorities, when it judged them to reflect the preferences of local people. Inevitably, however, it remained a creature of central government and, with its close involvement in the development, as well as the implementation, of Labour Government policy regarding CPA, CAA and performance 'league tables', it did come to be identified more closely with the government of the day than was healthy for its long-term interests.

The government's executive agents?

This chapter has presented a formidable array of powers and influences that central government can bring to bear on local authorities, both collectively and individually. To suggest – returning to the quote from the Commons Select Committee in the opening section – that they 'tilt the balance of power towards the centre' seems, if anything, a restrained understatement. Some of those giving evidence to the Committee suggested that indeed it was – like LSE's Professor George Jones (House of Commons, 2009a, para.11): 'What has been happening for the last 30 or so years is that increasingly the central government has seen local authorities as their executive agents, no different from other parts of the central government.' This concept of an agency relationship or model is one that will be taken up, and questioned, in Chapter 11.

Chapter 11

Central–Local Government Relations: The Practice

Local government fragmented, ministers in Wonderland

Chapter 10 was about what might be called the instruments of control in the relationship – in this case between central and local government: the various means of imposing their will that are available principally to ministers and central departments as a consequence of their superior constitutional and legal status. We now move beyond these formal legalities and look at the relationship in practice.

The centre, we know, can legislate, regulate, direct and exhort. But think what else we know. In England alone there were, in 2010, 354 local governments: large, elected, tax-levying organisations responsible for providing a very wide range of services, to standards partly determined by them, working nowadays with and through a multiplicity of partnerships from all sectors. Some, as it did not need the CPA or CAA to tell us, were doing these things better, and more efficiently and effectively, than others. Even a strategically focused, co-ordinated central government would have struggled to control as fragmented a local government system as England's has become – and those are not descriptions that most would associate with recent governments, as local government expert, Tony Travers, illustrated (2008):

> Imagine the scene: in the Children and Schools Department someone is complaining that there are hundreds of schools with surplus places. The demand goes out for local authorities to 'close under-subscribed schools'. Minutes later, another voice calls for action to protect threatened rural primaries. Councils are told to 'protect village schools'.
>
> Over the road, a minister is issuing an edict against the 'postcode lottery' in social care for the elderly: a full-scale inquiry is to be launched into variations from area to area. Nearby, in another department, plans are being implemented to curb local authority spending, with lower grant increases and tax capping.

You can stop imagining now – because there's no need. These things happen, regularly. In 2008, the Schools Minister did send one of those circulars (see p. 172) to education authorities, warning them to 'take very seriously' the 2006 Education Act's 'presumption that rural schools will not close'. And it did directly contradict the Every Child Matters guidance his department circulated two months previously, requiring councils to 'make the removal of surplus places a priority' and spend the money saved on raising standards in more popular primary schools (Dunton, 2008, p. 6).

Moreover, as Travers observes, the blame in such cases tends not to be aimed at central government for asking the impossible, but at councils for not delivering it. If only they were more capable and managed more efficiently:

> they would be able to close every under-subscribed school while simultaneously keeping open every rural primary ... provide everyone with above-average social care provision ... cut local tax by 50% while doubling expenditure on services. This is the kind of *Alice in Wonderland* world Ministers inhabit. They demand inconsistent behaviour by councils without even realising they are doing so.

The blame point is, we believe, a valid one, and it will get an airing in this chapter. But it is not the chapter's main purpose, which is less to bemoan the one-sidedness of the central–local relationship than to highlight its complexities and subtleties.

More complicated than physics?

The Nobel Prize-winning physicist, Albert Einstein, reckoned politics was 'far more complicated than physics'. If so, then the politics of central–local relations must be more complicated still – for the obvious reason that there are a great many diverse local governments and, what can be overlooked, also a lot of very different central governments.

We have rehearsed local government's diversity, and with that diversity come resources. Central government doesn't have a monopoly. Local authorities express their differences by having their own local knowledge and professional experience, their own political and policy agendas, their own service or spending priorities, and their own ways of doing things. They also communicate with and learn from each other. The constant danger – or delight – of seeking to say anything universally generalisable about 'local government' is that there is bound, somewhere, to be an exception.

Equally important is that, despite the UK's centralist political culture, central government itself is not a single uniform entity either. There are far fewer central government departments than local authorities, but they too have their own traditions, cultures and ways of working, as well as fundamentally different – and sometimes directly conflicting – approaches to local government. As Lowndes puts it (2002, p. 145): 'The "centre" is not joined-up and local councils experience a myriad of different cross-cutting and often contradictory relationships with central government departments and agencies.'

The Department for Communities and Local Government (DCLG) is local government's 'sponsoring' department, and would be hoped to be tolerably supportive. But, as Nick Raynsford indicated in an interview towards the end of his four years as Labour Minister for Local Government, other ministers and their departments can need almost constant cultivation:

> He admitted 'there was a genuine anxiety among some ministers about local government. One of my tasks has been to build confidence about its capacity to deliver.' He said there had been 'a significant change of attitude' at both the Home Office and the Treasury, with both co-operating in recent [departmental] reports respectively on neighbourhoods and performance. He remained tactfully tight-lipped about the DfES [Department for Education and Schools]. (Burton, 2005, p. 12)

For their part, those in local government are likely to feel more predisposed towards the DCLG, and even the Treasury – departments that deal with local government 'in the round' – than towards the DfES (now the Department for Education), the Department of Health and the Home Office, for whom local government can seem merely an inconvenient means to an end.

The reality is complex indeed – and will remain so, even after the disappearance of the Government Offices for the Regions (GORs). Not only is there a multiplicity of local authorities, a range of central government departments and policy areas, and a constantly changing party political dimension to consider. Account must be taken too of the many other appointed agencies and partnerships that make up the world of local governance. Our own 'sketch map' in Exhibit 11.1 is the crudest of simplifications. For a start, it omits, apart from the GORs, much of the regional tier of governance described in Chapter 6. But it should convey some impression of just how fragmented both 'central' and 'local government' really are. We have resisted, however, the temptation to re-label it a map of 'inter-governmental relations' for the same reason that we have retained 'local government' for the book's title. It is *primarily* a map of the links between central government departments and local authorities. The broken lines of communication symbolise the many and diverse relationships that can exist between each local authority and a range of central government departments. The unbroken lines signify that in practice much

Exhibit 11.1 Central–local government networks, 2009–10: a sketch map

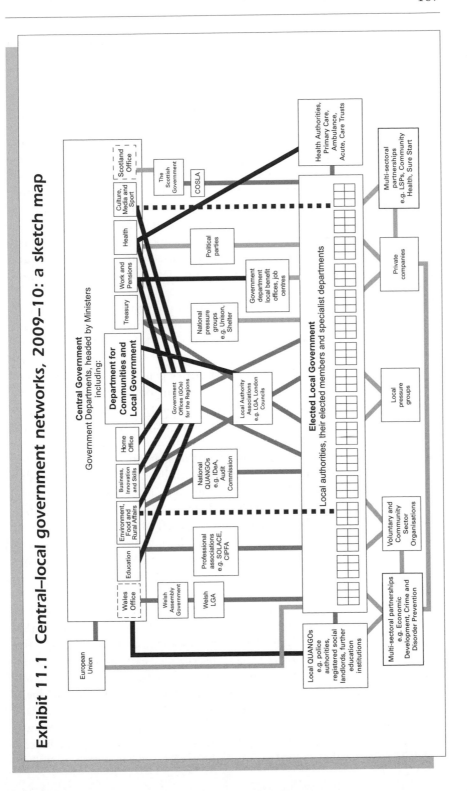

of this contact and attempted influence is necessarily channelled through 'umbrella' organisations and other agencies.

Interpreting central–local relations: changing phases

In principle, the *scale* of central intervention in local authorities' affairs could be quantified. It would be possible to add up – in the way Sir Simon Jenkins attempted for the Department for Education (see p. 172) – all the relevant Acts of Parliament, the plethora of regulations, circulars, guidance notes and statutory instruments emerging from Whitehall and doubtless conclude that the scale of intervention is massive. It is, however, far more difficult to assess the *nature* of the central–local relationship – partly because it changes over time, but mainly because even a 'freeze frame' at a particular point in time will contain, on detailed examination, more complexity than is initially apparent.

In previous editions of this book we identified five distinguishable C-initialled phases of central–local relations since the 1960s (Wilson and Game, 2002, p. 163, plus Exhibit on linked website). The period until the mid-1970s was 'Consultative': growing local service spending, much of it centrally financed, with local authorities generally left to their own devices. Accelerating economic decline brought phases of 'Corporatism' – with Labour governments trying to incorporate local authority representatives in securing voluntary expenditure restraint – followed in the 1980s by the 'Confrontation' and 'Control' that were the successive approaches of the Thatcher Administrations, captured in part in our 'funnel of local authority discretion' (see Exhibit 2.2). Persuasion hadn't worked, so ministers legislated for themselves total control over local spending. Authorities that challenged them, such as the GLC, were abolished, while the remainder were required to sell off their assets or invite the private sector to bid to take them over. With central financial control established, the Major Administrations ushered in a period of less overt aggression and more 'Conciliation', which in 1997 was inherited by New Labour.

New Labour came into power with high expectations on the part of an unprecedentedly Labour-dominated local government. The party's parliamentary and local politicians had both opposed, from their respective standpoints, the depredations of the Conservative years, and Labour councillors, while recognising that a partnership of equals was constitutionally impossible, hoped at least for a partnership of spirit and like-mindedness. In practice, the funding of local services was eventually greatly increased and their improvement became a major government priority, but there was no radical reduction in the central control and direction to which local authorities were subject. Indeed, quite the reverse: phrases such as 'micro-management', 'control freakery', and 'death by inspection' entered the local government lexicon early on – and stayed there (Stoker, 2002; Wilson, 2003).

In the Labour Government's third term, ministers themselves started to concede that the architecture of control and direction they had constructed might be somewhat excessive. They talked the language of localism, published White Papers with encouraging titles such as *Strong and Prosperous Communities* (2006) and *Communities in Control: Real People, Real Power* (2008), but generally, as in the *Central–Local Concordat* (see p. 168), their actions failed to match the rhetoric. They sought to persuade the Commons CLG Select Committee that various decentralising measures over the years amounted to a 'very dramatic swing of the pendulum in favour of localism' (House of Commons, 2009a, para. 23). But several of these measures – cutting the number of National Performance Indicators councils had to meet, reducing the reporting of local plans, refining the inspection system – amounted simply to modifications of the government's own former excesses, and Committee members were unconvinced. Their conclusion, following the evidence of most of their witnesses, was that 'central direction and control remain unchanged or even ... have increased' (para. 29).

Labour's mixed messages

The CLG Committee's tempered conclusion is hardly headline-making, but it seems a fair summary of the recent conduct of a complex relationship – reflecting what we endeavour to represent in the shaping of our funnel of local discretion as well as in Exhibit 11.2. The suggestion is that the Blair Government orchestrated its approach to central–local relations much more calculatedly and subtly than had the previous Conservative Governments – deliberately conveying, in fact, a mixed or dual message: tough and tender; hard cop, soft cop; or, as we previously described it, stick and carrot. The government had its analysis of local government's defects, and its modernisation agenda of required reforms. If local government embraced the reforms and the government's way of working, there were metaphorical carrots available. But for resisters and recalcitrants, there were hard cops wielding sticks. That was the theory. In practice, the whole 'command and control' regime was too tough and applied too uniformly, and the carrots were dwarfish and not terribly appetising. But this 'mixed message' approach does help to explain why, in Exhibit 11.2, several initiatives and policies show up, with different emphases, on both sides of the balance sheet.

Certainly, there is no shortage of ammunition for those arguing that centralism has increased, and that on the big issues the Blair/Brown

Exhibit 11.2 Labour's central–local relations balance sheet

Measures generally seen as being to local government's

Benefit	Detriment
Improved 'climate' of central–local relations, reflected by *Central–Local Concordat*	Central government's 'command and control' culture – and the assumption that its mandate and judgement are inherently superior to local government's
Scottish and Welsh devolution	
More stable 3-year grant settlements, with increased 'real terms' funding for local services, particularly from 2000	No major reappraisal of the role of local government and local democracy; ineffectiveness and one-sidedness of *Concordat*
Abolition of 'crude and universal' capping of spending and council tax levels	Increased funding of local government services lagged far behind that for the NHS
Some relaxation of capital funding controls	Local authorities increasingly 'commissioners', rather than providers, of several major services
Abolition of CCT, and priority given in Best Value and CPA to continuous improvement in service quality	Selective capping retained, unlike in Scotland, and revived by Labour ministers in 2004
Some 'freedoms and flexibilities' for high-performing councils under CPA – e.g. relaxation of inspection and plan requirements	No major financial reform, despite repeated promises; no relocalisaton of business rates, or increase in percentage of revenue raised locally; no reform of council tax; increased ring-fencing of grants
High overall CPA ratings have strengthened local government's bargaining position	Continued restrictions on capital funding force councils to transfer homes
	CCT replaced by Best Value, then CPA – more comprehensive, more interventionist
Introduction of power to promote 'well-being', and backing of Sustainable Communities Act	Discretion has to be 'earned', and in practice is only discretion to do what central government wants and approves
Restoration of democratic government in Greater London	Ever more targets, league tables, inspection and monitoring regimes, plus government insistence on partnership working
Promotion of local government's community leadership role through political management reforms, including mayoral referendums and overview/scrutiny procedures	Imposition of three restrictive models of executive management, and insistence on mayoral referendums
	Planning responsibilities of English county councils given to unelected regional bodies
	Little done to increase accountability of local quangos
Introduction of local public service and local area agreements	Dominance of central government priorities in public service and local area agreements

Administrations treated local government with a disdain bordering on contempt. Council tax remained unreformed, and the massive central–local imbalance in revenue funding barely changed. The Lyons Report's modest proposals on local finance were instantly shelved, and the Communities Secretary seemed to relish confirming to the CLG Committee that the government 'had no intention of responding formally' to the four-year inquiry it had initiated. Despite the party's vehement opposition to the very principle of tax- and expenditure-capping when introduced by the Conservatives in the 1980s, Labour ministers retained the powers and, from 2004, used them. Compulsory Competitive Tendering was abolished, but was replaced by the more interventionist regimes of Best Value and CPA. Targets and inspections went far beyond anything the Conservative Governments had contemplated. Even positive initiatives and reforms were driven and defined by ministers: models of executive management, performance assessment and partnership working.

The government's response would be that central prescription was necessary to bring about overdue change, and that the overall standard of local service provision is demonstrably higher than it was before 1997. Moreover, there was throughout a significant localist dimension to its reform agenda. The Local Government Act 2000 was prescriptive about executive forms of political management, but, with councils determining their own constitutions, there was more scope for operational distinctiveness than they initially appreciated. The same Act also gave them new powers: a new community leadership role, backed by the power of well-being, and the duty to prepare, with other local partners, what evolved into Sustainable Community Strategies. Councils' overview and scrutiny remits were extended first to NHS bodies and more recently to other local service providers. Council tax may not have changed, but, as will be seen in Chapter 12, local authorities now have three-year grant settlements and considerably greater freedom to raise capital finance. Some responsibilities have been lost to local government, but, as noted in Chapters 2 and 8, new responsibilities continued to be acquired.

These and similar developments indicate that a *purely* 'top-down' interpretation of Labour's period in office is simplistic – even if, as Pratchett and Leach suggest (2004, p. 378), the search for balance requires some delving beneath the surface: 'Despite a whole range of constraints, choice is a reality ... and extends across a whole range of policy areas. Often it lies in the detail of implementation rather than in wider strategic direction.' The authors also draw a distinction between the government's major policy priority areas, such as education, and the wide range of other local authority functions: 'There is much greater discretion outside the priority areas' (p. 378); blanket generalisations are dangerous.

The Department for Communities and Local Government (DCLG)

We referred above to the DCLG as local government's 'sponsoring' department. The easiest way nowadays to find out about government departments is through the annual reports they publish and present to Parliament. The DCLG's 2009 Report, with a similar upbeat slogan-title to those it gives its White Papers – *Community, Opportunity, Prosperity* – was only its third, because the department wasn't created until 2006. Before that date, local government was part of the expansive Office of the Deputy Prime Minister (ODPM), which in previous incarnations had been the Department for Environment, Transport and the Regions (DETR) from 1997 to 2001, and for Transport, Local Government and the Regions (DTLR) from 2001 to 2002. Government departments, in today's world, are restructured at least as regularly as local authorities, and their ministers are shuffled around more frequently still – to the perceptible detriment, in the view of the DCLG's own Select Committee, of effective government (House of Commons, 2010).

Its range of responsibilities makes the DCLG a large department. It sets and oversees policy on housing, planning, climate change and sustainable development, urban regeneration, the regions, homelessness and social exclusion, worklessness, fire and resilience, race and migration. Most of these functions, it should be emphasised, are exercised only in England, for, with devolution, in Scotland, Wales and Northern Ireland they are largely the responsibility of the respective governments and assemblies.

Measured by its core employment, though, the Department was not large even in 2009/10, with a headcount of 2,900, and, with this figure including those working in regional Government Offices (see below), and the Department facing overall budget cuts of up to 33% by 2014–15, its future would be a great deal slimmer. Certainly, it is a Whitehall minnow beside, for example, direct-service-providing departments such as Work and Pensions (121,000) or HM Revenue and Customs (92,000) (ONS, 2010a, table 11). On the other hand, in 2009/10 it slightly outnumbered the Department of Health's 2,300. The two departments are essentially similar: responsible for the nation's most important domestic public services and a large chunk of its public expenditure, but through other agencies – the NHS and local authorities plus, of course, the regional agencies and the many other quangos and partnerships encountered in Chapter 9.

The Department's name – combining yet distinguishing between two apparently similar concepts – is itself an irritant to some people. It was mocked by Sir Simon Jenkins, when it was first announced and when its two Cabinet Ministers, John Prescott and David Miliband, made, visually and politically, a strikingly distinctive couple (see cartoon, Wilson and Game, 2006, fig. 9.4 – also on linked website):

These two responsibilities would be considered the same in any normal country. The trouble for Miliband is that his boss regards them as complete opposites. To Blair 'community' is sugar and spice and all things nice, pink, soft and politically neutered. Local government is snips and snails and puppy dogs' tails. It is sweaty civic rooms and Old Labour councillors, the hoodies of the public sector. It is where people like John Prescott have punch-ups. Thus Miliband's task is to promote community but suppress local government ... a paradox that [he] cannot possibly resolve.

Jenkins was referring to the Labour Government's suspicion and distrust of local government and its concern to demonstrate its localist credentials and in some way 'empower' local people without involving elected councils and their councillors. But the division has also become a way for accountants to divide up the Department's spending. In 2005/6, of its nearly £50 billion current expenditure, £46 billion went on and was largely spent by local government, and just £3 billion on 'Communities'. In 2006/7, the Dedicated Schools Grant arrived (see pp. 212–3), and the DCLG immediately lost to the Department for Children, Schools and Families more than half the spending it previously controlled. By 2008/9, therefore, it had slipped down the departmental spending league table with a total budget of £29 billion, of which local government's share was £25 billion (HM Treasury, 2009, table 2).

David Miliband's departure ended the exceptional practice of a department other than the Treasury having two full Cabinet Ministers, but the position in 2009/10 came close, with 1 + 0.75 + 0.5. Secretary of State was John Denham, whose appointment, despite the chaos and carnage surrounding it (see Exhibit 11.3), was generally well received in the local government world – not least because he had been an elected member on both Hampshire County and Southampton City Councils. Such first-hand experience tends to be taken as a sign that a minister will at least understand local government, if not necessarily prove particularly adept at promoting its interests. John Healey's sideways move from Local Government to Housing came with an entitlement to attend all Cabinet meetings – hence the 0.75 – and Rosie Winterton could also attend when her specific ministerial responsibilities were on the agenda.

This arithmetic – imagining the potency of having three voices round the Cabinet table – was local government's way of trying to make the best of the circumstantial evidence that it had quite simply been forgotten during the crucial weekend of the ministerial reshuffle. Their Cabinet minister having resigned extraordinarily on the very eve of the local elections, there followed four days in which not even the DCLG knew whether a local government minister had been appointed and, if so, who it was. Setting aside considerations of the minister's work–life balance, there may have

Exhibit 11.3 Local government goes missing

The appointment of a Minister for Local Government, June 2009.

Wednesday 3 June – Hazel Blears **resigns** as Secretary of State for Communities and Local Government a few days after Prime Minister (PM) Gordon Brown describes some of her expenses claims as an MP as 'totally unacceptable'.

Thursday 4 June – **County and unitary council elections**; also European Parliamentary elections. Labour loses control of its last four English county councils – with only 22% of the national vote – in its worst-ever local election performance.

Friday 5 June – In the PM's ministerial reshuffle, **John Denham replaces Blears** as CLG Secretary, and John Healey switches from Minister of State for Local Government to Minister of State for Housing – the fourth in two years. No one becomes responsible for local government.

Elsewhere, Rosie Winterton is appointed Minister of State for Regional Economic Development and Coordination in the Department for Business, Innovation and Skills.

Monday 8 June – In the PM's list of further ministerial appointments, it is announced that Winterton's post is a joint one with DCLG. There is still no official mention of local government, but a DCLG spokesperson confirms that **Winterton will also be Minister of State for Local Government** – 'It is on the Number 10 website, so we are taking that as confirmation' (Drillsma-Milgrom, 2009).

been benefits in having the local government minister at the heart of government in Lord Mandelson's powerful ministerial team, and a regional co-ordination minister closely in touch with local government. It seemed odd, though, that no one thought to mention it at the time – even to the minister herself.

The DCLG ministerial team in the 2010 Coalition Government was headed by Conservative Eric Pickles, a local government heavyweight in every sense, with direct involvement in the sector dating back to his ruthless Thatcherite leadership of Bradford MBC in the 1980s. He slashed budgets and services, raised rents and charges, closed advice centres and sold off old people's homes, while teachers and caretakers, social workers and council officers lost their jobs (Vallely, 2009). His plan was to cut £50 million from the council's budget and the workforce by a third, and, while he would claim to have moved towards the centre-right during his parliamentary career, he will be hard to convince that there aren't substantial economies and efficiencies to be found in today's local government. His 'plain-speaking Yorkshireman' style – 'William Hague without the intellect'

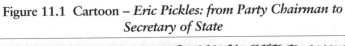

Figure 11.1   Cartoon – *Eric Pickles: from Party Chairman to Secretary of State*

Source: *Local Government Chronicle*, 19 February 2009.

was one description (Vallely, 2009) – is also popular with the party faithful, having, as party chairman, steered the recent Conservative electoral recovery in at least something of the style of James Bond villain, Ernst Stavro Blofeld (see Figure 11.1).

The Minister for Housing and Local Government was Grant Shapps, whose greater experience, it is fair to say, was with the former of those two portfolios. Greg Clark was an unusually well qualified Minister for Decentralisation. A former Westminster City councillor, he had also, while Conservative Head of Policy, co-authored a book with the fairly self-explanatory title of *Total Politics: Labour's Command State* (2003). The six-member team was completed by three junior ministers, all with significant councillor experience behind them: Bob Neill (GLC, London Assembly and Havering LBC), Liberal Democrat Andrew Stunell (Cheshire CC and Stockport MDC), and Baroness Hanham (former leader, Kensington and Chelsea LBC). The five ex-councillors made up a quarter of those in the first Cameron Administration – 15 Conservatives and 5 Lib Dems – three of whom were in the Cabinet, but none, perhaps unfortunately, in the six-minister Treasury team.

The DCLG has several London addresses, but its centre of operations is the glass-fronted Eland House in Bressenden Place, near Victoria Station, where ministers and most of the department's civil servants are based. It is at the centre of extensive formal and informal communications networks in Whitehall, dealing with any and all local government matters, or, as we phrased it earlier, with local government in the round. Numerous other departments, as shown in Exhibit 11.1, have their own specific dealings with local authorities, which are handled through formal and informal civil service meetings, and various ad hoc groups and committees. While the DCLG communicates directly with local authorities through directives and guidance, it spends a good deal of time consulting with broader representative bodies, chief among which is the Local Government Association (LGA).

The LGA Group – local government's national voice

Prior to 1997 there were three major English and Welsh local authority associations representing the three main classes of authority: county councils, metropolitan authorities and district councils. In 1997, after much agonising, it was decided that unification offered local government the best chance of making any political impression on national policy-making, and a unified LGA was created. Scotland already had a single association, the Convention of Scottish Local Authorities (COSLA), and there are Welsh and Northern Ireland LGAs, as well as a separate body for London local government, London Councils. Naturally, these associations are pivotal bodies in their respective central–local worlds, and no fewer than five of their present or past chairs feature among the 'movers and shakers' listed in Exhibit 1.2.

The LGA is a political body, in all senses. Its job is to represent the interests of all its more than 400 member authorities (including police, fire and transport authorities), who provide the bulk of its funding. Its leadership is in some ways similar to that of a 'hung' local authority, on which no single party has an overall majority. The political leadership reflects the parties' respective strengths in local councils across the country, so, having been Labour-led until 2006, it became increasingly strongly Conservative and in 2009/10 was chaired by Bradford councillor, Dame Margaret Eaton (see Exhibit 1.2, No. 10). Conservative councillors were in a plurality on the Executive and chaired a majority of the policy boards that steer the LGA's work. Some examples of its work can be seen in Exhibit 11.4.

The position of an association led by one party representing local government's interests to ministers of another party is not uncommon, and the LGA has a long-standing commitment to consensus working. In fact, its most recent publicised dispute was less a 'Big P' political one between the

Exhibit 11.4 The work of the LGA: a national voice for local government

Some of what the LGA felt it achieved in 2009:

- **Published** a report – *Delivering More for Less* – identifying £4.5 billion of potential annual savings achievable by reducing the 'unnecessary burdens Whitehall imposes on local authorities and by giving councils greater control over local spending decisions'.
- **Stopped** the government's 'fundamentally flawed' proposal for direct elections to police authorities.
- **Demonstrated** that allegations by the Equalities and Human Rights Commission that councils were not providing adequate services for victims of domestic violence were unfounded and based on flawed research.
- **Worked** with other members of the LGA Group – IDeA, LGE – to double the number of local government apprenticeships to 15,000 across the country.
- **Secured** £70 million to help some councils to compensate for their loss of central government grant funding resulting from recent migration trends, thereby making their local population statistics inaccurate.
- **Defended** councils that had lost money through investing in failed Icelandic banks against accusations of having acted recklessly, and worked with administrators, the government and Icelandic authorities to recover much of the money.
- **Launched** a national campaign aimed at recruiting and retaining children's social workers, following the exodus from the profession in the wake of the 'Baby P' case.

Main source: LGA (2009c).

parties than a 'small p' one between the political and managerial leaderships. The LGA's chief executive is generally a former CE of a large local authority, and the incumbent in 2008, Paul Coen, was eventually forced out, following a series of clashes with the leading politicians. It was a difficult period for local government, with the LGA having to respond to several 'front-page' stories – such as the death of 'Baby P' and the potential loss by councils of nearly £1 billion invested in failed Icelandic banks. But there were also differences over the future profile and organisation of the LGA, the CE favouring a broader role as lobbyist for public services as a whole, and the formation of a single 'local government services company', comprising the LGA and several other bodies linked loosely with it:

- *Local Government Improvement and Development* (formerly Improvement and Development Agency (IDeA))

    Funded mainly by central government. Works with councils to develop good practice, effective leadership, partnership working – through online communities of practice, leadership programmes and the Beacon Council/LIA scheme. Useful website – www.idea.gov.uk – for publications, councillors' briefings, glossary of local government jargon, and annually updated *Councillor's Guide.*

- *Local Government Employers*

    Represents local government employer interests to central government, government agencies, trade unions and European institutions.

- *Local Government Regulation*

    Oversees councils' regulatory services – trading standards, environmental protection, licensing and gambling, food safety and hygiene, animal health and welfare.

- *Local Partnerships*

    Works with councils to secure funding and accelerate the development of PFI schemes (see pp. 163–5), public–private partnerships, and complex projects.

- *Local Government Leadership*

    Helps leading councillors and senior officers to develop their leadership skills, through various regional and national programmes.

The tighter-knit company concept did not appeal to the LGA's political leadership, but these organisations have come together in a partnership – *The LGA Group* – and work jointly to lobby government and others for changes in policy and legislation, raising local government's public reputation, and assisting local authorities to improve and be innovative.

Government Offices for the Regions (GOs)

If the LGA is the national voice of local government, the nine Government Offices – co-ordinated by a Government Office Network Centre and Services (yes, GONCS) – were, until the new Coalition announced their abolition, the regional voice of central government. Set up in 1994 and much extended under the Labour Government, they brought together the regional services of 12 Whitehall departments, including the chief ones shown in Exhibit 11.1, with the result that policy can often appear more 'joined-up' regionally than it does at the national level. The GOs were the third main institutional arm – with Regional Development Agencies and Assemblies – in the regional tier of governance described in Chapter 5, and worked increasingly closely with local authorities.

Each GO had in 2009 an annual budget averaging between £10 billion and £12 billion, giving an approximate total of £100 billion, compared with a total local government expenditure in England of about £160 billion. This meant, should there have been any doubt about it, that GOs were the principal channel through which a sizeable proportion of government policy was delivered, particularly cross-cutting projects in areas such as regional economic development, environmental improvement, transport, health and education. They managed spending programmes directly on behalf of departments, monitored and gave feedback on the effectiveness of these programmes, linked departmental policies, and, particularly through the GONCS, provided what was once a largely absent regional voice in national policy formulation. They obviously played a vital role in the Labour Government's aim of reducing disparities between and within regions, and, with their responsibility for negotiating and overseeing LSPs, LAAs and MAAs (see Exhibit 9.3), their day-to-day links with local authorities grew closer.

With the change of government, however, their future immediately looked uncertain. Eric Pickles, in his first speech as Communities Secretary to the Local Government Association annual conference, warned of his policy to abolish the TLA – the 'Three-Letter Abbreviation'. LGA members looked startled, but the Minister was reminding them that he was already axing RDAs, CAAs, RSSs (Regional Spatial Strategies), and the GOL (the Government Office for London). It seemed unlikely that the remaining Government Offices would escape simply by having abbreviated themselves to GOs, rather than GORs, and they didn't.

Some conceptual models

This glimpse at GOs completes the overview of what we termed the working relationships between central and local government. It has been simplified in that most elements in the relationship have inevitably been treated summarily – and some squeezed out altogether. It has not – or not intentionally – been simplified in the sense of presenting a completely one-sided or unidirectional relationship, because that is not how we see it. On the contrary, it is a complex relationship, involving a large number of central and local government bodies, acting both individually and collectively, often with and through yet other bodies. All have their bargaining resources – knowledge, experience, legitimacy, authority – that they bring to the usually figurative negotiating table. The product of all these interactions – the overall balance or imbalance in the relationship – varies across time and across policies. The overall relationship can never be a stable, evenly balanced partnership, for all the constitutional and statutory reasons discussed in Chapter 10, but it is a long way from the simple top-down line management relationship of central office and field agencies.

Having sought to describe this complex relationship in practical, 'real-life' terms, the chapter's final section looks at how it has been depicted in some of the academic literature. In particular, it outlines a number of the models that have been applied to the study and interpretation of central–local relations. These models should be treated in much the same way – to use Loughlin's analogy (1996b, p. 53) – as maps. For, like maps, they are deliberate simplifications of the real world that should enable us to understand its complexities and find our way through them a little more easily.

Agency model

The agency model sees local authorities as having a completely subordinate relationship to central government: as arms or agents of the centre, with little or no discretion in the task of implementing national policies. From our accounts of the increasing bypassing of elected local government and the growing dominance of the centre, it might be supposed that the agency model is nowadays an accurate characterisation of reality – and that suggestion was indeed made at the conclusion of Chapter 10. Such an interpretation, though, ignores the substantial policy diversity that manifestly still exists among our local authorities. Central government does exercise tight financial control, but that control does not produce anything approaching uniform expenditure patterns or service performance. This can be demonstrated in many ways, but one of the most insightful is to compare – and then to try to explain – the financial and other statistics compiled each year by CIPFA (the Chartered Institute of Public Finance and Accountancy). All councils are required to produce such statistics, enabling their budget and service figures to be compared with those of other councils of the same type.

In previous editions, we presented quite elaborate summaries of these CIPFA statistics, to give readers an idea of their range and comparative potential (see, for example, Wilson and Game, 2006, Exhibit 9.6 – also on linked website). Happily, this is now unnecessary, for CIPFA itself now makes a good selection of its Statistical Profiles available on its www.cipfastats.net website – including those used by us in compiling Exhibit 11.5.

Exhibit 11.5 compares only metropolitan districts, but other authority types could serve equally well. The expenditure data selected are deliberately wide-ranging, sharing in common only that they are all per capita, rather than actual, and so control for most of the effects of population size. The immediately obvious contrast is between essentially statutory services, such as secondary education and social care, and those that are largely discretionary, where variations can, in both principle and practice, be almost infinite – and may well become even more extreme as the search for public spending cuts becomes increasingly urgent. But it is difficult to argue that all scope for local or political prioritisation has been removed from

Exhibit 11.5 Variations in local authority service statistics – Metropolitan Districts

The 36 English Metropolitan Borough Councils, 2009/10

Service*	Highest		Average	Lowest		Variation – highest ÷ lowest
Average council tax per domestic property	Stockport	£1,223	£980	Manchester	£802	1.5
Total service expenditure	Birmingham	£2,067	£1,730	Bury	£1,400	1.5
Education – Total	Oldham	£1,039	£911	Stockport	£704	1.5
Nursery schools	Salford	£73	£18	St. Helens	£1.20	60
Secondary schools	Rotherham	£435	£358	Knowsley	£192	2.3
Social Services – Total	Manchester	£671	£436	Bury	£344	1.95
Children's and families services	Manchester	£268	£140	Bolton	£90	3.0
Highways and Transport						
Structural maintenance	Barnsley	£25	£8	Rotherham, Leeds	15p	165
Street lighting	Sunderland	£30	£13	Barnsley	£4	7.3
Environmental health						
Waste collection	Wakefield	£34	£25	Coventry	£16	2.1
Public conveniences	S. Tyneside	£3	72p	Liverpool	7p	43
Culture and Heritage	Liverpool	£28	£14	Solihull	£1.80	16
Recreation and Sport	Sheffield	£61	£20	Trafford	£2.60	24
Library services	Newcastle	£42	£20	Wigan	£1.20	35
Council tax benefits administration	Barnsley	£40	£8	Coventry	£2.30	17

Note: * All measures are expenditure per head of population, unless specified otherwise.
Source: CIPFA (2009b).

local budgeting when, for example, per capita spending on social services can vary by a factor of two or three among councils in the same Greater Manchester metropolitan area.

These kinds of expenditure comparisons can be fascinatingly revealing, and, particularly if you are using your own local authority/ies, you may feel you can explain, or at least speculate about, the variations you will certainly find. Many factors may suggest themselves: political control, pressure group activity, differences in the geography, economy and socio-economic character of the area – or major events, such as Liverpool becoming European Capital of Culture in 2008. You may also want to question the statistics – whether, for example, secondary schools expenditure would be better calculated per pupil, or social services expenditure by client group, rather than per capita. Then there is the issue of whether high spending on waste collection or benefit administration is an indicator of high prioritisation or inefficiency. This brings us to the big limitation of all these statistics, which is that they are not, and do not purport to be, performance measures. They measure *input* – financial input – into the provision of a service, which may or may not relate to its quality or to the value for money received by local users and tax-payers. For that information we need to have *output* or, better still, *outcome* data.

The distinction is seen vividly in Total Place (see Exhibit 9.4), which first maps all the inputs of public money into an area and then, in the key part of the exercise, relates these inputs to outcomes and seeks to identify how the outcomes might be achieved or improved on by a more effective use of resources. It is seen too in the (quite separate) Oneplace website's reporting of Comprehensive Area Assessments (see pp. 180–1), whose data are all based not on inputs, but on Performance Indicators (PIs) of how an area is 'doing', how it is being served: what percentage of household waste is being sent for recycling, how many children's homes have been judged inadequate and so on, rather than how much cash has been spent on providing these services.

Neither type of data is intrinsically superior. Both are relevant if you are a tax-paying resident, and both are relevant too if, as here, the purpose is to question the agency model by highlighting the apparent extent of budgetary and policy discretion that exists among councils with the same formal responsibilities. Even in largely statutory services, councils clearly do vary in the priority they give and the efficiency they bring to different aspects of their service provision. They have, in other words, a degree of *choice,* which is why we suggest that, on its own, the agency model is a less than fully satisfactory representation of the central–local relationship.

Power-dependence model

This is an elaboration of the *partnership model,* which sees central government and local authorities as more or less equal partners. The partnership

Exhibit 11.6   The resources of central and local government

Central government	Local government
Controls legislation and delegated powers	Employs all personnel in local services, far outnumbering civil servants
Provides and controls the largest proportion of local authorities' current expenditure through formulae and, increasingly, specific grants	Has, through both councillors and officers, detailed local knowledge, expertise and experience
Controls individual authorities' total expenditure and taxation levels by 'capping'	Has limited powers to raise own taxes and set own service charges
Controls the largest proportion of local capital expenditure	Controls the implementation of policy
Sets standards for and inspects some services	Can decide own political priorities and most service standards, and how money should be distributed among services
Has national electoral mandate	Has local electoral mandate

Source: Based on Rhodes (1988), fig. 2.2, p. 42.

model itself is unsatisfactory in at least two respects. The concept of partnership tends to be left vague and imprecisely defined. It also disregards the constitutional difficulty of Britain being a unitary state, and local government being necessarily, therefore, a subordinate creation of the national Parliament. To circumvent these criticisms, academics have developed an alternative power-dependence model, which postulates that both central departments and local authorities have *resources* – legal, financial, political, informational and so on – that each can use against the other, and against other organisations (see Exhibit 11.6).

The model thus sees power in relative terms, hinging on a process of bargaining and exchange. The central–local relationship certainly isn't evenly balanced, but councils do have significant and exploitable assets of their own: local knowledge and professional expertise, networking and negotiating skills, and above all their position as the elected and concerned representatives of their communities. Its obvious appeal – not least to the presentation in this chapter – is that neither central nor local government are depicted as monolithic blocs. This arguable strength is also, though, one of its alleged weaknesses, and it has been criticised regularly (see, for example, Houlihan, 1988, p. 70; Cochrane, 1993, p. 25) for understating the superior power of central government. It is said to pay insufficient attention to the internal politics of organisations, and insufficient consideration to the broader (capitalist) economic and political system within which these inter-governmental relations take place. Such points should not be disregarded; nor are they by Rhodes (1986), perhaps the most prolific interpreter of the model, who saw it and the conceptual debate it generated as being of sufficient 'continuing relevance' to justify a 'revisit' (Rhodes, 1999, esp. chs 5 and 6).

Policy communities and networks

A limitation of both the agency and power-dependence models is that they are essentially 'bilateral', and therefore fail to embrace the complexities of inter-governmental relations that, as we saw in Chapters 8 and 9, are far wider than a simple central government–local authority axis. Both models focus on institutional or organisational relationships – at the inevitable expense of policy systems, policy communities and policy networks. The main point of studying political and governmental institutions should be to understand in a much better way how they interrelate to make and implement policies.

Our local authorities are multi-service organisations, and 'local authority policy making' – even in the age of cross-sectoral partnerships – still takes place for the most part within service-specific 'policy communities'

Exhibit 11.7 Policy communities

Characteristics of policy communities include:

- A limited number of participants with some groups consciously excluded.
- A dominant economic or professional interest.
- Frequent interaction between all members of the community on all matters related to the policy issues.
- Consistency in values, membership and policy outcomes over time.
- Consensus, with the ideology, values and broad policy preferences shared by all participants.
- Exchange relationships, with all members of the policy community having some resources.
- Bargaining between members with resources.
- The hierarchical distribution of resources within the participating organisations, so that the leaders can guarantee the compliance of their members.

Source: Based on Rhodes (1999), p. 143.

based on education, social services, planning and so on. The power-dependence model could be said to concentrate on the 'national community for local government', while substantially ignoring the multiplicity of other functional policy communities and policy networks.

Policy communities, as defined by Rhodes and Marsh, have the characteristics listed in Exhibit 11.7 (Rhodes, 1999, p. 143). It is easy to see from this listing the thematic continuity with the power-dependence model, and, with its emphasis on professional interests, a direct applicability to the profession-based world of British local government. Policy communities, in short, seem to have a closer congruence than superficially neater models with the complex and messy reality of local governance we have endeavoured to portray.

Chapter 12

Local Finance

Lady Godiva and other myths

One of many myths about local government finance concerns Lady Godiva, whose husband Leofric, Earl of Mercia, agreed to abolish the Heregeld tax on the local peasantry if she rode naked on a white horse through the streets of eleventh-century Coventry. Sadly, killjoy historians reckon that, real persons though they both were, the equestrian bit – and presumably the tax cut – was invented by medieval tourist development officers to attract pilgrims to the city. A more contemporary myth is that most of the money that councils spend is raised locally, through the council tax (Hansard Society, 2010, p. 126). Regularly, the guess – and it almost always is a guess – is between 50% and 70%, with the rest coming from central government. The key purposes of this chapter are to emphasise how the truth is *the precise reverse*, to indicate the consequences of what, from local government's perspective, is a debilitatingly adverse balance of funding, and to reduce the need for some of that guesswork.

The first part of the chapter outlines the basic elements of local finance and budget making. Specifically, it aims to provide information that will help readers interpret and understand their own council tax demands – but, it must be added, mainly readers living in England. Local finance in Scotland, Wales and Northern Ireland is broadly similar to the English system, but, administered as it is almost entirely through the devolved governments, certainly all statistics, unless otherwise indicated, should be taken as referring to England. The remainder of the chapter provides some recent historical and comparative context, not least to enable us to appreciate why, as noted at the start of Chapter 10, a body such as the Congress of Local and Regional Authorities of Europe (CLRAE) should see the system we have been describing as undemocratically centralist.

Your own tax bill

We start with the council tax, introduced by the Major Government in 1993 as a politically necessary replacement for the community charge or poll tax – of which more later. We suggest readers look at their own council tax demand notices and at the accompanying explanatory information

Exhibit 12.1 Some definitions

Billing Authority: A local authority empowered to collect, as well as set, taxes, through the **Collection Fund**. Council Tax is a property tax, and therefore billing authorities are those responsible for housing – shire and metropolitan districts, unitaries and London boroughs (see bottom line of Exhibit 8.1).

Precept: The amount of Council Tax that non-billing **Precepting Authorities** – county, parish, community and town councils, police and joint authorities – can instruct a billing authority to collect and hand over in order to finance their net expenditure.

Budget: A statement defining and costing a council's policies for the forthcoming financial year and beyond.

Finance (or Grant) Settlement: The government's announcement of how much grant funding it will provide for local government as a whole and individual local authorities, and what conditions may be attached.

Revenue (or Current) Expenditure: Used generally, as in 'Revenue Budget', Exhibit 12.3 – the day-to-day spending needed to keep services running: staff wages and salaries, books for schools, office equipment, petrol for refuse collection vehicles, heating bills in children's homes. Technically, **Current Expenditure** is defined as these running costs minus **Capital Financing Costs** or interest paid on loans.

Capital Expenditure: Spending that produces longer-term assets, often expensive, but the benefits of which will last beyond the following financial year: purchase of land, construction of buildings and roads, major items of equipment.

Gross Expenditure: The total cost of providing a council's services, *before* taking into account rents, fees and charges for services, and income from specific government grants.

Net Expenditure: Gross expenditure minus various forms of income – fees, charges and rents set by the local authority, and central government grants.

Capital Receipts: Income from the sale of capital assets.

Capping: A limit placed by the government on a council's budget, and hence on its Council Tax.

Community Charge: The local flat-rate personal tax used by councils from 1990–3; also known as the **Poll Tax,** after similar fourteenth-century flat-rate taxes.

Specific (or Ring-fenced, or Hypothecated) Grants: Central government funds distributed by individual departments to local authorities that must be spent on a specified service or programme. Most significant is the **Dedicated Schools Grant (DSG)**.

General (or Non-selective, or Unhypothecated) Grants: Funds that may be spent at the discretion of the grantees, local authorities themselves. The general **Revenue Support Grant** used to be an authority's largest single source of grant funding, but, with the arrival of DSG, this is no longer the case.

sent out by their council – particularly the details of the council's budget. If, perhaps as a student, you have no tax demand yourself, find one on Google Images, and it will probably lead you to a friendly council website and a much fuller explanation than we have space for here. With luck, you may unearth other goodies, such as a glossary or jargon-buster – a mini-version of which is provided here in Exhibit 12.1.

The vital figure on the tax demand is the amount you or your household are required to pay. Using Birmingham City Council's 2009/10 budget for illustration, this chapter will outline how that figure was calculated. Your council will, though, have provided its own explanation, in the various additional leaflets it sent out with the bill. These will include:

- the budget and spending plans of the *billing authority* that sent the bill, plus, since 2009/10, a summary of its forecast and achieved *efficiency performance*;
- similar information for any *precepting authorities*; and
- details from the billing authority of possible payment methods, appeal procedures, discounts and benefit entitlements.

This information is one of many ways in which local authorities are more open and accountable than central government chooses to be. The Inland Revenue provides no such literature about central government's spending plans with its tax returns.

Current and capital spending

Turning first not to the tax bill itself but to the accompanying budget or council tax leaflet, we encounter immediately some of the terms defined in Exhibit 12.1. *Budgets* are commonly thought of as annual events, but local authorities cannot possibly adopt such a limited time frame. They will plan at least three to five years ahead, and have been greatly assisted by the introduction in 2007 of what they hope becomes an established practice of 3-year, rather than annual, *Finance Settlements*. This brings us to the most fundamental feature of any council's budget: its division – for both legal and accounting reasons – into *revenue/current* and *capital* expenditure. Councils are more constrained than businesses; they can spend revenue account money on capital items, but not vice versa: they cannot, for example, sell off surplus assets to pay staff.

Far more of councils' spending goes on providing day-to-day services than on capital investment – roughly eight times as much in the most recent years (DCLG, 2009f, p. 21, chart 1.5f). Total local government expenditure in England in 2007/8 was just over £150 billion – £130 billion current, £20 billion capital (DCLG, 2009f, p. 2). That's £3,000 per person, and 27% of total public sector spending.

That 8:1 current:capital spending ratio is a key finance statistic, and one that has fluctuated greatly, and with great consequences. Throughout the late 1960s, the ratio was less than 2:1. For every £1 of councils' current spending, more than 50p was being invested in infrastructure for the provision of improved services in the future. In the 1970s the ratio started to rise, mainly because of relentless pressure by central governments on councils to limit their capital spending: 3:1 by the mid-1970s, 5:1 by 1980, at least 8:1 through the 1980s and 1990s, and peaking at 12:1 in 1999/2000. Ever-increasing private affluence alongside evidently growing public squalor, as J. K. Galbraith, the renowned American economist and author of *The Affluent Society* (1958), might have observed.

Under the 2001 and 2005 Labour Governments in particular, that trend was reversed in respect of both the NHS and local government. But how relatively small a step that reversal represented can be appreciated from Derek Wanless's 2002 Treasury study of the long-term financial needs of the NHS. He calculated that the cumulative under-investment in the NHS between 1972 and 1998, compared to the European average, had been a massive £267 billion (Wanless, 2002, p. 37). A rough calculation for local government services suggests at least as great an investment loss. If the current:capital ratio had been maintained from 1980 to 2000, not at the 1960s' 2:1, but at the 1970s' 3:1, there would, in today's money, have been at least an extra £200 billion of capital investment in England alone in each of the two decades. With the 2010 Comprehensive Spending Review cutting local authority capital funding by the equivalent of 45% by 2014–15, that investment shortfall can only increase.

As would be expected, the current:capital ratios of the major local government services reflect their very differing characters. Education, the police and social services are labour-intensive, with ratios of 10:1, 12:1 and 20:1, respectively; housing, by contrast, has a 3:1 ratio, while in highways and transport capital spending exceeds current (DCLG, 2009f, p. 3, chart K.2a).

If we followed strictly our own rationale, we would now move straight to current spending – the part of their budget leaflet of greatest concern to taxpayers and the topic that gets the bulk of councillors' attention. It will be our chief concern too, but we look first at councils' capital spending programmes, because they are the embodiment of any council's longer-term political and strategic objectives. They are financed very differently from current spending; and, once started, they can have major implications for subsequent years' current budgets.

Financing capital spending – major reform

We noted above how central governments have sought continuously to regulate local authorities' capital spending. In recent years, central government maintained tight control over three of the four main methods of capital financing: borrowing, capital receipts and capital grants. These capital constraints were resented by local government just as much as the similarly strict controls over current spending, and their relaxation in 2004 was the most important local finance reform the Labour Government had thus far introduced. Sadly, it was still the most important when the Labour Government left office in 2010.

Borrowing – welcome to Prudence

Until 2004, if a local authority wanted to borrow to finance any project whose cost would be spread over several years, it had to obtain a ministerial *Credit Approval*. These Approvals specified the maximum sums the council could borrow for investment purposes: not the maximum sum of a government interest-free loan or any other kind of loan, but the maximum that this elected and accountable body was permitted to borrow at competitive interest rates on the open market.

It took time, but eventually the Labour Government was persuaded to treat local authorities a little less like irresponsible children and entrust them in the 2003 Local Government Act with a *Prudential System*. Local authorities, provided they can service the debt themselves, may now borrow up to a level that *they* calculate they can afford, using a CIPFA Prudential Code. A little misleadingly, it appears in the budget not as 'prudential', but as *unsupported*, borrowing, because limited government assistance to cover borrowing costs is still available in the form of *Supported Capital Expenditure (Revenue)*. There is, of course, a government reserve power to impose borrowing ceilings, but the system itself encourages responsibility by forcing a council to consider value for money, its future revenue streams, and council tax implications at the time of borrowing, in a way that Credit Approvals did not.

Prudential borrowing has several benefits. Like CAA, it emphasises outcomes: councils focus on the outcomes they want to achieve, rather than on the inputs they were told they could afford. They can undertake self-financing investment – extending a leisure centre, for example, that will both earn additional income and create local employment. It also offers an alternative to councils who are wary of PFI deals (see pp. 163–5), and would prefer to own their assets, rather than pay for their use through annual revenue payments to a private sector partner. Larger authorities in particular seized the new opportunity, and for some it has become their largest source of capital finance. Birmingham, for example, modernised its National Exhibition Centre; Cornwall replaced three Torpoint ferries; and others renovated or built new schools, libraries and residential homes, and improved their housing stock. The biggest project by far, though, was Transport for London's £2.9 billion bond issue to finance station and line improvements, which sounded great unless one saw it cynically as the shifting of some of the massive pre-Olympic transport investment costs from the Treasury to London tax- and fare-payers (Gosling, 2004).

Capital receipts

Second, councils can finance capital spending through selling assets such as land, buildings and housing. Again, though, before 2004, governments limited the proportions of these receipts – 25% from housing sales and 50% from sales of other assets – that were 'usable' to fund new capital investment. Remaining receipts had to be 'set aside' to pay off outstanding debts. No part of a receipt now has to be set aside, though there is instead a *pooling system,* requiring local authorities to pay the government a proportion of the capital receipts from asset sales. As the saying goes: what the right hand giveth, the left hand taketh away at least a portion.

Capital grants

Up to a third of local authorities' capital spending – the biggest single fraction – is funded from the capital grants available from central government, other public bodies and private developers. Central government's in recent years have been predominantly specific or ring-fenced – for example, Sure Start, Early Years and Childcare; Building Schools for the Future; Homelessness; and AIDS/HIV – until the new Coalition Government decisively reversed the trend and removed the ring-fencing from almost £1 billion of non-schools capital grants. The National Lottery's grants database – accessible on the Department for Culture, Media and Sport website – categorises all its funding by local authority area, rather than institution, but some goes directly to the authorities themselves – for example, much of the £155 million distributed under the Big Lottery's Children's Play Initiative.

Then there is the EU, over a third of whose budget is distributed through its Structural Funds – the European Regional Development Fund (ERDF) and European Social Fund (ESF) – much of it to local government. ERDF grants in particular can be crucial to the viability of major developments – Birmingham's International Convention Centre and Symphony Hall, Cornwall's Eden Project near St Austell and Liverpool's King's Dock. The largest authorities therefore have long had their own Brussels offices, and many now have EU units dedicated to European working.

Revenue resources

As mentioned above, councils can also finance capital spending through revenue resources – the Housing Revenue Account for council housing maintenance and the General Fund Account for other services. In recent years, some councils have required their major directorates to set aside some of their revenue budget specifically to fund the structural maintenance of their building stock. But, like most other capital sources, this one too is bound to come under severe pressure from 2011/12, further constraining local authorities' ability to invest (London Councils, 2010, p. 6).

The capital budget

Councils' capital budgets can vary even more than their revenue budgets – from each other, obviously, but also from year to year, as has become very apparent with three-year Finance Settlements. Birmingham's 2009/10 capital budget (see Exhibit 12.2) is summarised here not for its typicality, but simply to illustrate some features to look for in your own authority's budget statement.

Current or revenue spending

How much to spend? On what? Where is the money coming from? The three basic questions just asked of our council's capital budget apply similarly to its much larger revenue budget. In fact, the answers should be more easily obtainable, as the main purpose of the tax demand literature is to present the council's revenue budget: its planned expenditure on day-to-day services in the coming financial year. Like everything else, budget leaflets vary from council to council, but you should find some figures set out under service or cabinet portfolio headings that resemble Birmingham's in Exhibit 12.3, even if the figures themselves are on a rather different scale.

We see from the first expenditure column of Exhibit 12.3 that the Council proposed to spend a total of nearly £3.4 billion in 2009/10 on its current service provision. Traditionally, by far the biggest slice of the budget of any local authority responsible for education was spent on precisely that: *education.* In these days of huge multi-service directorates, traditional budget headings such as 'Schools' or 'Education' are hidden away inside the Children, Young People and Families portfolio. A little digging, however, reveals that they occupy almost as dominant a place as ever. In Birmingham, schools' budgets, even tightly defined at £815 million, accounted for nearly a quarter of the authority's gross spending, and teachers' salaries alone took 17%. The big change has been in the funding of those budgets. After deducting income from fees and charges, most of the 'gross' figure would previously have appeared in the 'net' column, and had to compete with all the other services' claims for funding out of the council's large but general Revenue Support Grant. The arrival of the Dedicated Schools Grant (DSG)

Exhibit 12.2 Headlines from Birmingham's capital budget, 2009/10

1 Thanks to the 3-year finance settlement, the Council set a budget for 2009/10, and **provisional budgets** for the next two financial years.

2 The 2009/10 capital budget totalled **£549 million** – about **one-sixth** of the gross revenue budget (see Exhibit 12.3). This current-capital ratio of 6:1 was unusually low, because capital spending was unusually high (see item 5 below). The following two years' more typical budgets were for £430 and £437 million.

3 **Main sources of funding** for the 2009/10 budget: unsupported/prudential borrowing 42%; capital grants 25%; capital receipts 12%; supported borrowing 11%.

4 **Main areas of spending**: Housing 30%; Transportation and street services 16%; Children, Young People and Families 12%; Other 40% – see below.

5 Like many local authorities, though on a larger scale, Birmingham is engaged in a long-term **business transformation programme** – in partnership with the multinational business software suppliers Systems Applications and Products (SAP) – which is designed to increase the council's efficiency, improve the quality of its services, and save £670 million over a 10-year period. The year 2009/10 was a peak investment year, and therefore the biggest single capital allocation after housing (£164 million) was £142 million to the Deputy Leader's budget, to invest in new IT systems and redesign business processes. It was anticipated that borrowing costs would be met out of the future savings.

6 Other major investment programmes included £219 million over the 3-year period to maintain council housing at or above the Government's Decent Homes Standard; £193 million, mainly in 2011/12, for the building of a new central library; and substantial contributions towards the redevelopment of New Street Station, regeneration schemes in South Birmingham and Eastside, and the rebuilding or refurbishment of all secondary schools under the government's Building Schools for the Future programme.

Source: Compiled by the authors from Birmingham City Council (2009).

in 2006 ended all that. Now the council receives the DSG, covering all the £815 million and in fact a bit more. The 'schools' figure in the 'net' column virtually disappears, and the whole sum is distributed to the city's schools – regardless of any views councillors might have had about the relative priority schools education should have in this particular year.

Next biggest spender looks to be the Deputy Leader, but having a half-million-pound budget is not necessarily as empowering as you might suppose. From the local authority's viewpoint, it is as unempowering as the

Exhibit 12.3 Birmingham City Council's revenue budget and council tax, 2009/10

MAJOR SERVICES – by Cabinet portfolio/committee	Staff head count	Expenditure and Income (£ million)		
		Gross	Income	Net
Leader – incl. NEC, Convention Centre, Indoor Arena	800	174	121	53
Deputy Leader – incl. council tax and housing benefits	1,900	522	447	75
Adults and Communities – incl. older people, disabled	6,100	365	76	289
Children, Young People and Families – incl. schools	34,500	1,405	1,124	281
Equalities and Human Resources	600	17	11	6
Housing: General Fund – all services excl. council housing	400	106	91	15
Housing Revenue Account – council housing only	1,500	221	221	0
Leisure, Sport and Culture – incl. libraries, museums, parks	1,200	69	17	52
Local Services and Community Safety	300	113	104	9
Regeneration – incl. employment creation, business support	900	71	55	16
Transportation and Street Services – incl. refuse collection	2,000	160	70	90
COMMITTEES:				
Constituencies – 10 local committees with devolved budgets	3,300	118	18	100
Council Business Management	100	9	–	9
Regulatory – Public Protection, Planning, Licensing	700	32	15	17
TOTAL PORTFOLIO/COMMITTEE EXPENDITURE	(54,300)	3,383	2,372	1,011
Less: Capital financing costs, etc.				(41)
Plus: Contingencies (12), contribution to general balances (2)				14
COUNCIL'S NET BUDGET REQUIREMENT				984
Less: Formula Grant = Redistributed National Non-Domestic Rates (NNDR)				(536)
+ Revenue Support Grant (RSG)				(124)
REQUIRED FROM COLLECTION FUND				324
(Equals: 8% of Council's gross and 32% of net spending)				
Plus: West Midlands Joint Police Authority precept				29
Plus: West Midlands Fire Service precept				14
REQUIRED FROM COUNCIL TAX PAYERS				367
(Equals: Band D Council Tax of £1,238)				

Source: Birmingham City Council (2009).

ring-fenced DSG is disempowering. In both cases, the authority acts essentially as a local post office, passing on central government funding to recipients, as instructed from Whitehall – in this case, from the Department for Work and Pensions. Nearly four-fifths of the Deputy Leader's gross budget consists of *Council Tax Benefits* and *Housing Benefits* – rent rebates for council tenants, and rent allowances for private tenants – claimable by those on low incomes, according to rules set by the DWP but administered by local authorities.

The second biggest 'real' spender, therefore – in the sense of it having a major budget over which councillors can have a real say – is what until recently was known as *social services*, but which, as noted in Chapter 8 (see pp. 135–6), is now split between Children's and, usually, Adult and Community Services. There are some sizeable specific grants here too – to Early Years and Child Care, Lifelong Learning and Adults with a Learning Disability – but in Adult Services 'fees and charges' represent the biggest single income source to be set off against gross spending, and they amount to only 15% of the total. The result, as seen in Exhibit 12.3, is that Children's and Adult Services now take more than half of the council's net budget, the burden of which falls ultimately on council taxpayers. But what if central government grant funding is cut – as it will be from 2011/12 by 7% a year in real terms – and councils decide, or have it decided for them, that their council tax should be frozen? What, then, would happen to these supposedly statutory services?

Statutory, mandatory or discretionary?

We're quite keen on the dark cloud/silver lining approach to life, and, while councils themselves may be sceptical, there *are* silver linings to be glimpsed through the gathering clouds of threatened service cuts. There should be an increase in public consultation about council budget choices and priorities, if not in real participatory budgeting (see below) – in the course of which residents and voters may learn more about what their local authorities do and the services they currently provide. Councils may also start to do something that very few have done in the past: give some indications in their budgets of which expenditures are statutory – and therefore genuinely uncuttable – and which are discretionary. It is less straightforward than it might sound, but several councils have made commendable attempts (for example, Buckinghamshire CC, Havant BC and Breckland DC), and their examples should be followed.

The chief complication is that many major services – such as social services – are neither wholly statutory nor wholly discretionary. 'Statutory' sounds obvious – the council has to do it because it's the law. But, as noted at the start of Chapter 8, that law often just sets the framework for the provision of a new government service, with local authorities – if they are the designated providers – being left considerable discretion over both the level and organisation of the provision. 'Mandatory' provision is different again: regardless of the actual law, a council provides a service, or provides it to a certain standard, because not to do so would leave it open to possible legal challenge (Buckinghamshire CC, 2009, para. 12). Only then come the wholly discretionary services. It is a long list, even for a 'lower-tier' borough council such as Havant, but it includes some of the services that many local residents might see as being among the most important to their daily lives: community and leisure centres, free swimming sessions, play schemes, elderly health programmes, crime prevention, street lighting, markets, jobseeker support, parks maintenance, meals-on-wheels and public conveniences (Havant BC, n.d.).

In Birmingham's budget it is easy to see where these discretionary services are mainly located, and where future budgetary pressures are almost bound to pinch most painfully – in Leisure, Sport and Culture, Local Services and Community Safety, and Transportation and Street Services. In a two-tier system it is also worryingly easy: district councils have a disproportionate share. Schools are protected by their dedicated grant; children's services by their huge political and media profile; and adult services by their vocal, and voting, users. Planning and development control, housing and homelessness, environmental health and refuse collection can present themselves as being substantially statutory, or at least mandatory. But if a service is 'only' discretionary, it is vulnerable.

Precepts

Identifying the council's net spending requirements is just the first step in determining an individual's local tax bill. To the council-provided services listed in Exhibit 12.3 must be added the services provided by precepting bodies. In Birmingham – and the other six West Midlands Metropolitan districts – the two bodies whose precepts are separately identified on the council tax demand are:

- *The West Midlands Joint Police Authority* – now a separate Authority of 17 members: 9 councillors nominated by the district councils and 8 Independent members, including local magistrates, selected by the Police Authority and the Home Office. It receives a Home Office Police Grant, plus (like the City Council) a formula grant, that between them cover about three-quarters of net revenue expenditure.
- *The West Midlands Fire and Rescue Authority* – a joint board of 27 councillors nominated by their district councils. Its 2009/10 formula grant met two-thirds of its net expenditure.

These Authorities have their own capital and revenue budgets, the latter funded mainly through specific and formula grants. But they must fund the balance of their revenue budget through a *precept* on their tax-collecting district councils, divided among them according to their population size. These councils therefore have to collect from their local taxpayers, in addition to their own tax demands, these other monies, and then hand them straight over to the precepting authorities.

Birmingham's *total* net revenue requirement thus included, in 2009/10, £43 million that it had to collect, but over which it had no direct control (see Exhibit 12.3). This obligation can be irritating to councillors, who may have battled hard to keep down their own tax levels, only to have to take political responsibility for a level inflated by spending they were quite unable to influence. But their irritation is mild compared to that of some of their shire district council colleagues. For they have to collect a county council precept that may amount to at least 80% of their total tax demands, plus, in some cases, an additional few pounds in parish council precepts.

It is a built-in tension in the remaining two-tier parts of our local government system that it is not the English counties – with their bigger-spending education, social services and transport responsibilities – that are designated billing and tax-collecting authorities. The council tax is a property tax, and therefore most obviously collected by the local housing authorities, the much smaller and lower spending district councils (see Exhibit 8.1). This position will almost certainly be emphasised by district councils in their budget literature. Just look, they may say, at all the housing, leisure, environmental and community services we provide to enhance your quality of life, and all for the cost of a weekly cinema ticket.

Financing current spending

There are two final 'technical' adjustments to be made to the spending side of our council's revenue account, though both have clear political implications and should therefore involve councillors. It must be decided how much to set aside for any 'contingencies' – higher-than-anticipated inflation, flooding, a harsh winter necessitating winter gritting and additional road maintenance – and how much to keep as balances or reserves. With those adjustments made, Birmingham City Council's *total net spending requirement* for 2009/10 amounted to a formidable £984 million, or about £977 per resident. The obvious next question, then, is: where is it to be found? There is a kind of symmetry to British local government finance. We identified four main methods of raising capital finance, and there are four main ways of funding revenue spending.

Charges

Local authorities have always set fees and charges for the use of some serv-ices – passenger transport, car parks, home helps, school meals, leisure facilities and burials. They also collect housing rents. The 1989 Local Government and Housing Act enabled them to charge for any services apart from education, police and fire, elections and library book borrowing – part of the Conservatives' programme to increase local accountability by making consumers more directly aware of the cost and value of public services. In Birmingham's case, fees and charges in 2009/10 met 11% of the council's gross current expenditure – more than council tax – and housing rents a further 6.5%.

Most charges are discretionary, with councils deciding for themselves what to charge, or what they feel the market will bear. They can encourage the use of a service, such as adult education classes or day nurseries, by setting a *social* charge, below the full cost of provision. They can *just* cover the provision cost; impose a *means-related* charge based on ability to pay, as for some residential homes; or a *market* charge to maximise profit. Finally, they can try to limit the use of certain services, such as city centre car parks or cemetery burials, by imposing a *deterrent* charge.

Such decisions – for example, whether to subsidise a particular service, by how much and in what way, or whether to try to maximise profit – raise fundamental political questions. Quite properly, they offer councillors a ready-made subject for debate whenever charges and a council's charging policy come up for review. Different economic, social and political objec-tives will be argued, and sometimes intriguing policy decisions taken – which is why your council's Fees and Charges booklet is one of its few publications that you might just possibly contemplate for bedside reading.

Even the charges for standard services – car parking, leisure centres, refuse collection and public conveniences – can raise interesting issues, espe-cially if you know the area or can compare with other councils' policies. Why do some councils encourage their senior citizens to swim and exercise, while others extort as much as possible from them? Does your council charge for children's burials? Or sell composters and wormeries? More recondite services can be even more fascinating. Do car boot sale charges include the use of mobile toilets, or are they, as it were, a hidden extra? Why is the treatment of bedbugs and cockroaches more expensive than wasp and hornet nests? Does your council's dangerous wild animals licensing policy discriminate between vertebrates and invertebrates? As with the Audit Commission (2008, p. 15), you are likely to find that 'even very similar councils have very different approaches to charging' – evidence that, in this sphere at least, councils have by no means been stripped of all powers of decision and discretion. However, faced with possible spending cuts of up to 30% in the coming few years, that discretion is going to be tested to extremes, and all councils will find themselves considering charges, or higher charges, for services previously considered 'protected'.

Government grants

Grants, like charges, are a long-standing feature of local government finance, but we have already noted some significant changes in recent years. In previous editions, this chapter's concern with the budget process meant it focused mainly on one particular grant: the general *Revenue Support Grant* (RSG), which in Birmingham in 2005/6 provided 31% of the Council's gross revenue income, compared to 27% from specific grants (Wilson and Game, 2006, Exhibits 10.2 and 10.4). In 2009/10 the overall proportion of grant income had fallen slightly – from 58% to 54% – but, mainly through the introduction of the Dedicated Schools Grant, what now are termed *special and specific grants* had increased to 50%, while RSG had dropped to under 4%. At £124 million, it is hardly negligible, but nor is it the pivotal statistic around which the whole budget process for so long revolved. The change illustrates the different motives central government can have for paying grants to local authorities – most commonly, compensation or persuasion – and the way a grant's form will generally indicate its purpose.

Councils may be *compensated* for providing certain services that are acknowledged to be in the public interest and for which, therefore, local taxpayers should not have to foot the whole bill. In such cases, specific grants will ensure the money is spent exclusively on its intended purpose or recipients – for example, the Rural Bus Subsidy, asylum seekers, child and adolescent mental health services, and AIDS support. Councils are compensated too for their widely varying spending needs and taxable resources. Thus the *formula grant*, of which the RSG is now a part, is allocated through a formula that compensates authorities with adverse demographic and socio-economic characteristics, and local property profiles that limit the amount that can be raised in council tax. The rationale of the RSG is that local authorities should be able, and incentivised, to provide a common standard of service at broadly the same cost to local taxpayers across the whole country, but decisions as to precisely how this compensatory funding is spent should be left to democratically elected and accountable councillors.

The *persuasion* motive for grants can be seen as a straightforward wish by central government to influence some aspect of local spending: those who pay the piper expect to call the tune. Grants can be used to promote spending on certain services, to enforce minimum standards, to encourage councils to implement central government policy initiatives, and generally to push them in directions they otherwise might not go. As noted in relation to capital income, there was a trend in recent years for specific grants to increase as a proportion of central government funding, ministers of both main parties being keen to ensure that local spending reflected as closely as possible their national policy goals. The Dedicated Schools Grant was the extreme case, restricting significantly further the ability of councillors to pursue local priorities either in education or between education and other competing services.

Then along came Coalition Chancellor of the Exchequer, George Osborne, with, in the 2010 Comprehensive Spending Review, a grandstanding handbrake turn. In what he claimed as a 'dramatic shift in the balance of power between the centre and localities', he promised to remove the ring-fencing from all revenue grants from 2011/12, with the exceptions of local health, schools and policing, thereby cutting the funding streams to a local authority from a potential 90 to a maximum of 10. It reminded some observers of an old *Yes, Minister*-ish saying – 'Governments with money centralise and claim the credit; those without decentralise and spread the blame' – but a dramatic shift it undoubtedly was.

In recent years, the three-year Finance Settlement and the reduced importance of RSG have removed most of the drama from the event that, generally in December for the financial year starting the following April, used to be effectively local government's Budget Day. The relevant minister announced the total funding local government would have for that year, and anxious council treasurers would then calculate their own authorities' shares, principally in the form of RSG, and the consequences for the spending plans and eventual council tax that their councillors would be determining in their budget discussions. But if some of the drama has gone, the essential nature and significance of the process remain, as does its capacity to infuriate local authorities that feel they have been particularly, often uniquely, disadvantaged by the distribution 'formula'.

Councils in the South East claim the formula makes insufficient allowance for the higher costs of providing services and for the growing numbers of older people requiring intensive care. Those in popular tourist areas claim they are inadequately compensated under the national concessionary bus travel scheme for the elderly and infirm. Inner city councils argue that the formula's age and deprivation top-up for 'supported residents aged 90 and over' should recognise that older people living in urban areas require additional care earlier in their life cycle. Sometimes the special pleading works, sometimes not, but councils are bound to try – because grant distribution formulae are not value-neutral mathematical equations, but strings of weighted factors and indicators, almost every one of which has political, and usually party political, implications.

National Non-Domestic Rate/Uniform Business Rate

The third source of councils' revenue income is the second principal component, with RSG, of the formula grant: the *National Non-Domestic Rate*

(NNDR) or, as it is also known, the *Uniform* (*not* Unified, Unitary or Universal!) *Business Rate* (UBR). This came into operation in 1989/90, at the same time as the community charge – though with nothing like the same public outcry, despite being arguably the more constitutionally significant of the two tax reforms.

For almost 400 years, the one local tax available to UK local authorities had been a property tax, known as *the rates*. Its principles and administration were simple, which is one reason why some kind of property tax is to be found in most developed systems of local government (see Exhibit 12.6). Every property in the area – houses, flats, shops, offices and factories – was given a valuation: its *rateable value*. Each year, the council would calculate how much it needed to collect, in addition to the grant it would receive, to pay for the services it wished to provide, and would set an appropriate *rate poundage*: so much to be paid per £1 of each property's rateable value. Domestic ratepayers paid a slightly lower rate poundage than business ratepayers, because the government would pay a compensating subsidy for these to the local council.

In 1989 in Scotland and 1990 in England and Wales this whole system changed. Domestic rates were abolished and replaced by the *community charge*. Northern Ireland alone retained its rating system. The non-domestic rate was not abolished, but nationalised: hence the *National* Non-Domestic Rate. Now, each year, the government sets a uniform rate poundage for *all* non-domestic properties in England, and the devolved governments do the same in Scotland and Wales. Billing authorities continue to send out bills and collect the rates, but these are now paid into a central pool and redistributed to both billing and precepting councils on the same basis as RSG, with the payments being regarded as what they have become: another government grant. Former local ratepayers are now national tax-payers, and there is no longer any direct tax-paying link between local authorities and the businesses in their area – a development that even some business people regard as regrettable.

In 1989/90, non-domestic rates provided over a quarter of local government revenue income: more than that from domestic rates (see Exhibit 12.7(b)). At a stroke, therefore, local councils saw the proportion of their income they themselves controlled fall from over a half to barely a quarter: a fraction that was soon to decline even further.

Local taxation – the council tax

It will be obvious by now that the final source of councils' revenue income is their own local taxation: traditionally the rates, then the community charge, and since 1993 the *council tax*. Whereas rates were a tax on property, the community charge/poll tax was a tax on the individual: a flat-rate tax payable by most adults over 18. The council tax combines the two. It is

Exhibit 12.4 The council tax: key features

WHAT IS IT?	A tax on domestic property, not people, but with a personal element. There is one bill per household, with a 25% discount for single-person households and certain other property.
HOW MUCH?	Depends first on your property's valuation by the Valuation Office Agency. All properties were placed in one of 8 bands, A to H, in a fixed relationship with each other – A:D:H = 2:3:6. Band A, the lowest band, is for properties valued in 1991 at less than £40,000 in England, less than £27,000 in Scotland, and less than £30,000 in Wales. Band H, the highest band, is for properties valued in 1991 at over, respectively, £320,000 (England), £212,000 (Scotland), and £240,000 (Wales). Only Wales has revalued – in 2005 – stretching the bands and adding a Band I for properties over £424,000.
WHO SETS IT?	Each local authority, though in two-tier England, billing and collection are the responsibility of the district alone.
EXEMPTIONS?	Apply only to property, mainly if unoccupied – plus halls of residence, flats, houses occupied solely by students.
DISCOUNTS?	Relate to numbers and types of occupants, *not* ability to pay; 25% discounts for single householders; 50% discounts for under-18s, full-time students, apprentices and some carers. Most controversially, second-home owners: 10–50% discount at the council's discretion.
REBATES?	Up to 100% for taxpayers on low incomes.
WHO IS LIABLE?	The resident, aged over 18, with the strongest legal interest in the property.
NON-PAYMENT?	As with poll tax non-payment: appearance in magistrates' court, liability order issued by court, attempted recovery of money by council, imprisonment for up to 3 months (not in Scotland).
REGISTERS?	Unlike poll tax, no specific register required.
CAPPING?	Capping powers retained by Labour Government; reactivated in 2004/5.
NON-DOMESTIC RATES?	Still the 'nationalised' system introduced in 1989/90. Labour's pledge to relocalise reversed when in government.
IS IT FAIR?	No – and gets unfairer by the year. Inherently regressive: those in lower bands pay far higher proportion of their income than those in higher bands. Especially tough on fixed incomes – e.g. pensioners. Valuations massively outdated – average UK property price in January 2010: £165,000; London: £336,000.
THE FUTURE?	Who knows? Promised 2007 revaluation postponed indefinitely, first by Labour, then by Coalition. Likewise, Lib Dems' hopes for a local income tax. Lyons Inquiry thought system 'not broken', so no major reform needed, but in the medium term a revaluation and extension of bands. Coalition planned to abolish capping and replace with referendums triggered by councils raising council tax above levels set by ministers.

Figure 12.1 *Cartoon – Council tax assessment*

Source: Local Government Information Unit, *LGIU Briefing*, No. 55, December 1991.

a domestic property tax, but with the size of the bill depending partly on the number of residents as well as on the property's value, since taxpayers living alone get at least a 25% reduction, regardless of income (see Exhibit 12.4). Another difference from the rates is that each home is assigned to one of eight property bands, which in England have remained unchanged since the original 1991 valuation. This absence of reform justifies our recycling an old cartoon (see Figure 12.1) – though it misleadingly suggests a more rigorous exercise than actually took place. In fact, it was undertaken at such speed that it was tagged a 'drive-by' or 'second-gear valuation', with usually local estate agents driving up and down streets in second gear, giving approximate values to whole areas at a time.

As a policy failure, the Thatcher Government's introduction of the poll tax in 1989/90 was the domestic equivalent of the Blair Government's invasion of Iraq, with similar longer-term socially divisive effects. There were mass protests, marches and demonstrations – which were dismissed by the government, as in the similar situation over Iraq. It had huge and mainly damaging effects on many people's personal finances (see below), and brought not one but two major upheavals for council officers responsible for its administration and collection, with the number of tax bills sent out being first doubled and then halved within five years. But purely from the narrow viewpoint of a council's annual budget process, the key decisions remained essentially the same throughout all the changes.

The tax levied is still the final residual outcome of a process in which all the other elements are now known: your own council's spending plans, those of any precepting authorities, the amount you will receive in specific grants, fees and charges, the income you will get from the NNDR pool, your RSG. The sum outstanding has to come from the council's own local council taxpayers since, unlike their counterparts in most other countries, British local authorities have access to only the one local tax.

The last point is hugely important to the budgetary discretion of local authorities. An authority with access to several different local taxes, paid by different groups of taxpayers, has more options at its disposal than one forced to rely on a single tax and a single group of taxpayers. In most developed countries that is precisely what happens. Japanese prefectures and municipalities, for example, have taxes on residents, consumption (sales), enterprise (businesses), automobiles and their purchase, tobacco, property purchase, light oil delivery, mini-cars and motorcycles, and, if they have them, hot springs. New York's mayor has four major taxes – on property, personal income and general sales, plus a general corporation tax – and a fistful of minor ones, including a hotel tax, utility tax, commercial rent tax and property transfer tax. It may be, as Hambleton suggests (2005, p. 23), that such lists offer 'too many tax options for local politicians', but he is emphatic that this situation is greatly preferable to the situation in Britain: 'Compare this with the UK, where the council has only one tax – generating a small fraction of revenue spending. And, incredibly, even that is subject to capping by central government. Effective local leadership cannot be expected to prosper in such a constrained setting.'

Capping

Picking up Hambleton's observation, it could be argued that genuine local tax choice has in recent years been removed completely from British councils. In 1984, the Rates Act curtailed local authorities' already limited discretion still further through the capping process. The Act gave local government ministers the power to cap – that is, impose a statutory ceiling on – the planned budget or council tax of *any* local authority, and any police, or fire and rescue, authority that is, in *their* view, excessive; also the power to cap *all* authorities' budgets and taxes collectively.

Initially, Conservative ministers used their new power *selectively*, devising criteria each year that enabled them to pick out a dozen or so (mostly Labour) councils whose proposed budgets and rates they would then reduce. With the poll tax, though, capping rapidly moved from selective to *universal*, applying to all councils apart from parishes, with the capping criteria – maximum percentage budget increases – being announced *in advance*, in the Finance Settlement along with the other grant details. Each council thus knew, before it made its key budget decisions, exactly how much it would be permitted to spend and to raise from its own local taxpayers. Most then used these figures in effect as guidelines, and spent and taxed at their government-determined levels, which was both easier and cheaper than running the risk of being capped and having to prepare and mail out a completely new set of tax demands.

To local authorities of all political colours this universal capping was probably more offensive than the community charge/poll tax itself. It amounted to the government setting a spending ceiling for every council in the country, leaving locally elected councillors in the position of having the framework of their budgets, if not their detailed content, determined for them. Labour, having vehemently opposed the whole principle of capping in the 1980s, promised in its 1997 election manifesto that it would go – but not completely. 'Crude and universal capping' would be replaced by what presumably has to be described as discriminating and selective capping, as Labour ministers would 'retain reserve powers to control excessive council tax increases' – increases, that is, that they, rather than local politicians, voters or taxpayers, judged to be excessive.

This change came in the Local Government Act 1999, but received little attention until, in 2004/5, ministers decided to 'protect' the taxpayers of five councils by capping what they decreed – without having previously announced any criteria of acceptability – were 'unacceptable' tax increases being proposed by their councils. The following year's tax announcements coincided with the run-up to the 2005 General Election and local elections, and, in what was certainly interpretable as party electioneering, ministers capped the budgets and tax rises of eight councils – none with any record of wanton extravagance, and seven of which just happened to be Conservative.

The councils' proposed tax rises did breach the government's declared 5% threshold, but, significantly, all eight were districts. All therefore had modest-sized budgets, and most, even with their new tax yields, would still have had spending and tax levels below the national average. But ministers had spoken, and the councils were consequently – if nonsensically – forced to spend *additional* tens of thousands of pounds to mail out new tax bills and handle the associated administration, for what in one case was a 'saving' of under 10p per household per week.

One council, South Cambridgeshire DC, was so incensed that it applied for judicial review (see pp. 174–5) on the above grounds, plus the fact that 60% of respondents to the Council's own survey had supported the tax rise. Furthermore, the same government department that was capping its spending was also telling the Council to plan for a 33% population increase over the coming ten years. The application was, almost inevitably, denied, but the High Court judge expressed his personal sympathy and pronounced that the Council 'is not profligate. It is low spending and has given cogent reasons for the proposed increase in council tax'. But the law permitted ministers to act in the way they had – the law that is part of the framework of the most centrally dictated local financial system in Western Europe. The abolition of capping was one of the few short-term reforms proposed by the Lyons Inquiry in 2007, but ministers rejected it almost instantly and have continued to cap selectively – though almost all councils now just accept the nature of the regime and budget within what they guess will be the eventual criteria.

Budget consultation, participatory budgeting and tax referendums

As Birmingham's budget process neared completion, a couple of consultation meetings were held with representatives of the city's businesses and trade unions. Some previous administrations had made slightly more energetic efforts to convene meetings of local residents in an attempt to learn, more informally and discursively than in a 'tick-box' statistical survey, what their spending and service priorities were. But, with few exceptions, these gatherings were sparsely attended and not very productive, They were a world away, in every sense, from Porto Alegre.

Porto Alegre (or Happy Harbour, as we like to think of it) is a large city in Southern Brazil, credited with the invention, in the 1980s, of Participatory Budgeting (PB). PB started as one element in a more comprehensive reform programme to bring basic amenities to the most deprived sections of the city, and today involves tens of thousands of citizens coming together in large public assemblies to discuss and elect delegates, who then work with councillors and city officials to build, as much as possible, the city's annual budget from the bottom up. The PB concept, if not always the strongly democratic Porto Alegre model, spread across Latin America and has been taken up in Africa, Asia, and latterly the US and some European countries. Britain's insularity predisposes its citizens to disparage such innovations – what can a poor Brazilian city *possibly* teach us? – but there is now a PB Unit in the DCLG, thanks partly to the charity, Church Action on Poverty, and even a PB strategy (see www.participatorybudgeting.org.uk).

Most so-called PB projects are based around the devolution of relatively small community grants to neighbourhoods, council wards, or sometimes individual councillors, with residents voting on projects they would like to see adopted, and it may be that this 'community pot' model is better suited to our political culture than trying to persuade large numbers of residents to involve themselves actively in shaping their council's mainstream budget. At the same time, 'budgeting' properly involves weighing competing service priorities and their respective tax implications against each other, with, ideally, the decided package being put before voters in a proper election. The content is bigger than a 'community pot', and the process should be bigger than a referendum aimed simply at vetoing a proposed percentage council tax increase – a discredited idea of Michael Heseltine's from the early 1980s that the Conservatives revived, included in their 2010 manifesto, and that has subsequently become Coalition policy.

Under the Coalition proposals, any council from 2012/13 setting its council tax increase above a centrally set ceiling – set not by ministers, though, but 'approved in a democratic and transparent manner by Parliament' – would trigger an automatic referendum of all registered electors. They would then choose between the proposed rise and a 'shadow budget', which the council must also prepare within the defined limit. A 'No' vote would leave councils having to refund taxpayers or give a credit at the end of the tax year. Communities Secretary Eric Pickles introduced the scheme as a radical extension of direct democracy, making councils directly accountable to the local taxpayer. Others struggled to grasp how centrally driven referendums for councils exceeding centrally determined tax thresholds, paid for by those same councils and their taxpayers, furthered the government's commitments to localism and value for money.

Budget setting – managing the margins

Local budgeting, for local councillors and officers, has inevitably become an exercise in what Elcock *et al.* (1989) termed 'managing the margins' – the very tightly defined margins left to local councils' discretion, once ministers have taken all the major decisions on total spending, grant distribution, the NNDR poundage and possible capping criteria. There is an obvious temptation to see such a role as insignificant, even demeaning, but the temptation should be resisted – both by those in local government and by citizen-observers. As is emphasised throughout this book, the size, employing and spending power, and sheer community centrality of local authorities are such that even their marginal budgetary decisions have an important local impact. Central government may set the budgetary framework, but there is still scope *within* that framework – albeit much less than might be democratically desirable – for councils to respond to local needs and for councillors to pursue their political objectives.

To illustrate, we return to Birmingham's 2009/10 revenue budget, and complete the story of the setting of the city's council tax. As noted earlier, while the scale of Birmingham's budget is exceptional, the basic decisions underpinning it are essentially similar to those required of your own council. Council budgets nowadays are under continuous review, but the symbolic starting point for the 2009/10 budget was the December 2008

Commons announcement by the Minister of Local Government of the Finance Settlement: a 4.4% increase in total government revenue funding, and a Formula Grant increase of 2.8%. Birmingham's Formula Grant increase was above average at 3.3%. The minister then wrote to local authority leaders, giving them the details – and warnings (DCLG, 2008b). The letter is worth quoting, because it conveys eloquently where the power in this particular central–local relationship lies:

> As I said in the House, this is a tight settlement, but fair and affordable ... The Government expects the average council tax rise in England to be substantially below 5% in 2009/10, and we will not hesitate to use our capping powers to protect council taxpayers from excessive increases, including requiring authorities to re-bill if necessary.
>
> We are continuing the capping action taken against the Cheshire, Leicestershire and Warwickshire police authorities in 2008/09 by proposing maximum budget requirements in 2009/10 that will limit their council tax increases to around 3%. No other decisions about capping in 2009/10 have been taken, but it would be unwise to assume that the capping criteria set in previous years will be repeated. We intend to take decisions on capping after authorities have set their budgets.

The capping warning was quite unnecessary for Birmingham's Conservative–Liberal Democrat power-sharing administration. Since ending Labour's 20-year control of the Council in 2004, the Conservative leadership had prided itself on running an efficient, cost-cutting organisation with the lowest council tax of any major city in the country. It had made a public commitment three years earlier to limit council tax increases on a Band D equivalent property to 1.9% a year – until 2018 – and it wasn't about to break that commitment in only its fourth year. It was not a question, therefore, of starting from the previous year's service budgets, adding inescapable additional costs, then desirable improvements and developments, seeing what the sum totalled, and how much would need to come from the council tax. These things were done, but, like the notes of Grieg's Piano Concerto played by Eric Morecambe in the famous André Previn sketch, not necessarily in that order. Birmingham's budget process worked essentially from the answer backwards. There were, of course, protected and prioritised services – adult care, refuse collection and doorstep recycling, grounds maintenance, libraries – but the 1.9% took complete priority. In that sense it was unmistakably an exercise led by locally elected politicians, albeit within centrally defined boundaries. Had the Conservatives' Lib Dem partners or Labour been in control, both the process and outcome would have been very different – which is as it should be.

The final budget – an 80-page elaboration of Exhibit 12.3 – was approved formally by the full City Council on 24 February 2009. There had been a net revenue spending increase of 2.4%, producing once again a rise in council tax for a Band D equivalent property, *for City Council services*, of 'only' 1.9%, compared to a national figure of 3.0%. As described, this 1.9% has become so pivotal to the City's budgeting that it is important to understand just what it meant. It did *not* mean that Council spending, by any definition, had risen by only 1.9%; or that the sum required from the Collection Fund, even for City Council services alone, had risen by only 1.9%. Nor, most significantly, had the *average payment per property* risen by only 1.9%; in fact, the increase was 2.9%. Only the rise in that Band D equivalent rate for City Council Services had been kept to 1.9%.

There is nothing really underhand here. Band D is widely quoted for comparative purposes as representing the average property value across the country. The problem is Birmingham's. If Birmingham properties were equally distributed across the eight bands, the increase in the Band D equivalent tax and in the average payment per property would be the same. In fact, over half of Birmingham properties, as in many other authorities, are in Bands A and B. So, starting from a lower than average base, the percentage increase in the average payment per property is significantly higher. It's a neat trick if you can pull it off, and it's unreasonable to expect politicians not to try. What is questionable, we suggest, is not providing in the council tax leaflet the basic data about banding that would enable you, if you wanted, to work it out.

Presentation, however, is almost the least of the problems with the council tax and the local finance system generally. Important as they were, the tax and policy decisions made by locally elected politicians were *not* the major determinants of Birmingham's *overall level* of spending and service provision, or its overall level of council tax. They were managing the margins. The big decisions, once the responsibility of local councillors and their electorates, are today very largely determined by national politicians and civil servants in London. As shown in Exhibit 12.3, Birmingham council tax-payers in 2009/10 contributed less than a tenth of the Council's gross revenue expenditure. Go behind the figures, and this amounted to less than a fifth of its specific grant funding, less than was raised in sales, fees and charges, and much less than was paid by non-domestic ratepayers. Such a situation blurs accountability, leaving voters uncertain as to who is *really* responsible for any tax change for which they are asked to pay or vote. A 'gearing effect' also acts as a big disincentive for any local authority proposing to increase its net spending, because, with central government controlling all other sources of funding – grants and the NNDR – a 1% budget increase will require a 4%–5% rise in council tax.

If that were not sufficient, there are further disincentives. Until 2012/13, capping would remain in place, which Coalition ministers, though fiercely opposed to it in principle, indicated they were quite prepared to use. Then referendums would be available to veto tax increases. But first, in 2011/12, there was the freeze. The Scottish SNP Government had introduced a council tax freeze in 2008/9. Councils agreed to freeze their tax levels, and they received a compensating share of a sum set aside by the government. In 2010/11 the Scottish freeze was into its third year, and, embarrassing as it must have been to follow an SNP lead on anything, the Coalition copied it wholesale. If a council in 2011/12 froze or reduced its 2010/11 basic level of council tax, it would receive a grant equivalent of a 2.5% increase – though from precisely where in the government's budget was unclear. Most councils and council tax-payers seemed likely to see the choice, for one year at least, as a 'no brainer'. It is, however, unprogressive – in that Band G and H taxpayers benefit the most; it further undermines local budget and tax accountability; and, as we shall see in the next section, it is unrecognisably different from how most other countries organise their local finances.

How other countries do things

It was noted at the start of the chapter that local government accounts for just over a quarter of the country's total government spending, or about 9% of the gross domestic product (GDP). It sounds, and obviously is, a lot,

Exhibit 12.5 Britain's council tax – a small slice of an average cake, 2007/08

The cake

Total tax revenue as a percentage of GDP	Under 5%	5% – 20%	Over 20%
Over 40%	Netherlands (40, 4)	Austria* (43, 18) France (43, 12) Italy (43, 16) Norway (42, 13)	Denmark (48, 24) Sweden (47, 32) Belgium* (46, 29) Finland (43, 21)
30–40%	UK (38, 4.7) Greece (31, 1)	Portugal (37, 6) New Zealand (35, 6) Australia* (31, 18)	Germany* (36, 31) Spain* (33, 30) Canada* (32, 47)
Under 30%	Rep. of Ireland (28, 2)		Switzerland* (29, 42) Japan (28, 28) USA* (27, 34)

Local/state taxes as a percentage of total tax revenue   The slice

Notes: The first figure for each country is tax revenue as a percentage of GDP; the second is local tax as a percentage of total tax revenue. For federal and regional countries (*), the second figure = state/regional + local taxes.
Source: OECD (2009), table A, p. 19 and table 132, p. 230.

which is why, in any local authority area, the council itself will be among the largest employers, spenders and purchasers, and frequently *the* largest.

Compared with the financial muscle of other major local government systems, however, the UK, in football parlance, would be struggling in the Championship. A 'World Sub-central Premier League' would probably be headed by Canada and China, where, for differing reasons, sub-central government expenditure comfortably exceeds that by central government, followed by various other large and/or federal countries. A 'European Sub-central Premier League' would be headed by Denmark, with a local government sector contributing over 30% of GDP, followed by Sweden (25%), Spain, Finland and the federal systems of Belgium and Germany (all around 20%) (CEMR-Dexia, 2009, p. 6). In tax terms, the distinctions are even more striking. As shown in Exhibit 12.5, the council tax contributes a very small slice to a not particularly large national taxation cake. The UK, whatever its citizens may believe or are told, is a comparatively modestly taxed

Exhibit 12.6 Composition of state/local tax revenues, 2007 (percentages)

		Income and profits		Property	Goods	Other
		Personal	Corporate		and Services	
Federal countries						
Canada	State	37	9	5	37	12
	Local	–	–	94	3	3
USA	State	36	7	55	2	–
	Local	5	1	71	23	–
Belgium	State	67	–	23	0	–
	Local	71	–	17	12	–
Germany	State	43	9	6	42	–
	Local	53	27	15	5	–
Unitary countries						
Denmark		88	3	9	–	–
Finland		85	10	5	–	–
France		–	–	51	18	31
Italy		19	2	13	25	41
Japan		31	24	26	16	1
Netherlands		–	–	56	44	–
Spain		15	6	29	44	6
Sweden		100	–	–	–	–
UK	Pre-1989	–	–	100	–	–
	1990–3	–	–	–	–	100
	1993–	–	–	100	–	–

Source: OECD (2009), tables 136, 138 and *passim*.

country, and of every £1 of tax paid, less than 5p goes directly to local councils.

It is true that some European countries have smaller local government sectors than those in Britain – notably those in which teachers are employed by central, rather than local, government. But, since the introduction of capping and the 1989–93 tax changes – particularly the 'nationalisation' of business rates – there are few Western countries in which local government is more financially dependent on central government. The key to that situation lies, we suggest, in the data shown in Exhibit 12.6, where the detailed figures are in some ways less important than the evident overall message:

- In very few Western countries are local authorities forced to rely on only one source of local taxation.
- In most countries, local authorities can levy a variety of taxes on different groups of tax-payers and service users.
- The few exceptions are those, mainly Scandinavian, countries that rely very heavily on a broad-based and progressive direct tax: a local income tax.
- Britain has been unique in placing such a concentrated burden on *either* a property tax *or* a flat-rate personal tax.

The burden of a single local tax

Taxes, pronounced economist John Maynard Keynes, are the membership fee we pay to live in a civilised society: not inherently a 'bad' thing, as many politicians would have us believe, but a force for good, funding things we value, such as universal education, social services and public transport. It is when tax liabilities are inadequately or inappropriately shared that they come to seem burdensome. For British local authorities, the enforced reliance on a single local tax is burdensome in two senses: on the system itself and on those liable to pay it. As a local authority's responsibilities increase, more money is required from the same group of taxpayers, whose readiness to pay, and eventually their ability to do so, is finite. When, in addition, the single tax is either a flat-rate one or related only loosely to a tax-payer's changing income, problems are magnified. That, in essence, has been the story of post-war British local government.

The time-honoured rating system described in the previous section had been effective, but, in the post-war years, as councils took on increasing numbers of services, its limitations became apparent. Domestic rates were efficient, predictable, relatively easy to collect and difficult to evade. But, as a property tax, they were 'regressive' – not directly related to householders' or households' ability to pay. During the 1970s, as their rate bills increased year by year, and householders saw other service-users apparently 'freeloading', accusations of unfairness multiplied. The Conservatives, or more precisely the Opposition environment spokesperson – one Margaret Thatcher – produced a 1974 manifesto pledge to 'abolish the rating system within the lifetime of a Parliament and replace it by taxes more broadly based and *related to people's ability to pay'* (our emphasis).

Of that four-part pledge, half was eventually achieved, and half was not. Domestic rates were abolished, but after three Parliaments, not one. The replacement community charge – or 'poll tax' as it became known almost universally – was certainly more broadly based, being a completely flat-rate tax payable by almost everyone; but it was emphatically not related to ability to pay. The story of its introduction is a fascinating one (see Butler *et al.*, 1994; Wilson and Game, 1998, ch. 10), not least for the sheer chutzpah of ministers – and particularly the prime minister – in attempting to finance a sizeable part of a large-scale local government system through a personal tax that was unique in the Western democratic world.

The reason rating reform took a Conservative government ten years to introduce was that it had tried and finally exhausted other means of controlling local spending. The Thatcher Government came to power in what we have termed the 'corporatist' phase of central–local relations (see p. 188), and inherited Labour's policy of seeking to constrain local expenditure by reducing local government's *total* annual Rate Support Grant. This policy was ratcheted up in the Local Government Planning and Land Act 1980 by the unprecedented introduction of spending 'targets' and grant penalties for *every individual council.* If a council's spending exceeded by a significant amount its supposedly 'guideline' target, its grant, far from being increased, would be cut. In the mid-1970s, Rate Support Grant had funded over half of English local authorities' net spending (see Exhibit 12.7(a)), leaving councils themselves having to find only about a third (35%) through their locally-set domestic and business/non-domestic rates. But year by year, as their grant fell, many councils, rather than cut services, made up their income deficit by raising rates, often by formidable percentages: 27% on average in 1980/1 and 19.4% in 1981/2.

The government's response was threefold. First, a Green Paper examined a wide range of possible *Alternatives to Domestic Rates* (DoE, 1981) – local sales taxes; petrol, alcohol and tobacco duties; a local payroll tax; local income tax – and then rejected most of them, including a poll tax, on the grounds of impracticability. Second, and consequently, 'rate-capping' was introduced – in 1982 in Scotland and 1984 in England and Wales. The Rates Act gave central government complete control for the first time over the spending and taxing policies of some, and eventually all, local authorities – a constitutional development arguably more fundamental than the third strand of the government's action: the abolition in 1985 of the 'excessively' high-spending and high-taxing GLC and Metropolitan County Councils.

234

Exhibit 12.7 The changing composition of funding for English local authority net expenditure, 1975–2009

(a) 1975/6

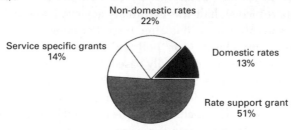

Non-domestic rates 22%
Service specific grants 14%
Domestic rates 13%
Rate support grant 51%

LOCALLY DETERMINED EXPENDITURE = 35%

(b) 1989/90

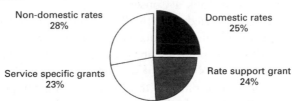

Non-domestic rates 28%
Domestic rates 25%
Service specific grants 23%
Rate support grant 24%

LOCALLY DETERMINED EXPENDITURE = 53%

(c) 1992/3

Non-domestic rates 31%
Community charge 15%
Service specific grants 23%
Revenue support grant 31%

LOCALLY DETERMINED EXPENDITURE = 15%

(d) 2008/9

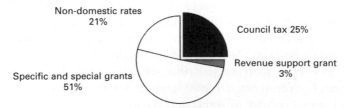

Non-domestic rates 21%
Council tax 25%
Revenue support grant 3%
Specific and special grants 51%

LOCALLY DETERMINED EXPENDITURE = 25%

Source: Data from DCLG (2009f) and similar earlier sources.

Poll tax – a short-lived policy disaster

There had been no mention of the rating abolition pledge in the Conservatives' 1983 manifesto. But, as the government continued to cut its general grant funding, the ratepayers' proportion of the local government spending 'pie' inevitably increased (see Exhibit 12.7(b)). It was time for another – this time uncompromising – Green Paper, *Paying for Local Government,* which outlined 'proposals for the most radical reform of local government finance in Britain this century' (DoE, 1986, p. 76). It was not exaggerating.

There were two main strands to the reform:

- *domestic rates* would be abolished, to be replaced by a Community Charge – a flat-rate payment by all adults aged 18 and over at a level set by individual local authorities; and
- *non-domestic rates* would be 'nationalised' – that is, set in future by *central* government at a uniform rate across the whole country.

The protests against the inequity of the community charge/poll tax were widespread and passionate, and the warnings about its operational difficulties – the maintenance of a rolling register and the problems of enforcement – were legion. Even ministers acknowledged that this Thatcherite 'flagship' policy would hardly be universally popular, but that only persuaded them to introduce it 'at a single stroke', rather than, as previously planned, phased in gradually as the rates were phased out. Accordingly, 'the most celebrated disaster in post-war British politics' (Butler *et al.*, 1994) was launched – on 1 April 1989 in Scotland and 1 April 1990 in England and Wales.

The average poll tax bill for 1990/1 was £363 per adult (about £800 in 2010, using an average earnings index) – 14 times higher than the sum envisaged in the 1981 Green Paper. There were three times as many 'losers' as 'gainers', the heaviest losers being pensioners and single-parent families in the smallest properties and with the smallest incomes. Tens of thousands were criminalised for the first time in their lives because of their inability or refusal to pay, and non-collection rates rocketed. In Scotland alone, more than 13 years after its abolition, £435 million was still outstanding – and was still being collected at the rate of £3 million per annum (Citizens Advice Scotland, 2007). The untried, untested tax proved to be simply unacceptable in practice. In November 1990, Mrs Thatcher lost the Conservative leadership – substantially because of the damage the poll tax furore was doing to her party. The new prime minister, John Major, despite his collective ministerial responsibility for the tax, was committed to its abolition, but first he had to neutralise it. This was achieved in Chancellor of the Exchequer Norman Lamont's budget in March 1991, in which he raised

Value Added Tax (VAT) from 15% to 17.5% to finance a cut of £140 in every poll tax bill in the country. Two days later, Environment Secretary Michael Heseltine announced the abolition of the poll tax and its replacement from 1993 by the council tax.

The financial, fiscal, economic and employment costs of the community charge/poll tax, massive as they were, can at least be estimated (see Wilson and Game, 1998, Exhibit 10.5 – also on linked website). The longer-term social and community costs, and the irreparable damage done to local government, are inestimable. The effects are still in evidence – in people's resistance to registration and census completion, in their disengagement from local government, and in the reluctance of some to pay even the initially obviously fairer council tax. Even more damaging to local government, though, was the two-stage switch – first the Uniform Business Rate, then the VAT increase – from local taxation funding over half of net local expenditure to its funding only one-sixth (see Exhibit 12.7(b) and (c)). In the ensuing nearly two decades, the proportion of locally determined expenditure has crept up to around a quarter (see Exhibit 12.7(d)). But that is still, as Hambleton put it, 'a small fraction' compared to most other Western European countries – too small, many observers would feel, to support a financially robust local democracy.

Instant interment ends hope of reform

The most obvious legacy of the post-1988 tax reforms is that British local authorities are still in the almost unique position of having access to just one, faulty, local tax. The council tax is neither big enough nor buoyant enough; it discriminates against those on low and fixed incomes, and is controlled and almost arbitrarily cappable by central government. For a self-proclaimed modernising and devolutionist government that was capable of embarrassment, the events summarised in Exhibit 12.8 would be a shameful tale indeed.

The keys to reform – the damaging imbalance in central–local funding and an inadequate council tax – were acknowledged explicitly in the government's 2001 White Paper. Ministers' first action, though, was to spend more than two years producing a Balance of Funding report (ODPM, 2004b) that added nothing of note to the far more comprehensive and challenging Layfield Report (1976). Then, in a way that even *Yes, Minister*'s Sir Humphrey Appleby might have found a touch audacious, they appointed another inquiry, and, as it approached completion, extended its terms of reference and deferred it yet further – to make quite certain that no legislation could be squeezed in before a General Election. Understandably, the sorry saga reminded one commentator (Grant, 2005, p. 14) of Samuel Beckett's play, *Waiting for Godot* – partly because Godot never actually

Exhibit 12.8 Balance of funding reform: nothing happened, thrice

What balance?

Actually the roughly 75:25 *imbalance* – between the national and local funding of local government's revenue spending. It distorts accountability through the 'gearing effect': a 1% spending increase requires a 4% council tax rise – thereby confusing local taxpayers and voters, who see no clear relationship between local taxes paid and services received.

Chronology of non-reform

2003 – A ministerial working group embarks on a **Balance of Funding Review**.

2004 – The **Review**'s bland report comprises an unoriginal rehearsal of options and a non-conclusion: any major shift in B of F requires a reformed council tax supplemented by relocalised business rates and/or a local income tax.

Nothing happens once – Minister announces further **Inquiry into Local Government Funding**, led by Sir Michael Lyons, former Chief Executive, Birmingham City Council. Lyons to report in December 2005 on the case for change and how best to reform council tax.

Nothing happens twice – In September 2005 the new Local Government Minister, David Miliband, announces an obviously electorally-driven decision to postpone indefinitely the 2007 revaluation of domestic property in England. Also extends Lyons' brief to include local government's future role and function, thus postponing the report.

Nothing happens thrice – 21 March 2007: the Inquiry's final report puts forward a carefully argued and deliberately incremental agenda of reforms; Local Government Minister Phil Woolas 'welcomes' the report and rejects almost all its proposals.

2010 – Labour Manifesto rules out revaluation in next Parliament, but promises (wait for it!) 'a cross-party commission to examine the future of local government finance' (p. 9:5).

What was never going to happen – the localist benchmark

Many in local government were disappointed by Lyons' calculated caution, and the LGA produced, prior to the report, its own reform package (LGA, 2004). It reads now like a town hall version of Sir Clive Sinclair's C5 electric tricycle, but it does serve as a benchmark for any future politicians contemplating describing themselves as localists:

- **Reverse the 75:25 central:local balance**, and improve the gearing ratio from 4:1 to 1.5:1, while still equalising across local authorities for their differing needs and resources;
- **A more equitable property/council tax** – involving a revaluation, and perhaps more bands, steeper ratios, regional bandings;
- **Relocalisation of business rates**;
- **Transfer of a proportion of national income tax to fund local government directly** – ideally through a progressive **Locally Variable Income Tax**;
- **Commensurate reduction in Revenue Support Grant**;
- **A basket of supplementary smaller taxes or charges** – for example:
  o **Localised vehicle excise duty** – councils retain receipts
  o **Local sales taxes** – on retail prices of certain goods or services
  o **Localised Stamp Duty** – on property transfers
  o **Land value taxes** – based on land ownership, not property occupation
  o **Tourist/bed taxes**
  o **Green/environmental taxes** – plastic bag tax, household waste generation charges.

Figure 12.2 *Cartoon – Lyons Report goes to an early grave*

Source: *Local Government Chronicle*, 22 March 2007.

appears, and partly also because of a famous review in which it was described as a play in which nothing happens, twice – except that here it was thrice.

When Sir Michael Lyons did finally produce his elegantly reasoned, ever-so-cautious, 400-page report (Lyons, 2007), almost all its carefully differentiated recommendations were lumped together and instantly buried – by a *junior* minister. The bespectacled gravedigger shown in Figure 12.2 is Local Government Minister Phil Woolas, assisted by then Chancellor of the Exchequer Gordon Brown, whose Treasury clearly could not contemplate the slightest loosening of its hold on even a 4.7% slice of the national tax pie.

It was insulting treatment of the report, its author and the world of local government – and wholly unjustified. Sir Michael had risked his own reputation in opting to produce a measured, non-confrontational report with a deliberately staged, developmental approach to reform. He didn't want to change the balance of funding (pp. 20–1), or give councils major new powers (p. 13). Council tax wasn't 'broken' (p. 21), business rates should stay centrally set (p. 28), and a local income tax was 'a choice for future governments' (p. 27). The most strident call was for a new central–local government partnership, in which the centre recognises the value of local choice and local government makes better use of its existing powers.

More specific reform proposals were grouped into essential short-term measures, desirable medium-term reforms, and more radical reform options for future governments. Essential reforms included the end of council tax capping; new powers for councils to charge for domestic refuse collection, and to levy a supplementary business rate; and a reduction in ring-fenced grants. In the medium term, council tax should be revalued, and the government should consider assigning a fixed proportion of income tax to local government, as well as the case for a tourist tax. A local income tax and the re-localisation of the business rate – which the LGA considered a priority option – were assigned to the longer term.

The groupings were ignored, and all major proposals were immediately ruled out or postponed indefinitely – with one exception: the proposal of greatest direct interest to the Treasury. From 2010, the GLA and upper-tier authorities could levy a Business Rate Supplement of up to 2p in the pound on the NNDR in order to raise money for local infrastructure projects. Largest of these is the London Crossrail project, to which the Supplement, modest as it is, probably owes its existence. It looked for a time as if the SNP Government might be able to embarrass Labour ministers still further by replacing the council tax in Scotland with a local income tax. But, having put the pledge at the centre of its successful 2007 Parliamentary election campaign, it was the SNP who became the embarrassed party, forced to postpone implementation until at least after the 2011 elections. On both sides of the border, therefore, the hastily conceived council tax remains unreformed, unrevalued and capped.

The Coalition's early contribution to this policy impasse was hardly encouraging. Its *Programme for Government* promised yet another 'review of local government finance' (p. 11). This review, Communities Secretary Eric Pickles informed the Commons Communities and Local Government Select Committee, would probably start work towards the end of 2011, but on what was not clear. They were 'not going to do another Michael Lyons, which was an excellent report; we are going to have to start making some political decisions about that' (House of Commons, 2010b, Q. 69). But some of those decisions, it seemed, had already been taken – by the Secretary of State himself. Council tax revaluation and a local income tax, both of which Sir Michael had commended for consideration, were apparently ruled out.

Part 2

The Politics and People of Local Government

Chapter 13

Local Elections: Christmas Tree Lights?

Why bother?

Of the several characteristics identified in Chapter 2 as distinguishing local authorities from other institutions of public administration, the most fundamental is the fact of their election, aspects of which provide the content of the next two chapters. Chapter 14 focuses on the products of the electoral process: the councillors, while this chapter looks in detail at that process: how elections are conducted, who votes, and how those votes are cast. They have been tagged 'the Christmas tree lights of British politics – one has to have them every year and they undoubtedly add colour to the scene, but are rarely that illuminating' (*The Times*, 3 May 2003, editorial). This chapter argues that their candlepower is underrated – and that the metaphor says more about the dismissive way in which the national media typically view and report – or, more commonly, ignore – local elections than it does about the elections themselves.

It is easy, though, to follow *The Times*' reasoning. Everyone knows that far fewer people vote in council elections than in even the 2001 and 2005 General Elections, with their record low turnouts of around 60%. Are not government ministers – real, as well as fictitious ones like *Yes, Minister*'s Jim Hacker – right when they suggest that: 'Local democracy is a farce ... Most people don't even vote in local elections, and the ones who do just treat it as a popularity poll on government in Westminster' (Lynn and Jay, 1983, p. 45). Certainly, local elections are not accorded much importance in Britain's national political life. Their results are analysed mainly for what they would mean *if* they had been produced in a General Election, rather than for what they *actually* mean: namely, councils changing political control, policies altering, and councillors winning and losing seats.

So why are we bothering to devote a whole chapter to them? The answer is simple. We do not believe that local elections should be dismissed as merely mini-General Elections, even when, as in 1979, 1997, 2001, 2005 and 2010, they are held on the same day. They are much more complex, and much more important, than a national popularity poll, or, as Margaret Thatcher and Tony Blair seemed to regard them, a handy aid for prime ministers seeking politically advantageous election dates. Our view of what

Exhibit 13.1 The who, when, how and why of local elections

When are local elections held?
Every May, normally the first Thursday of the month – *not,* as in many countries, at weekends or on a public holiday.

Can I vote?
Almost certainly – if you are 18, a citizen of Britain, Ireland or the Commonwealth, and not a convicted prisoner. Also EU citizens, peers and peeresses, who are ineligible in parliamentary elections.

Must I register first?
Yes, as for parliamentary elections. There is a continuously maintained electoral register – administered by your district, borough or unitary council, and specifically by the Electoral Registration Officer, who should require you to complete a registration form confirming **your residence in the electoral area.** Primitively and patently abusably, though – and with the commendable exception of Northern Ireland – this registration form is completed not by the individual voter, but by the head of household. Despite the estimated **non-registration** of 10% of the eligible population, 50% of 17–24-year-olds and private sector tenants, and 30% of BME British residents (Electoral Commission, 2010, pp. 2–3), it is an offence, with a potential £1,000 fine. More practically, it can also affect your credit rating.

Isn't there also a property qualification?
Not any longer. Non-residents used to be able to vote if they occupied land or property in an area, but this plural voting was abolished in 1969, except in the City of London.

So can I vote every year?
Easy question, ludicrously complex answer: it depends entirely on where you live. Most local authorities have **'whole council'** or **'all out'** elections every 4 years (when not postponed), though not on the same day; for example:

> English Counties (2009, 2013)
> London Boroughs (2010, 2014)
> Greater London Authority (2008, 2012)
> Scottish Unitaries (2007, 2012, 2017)
> Welsh Unitaries (2008, 2012)
> Northern Ireland – districts (2005, 2011)

But Metropolitan Districts have **'partial'** or **'by thirds'** elections – with a third of councillors standing for re-election in each non-county year: 2008, 2010, 2011, 2012, 2014. And some – English Unitaries and Non-metropolitan Districts – may choose their style of election. Elections by thirds have been chosen by 102 mainly more urban authorities, while 175 have whole council elections every four years (2007, 2011).

Whom do I elect?
The councillor(s) representing the particular area in which you live. All councils are divided into single- or multi-member electoral **divisions** (counties) or **wards** (districts, boroughs, and unitaries), each returning 1, 2 or 3 councillors for **4-year terms** of office. Starting with the London Mayor in 2000, there are also now a number of directly elected executive mayors, similarly serving 4-year terms.

$\rightarrow$

Exhibit 13.1 continued

When and where do I do it?
Traditionally, **on election day itself**, in your designated local polling station. Remarkably, you just turn up – no ID needed (outside Northern Ireland), not even the polling card you should have received. In 2000, **postal voting on demand** was introduced, leading to some increase in turnout and, in a few notorious cases, also in fraud. Several all-postal votes have been held, notably in mayoral and regional assembly referendums, and several e-voting methods have been piloted – internet, touch phone, SMS, interactive digital TV – with a view to eventual **multi-channel elections**.

Is voting easy?
Yes. In England and Wales completing the ballot paper is as easy as in parliamentary elections, as the same **plurality** or **first-past-the-post** system is used. You simply mark X against your preferred candidate (or candidates in a multi-member ward), and whoever gets the most votes is elected. Only in Northern Ireland – and, since 2007, in Scotland – is there a more voter-friendly opportunity to rank candidates in order of preference through the more proportional **Single Transferable Vote** system.

Counting is similarly straightforward, and councils' complete results are often available nowadays within a couple of hours of the polls closing.

Will I recognise the candidates' names?
Not necessarily – though you may recognise your existing councillor if s/he is standing for re-election. Your ward may have between 1,000 and 20,000 registered electors, so even the most diligent candidates may not have managed to visit you in person. But candidates have a free delivery of a brief, probably illustrated, 'election address', describing themselves and their policies; also up to six words of description on the ballot paper itself, which will usually be their party affiliation – no enhanced candidate photos, though.

Could I stand as a candidate?
Probably – provided you are 18, a British, Commonwealth or EU citizen, and have lived or worked in the council area for at least 12 months prior to your nomination. But there are disqualifications for convictions and bankruptcy, and, most controversially, if you are a paid employee of a local authority, you cannot also be elected to it, though you may be eligible to stand for a different authority. The 1989 extension of the latter disqualification, to prevent senior council officers and those in 'politically sensitive' posts from standing for election at all, was relaxed a little in the 2009 Local Democracy, Economic Development and Construction Act.

Would I have to be nominated?
Yes, again as for parliamentary elections – by 10 electors for the ward concerned.

Is it expensive?
Not terribly. It's cheaper to do badly than in parliamentary elections, since no forfeitable deposit is required. There is also a limit on each candidate's expenditure – £600 plus 5p for each registered elector since 2006 – though few report spending anywhere near their permitted limit.

Why is the system unnecessarily complicated?
Good question. It's simply historical accident, but it is, as the Electoral Commission have forcefully argued (2004), disjointed, discriminatory, confusing and effectively disenfranchising, since many electors simply don't know when 'their' elections are taking place. The Commissioners – and more recently the Councillors Commission (2007, Recommendation 18) – felt the case for simplification outweighed the merits for local diversity that we as authors favour in most other contexts. They recommended a uniform cycle of all-out 4-yearly elections across the whole of England. We agree.

local elections are, and are not, about can be summed up in the kind of 'before and after' editorials regularly produced by our more serious national newspapers, such as *The Times*. On the morning of an exceptionally bitterly contested set of local elections (3 May 1990), editorial readers were instructed:

> Today's local elections are about the running of Britain's cities, towns and county districts. They are not a public opinion poll. They are not meant to be a judgement on Mrs Thatcher, on her government at Westminster, or on the vexed matter of the poll tax. They are to select the men and women who are to run local administration. Those of all political persuasions who treat local elections as surrogate General Elections are merely playing the centralist game. They are enemies of local democracy.

Odd, then, and disappointing, that just two days later, the same paper's editorial should choose to play its own 'centralist game':

> Yesterday's election results showed, as predicted, that the public does not like the poll tax … The swing to Labour on a high turnout would be enough to give Mr Kinnock a good parliamentary majority.

Setting aside the fact that many voters demonstrably *did* like the poll tax, benefited from it, and voted accordingly, what happened to all those councillors running our cities, towns and county districts? The writer's assumption is that national and local elections are interchangeable. A key message of this chapter is that *they are not*. Local elections are local political events, and a great many voters, if not political commentators, clearly treat them as such. Far fewer actually use their votes than in parliamentary elections, but many of those doing so *consistently vote differently* in the two types of election.

They will vote on the basis of local, rather than national issues, and for or against the records or personalities of particular candidates, regardless of their party. We shall introduce some specific examples later in the chapter, but first we must outline how British local elections are in fact conducted – see Exhibit 13.1.

The case for whole council elections and individual registration

Undeniably, some aspects of our current local electoral arrangements – most notably, when they are held and how we register – are confusing and unsatisfactory. If you live in non-metropolitan England, you may well have to contact your district council's electoral registration office to find out whether yours are 'all out' or 'partial' elections, and when you therefore have your next chance to vote. Should it be the former, you may feel not only confused but also discriminated against, in having fewer opportunities to vote and influence the political composition of your council than your friend in a neighbouring district. While in many areas of life variety of local practice is commendable, it is not self-evident that the organisation of elections should be one of them. The Electoral Commission and more recently the Councillors Commission were surely right in favouring a uniform system, with as many voters as possible turning out on the same 'Local Election Day'.

There are arguments for and against 'whole council' elections. By giving councils a clear breathing space between elections, they may encourage policy consistency, forward planning, and reduce the temptation to defer politically difficult decisions such as school closures, tax increases or the siting of roads. They can, however, lead to dramatic changes in political control, producing large and sudden influxes of inexperienced councillors. Opponents declare that they dilute the political accountability that comes from politicians having to explain and justify their policies regularly to the electorate. But the harder and, for many, the clinching evidence is that turnouts are generally at least a few percentage points higher in whole council elections (Rallings and Thrasher, 2003; see also Exhibit 13.4), when, if you're really dissatisfied with your council's performance, you can 'vote the rascals out' in one go.

Just as the merits of local diversity can be exaggerated, so too can those of tradition. Unsecured electoral registration by household may have made sense when the Victorians had a property qualification for voters, and there was a significant adult illiteracy rate. Today it seems fundamentally wrong in principle, and democratically undermining in practice, for voters not to take responsibility for their own registration. Operated in conjunction with postal voting on demand – introduced in 2000 – it means that there is no effective check on who is applying for or receiving ballot papers, who is completing them, and under what kind of duress. It is an open invitation to fraud, potentially on a widespread and organised scale – as revealed in the Birmingham election trial (British Helsinki Human Rights Group, 2005; Parris, 2005), in which Labour candidates and their supporters were found guilty of having 'stolen' the 2004 council elections in two inner city wards by exploiting the many loopholes in the existing system.

Northern Ireland had already introduced individual registration in 2002, with voters having to provide personal identification information, as well as some form of photographic ID at the polling station. However, in the face of the advice of almost all those professionally – as opposed to politically – concerned about the integrity of the electoral system, the Electoral Administration Act 2006, while creating new offences of electoral fraud, stopped short of reforming the registration system in the obvious practical way that would largely prevent it.

It took a change of government to reform a system that Commonwealth monitors of the 2010 General Election officially found 'corruptible and open to fraud' (Royal Commonwealth Society, 2010, p. 4), and unofficially considered 'less secure than their own, and possibly the most vulnerable to corruption in the world' (Swinford, 2010). The Coalition intended making individual registration compulsory in 2014, with each person registering themselves and providing personal identifiers – date of birth, signature and national insurance number – that can be cross-checked before their name is added to the register.

The electoral system – should England follow Scotland?

This casual abandonment of the principle of the privacy of the ballot is a constitutionally important, but recent, concern, arising out of the government's rush to postal voting as a means of raising election turnouts. The greater and far more enduring controversy concerns the system itself: the *plurality* or *first-past-the-post* (FPTP) method of election. It is well tested and easily understood, and familiar to almost everyone through its long use in all governmental elections in mainland Britain. Yet there is also widespread resentment of its obvious deficiencies and biases and, as all the recently devolved institutions have adopted more proportional methods (see Exhibit 13.2), electoral reform for local, as well as national, government has inevitably become part of the constitutional reform agenda. The main arguments for and against FPTP in local elections are summarised in Exhibit 13.3.

We shall not add greatly to the extensive literature on electoral reform, but it is appropriate, given the confusion that manifestly exists about one of those citizenship subjects of which we should all have a basic understanding, to make a few key points. First, it must be emphasised that the choice of electoral systems, locally or nationally, is not simply between either FPTP or proportional representation (PR). It is probably most useful to think of there being four basic *types* of system, as outlined in Exhibit 13.2.

Second, by far the most common local electoral system in Western Europe is the party list – but *not* the closed, depersonalised, unalterable list system UK voters have been required to use in European Parliamentary elections. Most countries use either unblocked lists, enabling voters to express personal preferences for individual candidates, or an 'unordered' list, as in Finland, where, by voting directly for candidates, it is the electorate, and not the party 'selectorate', that determines the order in which parties fill their quotas of seats, and therefore who represents them.

Third, notwithstanding its international popularity, no version of the list system *per se* is likely to feature prominently in any debate on the virtues of PR in British local elections. For England (and possibly Wales), the principal

Exhibit 13.2 Basic types of electoral system

1 **Plurality (or first-past-the-post – FPTP) systems**
Vote for one candidate only, and the candidate with the most votes (a plurality, not necessarily a majority) wins.

2 **Majority/majoritarian systems** – for example, Alternative Vote (AV), Supplementary Vote (SV – used for mayoral elections), double ballot.

These are **preferential** systems, usually in single-member wards/constituencies – including council-wide constituencies for mayoral elections. The main aim is *not* proportionality, but to eliminate, through the counting, if necessary, of voters' second and subsequent preferences, the possibility of a candidate being elected on a minority vote – as, for example, two-thirds of all MPs were in the 2005 General Election.

3 **Proportional systems**

Any system, *necessarily* based on multi-member constituencies, which has as its aim the achievement of proportionality between votes cast and seats won.

There are **two main sub-types of proportional system:**

(a) **Party List systems** – which aim to represent **parties** in relation to their popular support, and in which any vote for an individual candidate is, at best, secondary to the vote for the party.
(b) **The Single Transferable Vote (STV)** – preferential voting in multi-member constituencies, the key objective being to provide voters with a choice of candidates *within* as well as between parties. Used in Northern Ireland and Scottish local elections.

4 **Additional Member Systems (AMS)** – aka **Top-up or Mixed Member Proportional (MMP) systems.**

Hybrid systems, combining single-member constituencies and party lists, 'additional' or 'top up' members being added to constituency members to achieve party proportionality in the elected body as a whole. Used for elections to Scottish Parliament, Assembly for Wales, Greater London Assembly.

choice would probably be between STV and some version of the Additional Member System (AMS) – the latter, of course, incorporating a party list vote as part of its hybridity. STV, in use for many years in Northern Ireland, has also been the PR system chosen for Scottish local elections from 2007 (though rejected by the Welsh Assembly), and could be introduced comparatively easily in England, where there are already many multi-member wards and divisions. In principle, it ought to appeal to those of all political persuasions who advocate maximum consumer choice.

Exhibit 13.3 The case for and against 'first-past-the-post' (FPTP) in local elections

For FPTP

- **Maximises the chance of a decisive electoral outcome**, with a single party having the full power to carry out its programme. Conversely, it minimises the likelihood of protracted post-election inter-party bargaining to form a minority or power-sharing administration.
- **Provides for a direct and personal councillor–constituent relationship**, unlike some systems of proportional representation, in which representatives may not be linked directly to any geographical constituency.
- **Encourages parties to be broad-based, tolerant and moderate**, and discourages the creation and proliferation of new and possibly extremist parties.
- **Is the easiest system**, both to understand and to administer.
- **There is no alternative system** on which there is widespread agreement.

Against FPTP

- **Distorts**, often grossly and even more than in parliamentary elections, the relationship between votes cast and seats won. Parties regularly win overwhelming control of councils on a bare majority, or even a minority, of votes.
- **Can effectively eliminate opposition**, producing councils on which opposition representation is either non-existent or too small to be seriously effective.
- **Wastes more votes** than almost any other system – with large majorities of votes often going to losing candidates or to building up needlessly large winning surpluses.
- **Reduces the incentive to vote**, by reducing the proportion of potential voters who feel they can affect the result, either in their own ward or in the council as a whole.
- **Undermines perceived legitimacy of councillors**, since many, like MPs, are elected on minority votes – and usually on smaller turnouts than MPs.
- **Is electorally inefficient**, using only voters' first preferences and giving them no opportunity to express their political opinions in greater detail.
- **Is socially and geographically divisive**, benefiting the two major parties in areas in which they are already strong.
- **Is politically divisive**, encouraging adversarial politics, with more attention being given to demolishing the opposition than to fostering inter-party understanding.
- **Does not prevent there being large numbers of hung (or 'balanced') councils** – but it can make post-election negotiation and co-operation on a hung council more difficult.
- **Can discriminate against women and ethnic minorities**, by making it harder for them to be selected and thus elected, though in fact female representation in British local government is higher than in some countries with PR systems.

AMS, however, is a form of election with which we are becoming increasingly familiar, and was the model advocated by the Jenkins Commission for the House of Commons, before the Labour Government reneged on its 1997 manifesto commitment to put the issue to a national referendum. It was also once favoured by the LGA, whose Local Government Additional Member System (LGAMS) would have had two-thirds of councillors directly elected by FPTP as ward representatives, with the remaining third chosen from open party lists of 'top-up' members (LGA, 2001). Advantages over STV are felt to be that ward sizes could be kept smaller, and that, if allocated on an authority-wide basis (as for the London Assembly), top-up members would have the distinctive and useful role of representing the council area as a whole.

Both systems could give independent and minority party members a better chance of election, and both would certainly increase substantially the already sizeable proportion of hung or 'balanced' councils – 114 out of 405 (28%) in Great Britain in 2010/11. Both would also end the practice under FPTP of many of the country's most important councils – especially the London and metropolitan boroughs – *never* changing political control (Game, 2004). Whether such outcomes are considered desirable depends on your personal political viewpoint. There is, however, plenty of evidence that hung councils can work eminently satisfactorily and may 'foster a more open and democratic form of local government than that typically found in majority controlled authorities' (Leach and Game, 1992, p. 152; see also Leach and Stewart, 1992; Temple, 1996; Game, 2004).

The Alternative Vote (AV), proposed by some electoral reformers for the House of Commons and on which a national referendum vote was scheduled for 5 May 2011, is, as shown in Exhibit 13.2, a majoritarian system, and would not produce the effects of a PR system. In the 2010 General Election, apart from ensuring that all MPs had majority support in their constituencies, it might have reduced the Liberal Democrats' under-representation by around 25 seats, chiefly at the expense of Labour. In local elections its likely impact would be similarly modest, doing relatively little to redress the disproportionalities between parties' vote shares and seat shares, particularly in strong one-party areas, and little to increase the election chances of 'minority' candidates of all descriptions. On the other hand, the very fact of the AV referendum focused public attention on the deficiencies of FPTP, which served as an encouragement to electoral reformers.

Turnout – the British cultural disinclination to vote

The one thing everyone thinks they know about local elections is that most people don't vote in them. They are right. The UK's 65.1% in the 2010 General Election did not put Britain quite at the bottom of the arbitrary

Exhibit 13.4 Turnout in local elections: the UK and Western Europe

	Average turnout 1980–94, % (n)		Most recent turnout % (year)		Change pre-1995 to date %	Most recent General Election turnout % (date)	
England						65.5	(2010)
London boroughs^{wc}	46	(4)	38	(2006)	−8		
Metropolitan boroughs^P	40	(11)	34	(2008)	−6		
County councils^{wc}	40	(4)	39	(2009)	−1		
Shire districts^{wc}	46	(4)	39	(2007)	−7		
Shire districts^P	41	(8)	39	(2009)	−2		
Scotland	44	(4)	54	(2007)*	n.a.	63.8	(2010)
Wales	50	(4)	44	(2008)	−8	64.8	(2010)
N. Ireland	55	(1)	63	(2005)*	n.a.	57.6	(2010)
Austria	81	(1)	73	(2004)	−8	82	(2008)
Denmark	75	(2)	69	(2005)*	−6	87	(2007)
Finland	73	(4)	61	(2008)	−12	65	(2007)
France	68		64	(2004)	−4	64	(2007)
Germany	71	(1)	60	(2008)	−11	78	(2005)
Rep. of Ireland	58	(2)	57	(2004)	−1	67	(2007)
Italy	85		75	(1999)	−10	81	(2008)
Netherlands	67	(3)	59	(2006)	−8	81	(2006)
Norway	67	(1)	62	(2007)	−5	77	(2005)
Portugal	65	(4)	39	(2005)	−26	60	(2009)
Spain	63	(1)	73	(2007)	+10	75	(2008)
Sweden	85	(3)	79	(2006)	−6	75	(2008)

Notes: n = number of elections on which an averaged turnout figure is based; ^{wc} = whole council elections; ^P = partial, usually one-third of seats only.
* indicates where sets of local turnout figures have probably been distorted by the elections having, exceptionally, taken place on the same day as national parliamentary, assembly or European Parliamentary elections.
Main sources: European Union, Committee of the Regions (1999, 2009); individual countries' statistical offices, etc.

league table of European countries shown in Exhibit 13.4, but, as ever, very close to it.

Exhibit 13.4 is not distorted by the compulsory voting countries – Belgium, Luxembourg and Greece – which are excluded, but it does require a cautionary health warning. Assembling collated local election statistics for other countries is tricky even for the experts: Colin Rallings and Michael Thrasher at the University of Plymouth's LGC Elections Centre. The figures in the first two columns of the Exhibit are therefore simply the best we have been able to put together for our purposes. Even so, the key points seem clear enough. The turnout in European countries' most recent local elections, though generally at least 5 points lower than in earlier years, was between 60% and 75% – or approaching double most UK figures, except when local elections happened to coincide with either parliamentary or national assembly elections. In almost all countries, fewer voters turn out for what are sometimes termed 'second-order' elections, for local councils and the European Parliament, but in England the local–national gap is currently between, say, 38% and 65%, whereas in Western Europe generally it is between about 65% and 80%.

What the UK figures suggest is that, while voting in local elections clearly has declined in recent years, by comparison with continental Europe, such voting *always was* a minority pastime. This idea upsets those who argue that today's low figures represent either a conscious or subconscious response of electors to the undermining and enfeeblement of local councils by successive central governments. Back in the days when a city council such as Birmingham's ran everything from education and trams to the gas and water supply, with its own municipal bank thrown in, *then* voters could see the point of voting and turned out in their droves – or so the argument goes. Well, not in Birmingham they didn't, as Exhibit 13.5 clearly shows.

The city may have had a golden age of municipal government, but, unless one includes 1950, when, for the only time since 1918, local turnout touched a hardly awesome 50%, it has never experienced a golden age of

Exhibit 13.5 What golden age? Birmingham local elections, 1920–2008

	Number of elections	Average turnout in contested seats (%)	Uncontested seats (%)	Candidates per vacancy
1920–9	10	42.0	17.7	2.1
1930–8	9	36.0	17.7	2.0
1945–50	5	44.4	0.5	2.2
1951–60	10	39.2	–	2.4
1961–72	12	32.4	–	2.9
1973–80†	7	36.1*	–	3.3
1981–90	8	41.2	–	3.6
1991–2000	8	33.0	–	3.8
2001–8	6	33.6	–	4.6

Notes: † = 1972–74: Reorganisation of local government in England;
* Excluding 1979, when general and local elections were held on the same day.
Main source: Phillips (2000), p. xxviii.

local electoral democracy. Nor, probably, did most other towns and cities. In Birmingham's inter-war years, more than one council seat in six was left totally uncontested – a proportion that would have been much higher still in rural and less party-politicised parts of the country – and those elections that did take place were mainly straight fights between Conservatives and Labour. Indeed, by that contestation measure, local democracy's heyday is right now. The numbers of uncontested seats, certainly in England (less so in Wales) are minimal by comparison with even thirty years ago, in the 1970s, and in many authorities – as in Birmingham – there are more minority party and independent candidates competing for each seat than ever before.

These two measures of electoral vitality – supply of candidates and voter turnout – need to be considered carefully by those keen to increase the British public's 'engagement' in local governance by increasing its voting opportunities. There are very few signs, certainly in England, that people disinclined either to stand or to vote in elections for councils responsible for setting local taxes and running a whole panoply of services – or, indeed, in parent governor elections at their own children's schools – are suddenly going to be enthused by elections for a police chief or a parks board. At best, the evidence in Exhibit 13.6 from elections to existing special-purpose bodies is ambiguous.

A few early turnouts in New Deal for Communities (NDC) board elections – in Bristol, Sheffield and Newcastle – were certainly striking in what are by definition some of the most deprived localities of the country. But these owed much to their being small-scale, intensively publicised postal votes, often undertaken over two days, with well-known local candidates (identified by personal photographs), and with voters having a very personal financial stake in the outcome. *Average* turnouts were less than 25% – lower than the figures expected in local elections in the same areas (Rallings *et al.*, 2004).

With Foundation Trust Board elections, it is the franchise itself that raises questions. In what will be described as a high turnout election, a few thousand voters will attempt to select up to twenty names from a list of several dozen – few, if any, of which they will recognise. Those elected, with perhaps no more than a large handful of first-preference votes, will then endeavour to represent the hospital's 'public', up to 99% of whom have not taken the minimum step necessary even to register as trust members. To strip councils of still further responsibilities in the cause of single-purpose 'participatory democracy' of this nature would seem, on the face of it, bizarre.

Returning to council elections, it was those in 1990 that produced the most recent peak in local turnout: 46% in Birmingham and over 50% in many districts across the country. Those figures, resulting largely from people's fury over their poll tax bills, offer us a basic insight into local voting behaviour. If and when people feel that what their council is doing

Exhibit 13.6 Elections to single-purpose bodies

Americanisation or community accountability?

US local government is characterised both by its exceptional number of governmental units, and by the service fragmentation that results. The Census Bureau's *2007 Census of Governments* recorded 89,500 local governments: 39,000 General Purpose (counties, municipalities, townships), and the remaining 50,500 Special Purpose.

These Special Purpose authorities are largely independent of their respective General Purpose governments. Best known are the 13,500 school districts, responsible not least for curriculum content. Others include local single-purpose bodies for drainage and flood control, housing and community development, cemeteries, libraries, parks and recreation. Their board or commission members are in the main directly elected.

The UK too has seen elections for single-purpose bodies and functions, and will see more. Labour ministers dropped plans to elect members to national parks and police authorities, but the Coalition Government has committed itself to implementing the controversial Conservative proposals for powerful directly elected police and crime commissioners, with existing police authorities of councillors and lay members becoming in effect panels of scrutineers. Also in 2010, direct elections were piloted to two of Scotland's 14 NHS health boards.

New Deal for Communities (NDC) boards

NDC was the Labour Government's 2001 flagship strategy to regenerate 39 of the country's most deprived neighbourhoods. Through the investment of £2 billion over 10 years, these NDC areas were empowered to tackle problems of unemployment, crime, educational under-achievement, poor health, and housing. Strategic direction came from a board elected by and from local residents.

Early elections attracted the interest of both participants and observers, who saw the 50% turnouts in some places as ushering in a new 'distinctively local brand of politics' (Shaw and Davidson, 2002, p. 5). Such figures, though, were the exception, notwithstanding the novelty, the exceptionally local scale, and the voters' personal stake in the project.

NHS Foundation (Hospital) Trust Boards

Foundation trust hospitals were introduced, controversially, by the Labour Government in 2004. Self-described as not-for-profit public benefit corporations, they would have greater financial and strategic freedom than traditional NHS trust hospitals. Numbering 129 by 2010 and providing over half of all NHS hospital and mental health services, they are controlled by boards of guardians elected by their 3 constituencies of members: staff, patients and, most contentiously, the public – those living in the trust's electoral area.

Staff and patient memberships are frequently 'opt out': people are registered and able to vote unless they opt out. But public membership, potentially millions in some cases, is 'opt in'. The turnout figures of up to 70% reported by the trusts and the independent regulator (www.monitor-nhsft.gov.uk) are in fact, therefore, perhaps 2 or 3% of the public supposedly served by the hospital – drawn, moreover, hugely disproportionately from ABC1 socio-economic groupings.

really can make a difference – particularly to their local tax bills – more of them will vote. It's not, as they say, rocket science – or even very sophisticated political science. But, even at a time of almost unprecedented hostility between local and central government, a time of protest marches, demonstrations, riots, regularly disrupted council meetings, and widespread civil disobedience, it was still only *a few* more – and nowhere near the numbers in most other European countries in normal years. As Britain's General Election turnouts consistently show, the country's national political culture does not lead to the populace being particularly dedicated voters in any form of election, and any search, therefore, for some magic key to increase local turnout *substantially* is likely to be in vain.

Three ways to increase turnout

The absence of a single magic key, though, does not mean that nothing can be done. There are three types of reform that, certainly between them, would surely both increase interest and turnout in local elections: reform of local taxation, the electoral system, and voting methods.

In one important respect, Mrs Thatcher was right about the community charge/poll tax. If, through paying local taxes, people felt that they had a stake in their community and could see a clear relationship between the tax they paid and the services their council provided, more of them would be inclined to vote. Where she was wrong was in making her flat-rate personal tax the *only* local tax available to councils. If, however, as fantasised in Exhibit 12.8, the present central–local balance of funding were reversed in local government's favour, and councils could call on several different local taxes, payable by different groups of taxpayers, the conditions would exist for a repeat of the poll tax effect. A council's budget and any changes to its principal tax levels would be tied closely to proposed improvements or cuts in services, competing parties could put forward alternative budget and service plans, and voters would have a meaningful choice to make.

That choice, though, is only truly meaningful if voters see themselves as having at least a fighting chance of replacing a council whose policies they dislike with one they prefer, which brings us back to the electoral system. In recent General Elections, it is estimated that up to 10% of eligible voters failed to register, while between 35% and 40% of those who did register stayed at home. Which is disappointing, but perhaps understandable, considering that 70% of those who did turn out cast what in effect were 'wasted' votes – for a losing candidate or contributing to an unnecessary surplus for the winner.

Local elections, using the same kind of plurality electoral system, are very similar. Millions of potential voters know that they live in wards and/or in council areas that are almost certainly 'safe' for one party or another. Whatever way they vote, or even if they don't bother, that party's candidate will win, and control of the council will remain unchanged. As has already been noted, more proportional electoral systems would do two things. First, they would take more account of an individual's vote preferences – either through a party vote as well as a candidate vote through the Additional Member System, or by considering their second and additional preferences with STV. Second, they would eliminate most wards and councils that are currently safe for any single party, making results and outcomes much less certain and reducing the perception of any individual vote being a waste of time.

In short, the '*Strictly*' effect would come into play, with the bonus that local elections are free. Millions of TV viewers pay up to 75p each time to vote for contestants in shows such as *Strictly Come Dancing*, *The X Factor* and *Britain's Got Talent* – not, presumably, because they like voting, but because they know that, if enough of them do so, they can extend Anne Widdecombe's 'dancing' or Jedward's 'singing' careers, or simply annoy Simon Cowell. Their votes can count. A PR electoral system in local government would also make more votes count and would almost certainly raise turnout by at least a few percentage points, as happens elsewhere.

The Labour Governments' refusal to give even as much consideration to the reform of the local electoral system as they did to that of the Commons was at least consistent – and perhaps not surprising, given that their power was derived largely from the FPTP system's ability to turn minority votes into massively inflated parliamentary majorities. The disingenuous dismissal from the outset was that the government 'does not view changes to the voting system as a panacea for the current weaknesses in local government' (DETR, 1998d, para. 4.26) – as if anyone were seriously suggesting that they were.

In their desperate search for ways of getting more British citizens to vote, it might have seemed a useful idea for ministers to look first to those countries whose different electoral systems manage to produce consistently higher turnouts – or, indeed, to those who use compulsory voting: about a sixth of the world's democracies, including Australia, Belgium, Greece and Turkey. However, they turned instead to the administration of elections and *methods* of voting. One of the Electoral Commission's earliest tasks after it was set up in 2000 was to organise and evaluate an extensive programme of pilot schemes, ranging from postal and different forms of electronic voting to the replacement of ballot paper serial numbers with barcodes. While barcodes *per se* are not great vote motivators, the pilots suggested that postal voting definitely could be (see Exhibit 13.7), and it quickly became a widely used option in all major elections, accounting for 15% of the votes cast in the 2005 General Election and nearly 19% in 2010.

Exhibit 13.7 General Election 2010 – the electronic election we never had

Piloting of alternative voting methods
Between 2000 and 2007, the Electoral Commission (EC) evaluated more than 150 pilot schemes, mainly by individual local authorities, testing out various innovations in the electoral process. Most of these pilots were of different voting methods – by post or electronically, by touchtone telephone, the Internet, digital television and SMS text messaging – but they also included electronic counting, extended voting hours and non-traditional voting locations.

Impact on turnout
The Government's main concern, particularly after 2001, was to raise voting turnout.

Postal voting seemed the most effective means – all-postal voting in pilot areas in the 2003 local elections, for example, appeared to raise turnouts on average by 15%, from 34% at the previous election to 49% (Electoral Commission, 2003).

Electronic voting, whether by electronic kiosks in polling stations or remotely, was generally liked by voters for the additional choice it offered, but made little significant difference to turnout.

'An e-enabled General Election sometime after 2006'
The Government's White Paper response to the EC's 2003 pilot evaluation launched a project – CORE (Co-ordinated Online Register of Electors) – to make local electronic electoral registers across the country fully interoperable, which would support a multi-channelled, 'e-enabled General Election sometime after 2006'(ODPM, 2003).

Which just might have happened, had the government:

- Not undermined voters' trust in the electoral system by rushing to introduce **postal voting on demand** in time for the 2001 General Election without adequate planning, public information, safeguards, or, above all, switching to a secure system of **individual registration**.
- Developed a coherent **electoral modernisation strategy**, as advised by the EC, and undertaken a full-scale public and stakeholder consultation.
- Designed a properly **planned programme of pilot studies** based on the requirements of the modernisation strategy, adequately financed and undertaken by local authorities of an appropriate size.
- Not so grotesquely **mismanaged the CORE project** that the delivery of a comparatively simple name and address database, after several years, was apparently shelved indefinitely.
- Avoided alienating voters further through a temporary fixation with **all-postal voting**, with ballot boxes 'consigned to the museum'.
- Listened to even some of the warnings from the US and elsewhere about the **security issues** concerning all forms of electronic voting and counting, and accepted that e-voting could be no more than one, relatively minor, channel in a multi-channel election.
- Responded seriously to the evidence of **large-scale electoral fraud** enabled by postal voting on demand, and followed Northern Ireland in introducing individual registration with personal identifiers at the first available opportunity.

It seemed that the combination of postal voting's novelty and unchecked availability did provide – at least to the tune of a few percentage points – the kind of quick and dirty solution to plummeting turnouts that Ministers apparently wanted. General Election turnout struggled back from just under 60% in 2001 to just over in 2005. Locally, while nothing changed overnight in the quality of either the government or the services that councils were providing, the overall 41% turnouts in 2004 for both the metropolitan boroughs and the shire district councils were the highest since the 1990 poll tax elections. No form of e-voting showed anything like the same impact on turnout, and the pilot programme stumbled to a halt, as the Electoral Commission lost patience with the Government's refusal to bring to the modernisation of elections the strategic thinking, integrity and finance that it merited (see Exhibit 13.7). In 2010, therefore, the country was probably further away from the full multi-channel election envisaged in 2003 than when we wrote this section in the book's previous edition.

Local votes, local issues, local candidates

As noted when discussing the Single Transferable Vote, certain types of reformed electoral system could have the effect of increasing the 'localism' of local elections. Independent, local or minority party candidacies can be encouraged, and electors given more opportunity to vote on local issues, on the merits or otherwise of the candidates, and generally to have a greater influence on election outcomes. But, while an extension of these practices would be welcome to many, they do all in fact *already* happen. Many voters require no exhortations from the editor of *The Times* (see p. 246) to treat local elections as genuinely local events.

This section of the chapter returns to our starting point by introducing some actual illustrations of local voting behaviour. A comprehensive study of the subject, Miller's provocatively entitled *Irrelevant Elections?* (1988), found that, even in the 1980s, when many more citizens identified strongly with political parties than they do in 2010, a great many voters treated local elections very much as *local* events. Over half of Miller's respondents claimed to be influenced in local elections more by local than by national issues, and two-fifths to vote more for individual candidates than for the party. In all, one in five electors reported voting for *candidates of different parties* in local and parliamentary elections – to which must be added the many more who supported candidates of the same party in the two sets of elections, but on the basis of different considerations.

A certain proportion of this differential voting behaviour will inevitably be self-cancelling; with some voters preferring Party A's candidate locally and Party B's nationally, while others do the reverse. There has, though, been a perceptible bias in recent years towards the Conservatives in parliamentary

Exhibit 13.8 Minor parties, local parties and independents

A few of the many smaller parties contesting, and winning, recent local elections:

GREEN PARTY – evolved from the Ecology Party (1975–85). Peaked in 1989 with 15% of the vote in Euro-elections, but has gradually increased profile and presence at all levels of government. 120+ councillors in 2010: Brighton & Hove (13), Norwich (13), Lancaster (12) + 2 London Assembly members, and, at last, 1 MP.

BRITISH NATIONAL PARTY – formed in 1982 from the National Front. Nick Griffin's 'respectable' leadership swapped its racism for 'ethno-nationalism' and a populist programme aimed at the disaffected from both main parties. 54 councillors in 2009, incl. 12 in Barking & Dagenham (B&D), slashed to 28 in 2010: B&D (0), Stoke-on-Trent (5) + 1 London Assembly member.

RESPECT – broad socialist party, whose name is its ideology: Respect, Equality, Socialism, Peace, Environmentalism, Community, Trade Unionism. Formed 2004, and within two years had 1 MP (George Galloway), 12 Tower Hamlets councillors, plus Salma Yaqoob in Birmingham. But, following a split with a Socialist Workers faction, down to 4 councillors in 2010.

RESIDENTS' AND RATEPAYERS' ASSOCIATIONS – longstanding alternatives to parties as a form of representative democracy. Historically strong in suburban Surrey – Epsom and Ewell, run by RAs since 1936, and Elmbridge; also East London/Essex – Epping Forest, Barking and Havering, where they have been part of power-sharing administrations.

MEBYON KERNOW – 'Sons of Cornwall' or, more prosaically, 'The Party for Cornwall'. Leftish and decentralist, rather than separatist. For a better deal for a neglected county, especially a Cornish Assembly, rather than new unitary council that cost them 9 former district councillors; would replace council tax with Cornwall-based local tax system.

HEALTH CONCERN – classic campaign group turned political party, with own MP 2001–10, Dr Richard Taylor. In 1998 campaigned to stop the downgrading of Kidderminster hospital and the loss of its A&E department. In 1999 deprived Labour of overall control of Wyre Forest Council. In 2000 was the largest group on the council and part of an anti-Labour governing coalition.

BOSTON BYPASS INDEPENDENTS – also a single-issue campaign group – for (surprise!) a bypass around Boston, Lincs. It became a multi-issue party, won 25 of the council's 32 seats in 2007, and became the first majority administration since 1972. Down to 18 councillors in 2010, following defections – mainly to the Better Boston Group.

MORECAMBE BAY INDEPENDENTS – formed in 1980s to campaign for a council separate from Lancaster City, but made such public impact that they ran the council from 1999 to 2003 as a minority administration. In 2009 gained their own Morecambe Town Council, and in 2010 were back running Lancaster in a Lab/LD/Green/MBI power-share.

COMMUNITY ACTION – loose-knit, Wigan-based association of (following splits) leftish localists. Sudden breakthrough in 2004, winning 18 seats on Wigan Council and becoming the opposition to Labour; but, after defections and expulsions, down to 4 in 2010. Interesting mix of policies: cancel Third World debt and save Wigan's population of ruddy ducks.

elections and towards non-Conservative parties locally, with the Liberal Democrats in particular polling consistently higher locally than nationally. We know this, because the 'synchro-elections' in 1979, 1997, 2001 and 2005 – when prime ministers Callaghan, Major and Blair, respectively, were forced or chose to call General Elections on a day already fixed for the year's local elections – enabled us to measure it. Millions of voters in these elections found themselves with two votes to cast: one for an MP and one for a local – usually county – councillor. By comparing constituencies in which each major party fielded candidates in both parliamentary and all local contests, we can see how a great many of them split their votes between candidates of different parties (Wilson and Game, 2006, Exhibit 11.8 – and on linked website).

Synchro-elections are fun, at least for political scientists, but for the present purposes they are not really necessary. There is plenty of evidence to be found of the impact of local electoral influences through the study of almost any set of local results. Start digging beneath the headlines and the aggregated figures, and you will be struck almost immediately by the diversity and apparent inconsistency of the detailed ward-by-ward results. One ward is gained by the Conservative candidate, while an adjacent, previously Conservative-held ward is lost. Labour win control of one council but lose control of several others. Third and minority party candidates and Independents win seats and even whole councils against all other parties (see Exhibit 13.8).

The June 2004 elections – baths and bus routes as well as Baghdad

For our illustrations of local electoral influences at work we have chosen 2004, the year mentioned above as having produced an unusually large turnout. It was unusual in other ways too. The local elections – for all metropolitan and 108 English unitary and district councils, Welsh unitary councils, the London Mayor and Assembly – were postponed from May, because of the earlier outbreak of foot-and-mouth disease, and coincided with the June European Parliamentary elections. The delay, though, was immaterial, because, as the electorate was told repeatedly by the national media, these elections would be all about the US/UK invasion of Iraq, and, if not, then about opposition to the EU and its proposed constitution. Any local issues would be submerged in what would be in effect a national opinion poll, the expected outcome being a heavy defeat for Labour councils and councillors, swept out of office on what would in reality be an anti-government or anti-Blair vote.

The post-election headlines suggested that this is exactly what did happen. Labour's results were among its worst ever. Its 26% share of the national vote was below that of both the Conservatives and the Liberal Democrats, it lost a total of 545 seats and its former control on 16 councils, including Newcastle and Doncaster – both for the first time in 30 years, Leeds, Burnley, Ipswich, Oxford, Cardiff and Swansea. The Lib Dems took Newcastle and Pendle (Lancs) and gained 239 seats. The Conservatives gained 315 seats and 12 councils, including Dudley, Trafford and Walsall metropolitan boroughs, and Eastbourne from the Lib Dems. End of story – *if* these elections really had been fought and won entirely on national issues.

Scratch beneath the headline figures, though, and you will quickly encounter anomalies. Among all their losses, Labour in fact *gained* 84 seats and as many as 7 new councils – including Hartlepool and Stoke-on-Trent, both led at the time by Independent elected mayors. Similarly, the Lib Dems' victories were qualified by the *loss* of 110 seats and 4 councils. Even the Conservatives lost 56 seats, including that of their group leader on the London Assembly, and, more significantly, they failed to prevent Ken Livingstone's re-election as London's Mayor.

As indicated in Chapter 5, Livingstone's win owed almost everything to his unique public profile and the well-regarded record of his first term of office, but, on a necessarily smaller scale, there would have been comparable 'local' factors of some sort at play in all the other results that deviated appreciably from the national trend. In Swansea, for example, voters were certainly disaffected, but more by the Labour council's closure of civic swimming baths than by the fate of Baghdad, while in Redditch it was voters' opposition, not to Saddam that swept Labour back to power, but to the Conservatives' plans to abolish concessionary bus fares for the elderly and vulnerable. In other places the story was sheer hard work by local party activists, as one Labour councillor in Birmingham defeated by a Lib Dem ruefully acknowledged (Coulson, 2005): '[It was] the culmination for them of ten years of serious leafleting, six or seven leaflets to each house ahead of each election, the quality of the leaflets greatly improved by the use of desktop publishing and fast Xerox copying.'

The point about all these local factors – let alone the micro-local issues, such as the number 14 bus route and new dog mess bins that a Milton Keynes candidate, Liz Campbell, found raised when she canvassed on doorsteps (Campbell, 2004) – is that they are completely unknown to national journalists and election 'pundits'. Perplexed, they resort to dismissing as 'freak' or 'maverick' any result that doesn't fit into their own national picture of what the elections were about. But, of course, they are not freak; simply the visible and perfectly rational products of voters' recognition that, on this occasion, it was not an MP they were being asked to elect, or a national government, but a local councillor and council to carry out local policies and provide local services. It is to these councillors that we turn in Chapter 14.

Councillors: The Voice of Choice

Public image – poor to invisible

In early 2009, Barbara Windsor's character, Peggy, in the soap opera *EastEnders*, was prompted – by the planned opening of a massage parlour near the Queen Vic pub where she was landlady – to stand as an Independent candidate for election to the fictional Walford London Borough Council. In the event, at the request of future-husband Archie Mitchell, she withdrew from the campaign ahead of their wedding, but a later storyline involved the London Mayor, Boris Johnson, visiting the Queen Vic, in an episode watched by 8 million viewers. Years before these momentous events, the Local Government Association (LGA) had lobbied hard to get an informative and sympathetic local government storyline into ITV's North Yorkshire soap, *Emmerdale*, and you can understand why. The image of councillors conveyed to TV viewers – even before the ninth *Dr Who*'s encounter with the alien, flatulent and definitely unelected Lord Mayor of Cardiff ('Boom Town') and her city centre nuclear power station scheme – has been not so much bad as awful. *Coronation Street*'s Councillor Audrey Roberts, handicapped by having to be unconvincingly scripted as an Independent on what in reality would be a party-dominated council, was self-important and manipulable. *EastEnders*' Ian Beale, in his brief membership of Walford Council, operated entirely self-interestedly and quite possibly corruptly. And the two outstanding 'state of the nation' drama serials of the 1990s – Alan Bleasdale's *GBH*, with Robert Lindsay, and Peter Flannery's *Our Friends in the North*, with Christopher Eccleston – both had councillors' abuse of power and corruptibility running through their storylines (see Brooke, 2005; Mahony, 2005).

This chapter explores – with a bit more information and balance – who councillors really are, what they do, and why they do it. In previous editions it opened with our suggesting that readers try to talk to one or two of their own councillors, to find out at first hand how they spend their time and justify their elective existences. We realise, though, that this can be easier said than done, given our exceptionally large local authorities and high citizen:councillor ratios. Perhaps surprisingly, 47% of a sample of British adults, surveyed in 2008, reckoned they knew at least a fair amount about their local council – compared to 38% who claimed a similar knowledge about the Westminster Parliament (LGA, 2008, p. 9). Asked about the councillors, though, they readily admitted widespread ignorance. Two-thirds had never met any of their councillors and couldn't name them, and even more knew either nothing at all (26%) or not very much (54%) about what they do (LGA, 2008, pp. 14–15).

Bearing such things in mind, in the fourth edition of this book we provided our own pen portraits of a handful of councillors as an introduction to what was obviously for many an unfamiliar world. Not in this edition, though – for two reasons. The minor one is that one of the book's reviewers made clear he didn't like them, because the councillors described were 'non-existent' and stereotypical. The latter they might have been, but the former definitely not; they were all very real, and most of them we knew personally. Curious readers can judge for themselves, as the most recent ones are now on our linked website.

The main reason for their removal, however, is that they are no longer necessary. Since we started, councillor profiles and self-profiles have become commonplace. Increasingly, councillors blog and use Facebook and other social media (see the 21st Century Councillor website on http://social-media.21st.cc). Both leading local government weeklies – *LGC* (*Local Government Chronicle*) and *The MJ* (*Municipal Journal*) – run regular councillor profiles. The LGA's *firstonline* weekly magazine has a 'day in the life of …' column to which councillors, among others, contribute. Then there is the *c'llr.* magazine – 'information and inspiration for councillors' – produced every two months by the Local Government Information Unit (LGIU) and, downloadable from the 'What we do' page on their website. Each issue has a 'My Patch' article featuring councillors who, like those below, are in some way noteworthy.

Yash Gupta (*c'llr.*, April 2010) was Thurrock's first ethnic minority councillor when initially elected in 1996. He arrived from India in the 1960s, worked as a teacher, became an educational psychologist, and won for Labour what he had been told was a safe Conservative seat. Since then he estimates he has dealt with 3,030 items of casework for his ward residents. By contrast, Hayley Matthews (*c'llr.*, November 2009) was just 22 when, fresh out of university, she was elected as a Liberal Democrat to Brent Council in 2006 for the area in which she grew up. When interviewed, she had recently taken over the portfolio for crime prevention and public safety in a Lib Dem/Conservative administration, and guessed she might be the country's youngest Cabinet member. She was wrong, however; Paul Holmes (*c'llr.*, February 2010) was elected as a Conservative councillor to Southampton City Council while still at university, aged 19. At 20 he became Cabinet Member for Children's Services and Learning, politically answerable for the education system that, as was no doubt frequently observed, he himself had left only comparatively recently.

Bob Bryant (*c'llr.*, January 2009) was a 38-year-old oil tanker driver with no special interest in politics when he suffered a massive stroke that left him wheelchair-reliant. Disagreeing strongly with his ward councillor's plans for the local hospital's stroke unit, he got himself elected on the Labour ticket to Halton Council (Cheshire), where he has developed an unofficial role as a tireless campaigner and spokesperson for the borough's disabled. Marisa Heath also changed career for the world of local government, but in her case from being a *Vogue*-featured teenage fashion model. She did an MSc in International Relations, and became a Conservative councillor, first on Runnymede Borough Council and then Surrey County Council, where, in 2008, she was the council's 'Looked-after children Champion'. She has also worked as a Parliamentary Officer, but, unlike many of her contemporaries, has no immediate interest in becoming an MP herself. She says, 'Local government is very undervalued. Looking after children is a vitally important service. My being involved in this service is more important than being a backbencher' (Hailstone, 2008).

It is a small cast list with which to start, but one comprising indisputably real people. They are not, we feel, stereotypical, and certainly not typical in any statistical sense. Three men, two women; three in their twenties, two definitely not; three on unitary councils, one from a London borough, and a dual county/district member; two Conservatives, two Labour, one Lib Dem; two executive members, three non-executives. Plenty of labels and contrasts, but what do they have in common – among themselves and with the other 21,000 councillors across the country?

Elected local politicians – the voice of choice

To begin with – and it is not quite the obvious statement it may appear – they are, all 21,000 of them, elected local politicians. Or rather, all 21,000 councillor seats on principal local authorities are held by elected local politicians. As shown in Exhibit 14.1, around one in eight in the latest census of councillors is, like Marisa Heath, a member on two local authorities – which means that the actual number of councillors is roughly 19,000. Dual membership is a questionable practice that all parties – Labour in particular – would prefer not to be as widespread as it is. But such is the shortage of competent candidates, prepared to spend half a working week on council-related business, that it has become a fact of life. Against that background, let us examine the three parts of our description in turn.

There was a time when the majority of members on many councils were unelected. Part of the reason was *aldermen*: usually senior and experienced councillors, who were appointed by the elected councillors to bolster their numbers by up to an additional third, and to add expertise and continuity. Their appointments were for six years – compared to councillors' then three-year term of office (now extended to four years).

They tended to take disproportionate numbers of committee chairs and vice-chairs, and never had to seek the support of, or face possible defeat from, a fickle electorate. They were undemocratic, but they unaccountably – in all senses – lived on until, apart from in Northern Ireland and the City of London, they and their Scottish near-equivalents, *bailies,* were finally abolished in the 1970s.

These unelected aldermen would have seemed even more anachronistic, had not many councillors themselves also never had to face an election. As noted in Chapter 13, the sorry truth is that, throughout most of the history of UK local government, thousands of council seats at each year's elections were filled by unopposed returns. By the 1960s, 40% or more councillors were winning or retaining their council memberships unchallenged.

There thus existed a double democratic deficit: up to a quarter of council members who did not have to be elected, and large numbers who should have been but were not. This is one local government deficit that has, since the 1972–4 reorganisation, been virtually eliminated. With more than 95% of seats in most parts of the country now being contested by more candidates than at any time previously, councillors, both individually and collectively, can claim with far greater legitimacy to be speaking as their community's 'voice of choice'. They are the instruments through which the residents of a particular geographical area have expressed their preferences for one set of candidates, policies, service standards and tax levels, rather than another.

Politicians all

Choice, preference, priorities ... they are the currency of politics, and those who translate them into practical policies are politicians. The third attribute of all our councillors – in addition to being at least nominally elected and representing specific geographical localities – is that they are politicians. All of them – even the small minority of self-styled 'non-partisans' and 'independents' – perform what Sir Lawrence Boyle, a key member of the Widdicombe Committee, termed the 'political function':

> all governments, be they central or local, have a two-fold function to perform: the service function and the political function. The service function consists of the provision of those goods and services that for one reason or another are supplied through the public sector. The political function, on the other hand, is the management and reduction of the conflict that arises out of the issues involved in the public provision of goods and services. It embraces such questions as *the scope, the scale and the quality of the public services and the manner in which their*

costs should be met. And it should be noted that it is easier in fact to remove the service function from local government than to remove the political function. Because the service function, as we know, can always be privatised, but *the political function cannot and should not be delegated. If the political function is removed from local government, it ceases to be local government*. (Boyle, 1986, p. 33, emphases ours)

That, surely, is what we expect of our elected representatives, national and local alike: that they debate and determine *themselves* – not delegate to unelected officials, or self-selected community forums – the distribution of our society's resources. Electors delegate the political function to them: to take on their behalf decisions about the building of houses, schools and roads, about levels of service provision and rates of taxation. That is their role and responsibility, whether or not they happen to have been elected under a party label. Most are; and we shall see in Chapter 16 how that party identity shapes almost every aspect of their work.

Representatives, not reflections

Councillors, then, are all local elected politicians. But what *kinds* of people are they, who have the apparent arrogance to wish to exercise *their* political will on the behalf of others, yet who are, at the same time, prepared to plead for the electorate's votes, and to risk ridicule and rejection? How like their own electors are they, or how different? The standard response tends to detail councillors' personal and socio-economic characteristics, as in Exhibit 14.1. There is nothing wrong with such data. They are relatively easily collected and categorised – in fact, there are regular councillor censuses – and they furnish us with measures of over- or under-representation of particular attributes in the councillor population. It is, for example, worth knowing – rather than merely suspecting – that there are fewer women councillors than councillors over conventional retirement age, and worth testing out those cartoon or essay-title characterisations: 'Councillors are male, pale and stale/rich, retired, redundant. Discuss, and illustrate your answer with statistics' (see Figure 14.1).

Such data, though, have their limitations. They can prompt misleading generalisations. They may obscure significant contrasts among councillors on different types of councils, and from different parties – though these can be checked in the detailed census tables available on the LGA website. They can also seem to imply that 'representative government' is more about trying to produce a socio-economic reflection of the electorate than about the representation of ideas and ideals. With these reservations in mind, we draw out a few key distinctions and implications – in the hope of *discouraging* the idea that there is a 'typical councillor'.

Exhibit 14.1 Personal characteristics of councillors, England, 2008

Party (percentage of 19,617 total)	(LFS)	All C'llors	Cons. (49%)	Lab. (22%)	LD (22%)	Ind. (6%)
GENDER						
Male	49	72	73	66	65	76
Female	51	28	27	34	35	24
ETHNIC MINORITY	11	3.4	1.5	8.9	2.4	1.2
Black (total numbers)		(97)	(7)	(66)	(18)	(4)
Indian		(206)	(53)	(132)	(17)	(2)
Pakistani		(121)	(21)	(77)	(23)	(0)
Other, including mixed		(210)	(57)	(86)	(43)	(7)
Total		(634)	(138)	(361)	(101)	(13)
AGE						
Under 30	21	2	2	3	2	*
30–49	36	18	18	20	20	12
50–59	15	23	20	29	25	19
60–69	13	39	41	36	40	43
70 and over	14	17	20	13	13	25
Average		59	60	57	58	63
EDUCATION – HIGHEST QUALIFICATION						
Degree or equivalent (NVQ 4/5, HNC, HND)	29	51	47	51	63	36
GCE A-level or equivalent (NVQ 3, ONC, OND)	15	12	13	9	10	11
GCE O-level or equivalent (NVQ 2, School Cert)	14	11	12	8	9	13
Trade apprenticeship/other	28	8	9	10	6	14
No formal qualifications	14	18	18	22	12	25
EMPLOYMENT STATUS						
Full-time paid employment	43	22	20	26	23	17
Part-time paid employment	14	10	8	13	12	6
Self-employed	8	16	21	8	14	18
Retired	22	44	46	40	42	53
Other (incl. unemployed, disabled, f/t education)	13	8	6	13	10	6
CURRENT OCCUPATION (excl. council work)						
Managerial/executive		37	43	29	31	40
Professional/technical		33	33	32	35	20
Teacher/lecturer/researcher		9	5	13	14	4
Admin/clerical/secretarial/sales		12	11	15	12	15
Manual/craft		9	8	11	8	21
TIME SPENT ON COUNCIL/POLITICAL BUSINESS (average hours per week)		(22)	(22)	(25)	(22)	(20)
DUAL MEMBERSHIP (of more than one principal council) (Total = 2,265)		12	11	10	15	8

Notes: LFS = National Labour Force Survey data.
Columns may not total 100%, due to rounding, and omitted categories.
( ) = actual number, not percentage; ☐ = significantly higher than for adult population.
Source: NFER (2009b), plus additional data downloadable from the LGA website.

Figure 14.1 *Cartoon – Councillor diversity?*

Source: *Local Government Chronicle*, 17 April 2008.

Gender

Most readers will surely find the gender figures in Exhibit 14.1 dispiriting, even if the proportion of women councillors has increased by about a half since the 1980s and, as ever, is substantially higher than that of women MPs (22% in 2010). In fact, though lagging well behind Sweden (45%), Norway and Finland (36/37%) and the UK's own PR-elected Welsh Assembly (47% from 2007) and Scottish Parliament (33%, down from 40% in 2003), Britain has more women councillors than most European countries (CEMR-Dexia, 2009, p. 15). Several councils, indeed, can boast gender parity, if not more – Great Yarmouth (77% women), Havering (72%), Islington (54%) – though there are others who seem not to have heard of the idea – Craven, West Somerset, Rushmoor (each 13/14%) (NFER, 2009b). Across the Channel, however, several countries – France, Belgium, Spain, Portugal – have followed much of the rest of the world in adopting gender quotas to increase the representation of women in both national and local government, and the pressure will surely grow on UK political parties to consider at least something equivalent (Game, 2009a).

Does such gender distortion matter? Inevitably, yes. Councils on which 75% of members are men simply do not pursue similar priorities and arrive in a similar way at similar decisions as would councils with even 40%, let alone 75%, of women members. The cliché illustration is that more women would mean better child-care facilities and fewer municipal golf courses. But there is much more to it than that. Women are the main users of council services. They make three-quarters of all calls to council departments. They are the majority of tenants, the family members who make the most use of swimming pools and libraries, who are the most likely to put the bins out for collection, and who are most affected by the quality of the local environment – inadequate street cleansing, poor lighting, dog fouling, pot-holed roads and pavements, inadequate public transport, and street crime. They are likely to have distinctive priorities and agendas; indeed, perhaps more likely to have agendas of any sort – because, some would claim, women are more interested in power for a purpose, rather than for its own sake.

If you still have doubts, try two simple questions. Why do most public buildings have far fewer female than male lavatories, instead of recognising, like the rebuilt Royal Opera House – a noteworthy exception to the rule – that roughly three times as much space should properly be allowed for women as for men? And why, as a Birmingham overview and scrutiny committee discovered, do so few public sector organisations have workplace policies covering the specific needs of breast-feeding mothers returning to work?

Ethnic minorities

An equivalent argument applies to the under-representation of ethnic minorities – a disappointing 3.4% compared with 4% of MPs in 2010 and 11% of all adults. While the election of black and Asian councillors in particular has increased markedly in recent years, their presence is still recorded more meaningfully, as in Exhibit 14.1, in absolute numbers rather than percentages.

But national figures in this instance are particularly misleading. What matter are the levels and details of representation in those areas with sizeable ethnic minority populations. In Birmingham, for example, there are more than 20 ethnic minority members on the 120-seat City Council. Twenty per cent might seem like a tolerable representation of the city's 30% ethnic minority population – until you consider the sheer diversity of that population: the African-Caribbeans; the Kashmiri restaurant owners, taxi drivers and textile industry outworkers; the Punjabi Sikhs, with their prominent role in the local economy; the small-business-owning Gujuratis from both India and East Africa; the Bangladeshis; Yemenis; Chinese and Vietnamese, and all the newer refugees – the Somalis, Sudanese, Afghans, Bosnians, ethnic Albanians, Kurds, Iranians, Iraqis, and the many more identifiable 'communities' in the city. Most of these groups are bound to feel unrepresented – not merely under-represented – on the City Council in any direct racial, religious or cultural sense, and if this is true in Birmingham, it is even more so in most other towns and cities.

Age

If age really did bring wisdom, our local government could compete with the Chinese gerontocracy, for the world of councillors is an increasingly middle-aged and elderly one. The three members in their twenties in our introductory sample are very much the exceptions. In the 1985 Widdicombe Committee survey reported in this book's early editions, over a quarter of all councillors were under the age of 45, including a third of Labour members and nearly a half of the then Liberals. Over 25 years that proportion has halved, to just 13%, compared with 48% of all adults. Labour and the Lib Dems are still the 'youthful' parties in modern-day local government, but even they have age averages of 57/58 – at least 7 years higher than those of MPs. The proportion of councillors aged over 60 (56%) is three times that of MPs – 19% in 2010 (Hackett and Hunter, 2010). In Scotland, the average age is slightly lower, but it is higher for English counties and was for Welsh councils until the Assembly approved a 'past service award scheme' of severance payments of up to £20,000 for older councillors, to encourage them to retire. Few councils, though, are anything other than visibly venerable, which is surely concerning for bodies whose responsibilities include childminding, children's centres, crèches, day nurseries, play centres, parent and toddler groups, pre-school playgroups, toy libraries and nursery schools.

Education

Partly as a result of their age profile, councillors as a whole are both better and no better educated than their constituents. Returning again to the 1985 Widdicombe survey, the proportion of councillors with no formal qualifications (23%) was half that among the adult population as a whole. Today those relative positions are reversed, and the proportion of councillors without qualifications exceeds that among all adults. There are still differences, though, in levels of qualifications, with 51% of councillors having a degree or equivalent, compared to less than a third of the general population. While such qualifications are not in themselves, of course, any measure of fitness or aptitude for government, education is presumably one characteristic on which most of us would be happy to see our elected representatives not perfectly reflective of the population at large.

Employment

Given the long-standing tradition of council membership being a voluntary and part-time activity, it is striking that only 38% of today's councillors are in full-time paid employment – a figure that varies in total very little across the parties, though the employed/self-employed balance predictably does. Part of the explanation of the major decline from 65% in 1976 and 54% in 1985 is obviously the fact that as many as 44% are now retired, compared to just 16% in 1976 (Gyford *et al.*, 1989, p. 51). The other key factor, as we shall see, is that councillors' allowances have increased significantly, to levels that can support, albeit modestly, a life-style as a full-time councillor. In the past, few councillors openly admitted to being 'full-time', no matter how many hours a week they put into the job. In the 2001 councillor census, at the advent of executive-based local government, more than 30% accepted the 'full-time' label, and, with over half in the 2008 census being in 'senior positions' and receiving special responsibility allowances, the number of effectively full-time councillors, especially on unitary and upper tier councils, must now be significantly higher still.

With their higher educational qualifications, it is not surprising to find councillors being drawn disproportionately from non-manual backgrounds in general, and from professional and managerial groups in particular. There is a correspondingly low proportion of manual workers: less than 10%, compared with nearly 30% of the adult population. The manual proportion of Labour councillors in particular has fallen, from 35% in 1985, and in recent years has been scarcely higher than that for all councillors.

Councillors' jobs and roles

We now know something about who councillors are. They come from all kinds of backgrounds and walks of life, and it is neither easy nor helpful to talk of there being a 'typical' councillor. So does it follow that there is no such thing as a typical councillor's job? Yes, it does. Different councillors will have their differing interests, motivations, skills, aptitudes and opportunities, and they will at least endeavour to spend their inevitably limited time in differing ways.

There is nowadays, unlike in the past, at least some guidance in most councils' constitutions (usually Part 2, Article 2) as to councillors' 'Roles and Functions', swiftly followed by their 'Rights and Duties'. These are of limited assistance, partly because of their blandness, but mainly because they are aimed consciously at 'all councillors', which, in the regime of executive-based local government, means that they cannot provide more than a very incomplete picture. With that proviso, however, we can construct out of these role lists a kind of composite starting description, as in Exhibit 14.2, not so much of the councillor's job, but of the job of councillors.

To balance its limitations, this kind of starting description has three considerable virtues. First, it is a neat distillation of what might otherwise be a lengthy catalogue of more specific councillor duties and responsibilities.

Exhibit 14.2 The job of (all) councillors

- To represent, be accountable to, and an advocate for, all their electors ...
- in formulating policies and practices for the local authority ...
- monitoring their effectiveness ...
- and providing leadership for the community ...
- while (of course) maintaining the highest standards of conduct and ethics.

Second, it takes us far beyond the traditional and apparently almost unthinking textbook distinctions that used to be made between 'policy' and 'administration': that councillors made policy and officers implemented and administered it, and ne'er the twain should meet. The sheer lack of realism underpinning this 'formal model', as we term it in Chapter 17, grated most with local government practitioners. Was it seriously imagined, on the one hand, that a small group of part-time, amateur councillors had the capacity – or even the inclination – to produce a 'policy' for every aspect of every council service *without* there being a necessarily substantial contribution from the numerous highly trained, experienced and generally well-paid officers whom they themselves employed? Similarly, were councillors really supposed, having delivered their policy pronouncements like proverbial tablets of stone, to stand aside and pay no attention as to how the policy was delivered and to its impact on their own local residents and electors?

This thought brings us to the third virtue of our starting definition, which is its expression in language that makes sense to councillors themselves. Councillor roles and 'role orientations' have long been a favourite topic of academic investigation, and some insightful studies resulted (Lee, 1963; Heclo, 1969; Hampton, 1970; Budge *et al.*, 1972; Dearlove, 1973; Jones, 1973; Corina, 1974; Newton, 1976; Jennings, 1982; Gyford, 1984). But so too has a positive lexicon of role labels: politico, delegate, trustee, representative, broad policy-maker, tribune, statesman, ministerialist, parochial, people's agent, policy advocate, policy spokesperson, policy broker, party politician, ideologist, partyist, facilitator, resister, politico-administrator, communicator, populist, conventional politician, community politician.

For the reader, such a proliferation of labels can produce confusion as well as enlightenment. From most councillors, though, the most likely response would be cynicism. Even if they recognised the actual words, they would never think of using most of them to describe the behaviour of either themselves or other councillors. They would, however, recognise and identify with the language of representation and accountability, policy formulation, performance monitoring and community leadership.

The councillor's 'traditional' job description thus embraces a wide variety of potential roles and responsibilities – as representative, policy-maker, scrutineer and community leader. Today, without further qualification, that simply will not do. With executive-based policy-making, and councillors having to be either part of their council's executive or not, some of these roles and responsibilities continue to be shared by all councillors, and all are exercised by some. But, for the first time, not all councillors are able even to claim that they have all roles. To explain, we shall examine each in turn.

Representative – on the grand scale

We start with the most fundamental role, yet sometimes the most over-looked. In our system of local government every councillor is elected by, and is accountable to, the residents of a defined geographical area, known as an electoral *ward* or *division* – 'constituency' being primarily a parliamentary term. With the exceptional scale of UK local government, these local electorates can be dauntingly large from the viewpoint of councillors trying to represent them.

Exhibit 14.3 lists only the 'old' EU countries, but its underlying message would hold, no matter how many other countries were added. We have proportionately fewer and much larger 'local' authorities than almost any other Western country, and, as noted, they are steadily becoming fewer and larger. Corollaries of this scale of 'local' government are that – with the single exception of the Republic of Ireland, the most centrally administered governmental system in Western Europe – we citizens have fewer councillors to represent us, and, as the figures at the start of this chapter confirm, we are less likely to know or be known by them. If anything, the figures in the final columns of Exhibit 14.3 understate the scale of the councillor's task. When many districts' multi-member wards are taken into account, an average English district councillor has an *electorate* of between 3,000 and 5,000, a county councillor one of up to 10,000, and a metropolitan district, unitary or London borough councillor one larger still. Multiply these figures by, say, 1.5 for total residential populations, and the reality is that in large city and unitary authorities councillors may represent wards of up to 25,000 people.

As with other aspects of the job, councillors themselves decide how much energy they put into the representation of their electorate. They do not *have* to hold surgeries or advice bureaux, or publicise their availability to deal with constituents' problems, complaints, queries and opinions. Most councillors, however, do choose to do these things, and much more besides. In which case, they are likely to find themselves acting in several distinct representational 'sub-roles', in addition to case-worker and individual problem-solver: as listener, advocate, ring-holder, facilitator and empowerer (Goss and Corrigan, 1999, pp. 13 ff.).

They *listen,* and talk of course, when they meet the various groups, organisations and individuals within their wards: tenants' and residents'

Exhibit 14.3 Britain's large-scale local government, by population per council

	Population (millions)	Number of first-tier (most local) councils	Average pop. per council	Total number of councillors	Persons per councillor
France	64	36,682 Communes	1,750	515,000	125
Austria	8	2,357 Gemeinden	3,540	40,570	200
Spain	46	8,115 Municipios	5,620	65,000	700
Germany	82	12,339 Gemeinden	6,655	198,000	400
Italy	60	8,101 Comuni	7,395	97,000	600
Greece	11	1,034 Dimoi, Kinotites,	10,870	18,600	600
Finland	5	348 Kunta	15,265	10,400	500
Belgium	11	589 Gemeenten/commune	18,180	13,000	800
Sweden	9	290 Kommuner	31,790	46,200*	200*
Portugal	11	308 Municipios	34,485	9,000	1,200
Netherlands	16	441 Gemeenten	37,280	9,600	1,700
Ireland	4	85 Counties, cities, boroughs	38,975	870	4,500
Denmark	5	98 Kommuner	56,040	2,500	2,000
EU 27	499	90,782	5,530		
(England)†	50	354 Counties, districts, etc.	141,000	18,200	2,750
UK†	61	434 Counties, districts, etc.	141,000	21,300	2,860

Notes: * includes Alternates, elected at the same time; † England and UK figures are for 2010 and for *all* councils, rather than just first-tier. To enable the most realistic cross-national comparisons, these figures exclude tiers of councils that, like the UK's parish, town and community councils, have only very limited service responsibilities and/or are not universal.
Sources: CEMR-Dexia (2005); The Local Channel (2009), pp. 4, 7; individual countries' sources.

associations, community groups, housing associations, youth clubs, local fetes, health and police authorities, local business people and journalists. They act as *advocates* in ensuring that the views, needs and problems of local people, particularly those likely to experience access difficulties, reach the appropriate sections of the council. Sooner or later they will be required to act as *ring-holder* in some dispute between individuals or groups, each convinced of the validity and justice of their case. They will go further and *facilitate,* by working with excluded, aggrieved or factionalised groups, bringing people together to discuss problems and jointly agree solutions. And on occasion they may *empower,* assisting local groups to organise, prepare and resource themselves in order to manage some council project or take over responsibility for a service. The 2007 Local Government and Public Involvement in Health Act added a dimension to the representative role in the form of the Councillor Call for Action (CCfA). If a local government or crime and disorder issue of concern arises in a councillor's ward and there appears no satisfactory means of resolution, they can bring the issue to the council's Petitions Committee and ultimately to an overview and scrutiny committee for review.

All these 'external' activities are capable of bringing relatively swift and positive outcomes and, very occasionally, an expression of gratitude from those benefiting. The rewards of 'internal' town hall or county hall work, especially for a non-executive member, may seem more diffuse, and it is easy to understand why many councillors find that their representational work is what brings them greater satisfaction (Barron *et al.,* 1987, pp. 73 ff.). Intriguing (in all senses) as he sometimes found meetings in Lambeth town hall, Jonathan Myerson, a member of the council's Labour minority group from 2002 to 2006, was one of those. Certainly, there has been no better contemporary insight into the councillor's representative role than that provided by his monthly *Society Guardian* columns. They merited preservation in book form, but most are still accessible – including 'The 10 best ways to waste a councillor's time' (which finally became 16); 'The world's most ungrateful refugee' (since we mentioned gratitude); and his final reflective piece, 'Farewell, my fiefdom' – on the *Guardian* website: just Google 'Jonathan Myerson councillor'.

For other first-hand accounts, several authorities, including Kirklees, Stockport, Tameside and Tunbridge Wells, have developed the useful practice of having their councillors produce regular or annual reports for their personal websites detailing what they have been doing, and what they feel they have achieved. More fun, though, and probably also more insightful are councillors' blogs, helpfully listed in *Total Politics' Political Blog Directory.* There were 135 in early 2010, the main parties' top three being: Alex Foulkes (Lib Dem – 'Lanson Boy'), Mark Bennett (Labour – 'According to Mark'), and Kingston Council's Alexandra ward members ('Alexandra Ward Conservatives').

Policy-maker

The mention of town halls brings us to the policy role of councillors – traditionally their work in committees and sub-committees in developing policy, for the authority as a whole and for particular services. They are assisted, informed, advised, and perhaps even steered, by their officers, but constitutionally they have the responsibility for giving strategic direction to the authority and for determining its policy priorities.

In the past, this policy or executive role, like that of representative, was shared by all councillors, though again the nature and impact of their contribution varied enormously. A committee might be chaired by a long-serving member, seemingly as conversant with the technical details of departmental policy as most of the professional officers, but include also a neophyte and perhaps minority party backbencher, still struggling to follow the procedure of the committee, let alone its agenda. All councils, however, organised their work through committees, and all councillors would find themselves appointed to at least one or two of these. All councillors could thus quite properly regard themselves as contributing to policy-making in at least some of their council's service areas, and all were collectively responsible for its policy as a whole. All too were potentially liable to be individually surcharged for supporting unlawful local expenditure, even when they themselves had received no personal benefit from the decision – quite unlike, say, a government minister who is demonstrably responsible for a major and extremely costly policy failure. The personal surcharge was finally abolished in the Local Government Act 2000, but, as recently as the rate-capping battles of the mid-1980s, 78 Labour councillors in Liverpool and Lambeth were surcharged a total, with costs, of over £600,000 and consequently bankrupted (Taafe and Mulhearn, 1988).

The far more comprehensive change introduced by the 2000 Act, though, was the executive/non-executive split in councillors' roles described in Chapter 7. From 2001/2 a small minority of councillors on most authorities became executive members – usually with responsibility for a specific service portfolio in a Cabinet or executive board chaired by either a leader or directly elected mayor – while the majority were non-executive members. But even if that portfolio resembled closely the title of a committee they formerly chaired, being a Cabinet member is very different from being a committee chair. The key point of the executive/non-executive split is to clarify publicly who is responsible for making particular policy decisions, and that is what executive members do: they make decisions and take public responsibility for them through the process of scrutiny by non-executive members. Some decisions will be taken collectively, by the cabinet as a whole, but others will be taken *individually* – in a way that previously was not legally permitted for even the most powerful committee chair.

Executive members, then, are now the key *policy-makers,* but that does not mean that non-executive members no longer have a policy role. They do, in several distinct ways. First, as ward representatives and perhaps members of area committees, they see and hear how the policies of the council and other bodies affect their own electors and localities. If a policy is not working as intended, or if service delivery is unsatisfactory, they are likely to be the first to receive complaints, and repeated complaints should feed into the process of policy evaluation and review.

Second, they are members of the *full council,* which, like councillors themselves, has a much changed and potentially enhanced role under executive government. The executive leads the preparation of the local authority's policies and budget, but the policy and budget frameworks have to be agreed formally by the full council. The full council has similarly to agree the many policy plans and strategies that authorities are required to produce: the best value and performance plan, children's services plan, community care plan, crime and disorder reduction strategy, and numerous others. Executive members take 'in-year' decisions on resources and priorities to implement agreed policies, but decisions not in accordance with the policy or budget framework, or that are not constitutionally the executive's responsibility, go to full council. The council also receives and debates all overview and scrutiny reports, which brings us to councillors' third main role, that of scrutineer.

Scrutineer

The policy process is best visualised as a continuous cycle – from initiation, through formulation, enactment and implementation, with the cycle completed by evaluation, the outcome of which may lead in turn to a further policy initiative or adaptation. The cycle does not stop with legislation or enactment, and nor do councillors' policy responsibilities. As John Stewart emphasises (1990, p. 27):

> Councillors are concerned not merely with policy, but with how policy is carried out, for in implementation policy succeeds or fails. Policy and implementation can never be completely separated. Policy is made and re-made in implementation.

The overview and scrutiny (O&S) function is *the* key non-executive role in the government's 'modernisation' of councils' political management, and its effective operation is arguably the real determinant of whether the executive/non-executive split is judged to be a success. The good news, therefore, is that it was given a considerably broader interpretation than at first seemed likely. Instead of an essentially 'inward-focused mechanism for holding the executive to account' (Leach and Copus, 2004, p. 334), it has become, at least potentially, 'a powerful set of arrangements for councillors to influence not only council policy, but also the policies of a range of public and private agencies'. In short, it has introduced into local government something that clearly ought to have existed previously but almost never did. The bad news is that it is the aspect of the new arrangements that councils and the non-executive councillors most affected have found it hardest to get working productively (see, for example, House of Commons, 2002, pp. 14–19; Rao, 2005).

Under the committee system, there had long been something called 'performance review', but it was almost invariably reactive and superficial – often delegated to a single sub-committee with responsibility for monitoring the council's performance across any and all service areas. O&S can and should be unrecognisably different: expansive rather than delimited, proactive rather than reactive, prospective as well as retrospective, creative and constructive as well as critical and blame-seeking (Audit Commission, 2001, p. 9; see also Exhibit 7.5).

Quite properly, councils decide for themselves how to organise the O&S function, though some requirements are non-negotiable. All O&S committees must reflect the political balance of the council, must meet in public, and must review all matters that are the responsibility of the executive, no members of which can be members of a scrutiny committee. Beyond that, the variety of practice is considerable. The average council has four 11-member O&S committees, but a fifth have only one committee, and the range extends up to 11 (CfPS, 2010, p. 3). Notwithstanding our emphasis in Exhibit 7.5 on the distinctiveness of the two functions, most councils nowadays have combined O&S committees. Similarly, while it is regarded as good practice to share O&S committee chairs according to the council's political composition, barely half (56%) actually do so, with Labour councils being particularly reluctant (CfPS, 2010, p. 5). It also seems disappointing that fewer than half of councils co-opt non-councillor members to their O&S committees, and that most of those that do withhold full voting rights from them.

In so far as their council's constitution permits, O&S committees set their own agendas. They can require executive members and council officers to attend their meetings and be questioned about what they are planning to do (policy review), what they are doing ('call-in'), what they have done (*ex post* scrutiny), and how effective it has been (service review). If unsatisfied, they can make recommendations for further action or amendments to either the executive or the full council. They can invite evidence from other individuals and organisations, and their powers have been extended over the years to enable and encourage them to investigate the performance of other organisations and partnerships in local governance – the health service, the police authority, registered social landlords, a PFI project, even the local university. As noted above, they are now also the ultimate recipients of Councillor Calls for Action.

The real effectiveness of overview and scrutiny involves non-executive councillors challenging not just the executive, but also their own party identities and loyalties. Majority party members have to work with colleagues from *other* parties in scrutinising and perhaps criticising publicly the performance of senior executive members of their *own* party. So too do members of parliamentary select committees; but, suggest Leach and Copus (2004, pp. 336–7), councillors in several respects have it significantly harder. First, the double role requires councillors both to hold executive members to account, and at the same time, in policy development mode, to work with them. Second, there is no real tradition in local government of questioning and cross-questioning ministers aggressively. Third, party group discipline can be even more entrenched and inflexible in local government than in Parliament. Fourth, local government's unified officer structure is expected to support both executive and scrutiny functions, which creates an almost inevitable role conflict.

All of this emphasises just how novel and alien O&S have been found to be by those familiar with, and perhaps skilled at, working the committee system. They *are* different; they are *not* easy. They will generally require training and the development of new skills, on the part of both members and officers. They will always require adequate and skilled officer support. And, perhaps the toughest condition of all, they require a substantial cultural change from party political groups and their members.

Community leader – or champion?

It is striking that none of the role labels listed at the start of this section included the word 'leadership', and it is a role that many councillors may not embrace readily. It is, however, one that is being pressed on them at precisely the time that councils no longer have the service-providing dominance in their areas that they once had. The full extent of this change is often unappreciated even by those caught up in it, as INLOGOV sought to illustrate in its evidence to a 2008 Commons Select Committee (House of Commons, 2009a, para. 1.7):

> Fewer and fewer services are provided directly by councils. Housing is the obvious example. But 120 councils have transferred services to leisure, arts or sports trusts – and more to private companies. Schools are run by governing bodies, or their head teachers, or the private interests that support academies. Buses are run by private companies, no longer by councils. Many important decisions are taken in partnership bodies, such as Local Strategic Partnerships, or their sub-committees that agree the targets for Local Area Agreements, that involve one or two councillors at most, and are heavily influenced by professional officers. The result of these changes is that non-executive councillors in particular are

far less involved in the fabric and detail of local decision-making than, until comparatively recently, they were.

Yet, as service provision has become more fragmented and councils work in partnership with other organisations in a network of community governance, councillors stand out increasingly as the only democratically elected pieces in the ever more complex jigsaw. They are the ones in closest touch with the electorate and service users; they are the ones likely to have to field inquiries about non-council service providers – health authorities, housing associations and primary care groups. If their particular local community is going to have leadership, over and above mere representation, where else is it going to come from?

The government's answer, to encourage councillors to embrace this new responsibility, is through their becoming 'community champions' (ODPM, 2005a, ch. 4) – in much the same way that they can boost their scrutineer role by becoming 'champions' of special interests, such as the elderly, the under-5s or the disabled. Or through reinventing the wheel, as Myerson (2005, p. 11) more or less put it, in his gentle mocking of the idea:

> Does John Prescott not realise that councillors are already champions? When you walk into a room and the officer has to address you as 'Councillor', that is accountability. It is not power, but it is championing with consequences.
>
> Of course, champions for disabled or older people are important, but *councillors champion everyone*. So maybe it does make sense to replace local councils with champions. But here is my idea: let's replace them with people called councillors. (Emphasis ours)

A split, but not a chasm

With community leadership, we have come full circle – back to one of what we described as jobs for all councillors. With the executive/non-executive split of councillors' roles, policy-making and scrutiny can no longer be so described, but a key message of the past few pages is that this is as far as the split should go: it is not a chasm. If one lists, as in Exhibit 14.4, the principal council arenas or councillors' potential roles, you will see that, numerically, most are still shared by executive and non-executive members alike. Moreover, given what we have argued about the interdependence of policy and implementation, and the policy developmental role of scrutiny, even the big arenas – Cabinet, O&S – should not be seen as entirely separate worlds. For either to function to optimum effect, collaboration is required. It may, for understandable reasons, be hard to cultivate, but it has to be sought.

Exhibit 14.4 Roles for all

Council arenas	Executive members	Non-executive members
ALL MEMBERS – SAME ROLES		
Representation of ward and constituents	✔	✔
Area committees – various devolved functions	✔	✔
Regulatory committees – e.g. planning, licensing	✔	✔
Standards Committee – to oversee standards of conduct	✔	✔
Appeals panels – e.g. on school admissions and exclusions	✔	✔
Appointments to outside bodies	✔	✔
Community 'champions'	✔	✔
Political groups	✔	✔
ALL MEMBERS – DISTINCTIVE ROLES		
Full council – debating and approving council's budget and policy framework	✔	✔
Full council – questioning and holding executive members to account	Being questioned	Questioning
EXECUTIVE MEMBERS ONLY		
Cabinet/executive	✔	
NON-EXECUTIVE MEMBERS ONLY		
Council Chair and Vice-Chair		✔
Overview and scrutiny	Attending when invited	✔
Supporting the executive – e.g. policy forums, cabinet advisory panels		✔

Source: Information from LGA (2000).

The workload

It is clear that, with more than 2,700 of us to every one of them, the job of a UK councillor in either a committee or an executive system is both multi-faceted and potentially extremely demanding. So how much time does it all take?

There is no simple answer. Like an MP, a councillor could 'get away with' doing an absolute minimum: attending the occasional council and scrutiny committee meeting and avoiding, as far as possible, all contact with constituents. Evidence suggests, however, that there are few such councillors these days, and that the more frequent behavioural pattern adopted is a maximalist and proactive one. *Married to the Council?* was the title of a 1980s' study of a sample of county councillors who, the authors found, spent between around 20 and 35 hours *per week* on their council duties

(Barron *et al.*, 1987, 1991), and there are no signs of their successors being any less committed in 2010.

Other studies, using different methods of recall and recording, have produced slightly lower figures. But recent councillor censuses have been strikingly consistent in showing, as in Exhibit 14.1 above, that the time spent now by members of *all types* of authority on their council and related political work is around 88 hours per typical month, or 22 hours per week. Such averages, though, must be read with care. Figures for executive members (113 hours per month) (Rao, 2005) and for most on urban and unitary authorities would be significantly higher, and those for shire district councillors rather lower. Figures for Scottish councillors would be much higher – 37 to 46 hours per week on average, depending on recording method, in 2005, and are likely to have risen since the 2007 change to STV elections and larger multi-member wards (Hexagon Research and Publishing, 2005).

Studies showed that up to two-thirds of councillors' time in the 1980s and 1990s was in some way meetings-related: attending them, preparing for them, and travelling to and from them. By comparison, constituency and community business occupied only about a fifth of their time – an imbalance that was one consideration behind the government's political management reforms, aimed at enhancing members' representational roles and reducing the time spent relatively non-participatively in committee meetings. The councillor census figures suggest there has been at least some change in the direction for which the government was hoping, with constituency work now taking up on average 7.5 hours per week, or a third of councillors' time (NFER, 2009a, p. 10).

Financial compensation

The jobs of councillor and MP may be similar in their open-endedness. However, in their financial rewards, as we have learned, they are emphatically different. MPs have had index-linked salaries (£65,738 in 2010/11), as part of an annual pay and allowances package totalling, for the *average* backbencher, well over £200,000. Such a sum, as can be calculated from the figures in Exhibit 14.5, would cover what many shire district councils pay out to *all* their members in the form not of salaries, index-linked or otherwise, but allowances – with details of individual members' expenses being easily accessible, incidentally, on council websites. Yet ironically, of the two groups, it is councillors, even under the traditional committee system, who have by far the greater and more immediate personal power – in the sense of contributing directly to decisions to spend budgets and allocate contracts of hundreds of millions of pounds. MPs can merely question, scrutinise, approve or disapprove the spending decisions of government ministers.

Exhibit 14.5 Councillors' remuneration – England 2009/10

History

1972 Attendance Allowances first introduced – £10 per day maximum.

1980 Special Responsibility Allowances (SRAs) payable to leaders, committee chairs, etc.

1991 Three allowances – flat-rate Annual Allowance, SRAs, and Attendance Allowance – available to every local authority, within limits defined by the Minister.

1995 Limits removed. Councils built **job description** for each councillor reflecting their responsibilities and payable at rate of the average non-manual wage.

The present system – from 2001

Individual authorities continue to decide own allowances. Local Government Act 2000 requires all principal councils to establish and maintain an **Independent Remuneration Panel** of at least 3 persons to advise council on: its scheme of allowances; the amounts to be paid; the pensionability of executive members' allowances.

Allowances **no longer** to be paid:

• Attendance Allowance – encouraged an 'attendance culture'.

Allowances that **must** be paid:

• **Basic Allowance** – flat-rate allowance paid to all councillors in recognition of their time commitments in attending council and party group meetings, meeting officers and constituents, and their incidental costs – use of home, private telephone, etc.

Allowances that **may** be paid:

• **Special Responsibility Allowance** – for executive members and other councillors with significant additional responsibilities, including at least one minority party member.
• **Carers' Allowance** – payable to councillors who incur expenditure for care of dependent relatives or children while undertaking 'approved council duties'.
• **Travel and Subsistence Allowance** – payable if felt not to be adequately covered in basic allowance.
• **Meetings Allowance** – payable to non-elected members co-opted or appointed to certain council committees and panels (for example, scrutiny committees, school exclusion appeals panels).

→

Exhibit 14.5 continued

The three elements of basic allowances

1 Estimate of hours required to perform the tasks expected of a non-executive member of the council.
2 Decision on the appropriate hourly/daily rate to be paid – e.g. median male full-time earnings: £28,720 pa/£531 per week (2010) – often adjusted to compare with local pay rates.
3 Decision on size of **Public Service Discount**: in recognition of the principle of council work as voluntary service, some proportion of hours should **not** be remunerated – usually between 20% and 50%.

Average allowances – some examples, 2008/09

	Basic	Lowest	Highest	Exec. Member	Leader
All authorities	£6,099	£1,500	£15,950	£9,710	£17,753
London boroughs	£9,739	£7,437 (Kingston upon Thames)	£11,596 (Croydon)	£22,028	£37,486
Metropolitan districts	£9,766	£6,121 (Trafford)	£15,950 (Birmingham)	£12,505	£26,405
Shire counties	£9,978	£7,086 (Northants)	£14,451 (Warwickshire)	£15,518	£27,290
Shire districts	£4,194	£1,500 (South Ribble)	£9,689 (Bolsover)	£6,083	£11,940
Unitaries	£8,076	£4,671 (Slough)	£11,643 (Hull)	£11,613	£22,477
London Assembly	£53,439	n.a.	n.a.	n.a.	See below

Some higher paid leaders, 2008/09

		£
Greater London Authority	Boris Johnson (Mayor)	145,350
Lewisham LBC	Sir Steve Bullock (Mayor)	79,670
Newham LBC	Sir Robin Wales (Mayor)	78,060
Hackney LBC	Jules Pipe (Mayor)	75,290
Birmingham City C	Mike Whitby (Leader)	70,960
Kensington & Chelsea LBC	Merrick Cockell (Leader)	66,480
Watford DC	Dorothy Thornhill (Mayor)	61,820
Middlesbrough Unitary C	Ray Mallon (Mayor)	59,700
Birmingham City C	Paul Tilsley (Deputy Leader)	57,300
Hartlepool Unitary C	Stuart Drummond (Mayor)	56,019
Manchester City C	Sir Richard Leese (Leader)	54,880

Main source: NFER (2009b).

Times, however, have changed. With executive councillors have come, on a modest scale at least, UK local government's first executive salaries – or, strictly speaking, 'pensionable remuneration', to emphasise that pensionable allowances do not make executive members employees of their authority. In earlier editions of this book we equated the annual allowances that most councillors received to the then maximum undergraduate student grant of under £2,500. While there are plenty of authorities where basic allowances are still well under £2,500 (£50 per week), a more accurate comparison these days is with the maximum student loan of around £5,000, or in London £7,000 (2009/10) – the average for all councillors in England in 2008 falling almost midway between the two at £6,099.

The reference to grants and loans is an apt reminder that, in its remuneration of councillors, as well as students, Scotland does things differently. The revised system introduced following the first STV council elections in 2007 is more centralised than England's, and, no doubt partly in acknowledgement of the apparent workload disparities noted above, more generous. In 2009/10, the basic councillor salary (the term is used more readily than in England), set centrally by the Scottish Government, was £15,838. As noted in Chapter 7, there are no directly elected mayors in Scotland, and a council leader's salary is in one of four bands, ranging in 2009/10 from £26,400 to £47,500 according to the local authority population. With few councils having opted for executive-based local government, all councillors with additional responsibilities are grouped together for remuneration purposes as 'senior councillors', and a limited number are paid an enhanced salary, again banded according to local authority size.

In contrast with Scotland, and unlike the situation prior to 1995, English local authorities are now entirely responsible for determining their own structures and rates of allowances, acting on the advice and recommendations of a local independent remuneration panel. It is these panels, therefore, who should take most of the responsibility for the rising national averages, their aim presumably being – like that of the government – to acknowledge the demanding nature of councillors' work, to attract a more diverse range of quality candidates, secure adequate support and training budgets, and assist family members with child care. Then, of course, there is the additional issue of recognising the greatly extended personal responsibilities of the leaders and executive members of particularly large urban and unitary councils and determining the appropriate remuneration for what are in some cases more than full-time posts.

A bunch of amateurs, the lot of 'em

The government hoped this more discretionary allowance system would address some of the existing disincentives to serving in local politics, while recognising that 'people do not enter public service to make their fortune' (DETR, 1998a). The 'recognition' was unnecessary: even the figures in Exhibit 14.5 are hardly beyond the dreams of avarice. But credit where it's due. The councillor census 'tick all relevant boxes' question on respondents' reasons for becoming a councillor now includes 'member allowances' as an option, and in 2008, 384 honest souls did tick it (NFER, 2009a, p. 33). However, in a total of nearly 47,000 ticks, they amounted to just 0.82% – suggesting that, even allowing for understatement, there must be other reasons. So what are councillors' motives? What drove them to start putting in these large numbers of hours for modest financial compensation and little public recognition?

Power, status, self-aggrandisement, ambition, compensation for personal insecurity, or even sexual inadequacy – the drives and motives attributed to politicians are legion, and mainly unflattering. They are not to be ridiculed or dismissed lightly, but this is not the place in which to speculate about councillors' essentially private motivations. Rather, we conclude this chapter in the way we started: with our own small cast list of members, whose apparent most proximate reasons for becoming councillor candidates seem, as it happens, to match closely the more frequently nominated reasons in the councillor census list.

The most frequently cited reason, not surprisingly, is 'to serve the community'. It is a catch-all cliché – almost to the extent of making one wonder about the 12% of respondents who chose not to tick it. But how else would one describe both the initial and ongoing drive of Yash Gupta, the Asian councillor acting as a tireless advocate for a ward of still very largely white residents, as well as a spokesperson for his own Indian and Asian communities? Next most popular box, ticked by 54%, was 'to change things' – like Marisa Heath in her work with looked-after children, and Bob Bryant, incensed by the plans for his local hospital's stroke unit. For others, the main driving force is 'political beliefs' (52%), as for the university Conservative supporter, Paul Holmes, and for Hayley Matthews, who, on returning home after graduation, 'decided to introduce myself to the local Liberal Democrats. I'd voted for them in the past and been attracted by their policies on the Iraq war, tuition fees and civil liberty' (*c'llr.*, November 2009). Having helped as a volunteer in a successful parliamentary by-election campaign with a view to becoming a party researcher or caseworker, she was invited to stand for the council, and the rest, as the saying has it, is history.

Hayley, like some of the others and 30% of the councillor census respondents, would probably also have ticked the 'because I was asked to' box. For it is a further regrettable consequence of our scale of 'local' government, with its massive authorities and electoral wards, relatively small numbers of councillors and heavy workloads, that all parties in almost all parts of the country struggle to recruit the numbers of quality candidates they would like. The same factors also help explain why those who are recruited suffer from the poor public image that was noted at the start of the chapter – on the part of a media and public who inevitably meet so few of them in person. In the circumstances, it is entirely understandable that councillors are inclined to resist the label 'amateur', even when it is used to clarify their distinctiveness from professional salaried officers, and especially if it is accompanied by any hint of carelessness or dilettantism. Which is a pity, because most of them at least really are 'a bunch of amateurs' in the true, original and etymological sense of the word: they do it because they love it.

Chapter 15

The Local Government Workforce

Beware (again) of generalisations

A key message in Chapter 14 was that there is no such person as a 'typical councillor', and that we should avoid making unthinking generalisations as if there were. There are – or were at the time of writing – over a hundred times as many employees of councils as there are elected members, so it is at least as important to avoid a similar trap with them. Which is one reason why this book's very first Exhibit takes the form it does – listing a small fraction of the hundreds of careers and thousands of job titles to be found within our multi-functional, multi-service local authorities.

We noted in Chapter 14 that in our large-scale local government system most people do not personally know their own councillors or, frequently, any councillors at all. Statistically, this is highly unlikely to be true of employees of councils. If you know 20 employed adults, the chances are that one or more will work full-time or part-time for a council. The chances are at least equally high, though, that they will not describe themselves as council *officers,* which is one reason why this chapter is entitled as it is, rather than being headed 'local government officers' or even 'the professionals'. When it comes to the making of policy or interacting with councillors, we shall add to what we have already said about the role of professional officers. We start, though, with a wider look at the whole local government workforce. It covers over 500 different occupational areas and more than 3,000 job titles, which means that many employees are *not* based in offices, or even indoors, do not have their lives governed by meetings, and would not remotely conceive of themselves as being bureaucrats.

Our own favourite council employee is Harry Venning's *Society Guardian* cartoon strip star, *Clare in the Community* (Wednesdays, along with the public service job adverts), who since 2004 has had her own award-winning radio series, played by *Smack the Pony*'s Sally Phillips. Clare would certainly never call herself an officer, but might well hit you if you questioned her professionalism. She is a college-educated, professionally trained and professionally responsible social worker, with all the compassion, care and conscience that such training imbues. She spends her

Figure 15.1 *Cartoon – The emotional frontline*

Source: Harry Venning, *The Guardian*.

days, and frequently evenings too, doing 'society's dirty work', confronting life on the 'emotional frontline'. She rarely sees a councillor or goes near her council's town or county hall, but works, probably from an outlying district office, as part of a five-member social work team. The team is mixed-gender and a real source of mutual support – even when managed, to the chagrin of Clare and her friend Megan, by a man. We encountered one of Clare's constant frustrations – shortage of resources – in Chapter 12, and she needs no *Local Government Employment Digest* statistics to tell her that social workers and care assistants are among the occupations that councils have long found it hardest to recruit and retain. She agonises regularly over the conflicting pressures facing the 'caring professions': the demands of her individual clients against those of the community, the battle between the requirements of care and of control. It is hardly surprising that, as in Figure 15.1, she sometimes finds it difficult to 'switch off'!

Some figures – the distinctiveness of the local government workforce

Careful readers will have noted the inserted clause in the opening paragraph: 'at the time of writing'. As the Coalition Government took office in May 2010, forecasters were competing to furnish the direst predictions for public sector employment generally, and local government employment in particular. By the time of the October 2010 Comprehensive Spending Review, some of the wilder forecasts had been modified, and expectations had settled at somewhere between 600,000 and 750,000 public sector job losses by 2015/16. Local government accounts for roughly half of all public sector employment in the UK – some 10% of total employment – but it would be wrong to make a prediction by simply halving the public sector figure. The LGA's expectations were local government job losses of at least 100,000 by 2014/15, while those of the unions – UNISON and the Public and Commercial Services Union (PCS) – were, not surprisingly, a great deal higher.

The 2009/10 'big tent' figure for UK local government employment – including parish councils, all police and local education authority staff – was 2.9 million by headcount, which equalled a full-time equivalent (FTE) workforce of 2.2 million (ONS, 2010b, pp. 1, 17), approximately 300,000 of whom (250,000 FTE) were in Scotland. Whatever the future, total employment has in recent years been a more stable figure than one might imagine. A loss of 250,000 jobs would equal the total fluctuation over the past twenty years.

There was a decline in numbers in the early 1990s, particularly following the LEAs' loss of control of further education institutions in 1993 and the creation of free-standing police authorities in 1995/6. With the election of the 1997 Labour Government, however, the downward trend 'bottomed

Exhibit 15.1 The local government workforce – professions, jobs, salaries and wages

Estimated number England and Wales, 2009	000s	Examples of median basic salary/wage	£000s
Teachers	512	Secondary school teacher	36
School support staff	496	School secretary	17
Social care staff	283	Social worker	30
Recreation and sport	67	Countryside, park ranger	20
Libraries and archives	34	Librarian	26
Planning and development	27	Building control officer	32
Youth and community work	22	Youth offending support worker	28
Environmental health	18	Environmental health officer	31
Culture and heritage	16	Archivist, curator	26
Trading standards	6	Trading standards officer	31
Administrative officers, assistants	181	Administrative officer	17
Cooks, catering assistants	73	Cook	14
Cleaners	55	Cleaner	12
School midday assistants	47	Midday assistant	12
Housing and welfare officers	38	Housing officer	25
ICT staff	52	ICT professional	28
Receptionists, PAs, secretaries,	42	Receptionist	15
Human Resources staff	39	Industrial relations officer	27
Refuse and salvage occupations	36	Refuse and salvage operatives	17
Nursery nurses	15	Nursery nurse	18
Caretakers	14	Caretaker	15
Security staff	11	Security guard	19
Gardeners, grounds(wo)men	11	Groundsman/groundswoman	15
Playgroup leaders, assistants	9	Playworker	16
School crossing patrol attendants	8	School crossing patrol attendant	12

Sources: Numbers – LGAAR (2009a); salaries – LGA (2009d).

Exhibit 15.2 Local government employment – Great Britain, 2009/10

Type of authority (2009) All numbers are headcount, and exclude police and fire services	Total (000s)	% of total	Average per authority	Part-time (%)	Female (%)	Part-time female (%)
Counties (34)	814	32	24,000	60	80	54
Shire districts (238)	133	5	560	34	53	25
Metropolitan districts (36)	539	21	15,000	49	75	44
London boroughs (33)	240	9	7,300	44	73	38
English unitaries (46)	381	15	8,300	53	75	48
Welsh unitaries (22)	165	6	7,500	50	72	43
Scottish unitaries (32)	306	12	9,500	39	67	35
Totals	2,578			51	74	45

Sources: LGAAR (2009b); Scottish Government (2010).

out' at just above 2.7 million, then rose steadily each year until 2007 – after which it fell, unlike total central government employment, which, largely through the NHS, continued to grow. Note the date: before the international banking collapse, the global recession and its aftermath. Even if these things had never happened, the local government workforce would have declined – albeit not on anything like the scale that now looks possible. Either way, it means that Exhibits 15.1 and 15.2 can be seen both as an outline of the key features of our local government workforce, and as an historical record of what it looked like near its modern-day peak.

The national collation of local government employment statistics is a difficult and imperfect art, which is why we have been unable previously to produce even the very sketchy picture contained in Exhibit 15.1. The top part, covering two-thirds of the workforce, comprises data derived mainly from surveys of various professional, occupational or negotiating groups, and emphasises once again the dominance of education and social services in UK local government. Well over half of all council employees in 2009/10 worked in education, and 20% in social care, so authorities responsible for those two services were necessarily big employers, and frequently *the* biggest in their area.

The employee numbers in the lower part of the Exhibit, necessary to complete the full picture, are extracted from the much broader Labour Force Survey, and should be treated with caution. The salary/wage figures, however, are sound: the latest available from the LGA's annual Earnings Survey, covering over a million posts. They are a forceful reminder that senior officers' alleged 'gold-plated salaries' in their 'fat-cat local authority fiefdoms' that so excite sections of the media (*Daily Telegraph*, 19 February 2010), certainly don't filter down to, for example, the lower paid battalions of school support staff: caretakers, midday assistants (yes, yes – dinner ladies) and school crossing patrol attendants.

Women and equal pay – local government's Christmas sprout

Even in summary form, as in Exhibit 15.2, the statistical profile of local government employment in 2009/10 was strikingly different from that of the private sector, or even of the workforce as a whole. Nationally, nearly three-quarters of all jobs are full-time; in local government half are part-time. Nationally, 15% of the workforce are aged under 25, in local government only half of that proportion. In the private sector the male:female ratio is roughly 60:40; local government's is 26:74. Nationally, full-time male employment constitutes nearly half the total, as in local government in the 1950s; in today's local government it is less than 20%. Nationally, part-time women workers are 20% of the total; in local government, 45%

– many of them doing at least three of women's traditional 4Cs – caring, cleaning, catering and cash registers – that have continued, notwithstanding equal pay legislation, to be undervalued and underpaid.

At first glance, local government's equal pay record appears relatively commendable. Across the whole economy, median gross pay for men in full-time employment in 2008/9 was £27,518, and for women £21,494, giving a gender pay gap of 28%. In the private sector, the pay gap was almost 40%. In local government it was 5.3% and falling fast (LGA, 2009d, p. 3). By anything other than the standards of other employers, though, local government's general record must be judged as dilatory and, towards some of the lowest paid workers in the country, literally degrading.

The Equal Pay Act, outlawing unequal treatment of men and women in terms of pay and conditions of employment, was passed in 1970. In 1997, the National Joint Council for Local Government Services (NJC) – representing local government employers and the main trade unions: UNISON, UNITE and GMB – negotiated a Single Status Agreement, intended finally, or at least by 2007, to implement the Act without wholesale recourse to employment tribunals. The aim was to develop, through systematic job evaluation schemes, a common pay and grading scale for all manual, administrative and clerical jobs, based on the principle of equal pay for women employed in jobs of equal value to those typically done by men.

Whatever may have been fondly imagined, Single Status was never going to be cost-neutral. There would be losers as well as winners, with local authorities having to find very large sums of money on top of their required efficiency savings, and without jeopardising their primary task of improving local services. They had to devise and negotiate a more expensive unified structure, and in addition compensate those discriminated against under the existing regime, while ensuring that the now 'downgraded' refuse collectors and road sweepers would not be penalised excessively – either through pay cuts or the withdrawal of the supposedly output-based bonus payments that tended to be the preserve of male-dominated jobs.

Righting a major long-term injustice is inevitably difficult, but 10 years was a generous time-frame, and in 2010 a fifth of councils had still not implemented a Single Status Agreement. Few emerge from the saga with much credit. Ministers set no staged timetable, enabling them to refuse to provide extra funding for back-pay settlements. They also capped, initially at a hopelessly inadequate £200 million, the total 'capitalisation' sum councils could borrow against their own assets: a figure that, even in 2006, would barely have covered the then estimated costs of Birmingham City Council alone. The generally male-run unions resisted any national campaign, giving the impression of putting men's wages – and Labour councils' interests – above those of their women members. So-called 'no win, no fee' lawyers rushed in to fill the vacuum, taking action against recalcitrant councils, against unions who had settled for less than maximum compensation, and trousering up to 25% of any payout.

The ultimate irony is that employment tribunals, which Single Status was designed to bypass, eventually took centre-stage. One decreed that up to six years' compensation should be paid for past injustice, instead of the two years that had become the norm – thereby adding further huge sums to councils' salary bills. Then, in 2010, 4,000 women won potentially the biggest pay-out of all in a tribunal judgement against Birmingham City Council. The tribunal found that thousands of women workers – cleaners, care assistants, cooks and clerks – were entitled to the same pay as men working as gardeners, refuse collectors and grave diggers, who had earned up to four times as much through large cash bonuses 'awarded' for tasks such as picking up refuse sacks and completing rounds on time. Adding insult to the financial injury of conceivably up to £3 billion, the tribunal criticised the council for wasting public resources in misguidedly incurred legal fees, and its senior management for having continually pushed the problem to one side 'like a disagreeable sprout on a Christmas dinner plate'.

Because they're worth it

At the other end of the local authority employment ladder too, pay is a contentious issue, increasingly exposed to the public gaze. Here, though, we are talking not of barely five-figure annual wage packets, but of 'employment packages' of negotiable benefits – pension options, private health insurance, company-leased cars – that, for plenty of the most senior officers nowadays, are very comfortably into six-figure territory and, it has seemed, pushing ever upwards. But again, regrettably, the record of many responsible for these matters has been less than exemplary, and emerging good practice has had to rely too much on external forces.

We have recorded previously how, just as councillors' remuneration has risen significantly since the arrival of executive-based local government, so has that in particular of the chief executives (CEs) of our largest councils (Wilson and Game, 2006, pp. 282–6). Considering the size of these councils, their multi-functional complexity, their public and political profile, and the emphasis placed on gaining and maintaining high 'star-ratings', this is hardly surprising: good managers of such organisations are bound to be at a premium. Councillors know this and are generally prepared to pay the 'going rate' for someone they judge to have the ability, experience and personality to lead and give strategic direction to their authority. Too often, however, all involved are coy about, or downright opposed to, revealing just what that rate is. For bodies spending public money and providing services to local taxpayers and citizens, such a lack of transparency seems inappropriate. Moreover, if freedom of information means anything at all,

Exhibit 15.3 Local government high earners, and some comparisons

Local authority	Chief Executive	Approx. salary 2008/09
Essex CC	Joanna Killian	265
Kent CC	Peter Gilroy	245
Newham LBC	Joe Duckworth	240
Wandsworth LBC	Gerald Jones	228
Kensington & Chelsea LBC	Derek Myers	225

	Comparable organisation	Number of staff – headcount	Gross revenue expenditure/ turnover (£m)	2008/09 salary of CEO (£000s)
Shire counties	Average	22,900	850	169
Public sector	British Nuclear Fuels	17,850	840	712
Private sector	Spirit Managed Pubs Ltd	23,200	760	7,800
Metrop. districts	Average	15,300	520	148
Public sector	University of Manchester	11,700	637	274
Private sector	BUPA Care Homes plc	16,900	472	694
Shire districts	Average	580	16	98
Public sector	Student Loan Company	1,250	69	172
Private sector	Canada Bread Ltd	470	30	233
London boroughs	Average	7,350	400	166
Public sector	HM Land Registry	8,900	380	155
Private sector	Clinton Cards Ltd	7,080	460	1,560

Sources: TPA (2010); SOLACE, 2009.

deliberate concealment is bound to fail sooner rather than later, by which time any opportunity of proactively making the most of the situation will have been lost. And so it has proved.

Exhibit 15.3 summarises the position. The top section lists information you might suppose would be on the respective councils' websites, but largely hasn't been. In 2008/9 these CEs, on the approximate salaries cited, were among the highest paid officers in UK local government. Others may have been paid more highly – but they and their councils persistently declined to reply to The TaxPayers' Alliance's freedom of information requests, in disregard of both the FoI Act and the Information Commissioner's ruling. The total remuneration of the five CEs themselves was probably more, but conceivably less, because they too revealed only their salary bands, rather than their actual salaries. The concerns of non-respondents ranged from the disclosure of specific details of remuneration being 'a gross invasion of privacy' to it opening their families and children to 'personalised attacks and mischief making' (TPA, 2009, p. 2). But in the climate of 2009 theirs was a doomed case.

Ministers, doubtless bearing in mind the plastering of their own remuneration details across national and international media, were suddenly keen on increased transparency and introduced one of those Statutory Instruments described in Chapter 10: *SI 2009/3322 – The Accounts and Audit (Amendment No.2) (England) Regulations 2009*, to be precise. In future, councils must publish in their annual statement of accounts the names of all officers earning over £150,000 – a threshold the Conservatives pledged to reduce to £60,000, if elected. Had the regulations existed in 2008/9, they would have shown, according to The TaxPayers' Alliance, at least 166 officers earning over £150,000, 31 getting more than the prime minister's then £188,000, and 24 receiving over £200,000.

This last group have an additional symbolic importance, for part of the brief set by the new prime minister, David Cameron, for the Hutton Review of Fair Pay in the Public Sector, was that there should be no more than a 20:1 ratio between the highest and lowest paid. The lowest paid, as shown in Exhibit 15.1, were earning in 2009 the equivalent of an annual wage of around £12,000 – except that most would in fact have been part-time on an hourly rate only a little higher than the then National Minimum Wage of £5.73 an hour (£5.93/£11,409 p.a. from October 2010). However calculated, it was far short of the 'living wage' of £7.37 an hour that the Family Budget Unit calculated was required to keep a two-earner family with two children – and very close to 1/20th of the salaries of top-earning CEs.

Which brings us to the lower section of Exhibit 15.3. For seriously offensive income disparities, argue local authority CEs and their 'trade union', SOLACE, you need to look elsewhere in the public sector or to private companies – the FTSE 100, for example, where 'the pay of Chief Executives is on average over 100 times that of *average* salaries in these companies' (Higginson and Clough, 2010, p. 3 – our emphasis). Then comes what might be termed the 'because we're worth it' defence – after the famous advertising campaign of the French beauty company whose name we are not permitted to mention. Critics, they claim, simply don't understand the exceptionally demanding, complex and publicly important work that council chief executives do. This may well be true, but it does raise difficulties, when, as noted in Chapter 7, numerous chief executives are already running two authorities at the same time, and when Communities and Local Government Secretary Eric Pickles believes that, in some cases at least, 'all of the position could be subsumed into the leader's role' (Dale, 2010). Moreover, even the most persuasive case for being worth it is probably lost, if you're not prepared to reveal how much 'it' actually is; people are bound to imagine it's shedloads.

Credit, then, to those CEs who, on their authority websites, chose to be completely open about their remuneration – including what they do to justify it. Basildon DC, Stratford-on-Avon DC, Swindon BC and Blackburn with Darwen BC were the first four listed when we Googled 'Council chief executive remuneration', and there were many others, but in mid-2010 it was still a long way from universal practice. That these CEs, in addition to outlining their roles and responsibilities, also mentioned the additional demands of attending evening meetings, working at weekends, being always 'on call' to cover emergency planning requirements and so on is in the circumstances wholly understandable. For invariably the chance is also taken to explain about the importance and impact of the council's role in the community, which has to be more productive than squabbling with the TPA over FoI requests.

It may also represent a glimpse of the future, if the thinking behind Italy's recent *Operazione trasparenza* (Operation Transparency) were to catch on. Go to the website of any of Italy's 8,000-plus *comuni*, and, with a single click on a home page link (*'Trasparenza, valutazione e merito'*), you can see the full CV and salary details of all senior and junior managers, their email and telephone contact details – and, among much else, a comprehensive absenteeism record for all operational units. For the present, the transparency 'rule of thumb' advocated by Emer Coleman, when Director of the London Alliances Project, strikes us as being on the right lines: 'If you can get it under Freedom of Information, you should publish it automatically. You can then enter into a dialogue about what people want' (Williams, 2010).

It will have been noted that the very top earner listed in Exhibit 15.3 was a woman CE, and it seems that at these lofty levels there isn't the financial discrimination against women – at least once actually appointed – that we saw in relation to councils' lowest paid employees. Getting there is a different matter. 21% cent of CEs in 2009 were women, compared with almost none 20 years earlier. It is unquestionably progress and, mercifully, far outstrips the 4% of women directors in FTSE 250 companies (Armitstead, 2010). It is, though, still adrift of the figures for senior civil servants (23% women), NHS and voluntary sector CEs (40% and 46%, respectively) (*Guardian Public*, April 2009). A 2007/8 study by the GMB union found 22 English councils where women constituted more than half of the top 5% of earners. But more typical seemed to be South Northamptonshire: widely publicised as one of the very few authorities where the leader, deputy leader and CE were all women – but whose senior management board turned out to be otherwise entirely male.

At most, this particular glass ceiling has been splintered. As for the ceiling confronting BME aspirants, it must still seem more like concrete. It is an under-publicised fact that the black, Asian and minority ethnic (BME/BAME) proportion of the local government workforce has in recent years been consistently below that of the workforce as a whole: in 2008,

7.1% compared to 9.3% (LGAAR, 2009b, pp. 12–14). If anything, local government's record of recruiting and advancing staff from BME backgrounds has been poorer even that it has for women – one result being that in 2008/9 there were just 2 BME CEs of Great Britain's then more than 450 local authorities.

An infinite variety

It was Shakespeare's Cleopatra who, according to Enobarbus, Mark Antony's lieutenant, embodied 'infinite variety', but – with the significant qualification identified in that last sentence – it is also not a bad description of the local government workforce. Moving from the top of the pile – the CE and chief officers, to whom we shall return shortly – we come to the middle-ranking managers and professionals who combine an expert knowledge of a particular service or support function (for example, finance, law, personnel, IT) with experience of overseeing the resources and employees of the authority. The number and range of both top and middle management posts are considerable – with descriptions sometimes verging on parody: the Children's Services Director, who must 'find new ways to engage young people, and champion consultation exercises that are more than empty gestures'; the 'outward-facing, but usually non-operational' Executive Director of Community Services; the Waste Enforcement Manager, required to have a 'passion for tackling environmental crimes'; and many more (see Wilson and Game, 2006, Exhibit 13.3; also on linked website). The final element in this group of senior managers and salaried professionals are those with professional training operating at the service frontline, such as teachers, field social workers, environmental health officers and development control planners.

Beneath the top managers and salaried professionals are the 'worker bees': a vast network of employees in a variety of lower-status clerical, manual and non-manual jobs. These are the 750,000 ATC (administrative, technical and clerical) 'white-collar' staff – clerical assistants, technicians, nursery nurses, welfare assistants – and the million or so full-time or part-time manual workers we encountered above, being slowly and at times painfully fused together into a Single Status. These are the people who clean streets and schools, are caretakers, council gardeners, home helps and road maintenance operatives, who are already on low – sometimes even reduced – wages, and few of whose jobs were anywhere near the lists of those being 'protected' from cuts by the incoming Coalition Government. With many having to rely on state benefits to the low paid in order to survive, the surprise must be not that 2002 saw the first national strike of local government workers for 23 years, but that it has not become a more frequent event. It may yet.

The world of senior management

We turn now from those who actually provide the services of a local authority to those whose job is to manage them: the senior officers at the top, rather than the front-line, of the organisation. As departments become ever less tied to single services, chief officers are expected to play a corporate as well as a departmental role, and may well not even come from the department's dominant profession. Those at the very top are likely to be appointed at least as much for their managerial skills and experience, including that acquired abroad or in the private sector, as for their professional qualifications and expertise.

There are at least four distinctive dimensions of the senior management role, summarised in Exhibit 15.4.

Exhibit 15.4 The senior management role – four dimensions

- Exercising professional influence.
- Supporting, advising and monitoring politicians.
- Representing the authority's interests externally.
- Managing staff and resources within the authority.

Exercising professional influence

Senior local government officers may now spend most of their time as managers, but still the majority are trained and qualified professionals: solicitors, treasurers, architects, planners, engineers, housing managers, education administrators, social workers and so on. Professionalism in this sense remains a hallmark of British local government, and one of its most powerful forces. Its most prominent signs are probably the dozens of professional bodies involved in virtually every sphere of local government activity, from administration to waste management, including the following small selection:

- SOLACE – *Society of Local Authority Chief Executive and Senior Managers* – local government's leading professional organisation; CEs' union. Has professional arm, SOLACE Enterprises Ltd, which sounds straight out of James Bond, but more mundanely undertakes consultancy, interim management, recruitment and training.
- ACSeS – *Association of Council Secretaries and Solicitors* – for managers of all corporate governance functions: legal, administrative, democratic, scrutiny, standards.

- CIPFA – *Chartered Institute of Public Finance and Accountancy* (pronounced 'sipfa') – training and standards-monitoring body for public sector accountants.
- PPMA – *Public Sector People Managers' Association* – formerly the more exclusive, if also more memorable SOCPO, the Society of Chief Personnel Officers.
- SCALA – *Society of Chief Architects of Local Authorities.*
- ADASS – *Association of Directors of Adult Social Services.*
- AEA – *Association of Electoral Administrators.*
- CIWM – *Chartered Institution of Waste Management.*

These bodies are, of course, key members of their respective policy networks and communities (see pp. 204–5), but they have other roles too. They are, as Rhodes noted (1988, pp. 214–15), 'organised as "learned societies", in which capacity they recruit and train personnel, organise conferences and seminars, produce research and publications and, as with any other organised group, proselytise and lobby for their interests'. They are also 'trade unions and … can use working to rule and strikes as a means of influencing the government. In effect, therefore, the professions can have three bites at the cherry of political influence.'

The influence of senior officers as professionals can thus be considerable, particularly in policy areas where complex technical knowledge is at a premium and of consequential value to central government. In such situations there is, as Gains *et al.* put it in 'bureau-maximising' terminology, an 'information asymmetry' in their favour (2008, p. 651):

> Local authorities administer the services of housing, education, public health, consumer protection, social services, local roads, waste collection and disposal – all of which require expert administration according to professional standards and national rules … The relatively large scale of English local government and the extent of national direction of policy and spending make for an extensive information advantage for local permanent bureaucrats. They operate in a highly professionalised environment and in the context of strong claims for expert knowledge, with established powers over appointments and the ability to regulate workflows in their bureaus. Moreover, as gatekeepers for nationally led policy initiatives and legislative demands, they play a central role in setting the agenda of local decision-making. Indeed, through their professional and managerial associations, they have a considerable influence on the direction of policy, in particular the technical detail of nationally imposed interventions.

Much of this book has been about 'nationally imposed interventions' – the introduction of private sector competition through CCT and its successors, tax- and expenditure-capping, partnership working, targets and perform-ance measurement, and now efficiency savings and the management of declining resources. Neither generalist civil servants nor most councillors have the combination of professional, technical and local knowledge required to implement these initiatives that senior officers possess. They are bound to be influential, and, without at all underrating their local advocacy role, that influence is more likely to constitute a force for centralism than for localism, promoting homogeneous standards, rather than local diversity (Rhodes, 1988, p. 225).

Working with politicians

The relationship between senior officers and councillors is explored in Chapter 17. Senior officers are likely to be involved in the process of devel-oping strategies and policies for the authority. Much of their time is taken up in writing reports for Cabinet members, meeting with councillors, and liaising with officer colleagues in other departments to provide policy advice and guidance. They also, necessarily, have extensive *delegated powers* in respect of their particular services – set out these days, of course, in the council's constitution. Executive members, however, also have dele-gated powers now, both individually and collectively, and the outcome of the negotiation of, in particular, the most sensitive of these delegations – planning permissions and certain categories of licence – has provided a new indicator of the officer or member dominance in the running of an authority.

Another recent development has been the *monitoring role* of senior offi-cers in relation to the performance of the council and councillors. Part of the Conservative Government's response to the 1986 Widdicombe Committee Report was to require local authorities to appoint a monitoring officer – usually the chief legal officer or council solicitor – responsible for reporting directly to the council on issues of legality, financial probity and alleged maladministration. The Local Government Act 2000 extended these responsibilities, and a monitoring officer is now charged with promoting and maintaining high standards of conduct within the local authority, and with ensuring that executive decisions, together with all relevant back-ground documentation, are made available publicly.

Senior officers stand at the heart of the decision-making processes of local authorities. Their delegated and monitoring responsibilities give them some powers, but above all it is their ability to influence the choices, thinking and approach of leading councillors that gives them real decision-making influ-ence. Their proximity to the formal holders of decision-making authority – executive councillors – gives them an opportunity for influence not afforded to such a degree to employees in the lower ranks of the organisation.

External relations

Managing relations with the world outside the council has become an increasingly important part of the daily workload of senior officers in an era of growing collaboration, local partnerships and supposedly 'joined-up' government. Links with central government regional offices, local authority colleagues in other areas, conferences and debates within professional associations all contribute to a powerful network of influence for the modern senior officer. They constitute important sources of information and ideas, and provide a national forum in which senior officers can present themselves as policy entrepreneurs and learn from the knowledge and experience of others. More generally, they enable officers to make sense of the local government world and to put the work of their own department, profession and council in a broader context.

As described in Chapter 9, partnerships are today an integral part of the world of local governance. Senior officials in social service departments are thus in regular touch with voluntary groups and agencies. Land-use planners will represent the authority in public meetings and debates. Housing officers will attend numerous meetings with tenants' associations and community organisations. In contrast to the position in the 1970s, these senior officers have come to expect a relatively 'rough ride'. In today's consumer culture, people are less willing to accept professional explanations of what is best, and far more prepared to question the policies and actions of the local authority. The need to consult with the public on a wide range of issues has also meant greater interaction than ever before with the local population.

Internal management

As we have seen, the role of senior local authority officers is nowadays a managerial, as well as a professional, one. Effective chief officers and senior managers in local authorities exercise a range of skills – in strategic management, decision-making, political awareness and sensitivity, leadership, business and commercial practice, negotiation – that go far beyond anything required in their professional qualifications.

The new executive structures have, in most authorities, affected the role of senior officers significantly – more so than was sometimes initially understood. Executive members are more involved in day-to-day decision-making and management, and officers correspondingly less so. The tensions inherent in senior officers' responsibilities to serve both the council as a whole and the current political leadership have increased. Inevitably, however, there will continue to be considerable differences in the operational styles and practices of what are, statutorily, identical authorities. It would be both naïve and premature, therefore, to start playing down the influence of senior local government officers in policy-making, whatever the formal position might be. Their knowledge and expertise mean that, along with senior councillors, they remain of central importance.

From model employers to flexible employment structures

For much of the post-war period, local authorities had an image as 'model' or 'good practice' employers, but the period from 1979 ushered in changes. Local government was subjected to commercialism and competition – most notably in the form of compulsory competitive tendering (CCT). With these changes came private sector management ideas and personnel practices such as performance-related pay, staff appraisal procedures, and decentralised negotiating and consultative arrangements. Authorities found it difficult to maintain national pay and conditions in services subject to competitive tender, and there was a movement away from formal systems for the management of industrial relations towards more ad hoc approaches reflecting the organisational interests of management (Leach *et al.*, 1994, p. 199).

The realities of CCT meant that it became increasingly difficult for local authorities to maintain the 'model' employer tradition. If the choice were presented as one of aspiring to best employment practice, but at the possible loss of a vital contract and the associated jobs, councillors would understandably fight for the contract. In response to such dilemmas and the changing environment, local authorities developed various ways of introducing greater flexibility into their employment practices.

Chief officers were given greater discretion to employ and deploy staff, with councillors' involvement being confined to the most senior appointments. Contracts and job descriptions became less tightly defined, making it easier for clerical and administrative staff in particular to be transferred between departments, and for new working practices to be introduced. Increasing numbers of chief executives and senior officers were recruited on fixed-term contracts and with company-style benefits packages. In another echoing of the private sector, performance-related pay (PRP) for senior managers was introduced by some authorities – by no means all Conservative – with merit bonuses or awards for exceptional performance. More widespread, and beneficial to both the employees and service users of an authority, were the adoption of more flexible working hours and conditions – flexitime, job-sharing and home-based working all taking off earlier in local government than in the economy as a whole.

The future – global recession, national impact, local response

The past, it is said, is a foreign country. The past here is the above paragraph that closed the main sections of this workforce chapter in the book's previous edition (Wilson and Game, 2006, p. 293). Since it was written in 2005, local government services and their providers have experienced at least five years' worth of significant changes and innovations: less direct provision, more commissioning (see Chapter 2); councils' efficiency-driven bids for unitary status (Chapter 5); Gershon efficiency savings, outsourcing of back-office functions, sharing of services and managements (Chapter 7); more user choice and personalisation of services (Chapter 8); more partnership working and the Total Place initiative (Chapter 9). On top of all these have been the global recession and ensuing structural budget deficit. Collectively, they have changed the foreseeable future to the extent that it might almost be that of a different country.

With a complete change of national government adding to the uncertainty, and a new three-year grant settlement due to start in 2011/12, no one in 2010 could know how severely and in what ways local government and its workforce would be affected, and in what shape they would be in a further five years' time. Some things, though, are certain. First, the directly employed local government workforce will shrink, significantly. Second, the shrinkage will vary considerably from one council to another. Third, all should be better prepared to respond to their particular sets of circumstances than they would have been previously. These are the themes of this final part of the chapter: we are facing the consequences of global events that will impact on all UK citizens, but that in many ways will be most efficiently and effectively dealt with at the local level – indeed, by the elected local authorities.

Job cuts – inevitable but not uncontrollable

Virtually all the trends listed above point in an essentially similar direction, so it was no great predictive feat for a 2007 IDeA discussion document to suggest that 'the directly employed local government workforce is likely to reduce gradually in size over the next three years' (p. 11). The impact of the recession was to change the scale, speed and time-frame of that prediction. In March 2010, a BBC English Regions survey of a limited sample of councils found that one in ten council jobs could be cut over the next five years, leading to aggregate projected job losses of between 100,000 and 180,000 (Deal, 2010). Almost all major councils that could be persuaded to reveal any hard figures estimated cuts running into the thousands.

As always with local government, however, a careful look at and behind these headline figures uncovered a more complex picture. First, there were regional variations. A 2009 LGA survey found that, while a third of councils in the East region had already made staff cuts, two-thirds of those in the South West had done so, and more than 55% in the North West and West Midlands (LGA Media Release, 26 February 2009). As the impact of public spending cuts becomes even fiercer, those regions, particularly areas of the north and north-east, where almost all recent job creation has been in the public sector, will suffer disproportionately.

Then there are the different types of councils, with their differing services and income sources. Unitary and metropolitan councils, for example, have a wide range of services – some high on the government's 'protected' list, the larger ones substantially grant-funded – and receive about 70% of their income from grants. For district councils, with their narrower range of largely 'unprotected' services, grants contribute only 40%, and they are relatively much more dependent on locally generated income: council tax, fees and charges. Most of these income sources – planning fees, land searches, commercial rents, sales of property and capital assets, car-parking, leisure services – will have fallen during the recession, leaving many district councils already struggling financially more than their larger neighbours – the more so if theirs is an area with a weak economy and high deprivation (Audit Commission, 2010b, esp. chs 3 and 5).

In some service areas the almost constant problem is not redundancies, but rather recruitment and retention. Our description of Clare, the overburdened social worker, at the start of this chapter was all too true. In the 2009 *Local Government Workforce Survey*, the ten occupations for which the most local authorities reported recruitment difficulties were children's social workers (72% of authorities) – followed by adult social workers (48%) (p. 25). Of course, if you are a shire district council, with no responsibility for social services and education, shortages of social workers – or of teachers or school crossing patrol attendants (25% each) – will not worry you unduly. But difficulties in finding and retaining planners (44%), building control and environmental health officers (32% and 35%, respectively) certainly will.

Councils' financial and economic situations vary greatly, therefore, and so do their councillors' politics. In the case of a normal-scale funding gap, the debateable options would probably range from maintaining services, by increasing council tax and/or fees and charges, through to more or less severe service cuts, accompanied by permutations of job losses, demand management and efficiency savings. The efficiency savings might themselves range from the quickly implementable – freezing recruitment, retraining existing staff, reducing maintenance, postponing new projects, to the longer term – sharing procurement and other back-office functions, better asset management, outsourcing (Audit Commission, 2010b, ch. 6). Labour councils in particular are likely to contest the very principle of job cuts, emphasising the social, health and local economic costs of unemployment, and citing studies showing how each £1 earned by averagely paid council workers generates far more than an additional £1 of spending in the local economy (see, for example, APSE, 2008; CLES, 2010). Recruitment freezes too are easily attacked, using statistics like those in the previous paragraph, for their arbitrariness and frequently inefficient consequences – the work of departed personnel either being done by people unfamiliar with it and to the detriment of their own work, or not at all.

But a £160 billion budget deficit is not a normal-scale funding gap. Moreover, the new government eliminated potentially the most 'democratic' response option of all by freezing council tax from 2011 for at least one year and preferably, with local authorities' compliance, for two. This time, all councils, whatever their circumstances and their politics, are bound to consider all remaining options, and their eventual policy packages will comprise combinations of the shorter and longer term, the more and less politically palatable, but always including some provision, over some time period, for reductions in workforce numbers.

As ever, some will manage this crisis and contraction better than others. All councils should be relatively better-equipped than in the past, as there has been more strategic planning and preparation for this post-recession period, and the LGA nationally (LGA Group, 2010) and most individual councils have in place something recognisable as a 'workforce strategy'. But, just as some authorities have suffered serious financial losses through dragging their feet over Single Status Agreements, some will manage less well the balance between reducing their wage bill and retaining a workforce of the scale and with the skills they require. Others will be more effective in negotiating with their staff and unions flexible working practices, voluntary reductions in hours, reduced overtime, changed entitlements to annual increments, even pay freezes – thereby limiting redundancies and their additional impact on the local economy.

One rough and ready test of the progressiveness of your own authority's human resources or workforce strategy is its adoption, or otherwise, of a Total Reward(s) approach to pay and benefits. There is nothing very new about Total Rewards, and it has been promoted in local government since at least 2007 (LGE, 2007). Nor is it remotely complicated: simply the recognition that pay is not the only workplace motivator, and that there are other tangible and intangible rewards that employers may use to attract, incentivise and retain staff. Depending on the job, a total reward package might include flexible benefits, career development opportunities, a challenging role at work, recognition of achievement, personal office space, or the chance to work from home. A Total Rewards employer should be able to engage with individual employees, understand their reward preferences, have them understand the value of the rewards they already receive – not least the cash value of the local government pension scheme – and provide a reward package that best suits their circumstances. In 2009, 28% of councils had already implemented a Total Rewards approach (10%) or planned to in the next two years (LGA Group, 2010, p. 27). It seems a reasonably hypothesis that these councils will be among those that manage best to maintain their workforce numbers and minimise their overall redundancy costs.

Chapter 16

Political Parties

Introduction

Like it or not – and this chapter concludes by examining both sides of the case – political parties and party politics are a central feature of contemporary local government across most of the UK, and will continue to be so for the foreseeable future. In the overwhelming majority of councils it is within closed party group meetings that the serious policy debates take place and key decisions are made, rather than at the formal open public meetings of the council, democratically important as these are. The first part of the chapter outlines the current political landscape of local government and some of its history, including the impact of small parties and Independents. It then compares the organisation and operation of the main parties, inside and outside the council, and concludes by examining the role of the national parties and their respective policies in relation to local government.

Party systems and the survival of non-partisanship

It is important to strike the right balance when dealing with party politics in local government. Understate its significance, and one risks completely misunderstanding how and where many of the most important council decisions are actually made. Overstate it and one then falls into the trap of assuming that all councils are run on tightly disciplined party lines, and that all decisions are party-based. The truth is that, as with almost everything to do with local government, there is great variety of practice. Nothing is universally true of all authorities, as can be seen in outline in Exhibit 16.1, which summarises the range of party, and non-party, systems in Great Britain in 2009/10.

In the metropolitan areas of the country, in all the remaining English counties, most unitaries, and the larger shire districts, there are *fully developed party systems*. These days seven-eighths of all councils come into this category – those in the bottom four main rows of Exhibit 16.1. The great majority of councillors in these authorities are elected under the labels of national or nationalist political parties and, once elected, they organise themselves into separate party groups. Independents and representatives of small parties find it hard to get elected to these councils. With the notable

Exhibit 16.1 Party systems in local government – Great Britain, 2010

Party system and definition		England					Wales	Scotland	Great Britain	
		Unitaries	Counties	Non-Met. Districts	Met. Districts	London Boroughs	Unitaries	Unitaries	Total	%
Completely/predominantly non-partisan (60% or more seats held by Independents)		–	–	1	–	1	3	3	8	2
Weak partisan (20–59% seats held by Independents)		5	–	20	1	1	10	3	40	10
Multi-party/fragmented (20% or more seats held by third party/parties)		12	2	19	17	1	5	16	72	18
Two-party (80% or more seats held by two parties, neither more than 60%)		16	2	51	7	11	2	10	99	24
One-party dominant (60–75% of seats held by one party)	Con	13	16	48	1	3	1	–	82 ⎫	
	Lab	3	–	2	6	5	1	–	17 ⎬ 108	27
	LD	–	–	9	–	–	–	–	9 ⎭	
One-party monopolistic (75% or more seats held by one party)	Con	5	7	48	–	5	–	–	65 ⎫	
	Lab	1	–	–	4	5	–	–	10 ⎬ 79	19
	LD	–	–	3	–	1	–	–	4 ⎭	
Total		55	27	201	36	33	22	32	406	100

Source: Data from Edkins Family Index Page, Local Council Political Compositions. Available at www.gwydir.demon.co.uk/uklocalgov/makeup.htm; accessed May 2010.

Exhibit 16.2 Party affiliations of councillors – Great Britain, 2010

Party affiliation	Unitaries		Counties		England Non-Met Districts		Met Districts		London Boroughs		Wales Unitaries		Scotland Unitaries		Great Britain 2010		Great Britain 1997/98	
	No.	%	No.	%	No.	%	No.	%	No.	%	No.	%	No.	%	No.	%	No.	%
Conservative	1,389	44	1,262	68	5,123	57	579	24	716	38	174	14	143	12	9,406	45	4,449	20
Labour	792	25	148	8	1,098	12	1,221	50	876	47	346	27	350	29	4,831	23	10,643	48
Liberal Democrat	676	22	346	19	1,832	21	521	21	246	13	157	12	166	14	3,944	19	4,756	21
Nationalist Parties	–	–	–	–	–	–	–	–	–	–	207	16	361	30	568	3	301	1
Independents and others	285	9	102	6	846	9	124	5	23	1	380	30	202	17	1,962	9	2,153	10
TOTAL	3,142		1,858		8,919		2,445		1,861		1,264		1,222		20,711		22,302	

Notes: 'Others' include Ratepayers' and Residents' Associations (126), Greens (119), BNP – British National Party (28), Liberals (25), UKIP – UK Independence Party (21), ICHC – Independent Community and Health Concern (10), and other small local parties.
In Northern Ireland, party affiliations of the 582 district councillors elected in 2005 were: Democratic Unionist Party, 182; Sinn Fein, 126; Ulster Unionist Party, 115; Social Democratic and Labour Party, 101; Alliance, 30; Greens, 3; Independents and others, 25.
Figures for the London Boroughs exclude the 157 members of the Common Council of the City Corporation of London, which claims to have no party politics.
Sources: Data from Rallings and Thrasher (2010); Edkins Family Index Page – Local Council Political Compositions. Available at www.gwydir.demon.co.uk/uklocalgov/makeup.htm; accessed May 2010.

exception of the representatives of Havering's long-standing Residents' Associations, few London boroughs have any councillors at all from outside the three main parties. The same is not true of the PR-elected London Assembly (see Exhibit 5.4), but it was the case in 2010 for almost a quarter of the other English councils.

In the more rural areas of England, and in Wales and Scotland, the picture can be very different. As Exhibit 16.1 indicates, there are plenty of English district and Scottish and Welsh unitary councils with *weak party systems* – 10%, using a definition that deliberately distinguishes between

Exhibit 16.3 Four forms of developed party system

1 **Multi-party or fragmented** – relatively few Independents or 'others', but council seats divided among several party groups. Most of these councils will be 'hung' or 'balanced', in the arithmetical sense of having no single party with an overall majority. Their actual forms of administration can vary greatly – from single-party minority rule, through all possible permutations of 'power-sharing' arrangements. In countries with PR electoral systems, multi-party hung councils are the norm, as in Northern Ireland (see Exhibit 16.4, footnote) and now Scotland, where in 2010 there were just three councils with single-party majorities, all Labour: Glasgow, Midlothian and North Lanarkshire. England's first-past-the-post (FPTP) system reduces their number, but they still make up between a quarter and a fifth of the total, reflecting the fact that it is far easier for third and minor party candidates to win elections in the smaller wards and divisions of local councils than in parliamentary constituencies.

The impression given by much of the Westminster-centric media and many MPs, following the 2010 General Election, was that a power-sharing government was some utterly alien phenomenon. In fact, in council cabinets across the country in 2009/10 the parties could be found working together in almost every imaginable combination: Conservatives and Lib Dems (Birmingham, Leeds, Brent, Camden); Labour and Lib Dems (Kirklees, Wirral, Waltham Forest); Labour and Conservatives (Cumbria, Stockton-on-Tees); and all three parties (Sefton, Lancaster).

2 **Two-party** – relatively few third party and Independent members, council seats being split fairly evenly between the two leading parties. Depending on the actual party balance, some of these councils will also be hung. In others, control will swing regularly from one party to the other.

3 **One-party dominant** – one party holds a decisive majority of seats, and will expect to run the council most of the time.

4 **One-party monopolistic** – self-explanatory; the extreme product of our electoral system, one party having unbroken, and often effectively unchallenged, control of the council. Two London boroughs in 2010 were 100% (Labour) monopolies: Newham, and Barking & Dagenham.

'Independents' and candidates of small parties – and still a few that are actually or effectively *non-partisan,* almost all councillors having stood as Independents of some description. Traditionally, perhaps the best examples of near-complete non-partisanship have been the three Scottish Island authorities: Orkney, Shetland and Eilean Sair (the Western Isles). But predominantly non-partisan district councils survive in several areas of the country that are not parts of any Celtic fringe: Cumbria, Lincolnshire, Nottinghamshire, Staffordshire and Surrey.

This brings us to *developed party systems,* which both arithmetically and organisationally can be divided into at least four types, as in Exhibit 16.3.

Conservative recovery, and its limits

There are versions of Exhibits 16.1 to 16.4 in previous editions of this book, most interesting for comparative purposes probably being those referring to 1997, the year Labour came to power nationally (Wilson and Game, 1998, pp. 260–3). Illustrative summary columns have been added to Exhibits 16.2 and 16.4. In 1997/8 there were no fewer than 146 'one-party monopolistic' councils, just three of which were controlled by the Conservatives and 126 by Labour, as were 65 of the 97 'one-party domi-nant' councils. Of the 36 metropolitan districts, 24 were one-party monop-olies, all Labour; similarly 10 of the 15 in London. Labour had over 10,600 councillors: more than the Conservatives and Lib Dems combined.

Notwithstanding the significant local dimensions to local elections iden-tified in Chapter 13, all parties in power nationally expect to lose council seats to protest votes. The Conservatives, though, had surpassed such expectations. Since the Thatcher Government came to power in 1979, the party had lost nearly two-thirds of its councillors and almost 95% (242) of its councils – a process that is fascinatingly plotted, year by year, in the LGC Election Centre's sequence of Local Council Control animated maps or cartograms (Google 'mapping elections'). By 1997, the Conservatives trailed in a poor third place, with fewer councillors than the Lib Dems and controlling fewer than half of their number of councils: statistics that constitute a useful baseline from which to measure the transformation of the local political landscape during three terms of Labour government.

Nearly three-quarters of those 191 Labour fiefdoms had gone by 2005/6 (Wilson and Game, 2006, p. 298), and in 2010, as Labour left office, their number was down to 27. It had taken the Conservatives virtually all 13 years of parliamentary opposition, but they had regained what they would consider their historically rightful position as the pre-eminent party of local government. It was they who now had more councillors than the other two major parties combined (see Exhibit 16.2) and who controlled, on their own, more than 200 councils, plus a further 46 they ran either as a single minority party (16) or in a power-share with one or more other party groups (see Exhibit 16.4). Numerically, it might seem, all lost ground had been made up – but again a more careful look, especially at Exhibit 16.4, produces qualifications.

In the English counties, Conservative domination was virtually absolute. The sole exception was Cumbria – Conservative-led, but where the party was merely the dominant partner in a power-sharing administration. Two-thirds (135) of the districts in those counties were also Conservative controlled, while Labour's majority control was confined to six districts, and just three south of the Midlands – Hastings, Oxford and Stevenage. These results had been produced by a series of worst-ever local election performances by Labour, in which the party's national equivalent vote share fell from 26% (2006, 2007), to 24% (2008), then to 22% (2009) (House of Commons Library, 2009c, p. 11).

Across in the metropolitan district column of Exhibit 16.4, however, the picture is quite different. Here Labour controlled 16 councils to the Conservatives' 3 – Dudley and Walsall in the West Midlands and Trafford in Greater Manchester – and had more than twice the number of councillors. These metropolitan districts emphasise the huge north–south political division we have seen also developing in our parliamentary representation in recent elections. The contrast with 1979 – the last time the Conservatives ousted Labour from government – is striking. The Conservatives then were in a similar overall ascendancy, but part of that ascendancy was their control of 11 metropolitan districts to Labour's 18, and their almost 1,000 councillors to Labour's 1,300. The major parties, in short, were relatively much more evenly balanced, as was also reflected in Labour's control of 49 shire districts – eight times its 2010 total – to the Conservatives' 166 (Butler and Butler, 2006, pp. 238–9).

The alienating and disempowering consequences of this political polarisation seem even more serious in the context of local government than in parliamentary representation. It meant, in 2010, that in over half of England's most important local authorities – the 27 county councils, with almost 50 members each – Labour supporters were represented by three or fewer councillors. In 78 of the 201 shire district councils there was no Labour representation at all: not a single councillor. But hundreds of thousands of Conservative supporters in most of the metropolitan districts went similarly under- or un-represented: one seat on Manchester's 96-seat council, and none at all in Liverpool, Sheffield, Newcastle upon Tyne, Gateshead and Knowsley. In short, the Conservatives' recovery of their local government position, significant as it was, left the party still comprehensively excluded from much of the country's urban government – thanks, substantially, to an electoral system the reform of which it continued to oppose.

There is, therefore, a certain irony that the chief beneficiaries of this

Exhibit 16.4 Pattern of control of local authorities – Great Britain, 2010

| | England | | | | | Wales | Scotland | Great Britain | | | |
| | Unitaries | Counties | Non-Met Districts | Met Districts | London Boroughs | Unitaries | Unitaries | 2010 | | 1997/98 | |
Party affiliation	No. %	No. %	No. %	No. %	No. %	No. %	No. %	No. %		No. %	
Conservative	24 44	26 96	135 67	3 8	11 33	2 9	– –	201 50		23 5	
Labour	10 18	– –	6 3	16 44	17 52	2 9	3 9	54 13		205 47	
Liberal Democrat	3 5	– –	18 9	2 6	2 6	– –	– –	25 6		50 11	
Nationalist parties	– –	– –	– –	– –	– –	– –	– –	– –		4 1	
Independent	– –	– –	4 2	– –	1 3	5 23	3 9	13 3		25 6	
No overall control	18 33	1 4	38 19	15 42	2 6	13 59	26 81	113 28		134 30	
Total	55	27	201	36	33	22	32	406		441	

Notes: 'No overall control' is a purely arithmetical definition of councils on which no single party has more than 50% of all seats. It may therefore include councils on which a single party holds exactly half the seats and, through the casting vote of the mayor or Chair of the Council, may be in a position of effective overall control.

Of the 70 non-mayoral English authorities under no overall control, 32 (47%) were governed by **minority administrations** (15 Conservative, 8 Labour, 9 Lib Dem), and the remaining 38 by various permutations of **power-sharing** arrangements: 24 involving two parties/groups, 8 involving three, and 6 involving four or more.

In Northern Ireland, where local elections are by the proportional Single Transferable Vote (STV) system, all 26 councils in 2005 were under no overall control, as defined above, with the exception of Ballymena (DUP).

Sources: Rallings and Thrasher (2010); Edkins Family Index Page – see Exhibit 16.2.

Conservative metropolitan exclusion were the Liberal Democrats, parliamentarily the long-term victims of the first-past-the-post electoral system. Back in 1979, the Lib Dems' predecessors, the Liberals, had 4% of Great Britain's then 25,000 councillors (House of Commons, 2009c, p. 12), and controlled just 2 of its more than 500 councils. First in alliance with the Social Democrats (SDP), then as the Lib Dems, the party gradually developed distinctive local electoral strategies – as it had done for parliamentary by-elections – and areas of strength that it could target, so that its share of council seats following any set of local elections began to reach the 15–20% national vote share it consistently received. In 1987 the number of Lib Dem councillors overtook 'Independents and others'. In 1995 they overtook the Conservatives for the first time, and by 1996 'had amassed a total of more than 5,000 councillors and majority control in more than 50 councils. [They were] without question the second party of local government' (Rallings and Thrasher, 1997, p. 132).

Then, as in turn the unpopularity of the Blair/Brown Governments increased, the Lib Dems started both to outpoll Labour and to win majority or part-control of some of the urban authorities that the party had controlled previously, sometimes for generations. Disaffected Labour voters in these areas turned to the Lib Dems, much as disaffected Conservatives in the south and south-west had done a decade earlier. In 2010, in each of the above-mentioned six councils on which Conservatives were virtually or completely unrepresented, the Lib Dems were either part of the administration or the main opposition. In Newcastle they had majority control; in Sheffield, minority control; and in Birmingham, Calderdale, Oldham, Rochdale, Sefton, Wirral and Wolverhampton they were partners in power-sharing coalitions. Numerically, they may not have qualified as the second party of local government, but, with far more county and shire district councillors than Labour and nearly as many metropolitan district councillors as the Conservatives, they could claim a more balanced representation across the country than either of the other two.

The history and spread of local party politics

The present-day hold of party politics on *so much* of the country's local government is a comparatively modern phenomenon. Party politics per se has a history in many towns and cities dating back at least as far as the Municipal Corporations Act 1835 (see Chapter 4), but its spread outside those areas is generally much more recent. We should therefore view the emergence of a more politicised local government as 'a steady long-term trend, beginning in the nineteenth century, spreading in this century first through the major cities and then, if less evenly, to the shires' (Young, 1986a, p. 81). The trend has been well described in recent years, by Young

Exhibit 16.5 The party politicisation of local government

1 **Diversity** (1835–late 1860s) Many of the new municipal councils were dominated and split by party politics, but there was no uniform national pattern. 'Tories, Whigs, Conservatives, Liberals, Radicals, Chartists, Improvers and Economisers offered varying prescriptions in different towns' (Gyford *et al.*, 1989, p. 7). Main divisive issues: role of religion in educational provision; levels of municipal spending; drink/teetotalism.

2 **Crystallisation** (1860s–1900s) Administrative rationalisation of local government was accompanied by a channelling of party politics, where it existed, into a predominantly Conservative–Liberal contest. Key catalyst: Joseph Chamberlain's Birmingham Liberal Association (1860s), as both a successful electoral organisation and a radical pioneer of municipal collectivism – local government's proactive involvement in gas and water supply, slum clearance, public health, parks and gardens.

3 **Realignment** (1900s–1940s) Labour displaced the Liberals as the principal radical force in local government, offering 'a distinctive municipal programme: better wages and conditions for council workers, provision of work for the unemployed, public baths and laundries, and adequate housing for working class families' (Gyford *et al.*, 1989, pp. 11–12). Anti-socialist response was orchestrated by the Conservative Party through various local groups of Moderates, Progressives, Municipal Alliance and Ratepayers.

4 **Nationalisation** (1940s–1970s) Of local-government-run public utilities and hospitals, and of local party politics. Growing involvement of the national party organisations in local government; local elections fought more on national issues and personalities; but most county and rural district councils still organised on non-party lines.

5 **Reappraisal** (1970s onwards) Rapid growth and change in the character of local party politics following local government reorganisation. Quantitative change – increasing numbers of party-dominated councils and declining numbers of Independents – accompanied by qualitative change, through the formalisation of local party organisation and intensification of policy debate.

Source: Information from Gyford *et al.* (1989), ch. 1.

himself and by Gyford (Gyford *et al.*, 1989), who usefully identifies five stages to the story, summarised in Exhibit 16.5.

Our chief concern here is with Gyford's final Reappraisal stage, incorporating both a quantitative extension of the scale of party politics in local government and some fundamental qualitative changes in its character. Much of the quantitative change occurred suddenly and immediately upon reorganisation in the early 1970s. Previously, about half the councils in England and

Wales, and two-thirds of those in Scotland, could be defined as 'non-partisan', in that over half of their elected members resisted all conventional party labelling. There was, as ever, an urban–rural divide: between two-thirds and three-quarters of urban councils being run on party lines compared with one-third of county councils and just 10% of rural district councils.

Reorganisation inevitably involved the merging of many non-partisan authorities with others having stronger partisan traditions. The latter almost invariably prevailed, and following the 1973/4 elections the proportions of predominantly partisan authorities rose immediately, to nearly 80% in England and Wales and to over 50% in Scotland.

In the succeeding few years this trend continued, with the Conservative Party in particular insisting that all party sympathisers stand as official party candidates and not, as often happened previously, as Independents. As has already been noted, Independent councillors – that is, those actually standing as Independents – still survive in larger numbers than is often recognised, but Independent-run councils have been inexorably squeezed, and in Scotland and Wales the screw was tightened further by the mid-1990s' reorganisation of local government. In both countries there are now, in the much larger unitaries, fewer Independents than there were previously, though this trend has been more than counter-balanced by the increase in SNP and Plaid Cymru councillors (see Exhibit 16.2).

The English equivalent has been the gradual, if sporadic, increase in the representation of the 'others', who used to huddle anonymously under the 'Independents and others' umbrella. Independents themselves, though, form a far from homogeneous group. Copus and colleagues identify several varieties, distinguishable mainly by their readiness to join and work with other like-minded souls both before and after their election (Copus *et al.*, 2008, 2009). At one end of the spectrum are the 'fully independent' – the indeflectable non-joiners. At the other end are the 'conjoiners', equally opposed to the trappings of party politics – for which, they insist, there is no place in local government – but who recognise the benefits, to themselves and their constituents, of collaboration. The Ashford (Kent), Barnsley, and Canvey Island (Castle Point, Essex) Independents are, among others – see the Independent Network on www.independentnetwork.org.uk – all conjoiners. They register with the Electoral Commission, enabling them to campaign as a group. They can ensure themselves committee places, hold group meetings and promote agreed policies on council-wide issues, while still resisting all suggestions of party discipline and whipped voting.

'Others' come in even more shapes and sizes (Game, 2007b). There are the relatively and absolutely small national parties, from the Greens, UKIP and the BNP to the Justice Party, Christian People's Alliance, English Democrats, and the Monster Raving Loonies. There are the local and single-issue parties, such as those included in Exhibit 13.8; and the professedly 'non-partisan' residents' and ratepayers' groups. They add to the diversity of British politics, and with 'Independents and others' contributing over a fifth of the 28,000 candidates in the 2007 nationwide local elections – and not forgetting the six elected mayors (2010) – their collective voice is becoming louder.

Party politicisation in practice

There is much more to understanding the party politicisation of local government than simply adding up the numbers of party-dominated councils. If we describe a council as 'party politicised', we should expect to find certain features of organisation and modes of operation. These are not new; they developed gradually, most notably under the direction of Labour's influential London leader, Herbert Morrison, in the 1920s and 1930s. Morrison's model party system, described by one of his biographers, George Jones (1975), comprises at least seven elements, as listed in Exhibit 16.6.

Exhibit 16.6 The Morrisonian model party system

Herbert Morrison, Home Secretary during the Second World War, and Deputy Prime Minister 1945–51, was from 1934–40 Leader of the London County Council, and, before David Blunkett, one of the very few to have reached the top rank of the party through local government (Donoughue and Jones, 2001, p. 63). It was, though, as the organising Secretary of the London Labour Party during the 1920s that he developed and propounded the following basic precepts of local party organisation:

1 **The selection of candidates** by local committees of party members.
2 **The formulation of a distinctive policy programme** by a local party group, usually comprising a mix of councillors and local party representatives.
3 **The production of a party election manifesto** to which all party candidates are expected to adhere, both during the election campaign and once elected.
4 **The attempted implementation of the manifesto** in the event of the party winning a majority of seats on the council.
5 **The organisation of councillors into party groups** for the purposes of determining Cabinet and committee memberships and other positions of leadership and responsibility, developing and co-ordinating party policy, determining strategy and tactics, and ensuring group discipline.
6 **The election of a group leadership**, comprising an individual leader and normally a committee of group executive officers, by members of the party group.
7 **The convening of pre-council and pre-committee party group meetings** to enable party group members to agree on policy and plan their debating and voting tactics.

This party political dimension is rarely included in diagrammatic representations of the organisation of councils because, in the past, it would inevitably have complicated an otherwise fairly straightforward, if simplistic, picture of officers and departments servicing committees of councillors who made policy decisions that were then approved publicly in full council. We ourselves sought to address this complication and, in the interests of realism, to show not only where party politics fitted into the policy-making process, but also how in many councils it in fact drives it (Wilson and Game, 1998, Figure 16.1, p. 268).

The party groups, often omitted completely, featured almost at the centre of our illustration – as they would also for Copus (2004), who compares the group to a Leviathan, reaching 'into all facets of council politics and into the wider public realm' (p. 93), though whether the analogy is with the biblical sea monster or Thomas Hobbes' all-powerful state is left for the reader to decide.

The party groups and their respective sizes are the direct outcome of the local elections and, unless there is a directly and separately elected mayor, will determine who is to run the council and how. If one party has an overall majority of seats, its elected leader will become Leader of the Council – now, following the 2007 legislation (see Chapter 7), for four years, rather than an annually renewable term of office – and the chair of a normally single-party Cabinet or executive committee. The Leader, formally at least, determines the size of the Cabinet – between 2 and 10 members – the allocation of policy portfolios, Cabinet members' individual and collective decision-making powers, and will appoint a Deputy, similarly for a four-year period. The party's manifesto becomes in effect the council's agenda, to be translated into practical policy proposals by the relevant officers and departments, as directed by the Cabinet.

Cabinet meetings are open to the public, publicised in advance, and nowadays will often open with some kind of public forum or question time. Topics generally have to be submitted in advance, so spontaneity is limited, but, with councils increasingly webcasting full council and other significant meetings, citizens may get the chance to see themselves on the telly. As under the committee system, public meetings those of the Cabinet and committees are normally preceded by private party group meetings at which members debate agenda issues more forthrightly than they might in public, and will determine their tactics: which issues to focus on, who will speak and, if any local journalists are there, what they hope to have reported. Regrettably, a decade into executive-based policy-making, we have less systematic knowledge than we might have about what actually takes place at these pre-Cabinet and pre-committee meetings: whether, for example, in most councils, party groups meet to discuss forthcoming executive decisions, and whether group decisions are binding on Cabinet members. Until we do, we cannot claim a proper understanding of how councils are *really* working, because, as with committees, one needs to visualise the 'unofficial' organisation of the political parties superimposed completely on the council's 'official' policy-making structure.

A hung council, in which there is no overall majority party, will inevitably operate differently in practice, but not in principle. There may have to be negotiated compromises on manifesto proposals. Cabinets and executives may comprise members of two or more parties, and of course no votes in any arena can be won simply by a party exercising tight party discipline over its own members. Officers may find themselves dealing with and briefing spokespersons from two or three different parties. Those parties, though, and councillors' party affiliations, remain at the heart of the policy process.

Organisational and operational differences

Any political party would recognise most of the elements in Morrison's model party system, different though actuality often is from theory. For example, local parties will inevitably vary in their size, resources and sheer capability – ranging, to use Copus's taxonomy, from the omnipotent, through the 'functioning-mechanistic' and resurgent, to the dormant and downright moribund (2004, pp. 68–70). Very few local parties, though, find recruiting easy, and a dearth of willing and capable volunteers may well 'informalise' candidate selection procedures. Manifestos can vary greatly in length and specificity, and party discipline also varies, some groups treating potential or actual voting dissent with considerably greater tolerance than others (Gyford *et al.*, 1989, pp. 172–5; Copus, 2004, pp. 104–11). But there are also some *systematic differences* of formality and emphasis across the political parties.

The fundamental difference between the Labour Party on the one hand and the Conservatives and Liberal Democrats on the other derives directly from their contrasting origins and objectives. Labour is a programmatic, constitution-based, ostensibly democratic party whose local operations are governed by a set of *Model Standing Orders for Labour Groups*. Some local parties will adhere more rigidly than others to these Standing Orders, but there is a greater uniformity of practice than is found across the other two parties – more uniformity, for example, in the selection of council candidates, which is by ward parties, but only from a *panel of approved candidates*, drawn up by the local party executive committee from ward party or union branch nominees, the whole process being overseen by the regional party. Conservative and Lib Dem selection processes, by comparison, are considerably more relaxed, with ward branches left much more to their own devices and with less emphasis placed on the prospective candidate's party experience, or even membership.

For Labour, as prescribed in the Morrisonian model, policy-making, including the drafting of the manifesto, is constitutionally not the exclusive responsibility of the party group on the council, but one shared jointly with the *local party*. Non-councillor representatives therefore have a right of non-voting attendance at group meetings; group nominees are expected to report back to the party, and there are regular joint meetings. For Conservative councillors, policy is determined by the party group, then possibly (or possibly not) discussed with the constituency's Local Government Advisory Committee, if such a body formally exists. Not surprisingly, Labour party groups on councils tend to be run more tightly, with generally more insistence on internal discipline, than either Conservative or Liberal Democrat groups. For Labour, as Copus puts it, 'all issues are whip issues' (Copus, 2004, p. 129; see also Leach, 2006, ch. 7). Which means, in turn, that there is significantly greater potential for internal party conflict, comparable to that at national level between the Parliamentary Labour Party (PLP) and the Conference-elected National Executive Committee (NEC), with party activists concerned to prevent councillors becoming 'sucked into' the council and being deflected by professional officer advice from manifesto priorities.

The Conservatives evolved over a much longer period than Labour and have traditionally been less rule-bound in their organisation. The party does, however, produce *Model Rules for Conservative Groups* that are wide-ranging. The distinction across the parties today is not so much the existence of such rules, but rather their compulsory/voluntary status. Labour groups must adopt the model standing orders in their entirety, while Conservative model rules have compulsory and voluntary elements to them. Additionally, the Conservatives, while still not as rule-bound as Labour, are today far less flexible and much more structured than in the past. There are also model standing orders for Liberal Democrat groups, produced by the Association of Liberal Democrat Councillors (ALDC), based at Hebden Bridge in West Yorkshire. But here there is a real difference. Lib Dem groups can only be exhorted to adopt them, and many councillors seem barely aware of their existence. Liberal Democrats too tend instinctively to favour structural flexibility and to resist externally imposed discipline, though the ALDC endeavours to foster the virtues of group organisation and coherence.

Leadership differences

An obviously related dimension of party difference is that of the parties' attitudes towards leadership. These are as distinctive locally as they are nationally, and the differences may well have grown with the arrival and subsequent strengthening of executive-based policy-making, designed as it

Exhibit 16.7 Leadership in early Leader/Cabinet councils, by political party

	All (%)	Con (%)	Lab (%)	LD (%)
Measures of leader autonomy				
Leader chooses members of the Cabinet	34	55	28	18
Leader allocates Cabinet portfolios	54	67	57	53
Leader takes at least some executive decisions alone	38	47	31	47
'Concentrated' leadership – leader does all three of above	16	28	12	–
'Diffused' leadership – leader does none of above	27			
Leadership/scrutiny typology				
Individual leadership + robust scrutiny	16	25	10	13
Individual leadership + weak scrutiny	26	(35)	21	27
Group leadership + robust scrutiny	33	19	(44)	(40)
Group leadership + weak scrutiny	26	22	26	20

Notes: 'All' councils column excludes the 27% of the sample under No Overall Control.
◯ = modal executive style.
Source: Stoker *et al.* (2003), chs 5 and 9.

was to empower local leaders and give them a more visible and accountable public profile. Professor Gerry Stoker and colleagues (Stoker *et al.* 2004) were the official DCLG-sponsored monitors of the new political management arrangements, and their early findings suggested that, certainly among the great bulk of councils that opted for the Leader/Cabinet model, party-distinctive styles of leadership were very much carried over from the committee era. Leader-dominated executives were found more in Conservative authorities, while multi-actor or team executives were more common in Labour and Lib Dem authorities. The numbers underpinning these distinctive leadership styles can be seen in Exhibit 16.7, and brief descriptions of the styles in Exhibit 16.8.

Focusing on the three measures of leadership autonomy in the first section of Exhibit 16.7, it was found that in 34% of Leader/Cabinet authorities, the Leader was allowed to select Cabinet members; in 54% to allocate portfolios; and in 38% to take policy decisions without consultation. Combining these measures into a single continuum, 16% of predominantly Conservative leaders were found to have full autonomy, while 27% of predominantly Labour and Lib Dem leaders had, by this definition, no freedom of individual action. From ministers' perspective, therefore, over a quarter of councils – particularly those controlled by their own party colleagues – were failing to take full advantage of the strong leadership levers they had been given. These councils had supposed they were being given a free choice over whether to opt for the government's obviously

Exhibit 16.8 Three executive leadership styles

Leader-dominated executive	Cabinet members work to the leader, who takes responsibility for the overall direction of policy. Role of the Cabinet is to advise on policy development and monitor progress of implementation. Can result in fewer full Cabinet meetings and more 'bi-laterals' between the leader and individual portfolio holders. Leader will be the key contact for external partners, and may choose to have own independent sources of policy advice.
Multi-actor executive	Cabinet members have extensive delegated powers, operate with considerable autonomy from each other and from the leader, and are expected to provide leadership themselves in their respective policy areas. They will develop their own networks and meet independently with external partners. Leader's role is to maintain a corporate approach and ensure that Cabinet members' efforts join up to form a coherent policy. Individual Cabinet members are the 'default clearing point' in decision-making.
Team executive	Leader and Cabinet work together, with a view to collective decision-making. Full Cabinet meets regularly and possibly at length, and individual decision-making is checked back with the Cabinet as a whole. Leader's aim is to ensure and manage consensus, and give a collective drive to council policy.

Source: Information from Stoker *et al.* (2004), pp. 39ff.

preferred model of strong, high-profile individualistic leadership, or for a more collective, inclusive, democratic model. They were mistaken – as was made clear in the 2006 White Paper and the 2007 introduction of revised 'strong leadership' models (see pp. 110–12).

In the lower section of Exhibit 16.7, Stoker *et al.* (2003) incorporated an assessment of overview and scrutiny (O&S) arrangements, to provide a more rounded picture of leadership styles from the viewpoint of the authority. The assessment was based on several factors – the independence of O&S from the executive, its readiness to explore innovative forms of service delivery, and the quality of officer support it received – that could be combined into a crude index of what we have termed 'scrutiny robustness'. Put this together with the 'leader autonomy' index, and one has a 2 x 2 leadership/scrutiny typology, which, as shown by the encircled figures in Exhibit 16.7, correlates at least loosely with these authorities' party control.

Policy differences and manifestos

These variations in how our main political parties organise themselves and operate are real and important, but ultimately what matter are the policy differences. As emphasised throughout this book, local government, its structure, functions and financing, these days occupy a prime place on the UK national political agenda. Accordingly, no party's General Election manifesto is complete without a selection of pledges concerning the further changes it will impose on local government, should it be elected to office.

In 2010, the three parties' manifestos all followed the modern trend of being ludicrously long (100+ pages on average) and expensive (£5, if it wasn't possible to download them), and, having been swiftly outdated by the *Coalition Agreement*, they may well be remembered in future less for their content than for their covers: the Conservatives' austere blue hymn-book-style clashing dramatically with Labour's extraordinary retro-homage to Soviet propaganda. As might be expected of the chief opposition party, the Conservatives' *Invitation to Join the Government of Britain* was the longest manifesto. There was a statistical oddity, in that the party, whose big appeal was intended to be the contrast between its localist plans and Labour's centralist record, actually used the word 'local' fewer times than either of its rivals (*The Guardian* datablog). But more relevantly, the key local government section of the manifesto – prefaced, incidentally, by a 'blob' diagram based on data similar to those in our own Exhibit 14.3 – contained the greatest concentration of more or less specific pledges.

Several of these pledges we have already encountered, carried forward as they were from the party's 2009 Green Paper, *Control Shift*: no more large unitary authorities, abolition of 'the entire bureaucratic and undemocratic tier of regional planning', directly elected mayors and police chiefs, a 'general power of competence' for councils, scrapping Labour's regime of centrally set targets and inspections. Other policies too supported the party's localist credentials: a 'community right to buy' scheme, to enable the protection of community assets such as post offices and pubs, threatened with closure; 'ending' the ring-fencing of grants; councils permitted to keep above-average increases in business rate revenue; financial incentives for councils to build new homes; and residents able to instigate local referendums.

But also carried forward from the Green Paper was what many of its local government critics had seen as its biggest weakness: the absence of 'root and branch' financial reform. There was no mention of shifting the funding imbalance through which councils are dependent on the Treasury for 80% of their income. References to council tax were limited to an initial two-year freeze, imposed 'in partnership with local councils', and subsequently the right of citizens 'to veto any proposed high council tax increases' – neither of which could truly be described as a radical 'control shift' to democratic local government and its elected representatives. The other two parties at least promised further reviews, intended in the case of the Lib Dems to lead to the piloting and subsequent introduction of a local income tax, based, unlike council tax, on people's ability to pay (p. 90).

None of the manifestos, it might redundantly be added, gave any hint of the make-up of the £1.2 billion of savings/cuts (£800 million in revenue) that would be demanded of local government within weeks of the election – from the £311 million from locally delivered children's services to, as the LGA inevitably described it, 'pulling the plug' on free swimming for the under-16s and over-60s. The headline pledges that were made can be compared in Exhibit 16.9.

The contrasts and disputes among the parties can be just as great at local elections as at General Elections. Councils are more restricted as to what they can do than they used to be. They cannot raise taxes as they might wish, and their influence over major budget expenditures may be limited to the margins. But, as emphasised in Chapter 12, budget margins of organisations the size of the UK's major councils are themselves sizeable enough for their spending increases, or cuts, to have a far from trivial impact on those whose lives are directly affected.

Local elections thus continue, quite properly, to be run in such a way as to acknowledge that the outcome makes a difference. Manifestos and candidates' election addresses are likely to be based on the respective parties' national policies, with appropriate adaptation to local issues and circumstances. The atmosphere and conduct of the election will be set by the party defending its record and those challenging it – as in our illustration of the 2009 County Council elections in Northamptonshire. Labour had controlled the 73-seat council from 1993 until the previous elections in 2005, when the Conservatives had won majority control, with 45 seats to Labour's 21 and the Lib Dems' 7 – the highest total the latter party had ever achieved. All seats were contested in elections held on the same day as – and overshadowed by – those for the European Parliament. The Conservatives were well ahead of Labour in the opinion polls, and few neutral observers would have expected anything other than a thumping Conservative victory, which is precisely what materialised – the Conservatives on 56 seats, Labour lost all but 6 of theirs, and the Lib Dems overtook them with 9.

Notwithstanding their differing prospects, all three parties produced attractive, detailed, locally-focused manifestos, with those of the Lib Dem and Labour parties running to 12 and 15 pages, respectively. Each comprised a mix of thematic priorities and specific policy pledges that, as can be seen in Exhibit 16.10, was clearly distinguishable from those of the other two parties.

If ever there were conditions likely to suppress local variations across a set of local elections, it was in 2009. The elections were confined to the already Conservative-dominated English counties plus 7 unitaries, they

Exhibit 16.9 The national parties' local government manifestos, 6 May 2010

	Conservatives	Labour	Liberal Democrats
Democracy	Scrap Labour's plans for further unitaries; 12 largest English cities to have referendums on directly elected mayors; replace police authorities with 'directly elected individual' to set policing priorities.	'Stronger local government, with increased local democratic scrutiny over all local public services' (9.2).	'Fair votes' – i.e. PR – for English local elections; direct election of police authorities; local elected health boards to take over PCTs' commissioning role.
Regions	Abolish entire undemocratic tier of regional planning; councils and businesses to have power to form Local Enterprise Partnerships, instead of RDAs; more powers for London Mayor and boroughs.	Promote city regional authorities, with powers to improve transport, skills and economic development, and referendums for directly elected mayors.	Abolish Government Offices for the Regions; RDAs to focus wholly on economic development; support establishment of Local Enterprise Funds and regional stock exchanges.
Finance	Two-year council tax freeze, then voters able to trigger referendums to limit tax rises; councils to keep above-average increases in business rate revenue; end ring-fencing of grants.	Council tax capping to continue; cross-party commission to review future of local government finance; reduce ring-fencing.	Review finance, with view to replacing council tax with 'fair tax' based on ability to pay; pilot Local Income Tax; relocalise business rates; reform public sector pensions.
Powers to local government	'Unprecedented redistribution of power from the central to the local' (p. ix); councils to have 'general power of competence'.	New powers for social, affordable housing, climate change, and to work with NHS in new National Care Service.	Enable councils to borrow money against assets to build new council homes; more powers to regulate bus services to meet community needs.
Inspection	Scrap Labour's 'hundreds of process targets' imposed on councils; end bureaucratic inspection regime; curtail planning inspectors' powers.	Reduce central targets and indicators; enhanced scrutiny powers for councillors.	Scrap nearly £1 billion of central government inspection regimes on local councils.
Education	All schools, incl. primaries, to have chance to achieve Academy status; new 'pupil premium' for children from disadvantaged backgrounds; halt ideologically-driven' 'closure of special schools.	More spending on Sure Start, free childcare, schools and 16–19 learning; more free nursery education; more innovative school providers.	Invest £2.5 billions in 'pupil premium'; local authorities to have strategic role in schooling, including oversight of admissions and performance; axe rigid national curriculum.

Exhibit 16.10 Contrasting local manifestos

Priorities and pledges from the major party manifestos for the Northamptonshire County Council elections, June 2009

CONSERVATIVE priorities:

- A prosperous economy to protect and create jobs across the county.
- Give elderly people a wider choice of better quality care.
- Provide young people with richer education, life experiences and opportunities.
- Strong emphasis on partnership working and value for money.
- Smaller government, low taxes, reducing costs and waste.

Some specific pledges:

- Develop partnership with Cambridgeshire County and Slough Borough Councils to deliver services more efficiently.
- Extend 'In Control' scheme to help another 1,000 people have control over their care.
- Provide £500,000 p.a. for extra Police Community Support Officers.
- Introduce smart card payment system for residents using public transport.

LABOUR priorities:

- Regenerate town centres – so getting people back to work.
- Youth activity centres in each town and a youth worker allocated to every neighbourhood.
- Restore free meals-on-wheels to the most vulnerable people, who need them the most.
- Concessionary £1 'anywhere in the county' bus fare scheme for all young people under 21.
- Cap council tax below inflation – and give £50 cash refund for pensioners over 75.

Some additional pledges:

- Provide £500,000 capital grant towards a children's hospice.
- Reprioritise capital programme to rebuild two secondary and six primary schools by 2013.
- Make the council carbon-neutral in four years, through energy audit of council premises, planting 10,000 new trees, and more wind- and solar-powered street lights.

LIBERAL DEMOCRAT priorities:

- Improve school standards.
- Tackle waste to keep council tax down.
- Fix roads and pavements.
- Better support for elderly and vulnerable people.
- Community and restorative justice for offenders.
- A council closer to people, not to faceless bureaucracy.

Some specific pledges:

- Develop a more balanced mix of secondary schools, with more vocational alternatives.
- Seek developer contributions to help fund a fuller network of cycle routes.
- Strongly oppose the government's unrealistic development targets in the Milton Keynes & South Midlands Growth Area, which includes Northamptonshire.

Source: Conservative, Labour and Liberal Democrat Manifestos, 2009. Available at www.telegraph.co.uk/news/newstopics/local-elections/5345770/Northamptonshire-county-council-local-election-2009.html.

coincided with the Euro-elections, and they took place with Labour's popular support at virtually its historically lowest ebb. It was unsurprising, then, that the results were far more uni-directional than is usually the case with a nationwide set of local elections. The Conservatives gained control of 7 councils, won an additional 285 seats, and lost almost nothing. Labour and the Lib Dems lost both councils and seats and won very little – though the Lib Dems did take control for the first time of the traditionally Labour-dominated Bristol City Council.

Actual voting patterns, however, were clearly different from what they would have been at a General Election. The Lib Dems, with an estimated national vote share of 25%, probably did relatively better, and Labour, with 22%, relatively worse. More obviously, of the nearly 7 million votes cast, the Greens, UKIP and Independents each won over 300,000 votes, and the BNP a further 170,000 – a total of nearly one vote in five going to candidates *not* representing the three main parties. As ever, a significant proportion of electors had cast 'local' votes in these local elections. With an electoral system that rewarded the combined 11.7% of votes won by the Greens, UKIP and the BNP with more than 1.2% of seats, the proportion might well have been higher.

The pros and cons of party politics

It is at election time that we see most clearly both the positive and negative features of the extensive role played by party politics in modern local government. We have already alluded in Chapters 3 and 13 to some of the claimed positive features, notably the contribution of parties to political education and participation. These, and the other claims set out on the left-hand side of Exhibit 16.11, make a strong case, yet it remains one that many find unpersuasive. When asked, as in the 1985 Widdicombe Committee survey, the majority of respondents (52%) said they would prefer local councils to be run on non-partisan lines, with only a third (34%) feeling that a party system is better (Widdicombe, 1986b, p. 88). We need to examine, therefore, the other side of the coin, which is why Exhibit 16.11 takes the form that it does.

Set out in this way, the arguments may seem to be evenly balanced. You must draw your own conclusions, preferably with reference to your personal experience and impressions, while we, as academics, could continue to fence-sit. On this occasion, however, we won't. Rather, we shall conclude by making two points. First, bearing in mind the historical trends we identified earlier in the chapter, we would suggest that the comprehensive party politicisation of most of our local government is not only here to stay, but in recent years has been reinforced by the trend towards ever larger and unitary authorities.

Exhibit 16.11 The pros and cons of party politics in local government

The merits and benefits	The counter-claims
• **More candidates, fewer uncontested seats** in local elections.	• **More party candidates, fewer Independents** – the major parties' resources give them too much advantage over small parties and Independents.
• **More active campaigning**, more information for electors, more debating of the issues.	
• **Clarification of the issues**, as the parties are challenged by their opponents to justify their arguments and assertions.	• **Less electoral enlightenment** – voters want rounded debate of issues and dislike politicians' apparent belief that their party alone possesses the answers.
• **More citizen awareness of and interest in local government** – both in general and in their own local council in particular, resulting probably in a higher electoral turnout.	• **Electoral boredom** – electors stay at home, invoking 'a plague on all their houses', or are unmotivated by an outcome that seems a foregone conclusion.
• **Stimulation of change and initiative** – as parties with their underlying principles and collective resources develop policies to put before the electorate.	• **Less public involvement** – the many citizens not wishing to join a political party are excluded from decision-making in their own communities.
• **More opportunities for public involvement in community life**.	• **Nationalisation of local elections** – what should be local campaigns focus too much on national issues and personalities.
• **Enhanced accountability** – parties and their candidates make public pledges, which, if elected, they must seek to implement, and for which they can subsequently and electorally be called to account.	• **Reduced representativeness of councils** – winning parties take all positions of responsibility and seek to implement their policies to the exclusion of all others.
• **Governmental coherence** – following a decisive election, a single-party administration, clearly identifiable by electors and council officers, is able to implement the policies on which it was elected.	• **Excessive party politicisation of issues** – parties feel obliged to adopt adversarial positions on subjects better discussed consensually.
• **Enhanced local democracy** – the existence of electorally endorsed party policies and programmes reduces the potential policy influence of unelected and unaccountable officers.	• **Parties demand loyalty and voting discipline from their members** – councillors appear to represent their parties, not their voters, particularly when the party makes a decision with which voters disagree.
• **Parties are the best scrutineers** – of each other's policy performance and ethical behaviour.	• **Exclusion of professional advice** – most key decisions are made by party groups, usually without professionally trained and experienced officers in attendance.

Second, we would refer back to the assertion made in Chapter 14: that politics, properly understood, is at the heart of what local government is about. It is about the management and resolution of the inevitable conflict of local views concerning the provision and distribution of goods and services. Without necessarily agreeing with the respected colleague of ours who insists that the definition of an Independent is someone who can't be depended upon, we suggest that there are democratic benefits in these conflicting views being marshalled and articulated openly by consciously accountable politicians, rather than by self-styled 'non-political representatives', whose motives and political objectives may remain publicly unspecified. Indeed, as former Secretary of State for Communities and Local Government, Hazel Blears, put it: 'Without political parties and local politicians, we would have no functioning local democracy' (Blears, 2007).

Of course, that democracy would function much more effectively if, for example, the parties could attract far more citizens to become active members, so that they didn't appear so narrow and unrepresentative of those whose votes they seek; or if we had an electoral system that made it easier for Independents, and candidates of small and local parties, and representatives of popular interests, to get elected; or if we had a scale of local government in which there were far more smaller and genuinely local councils to which they could get elected. As this book has indicated, these conditions are not unrealisable, for there are plenty of countries in which similar situations exist. For the present, however, the UK's party-based local government system is all the populace has, and, imperfect as it might be, both the system and its party operatives deserve a more positive recognition than they are generally accorded.

Chapter 17

Who Makes Policy?

The internal and informal politics of policy-making

Chapters 14 to 16 examined three of the key elements in a council's policy-making process: elected councillors, the officers who advise them, and the political party groups of which most of them are members. But these were essentially static examinations, or snapshots. This chapter brings them together, focusing on their collective *raisons d'être*: the actual determination of policy. It is a process that has been transformed structurally by the advent of political executives held to account by an overview and scrutiny regime. Executive members are now held personally responsible and accountable for decisions relating to the management and delivery of services in a wholly different way from committee chairs under the previous system.

These changes have not, however, invalidated everything previously written about policy-making in British local government: about the centrality and subtleties of the member–officer relationship, the critical importance of a council's 'party arithmetic', and, not least, the attempts by some academics to conceptualise these inter-relationships. The purpose of this chapter is to review and, where necessary, refine what we know about the *internal and informal* influences on policy-making. Much of the framework of local government policy these days is laid down by central government. But we have seen how local authorities can still pursue policy priorities, respond to specific local circumstances, and launch their own initiatives. This chapter explores the extent to which it may be possible to make some general statements about how, within town halls and county halls across the country, these things are done.

Analytical models

Three main analytical models have been widely used to describe the distribution of power and influence inside local authorities. Each is considered briefly, along with a further model based on insights from central government, before the discussion broadens into an examination of a variety of 'real-life' influences on the policy process.

The formal model

This model derives from the 'legal-institutional' approach that once dominated the study of local government. Its proponents saw power relationships in formal terms and focused on the formal structures of decision-making – the council, its committees and departments. The model could hardly be simpler: councillors make policy, while officers advise them and carry it out. No overlaps or qualifications are countenanced.

Advocates would argue that, if people understand the formal, legal position, they understand reality. Critics would retort that reality, and certainly political reality, is considerably more complex, as has already been suggested in our discussion of councillor roles in Chapter 14. A model that sees councillors making policy through the council, while officers merely advise and implement, tells us more about what perhaps *should* happen than about what *actually* happens. It fails to recognise the complexity within, and the organisational variety among local authorities – lacking what Gains would term 'institutional interpretivism' (2009, p. 50). It nevertheless, she acknowledges, 'highlights the normative and legalistic "rules of the game" and the political and authoritative resources which elected politicians hold' (p. 51).

One must beware of dismissing even an overly simplistic model as worthless. The confrontational Thatcher years saw real assertiveness by councillors of both the New Urban Left and the Radical Right – including several whose names are still in the public eye today. At the GLC there was Ken Livingstone and his deputy leader, John McDonnell, one of the 2010 Labour leadership contenders. Islington London Borough was led by Margaret Hodge, later Minister for Children, and in 2010 the first elected chair of the Commons Public Accounts Committee. David Blunkett was leader of Sheffield City Council, the so-called 'People's Republic of South Yorkshire', while across in West Yorkshire the Coalition Government Communities Minister, Eric Pickles, was plotting his Thatcherite 'Bradford Revolution' – as fascinatingly recounted by Tony Grogan in *The Pickles Papers* (1989). One of the few things that these outstanding local politicians might have agreed upon is that councillors and officers have different roles, and it is the former who are elected to govern. They set out to run their authorities in the way that the formal model delineates.

The technocratic model

A rival to the formal model has been the technocratic model, which views *officers* as the dominant force in local politics. Their power resides, it is asserted, in their control of specialised technical and professional knowledge, unpossessed by and possibly incomprehensible to part-time, amateur, generalist councillors.

This model too, however, is something of a caricature and should not be accepted uncritically, especially in the age of executive local government. Highly paid, professionally trained officers, heading large directorates and departments, with all the staff and other resources of these organisations at their disposal, can appear formidable to the inexperienced, newly elected councillor. But the relationship is not all one-sided.

Plenty of leading and long-serving councillors, particularly those in virtually full-time executive positions, have the experience, knowledge and political skill to assert themselves effectively in negotiations with officers. Moreover, even the neophyte councillor comes with that vital source of democratic legitimacy that no officer, however senior, can ever have: the authority of having been *elected,* on what is now an endorsed political platform, to represent all the citizens of their locality.

Exhibit 17.1 is a balance sheet of the respective resources of officers and councillors – a little like that in Exhibit 11.6 in which we compared the resources of central and local government. It was argued there that local

Exhibit 17.1 The resources of officers and councillors

OFFICERS	COUNCILLORS
• Professional knowledge, training, qualifications	• Political skills, experience; possibly training, expertise, qualifications in own field of work
• Professional networks, journals, conferences	• Party political networks, journals, conferences
• Full-time, well-paid employee of council	• Spends an average of 20 hours per week on council work, far more if on the Executive
• Resources of whole department	• Resources of whole council
• Knowledge and working experience of other councils	• In-depth (possibly lifetime) knowledge of own council, ward, its residents and service users
• Commitment to professional values and standards	• Commitment to personal and political values, to locality and community
• UNELECTED 'servant of the council' – appointed to advise councillors and implement their policies	• ELECTED on political manifesto to make policy and represent hundreds/thousands of residents and service users

government has access to more resources than is sometimes suggested, and so it is with councillors in their relations with officers.

It is apparent from Exhibit 17.1 that it has been the politicisation of local government, and particularly its intensified *party* politicisation since the 1970s or 1980s, that has done more than probably anything else to shift the balance of power between officers and elected councillors. We come back again to the rise during the 1980s of ideologically committed and politically skilful councillors of both the New Left and the New Right, which inevitably served to check any independent policy aspirations of officers. In the 1990s, for example, ruling Conservative Party groups in Westminster LB, Wandsworth LB, Wansdyke DC in Avon and Rochford DC in Essex were notably assertive in the introduction of competitive tendering and the enabling/purchasing philosophy – just as a decade earlier the 'municipal left' had introduced public transport and council housing subsidies, job creation and anti-discrimination policies.

Notwithstanding such examples, the professional knowledge and technical and administrative experience possessed by officers remain tremendous resources, equipping them to act as powerful policy-makers *in the absence* of any positive policy lead from members. Their influence can be especially strong in smaller rural authorities, where party politics may be less highly developed and less of a policy driving force. As professionals, officers are always there to fill any policy vacuum. It is up to councillors to set their own clear localist policy agendas and thus to ensure that there is no vacuum.

The joint elite model

Claiming to be more truly reflective of actual practice than the formal or technocratic models, the joint elite model argues that policy-making is dominated by a small group of leading majority party councillors (now invariably located in the Cabinet) and senior officers, with minority party and what we now call non-executive members and junior officers being only marginally involved.

It was an interpretation that found support in several empirical studies. Saunders' research in Croydon (1980, pp. 216–30) revealed a picture of town hall politics where chief officers and political leaders worked as 'close allies', maintaining a powerful control over policy-making. Cockburn's study of Lambeth saw the backbencher 'excluded by the high-level partnership between the leadership and senior officers' and consequently taking 'little part in the policy planning process'. Council decision-making was, Cockburn maintained, dominated by 'a tightly-knit hierarchy under the control of a board of directors [the chief officers] in close partnership with a top-level caucus of majority party members' (Cockburn, 1977, p. 169).

But the joint elite model too had its critics, who questioned the virtual monopoly of influence apparently attributed to this elite. Young and Mills (1983) argued that the very exercise of routinised power by those at the top of a hierarchy makes them less likely *sources of policy change* than those lower down. These 'junior actors' learn from direct operational experience and often have the creative energy necessary for the development of new initiatives. Important though leading councillors and officers in any authority obviously are, a thorough understanding of the policy process requires a recognition that they will rarely constitute a united cohesive group sharing a common agenda. In the real world, relationships are more complex and frequently characterised by tension and conflict.

For Gains (2004, 2009), the problem with all three of these models is that, while each 'may reflect the position in one authority at a particular point in time, they cannot capture the dynamic and variable power relationships which can be found across local government either as a whole or over time' (2009, p. 52). What was needed was a 'dynamic dependency' model.

A 'dynamic dependency' model

Quite apart from their individual limitations, all three of the above models date from the committee system era. It is therefore worth reflecting on what might be termed an early 'post-modern' analysis: an attempt to adapt elements of these earlier models, most notably the resource-based technocratic model, to local authority differences in the implementation of the political management changes introduced by Labour's 'modernisation agenda'.

From her perspective as a member of the University of Manchester's Evaluating Local Governance (ELG) project, Gains drew on the literature on central government bureaucratic political relations (for example, Rhodes and Dunleavy, 1995) that stressed the importance of 'formal and informal institutionalised rules in structuring action and influencing outcomes' (Gains, 2004, p. 94). At the local level, these 'rules' include institutional understandings or 'inheritances' concerning the departmental and hierarchical nature of local government, the understanding that officers are politically neutral and serve the whole council (Stewart, 2000); also shared 'world views', such as the Thatcher-instilled drive for economy, efficiency and effectiveness, and 'New Labour's 'steering centralism' and its commitment to targets, performance measurement and partnership working.

Gains' 'dynamic dependency' thesis is that all behaviour, including that of councillors and officers, is the outcome of the interplay of these institutional understandings – which in part are institution-specific – and the actors' skill in exercising their respective resources: the political resources of the council leader *vis-à-vis* senior managers, the strength of the party group and so on (2004, p. 95). Dynamic dependency analysis, Gains suggests, provides a better understanding than more static models of how and why member–officer relations differ both across authorities and over time. More specifically, it can help to explain the 'huge variety of formal institutional arrangements adopted to enact the 2000 Act' that were found by the ELG surveys (Gains, 2004, p. 98): how the delegation of decision-making powers to individual portfolio holders was more likely in Conservative and county authorities; why Labour authorities were more likely to have dedicated officer units supporting the scrutiny function; and how, generally, officers appeared to respond initially more positively than councillors to the abolition of the committee system (2004, pp. 98–100).

Like all models, dynamic dependency has both strengths and weaknesses. But, unlike the joint elite model, it does not assume shared values or a shared agenda, and it emphasises how local history and political culture will vary along with, for example, the political resources of a council leader, the strength of the party group, and the clout of the professional officers. Moreover, it does not see the balance of power between, in our case, officers and members, in zero-sum terms, but rather as a dynamic and dependency-based relationship, varying from one institutional setting to another. It thereby adds a helpful nuance to our understanding of local policy-making.

Broadening the debate – additional influences on policy-making

There is more, though, to an understanding of the distribution of policy influence in a local authority than simply an analysis of the activities of the most senior players. Other factors need to be incorporated if a model is to depict anything like the full complexity of internal power relationships. That is the purpose of the remainder of this chapter: to add to, qualify and generally complicate the models outlined above, and in doing so to identify some of the additional influences on policy-making. Our focus will be on those authorities that now have executive management structures, rather than those smaller English shire districts (with populations of fewer than 85,000) that opted for 'streamlined committee systems', though in practice many of these smaller authorities will face similar influences. Exhibit 17.2 provides a diagrammatic presentation of the ideas covered, which comprise:

- *Intra-party influences* – relations *within*, in particular, ruling party groups, and between groups and the wider party;
- *Non-executive influences* – the evolving roles of 'backbench' or non-executive councillors;
- *Inter-departmental influences* – relations between and across departments and professions;
- *Intra-departmental influences* – relations within departments; and

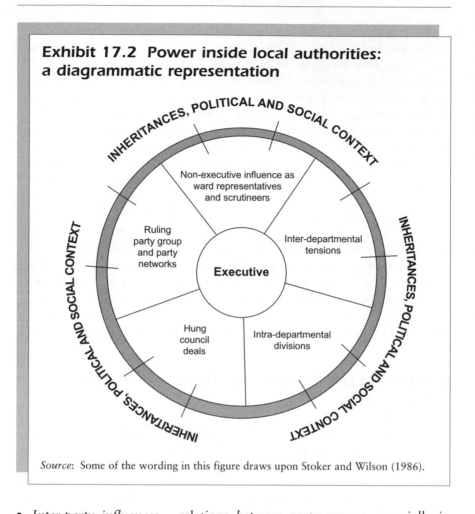

Exhibit 17.2 Power inside local authorities: a diagrammatic representation

Source: Some of the wording in this figure draws upon Stoker and Wilson (1986).

- *Inter-party influences* – relations *between* party groups, especially in hung authorities, where they have to take account of one another.

The ruling party group and party networks

It was noted in Chapter 4, in relation to the Widdicombe Committee, and in Chapter 16 that UK local government has a deep-rooted cultural reticence towards the recognition of political parties: an irritating coyness about acknowledging their very existence, let alone the obviously fundamental role they play in shaping and determining the policies of most local authorities. Most councillors are elected under party labels; they meet as groups before most public council and committee meetings, then vote together at those meetings; the sizes of the groups determine who controls the authority. Yet, try finding out on many councils' websites the party composition of the Cabinet or executive – always vital information, and, especially on a hung or balanced council, far from self-evident – and the information *per se* is regularly unavailable. It should be one click from the home page, yet often it is necessary to search through the perhaps 10-member Cabinet, councillor by councillor, and work out which configuration of parties is actually running the council.

When the ruling group is eventually identified, one will have located, as indicated in the previous chapter, a significant influence on policy-making – and not just among its leading and executive councillors. Few party groups are homogeneous. As Copus enticingly puts it: 'whilst the group presents a united face to the public and political opponents, the reality can be much more exciting' (Copus, 2004, p. 101). The ruling Labour group on Leicester City Council at the end of the 1980s was unusual in the formalisation of its factionalism, and in the fact that the party leader, Peter Soulsby, was one of the few members who belonged to none of them, but it was by no means unique. There were in effect four caucuses within the group (Leach and Wilson, 2000, pp. 128–9):

- The 'left', about 13 in number, who met in a local pub, with formal agendas, in advance of Labour group meetings;
- The 'black' caucus of about 8 members, including one white Muslim councillor, which also held formal pre-meetings;
- The 'right' – again about 8 members, largely from Leicester West parliamentary constituency, less formally organised than the left and the black groups; and
- The 'non-aligned' group, of between 6 and 8 members.

Most party groups manage their internal schisms more informally, but, as Copus observes (p. 102), that doesn't stop councillors regularly alleging that their group is dominated by one 'mafia' or another: the members from one section of the authority, from one union, profession, generation or class. Factionalism, however, is no bar to policy influence. Policy initiatives can emerge from the backbench/non-executive members of a group, who can also veto or refer back leadership proposals with which they disagree. Stoker (1991, p. 98) notes that, while over many issues and for most of the time, a group may 'simply endorse decisions taken elsewhere, at the very least senior councillors and officers must be careful not to offend the core political values and commitments of backbenchers. The role of party groups in local policy-making is a potentially crucial area for decision-making.'

Party groups nowadays expect to be consulted and listened to, and leaders – other than directly elected mayors – have to cultivate their support continuously, even if they don't any longer face annual re-election. Upset just one or two group members and they may decide to leave; alienate a majority and *you* may have to. Defections and cases of 'crossing the floor' of the council chamber are numerically far commoner, if less publicised, than in parliamentary politics, as evidenced in almost any local election listings. Even discounting all the plain, unvarnished 'Independents', there will be plenty of candidates describing themselves as 'Independent Conservative', 'Socialist Labour', 'Independent Liberal Democrat', even 'Independent Green', and suggesting that their favoured parties cannot accommodate the ideological purity of their views – or perhaps just them personally.

On occasion, party groups will flex their muscles and remove the group leader. This can be a heartless process, especially when the relevant group meeting comes, as often occurs, immediately after an election. The best known case was 'Red Ken' Livingstone's displacement of the more right-wing Andrew McIntosh as leader of the Greater London Council in May 1981, within 24 hours of McIntosh having led the Labour Party to electoral victory (Livingstone, 1987, pp. 3–4). The clash there was a mix of ideology, policy and personal style, and some permutation of these factors is probably at the root of most leadership challenges. However, executive-based local government has changed internal group dynamics, particularly for a party in power, and there is now an institutionalised separation of the leader and the group. Several recent cases, therefore, have a distinctively twenty-first century feel to them.

In 2005, Labour group members on Hull City Council conducted an overthrow in stages, first removing the power of their leader, Colin Inglis, to appoint his own Cabinet, then a fortnight later replacing him completely with a former leader, Ken Branson. In 2009, the challenge that cost Richard Shepherd his leadership of the ruling Conservative group on Charnwood Borough Council was prompted by an Audit Commission report criticising the authority's leadership and its 'limited ambition' for the future. Also in 2009, Kate Dean, Lib Dem leader on Aberdeen City Council, was ousted in a party coup following an Accounts Commission public inquiry into the council's financial affairs. Leaders or executive members who owe their elected positions to their group can expect to be reminded regularly of the fact – which is one powerful reason why so many councillors oppose the very principle of directly elected mayors, whose first accountability is to the electorate as a whole, rather than to them.

The *local party network* also requires consideration. Links with the wider party organisation can be a valuable resource for individual group members, especially in the Labour Party, where such networks have a greater policy significance, with local election manifestos, for example, being drawn up in consultation with non-councillor party members. It was thus the district parties in Walsall and Rochdale, rather than the party groups on the council, who were the real originators of the decentralisation policies in those boroughs. Local councillors and council leaders must respect the role of the wider movement; disregard can easily lead to conflict.

Non-executive councillors

It might have been better if the essentially parliamentary term 'back-bencher' had never been applied to the very different world of local government, where, in the traditional committee system, no councillor constitutionally had more decision-making authority than any other. 'Backbencher' misleadingly and demeaningly suggests a hierarchical role division where none existed legally. On the other hand, 'frontline' councillors, given official recognition in the 2007 Local Government and Public Involvement in Health Act, strikes some, including Dame Jane Roberts, former leader of Camden LBC and Chair of the 2007 Councillors Commission, as even worse:

> It's language from the trenches. It suggests holding an enemy back, rather than engaging with the community. It also implies that the community engagement function is not for the likes of executive councillors. It suggests that formal decision-making is best carried out away from direct and immediate experience of community life. I believe councillors' rootedness in, and feel for, the community they represent should inform all council activities. (IDeA, 2007b).

We shall therefore continue, despite the term's inherent negativity, to talk mainly of 'non-executive' councillors, who now have four distinct roles through which they can play a part in shaping policy, if not in actually taking policy decisions. Like all councillors, they are representatives of their wards and constituents, community leaders – Jane Roberts' community engagement function – and members of full council; and, as non-executive members, they are also overseers and scrutineers.

In promoting or defending local ward interests, councillors can enter the policy arena in all kinds of potentially influential ways. In one of the best recent depictions of councillors' ward work, shrewdly entitled *Cabinet Member for Your Ward,* three Liverpool Lib Dem councillors describe their many ways of influencing and in some cases changing policy, from the ultra-local to the national (Kemp *et al.*, 2009). Ultra-local examples might include negotiating free school lunches for 'lollipop' men and women, challenging officers' proposals for road resurfacing and traffic calming measures in their ward, and obtaining lottery funding to develop a disused building for community use. National policy influence would probably be headed by the 2005 Clean Neighbourhoods and Environment Act (Section 2), which legalised Liverpool City Council's popular initiative of alleygating – cutting crime and anti-social behaviour by gating off the ends of the thousands of alleyways giving rear access to rows of terraced houses. In what they call their treatise, the councillors emphasise the city hall–ward balance that they feel should characterise their work. The policies that affect their constituents and that they seek to influence are made in city hall, but the information, the partner agencies and networks needed to bring that influence to bear are largely in their wards.

It was one of the Labour Government's insistent claims for executive local government that it would enhance councillors' ward and community roles, and their unique position as conduits of their constituents' views to the council. Freed from some of their former committee work, non-executive members would be expected to consult with their communities on the development of policy, on the regular reviews of Best Value and the development of the Best Value Performance Plan, and on any other community-relevant initiatives, and, as discussed in Chapter 14, act as community leaders or champions. For their part, councils were charged with ensuring that appropriate procedures were available for members to 'feed-in' the views of their constituents to the policy development process.

The message received strong reinforcement in the 2007 Local Government and Public Involvement in Health Act with the introduction of the Councillor Call for Action (CCfA) and 'Section 236' powers. CCfA, referred to in Chapter 14, enables members to ask for discussions at scrutiny committees on issues where local problems have arisen and where other methods of resolution have been exhausted. Section 236 of the Act provides for councils, if they choose, to delegate powers to individual councillors to carry out any function of the authority that relates to their ward. It would thus extend the power that some councillors already have to spend modest amounts of money on ward issues by enabling them, for example, to supplement local safer neighbourhood teams with additional officers, to effect street repairs and improvements, or to take local action on issues such as child obesity and diet.

Executive-based local government's biggest contribution, though, to the enhancement and transformation of the non-executive councillor's role was intended to be Overview and Scrutiny. Properly exercised, a council's O&S arrangements would be about far more than evaluating existing policy and holding the executive to account *after* the event – knowing whom to blame – important and satisfying though that is. The opportunities are there for the 80% or more non-executive members to contribute *prospectively* to the development of policy *before* it is finalised (see Exhibit 7.5 and 17.3). O&S are rightly presented as integral to effective executive government, and their potential impact is almost limitless, because they offer the non-executive members who exclusively run the process the possibility of reviewing, scrutinising, reporting on and making recommendations concerning any past, present or future policy or action of the council, or any matter affecting the council's area or its inhabitants.

It was emphasised in Chapter 7 that, for the full potential of O&S to be realised, at least three conditions are required. First, councillors themselves must approach the process positively, acknowledging that not being part of

Exhibit 17.3 Policy influence of Overview and Scrutiny – Birmingham City Council

Exceptional structure

Birmingham's 120 councillors make it the largest council in the United Kingdom, and the 110 non-executive members explain its exceptional structure of 10 O&S committees that broadly match the portfolios of the 10 Cabinet members. O&S activities that can influence the development and implementation of council policy include:

- monitoring the performance of council services;
- reporting on draft Policy Framework plans and strategies;
- undertaking policy development tasks at the request of the Cabinet or Council; and
- undertaking Scrutiny Reviews.

Examples of Scrutiny Reviews, 2009/10

Road Safety (Transportation & Street Services Committee)
To examine how the city's recent record of significantly reducing road traffic casualties could be carried forward through a combination of engineering advances, education and enforcement campaigns. Ideas examined included 20 mph zones in all residential areas, and the introduction of 'shared space' schemes that break down the rigid separation of drivers and pedestrians.

Effectiveness of Sex and Relationship Education (SRE) (Children & Education) – jointly chaired and undertaken by UK Youth Parliament members co-opted to the committee. Challenged the Council's model of SRE provision, proposing a clearer focus on relationships, meaningful consultation with parents, and more pupil involvement.

Partnership working to tackle gang violence (Equalities & Human Resources)
Reviewed the work of the Birmingham Reducing Gang Violence partnership, established by the Council and the police following two high-profile gang shootings in 2003. Made recommendations concerning the Council's future role – including the Cabinet Member for Local Services and Community Safety having responsibility for operational matters concerning gangs.

Additional policy areas reviewed in 2009/10 included:

- Reducing the impact of drug and alcohol misuse;
- Housing provision for older people;
- Allotments;
- Child victims of domestic abuse;
- Swine flu preparedness; and
- Improving school leavers' functional literacy and numeracy skills.

the executive can be *empowering* at least as much as disempowering. They must realise too that new skills are likely to be expected of them, which for most will mean serious training. Instead of, as often sufficed in the past, passively processing officer reports, they should now be assessing and probing, working collaboratively to draw out evidence and views from witnesses, and understanding performance indicators, comparative data and financial processes in a way that few will have done previously (Audit Commission, 2001, p. 24).

Second, members need to learn also new ways of working – constructively across the party divide. Their role as scrutineers, even if they are members of the same party as the executive, is not to defend the party line, but to explore, critically if necessary, ways in which the council can better serve its community. It is vital, therefore, that party 'whipping' and tight disciplinary regimes be relaxed – something that does not come easily to members who may have spent their entire adult lives opposing just about everything for which their political opponents stand.

Third, effective scrutiny requires, in addition to committed and trained members, *dedicated* officer and resource support – in both senses of the adjective. The executive's demands must not be allowed totally to hold sway. Sufficient and sufficiently senior officers need to be allocated specifically to the scrutiny process, and, like members, they need to view the assignment positively, and not as some kind of second-class, career-blocking posting, inferior to working for the executive. Adequate financial support is needed too, and there is a real worry that councils that have been reluctant in the past to recognise the support requirements of O&S are hardly likely to in a much more financially pressured future.

No one who understands local government would claim that these conditions are easily met. As may be sensed from Exhibit 17.3, O&S has the capacity to offer non-executive members a considerably more stimulating existence than traditional committee work generally did – provided it is embraced wholeheartedly. Patently, that has not always been the case, which explains why it is the element of executive arrangements that most authorities, and particularly their non-executive members, have found it hardest to operate effectively (see, for example, Leach and Copus, 2004; Snape, 2004; Leach, 2009).

The former Labour Communities Secretary, John Denham, described O&S as 'in many ways, a lion that has failed to roar'. The minister's quote came in his speech launching the 2009 DCLG consultation paper, *Strengthening Local Democracy*, the conclusions from which formed the basis of the Local Authorities (Overview and Scrutiny) Bill that was introduced towards the end of the 2009/10 parliamentary session. It was inevitably overtaken by the election, but its main proposals can be seen as reflecting the outgoing government's view of what was needed.

O&S committees currently have powers to require information from their own councillors and officers, from local NHS bodies, and from organisations involved in the prevention of crime and disorder, who can be required to attend and to respond formally to reports and recommendations. Most other bodies – including a council's LAA partner authorities – aren't compelled to attend or do more than 'have regard' to recommendations. The Bill would have strengthened the obligations on some of these external organisations when carrying out functions relevant to the local authority area: a positive step certainly, but whether it would have elicited from the king of beasts much more than an approving growl seems unlikely.

Inter-departmental tensions

Most councils have more than one O&S committee or panel, but not one for every major department. In this way, local government practice differs from that of the mainly departmentally-linked select committees in the House of Commons. Councils have generally been readier to recognise that many of the most urgent and intractable problems they face – the so-called 'wicked issues' of social exclusion, environmental sustainability, community safety and so on – cannot be pigeonholed neatly into service-specific departments and committees. They have therefore set up more open-ended and flexible scrutiny arrangements, often with some formidably all-embracing titles – Safe, Strong and Inclusive Communities (Cumbria); Health Overview and Crime Reduction (Shropshire); Built Environment, Business, Enterprise and Skills (Westminster); Quality of Life (Bristol). Others, like Sunderland, have linked their O&S committees to the council's strategic priorities: Children, Young People and Learning; Community and Safer City; Environment and Attractive City; Health and Well Being; Prosperity and Economic Development; Sustainable Communities.

Such developments should not be taken to imply that departmental identities and boundaries are no longer of much significance. Departments remain the main units of a council's administrative organisation, and, as ever, they represent different interests and inevitably have different, and potentially conflicting, sets of priorities. Particularly at times of zero growth, or service and staffing cutbacks, these differences surface and can lead to arguments across departments in the fight for scarce resources, and conceivably for departmental survival.

There are also instinctive *professional rivalries* – between, for example, the technical departments involved in land development: 'Planners, architects, housing managers, valuation officers and engineers all claim an involvement and there is a long history of rivalry between these professions' (Stoker, 1991, p. 102). Dominance of specific departments and professions will inevitably change over time; unacceptable policies will be delayed and favoured policies will be accelerated. Increased professionalisation within the local government service has meant that inter-departmental tensions are never far from the surface and will spill over into the policy sphere with some regularity.

According to Pratchett and Wingfield (1996), the dual impact of market competition and the internal reforms associated with the advent of the 'New Public Management' has been some erosion of the public service ethos in local government. The divisions of functions between client and contractor engendered by market competition have led to increasingly antagonistic and adversarial relations between different parts of the same organisation, encouraging more reticent and secretive behaviour within local authorities. Employee loyalty is frequently perceived nowadays to be to a specific 'cost centre' rather than to the broader authority.

Intra-departmental divisions

Intra-departmental divisions are a further factor in the policy-making equation. Individual departments are frequently no more homogeneous than are party groups. The size and diversity of many departments mean that, in effect, the span of control a chief officer can exercise must be limited, thereby providing junior officers, often with greater technical expertise by virtue of their more recent training, with scope for influence.

Most departments in larger local authorities consist of hundreds, even thousands, of employees in a range of relatively separate hierarchies and organisational divisions. Indeed, given the trend, noted in Chapter 7, of merging several departments into a much smaller number of strategic directorates, there is increasing scope for competing priorities and internal friction *within* a single management unit. Leicester City Council's Development, Culture and Regeneration Department, for example, combines the former departments of Cultural Services and Neighbourhood Renewal, and Environment Regeneration and Development into a unit with more than 3,200 staff and four divisions – Culture; Environmental Services; Planning & Economic Development; Regeneration, Highways and Transportation – which, as the department's web page justly claims, 'provide between them a large proportion of the council's visible public services'. In such contexts, senior managers play the role of directors of far larger groups of more disparate, if loosely related, services than would have been the responsibility of their predecessors.

Divisions within departments can also arise with the spread of decentralised management and service delivery. Area-based housing officers, for example, may develop a dual loyalty: to the local authority but also to their own operational area and its residents. Conflict is by no means uncommon between area offices and central departments, or between a number of decentralised area offices. Nor is it unknown for officers working in decentralised offices to develop close ties with local ward councillors – another source of potential influence for junior officers. Failure to incorporate *junior* officials in any model of decision-making inside the town hall is to ignore a group which can, on occasions, be influential.

Hung or balanced councils

The prevalence nowadays of hung or balanced councils – those on which no single party has an overall majority of councillors – raises further questions about the adequacy of the joint elite model, which assumes the existence of a small group of leading majority party councillors. In 1979, 14% of councils in Great Britain were hung; in 2010 the figure was double that (see Exhibit 16.2). If, in the future, Scotland's introduction of proportional representation for local elections were to spread to the rest of Great Britain, the number of hung councils would almost certainly double again, to approaching two-thirds of the total (Leach and Game, 2000, ch. 2).

Even in the absence of electoral reform, though, in large numbers of councils party groups already *have* to take into account each other's policies and actions; otherwise, any proposal they put forward could in principle be defeated at any time. First, however, they need to determine among themselves how council business will actually be conducted. With a committee system there were several possibilities:

- *Minority administration* – where one party, usually the largest, took all committee chairs and 'governed' as if it had an overall majority;
- *Power-sharing* – where two or more parties agreed to share committee chairs, but without, usually, any more far-reaching agreement on a shared policy programme: a deal or arrangement, therefore, rather than a formal coalition; and
- No *administration/rotating chairs* – where there were no permanently held chairs, the positions being rotated among the parties for procedural, rather than policy, purposes.

Executive government changed the 'rules of the game' completely, imposing altogether different demands on a hung council and requiring substantially different solutions. Under the committee system there was no easily identifiable 'executive': no functional or constitutional equivalent of a Cabinet, with seats and portfolios that could be bargained over in negotiations about the formation of a governmental coalition. With committee chairs having no individual decision-making power and relatively little additional remuneration, the arena of coalition negotiation, in so far as there was one, was the 'legislature' – the council chamber – rather than the executive.

With executive local government – and its important by-product of enhanced remuneration for executive members – the 'no administration' option, for a start, ceases to be either a possibility or, even if it were, an attraction. Councils are required to adopt some form of executive, mayoral or otherwise, and those executive positions offer what coalition theorists would call the twin incentives of *policy influence* and the *benefits of office* (Laver, 1989, p. 19). So, while the negotiations now facing party group leaders on a hung council may appear to resemble those that would have taken place under the committee system, and while even the available options may appear to be similar, what is at stake is very different indeed.

Thanks to the inter-party comings and goings following the 2010 General Election, everyone is now an armchair expert on the considerations confronting politicians required to construct a viable administration from the arithmetic of a hung Parliament or council. In local, as in national, government, the basic options are a one-party Cabinet – equivalent to a minority administration under the committee system – even though that party could be defeated in full council at any time, or some kind of two- or multi-party coalition Cabinet. In recent years – perhaps reflecting the sense that the main parties are ideologically closer to each other than previously – there has been a definite trend in local government towards coalitions, or, as they tend more usually to be known, power-sharing arrangements. So, in 2010, while the Conservatives and Liberal Democrats were negotiating their national coalition, many similar deals were being struck locally. As indicated in Exhibit 16.2, of the 70 non-mayoral English authorities that were hung, 32 (47%) were governed by single-party minority administrations and 38 by various permutations of power-sharing arrangements – several of them much more complex than anything contemplated seriously at national level.

A more detailed look at the composition of some of these arrangements also sheds interesting light on coalition theorists' *a priori* hypothesis that, with the change from committee to executive systems, coalition formation would become more arithmetically rational and therefore predictable. The UK committee system used to confound coalition theorists. The absence of any executive body or Cabinet to act as a significant prize deprived them of their core assumption about politicians being, above all else, office-motivated, and frequently made a nonsense of their typical 'minimum winning coalition' (MWC) predictions – that parties will form ideologically compact coalitions that can claim a majority with the fewest possible members.

The 2010 national coalition is an MWC only in the sense that, if either party were to withdraw, the majority disappears. It was not, given the distribution of seats following the election, arithmetically the *minimum* winning coalition, and, certainly according to critics, was not ideologically compact either. A possibly more ideologically coherent MWC was in principle negotiable between Labour (258 seats), the Lib Dems (57), the Scottish and Welsh Nationalist parties (9), and the Northern Ireland Social

Exhibit 17.4 Some hung council administrations, 2010 – how could you guess?

Metropolitan borough council	Con	Lab	Seats LD	Other	Administration
CONSERVATIVES largest party					
Birmingham	45	41	31	3	Con/LD
Bury	23	20	8		Con minority
Calderdale	21	10	17	3	LD/Lab
Wirral	27	24	15		Con/LD
LABOUR largest party					
Bradford	32	39	14	5	Lab minority
Kirklees	19	24	20	6	Lab minority
Leeds	22	41	21	8	Lab minority
Wolverhampton	26	29	5		Con/LD
LIB DEMS largest party					
Rochdale	11	22	26		LD/Con
Sefton	15	23	28		LD/Lab/Con

Democratic and Labour Party (3). But it was hardly compact and arithmetically would have been flimsy in the extreme. The Conservatives' 306 seats, though, added to the Lib Dems' 57, produced an arithmetically robust coalition, leaving time to test its ideological strength. It was in fact the kind of outcome that used to emerge frequently on hung councils, and would frustrate coalition theorists by appearing to owe at least as much to the personalities of the leading councillors as it did to either the detailed party arithmetic or respective ideologies (Mellors, 1989; Leach and Stewart, 1992). Moreover, to judge from the small sample of metropolitan boroughs in Exhibit 17.4, not much has changed.

In the case of each major party, it would seem almost impossible to predict from the arithmetic alone what kind of administration would result from its being the largest single party in a hung authority, or even whether it would be part of the administration at all. The theoretician's notion of the MWC would seem frequently to be an irrelevance, and even the idea of maximising the size of Cabinet, or the largest party's proportion of seats in it, is regularly resisted.

Any form of hung council administration is likely to involve far more extensive inter-party contact and negotiation than is seen in most majority-controlled councils. Officers too – particularly the chief executive and chief officers – have to assume different roles, working with and briefing spokespersons from possibly several parties rather than from just one. They may, indeed, perform a role of broker, bringing the different parties together in order to negotiate some policy or procedural agreement. And, of course, non-executive members find their position is enhanced, as every council vote becomes precious. Bargaining becomes the order of the day because there is no one-party elite of members who can be sure, unaided, of delivering a policy programme.

Conclusion – constantly shifting alliances

The conceptual models presented in the first part of this chapter – the formal, technocratic, joint elite and dynamic dependency models – provide useful insights into local policy-making, but they have their limitations. While the arrival of executive government has generally greatly strengthened the positions of leading councillors and senior officers, it is misleading to see the policy process as being confined to this elite. While their centrality is not questioned, their exclusive dominance certainly is. Local authorities are political institutions, in both the 'big P' and 'little p' – the partisan and the broader senses of the word. They incorporate a whole range of additional actors and influences that may impinge on policy-making, depending on an authority's traditions, culture, leadership, political balance and so on. The policy process in the real world is complex and changeable. It can be regarded as a series of shifting alliances, forming and re-forming over time and from issue to issue. These networks and alliances vary enormously, but they are by no means solely the preserve of the political executive and the officer elite.

Chapter 18

Voluntary and Community Groups

Bowling in groups

A curiosity of the modern age of individualised and privatised lifestyles, of iPods, MP3 players, and mobile everything, is not just that organised groups and group activity still exist, but that they have almost certainly increased in recent years. On the face of it, this seems to conflict with the mass of evidence produced by US Professor Robert Putnam in his famous mapping of the alleged breakdown of civic and social community engagement in modern America, *Bowling Alone* (2000). There is no equivalent body of data for the UK, but what there is would seem to question the direct comparability of the two societies. We appear not, at least to the same extent, to have withdrawn from the social interaction of our equivalent of American bowling clubs and leagues and taken to doing it alone.

The independent Power Inquiry, like other recent commentaries, differentiated between *electoral activity* – declining in recent years – and *pressure activity*, which included a wide array of activities designed to influence decision-making without seeking electoral advantage, and which, if anything, had increased (Power Inquiry, 2004, p. 12). Apparent evidence, directly relevant to our concerns, comes from several detailed investigations of group activity in particular regions, listed helpfully on the website of NAVCA, the National Association for Voluntary and Community Action. The mapping studies listed in this book's previous edition (VONNE, 2000; Lewis, 2001; Voice East Midlands, 2003) have since been joined by others in Central London, Greater Manchester, the West Midlands, Leeds, Halton, Wandsworth and no doubt more besides. Typical headline findings are those from the latest Brighton and Hove Community and Voluntary Sector audit (2009), which found, for a population of a quarter of a million, 1,600 local organisations, employing 8,000 people, and contributing £96 million annually to the local economy, plus more than 19,000 volunteer positions donating in effect an annual salary bill that the CVS Forum calculated at £24 million.

More dated now, but especially interesting for its comparability across time, was the 1998 survey of Birmingham's voluntary sector by Maloney and colleagues. Taking as their baseline Newton's study of Birmingham in

Exhibit 18.1 Voluntary and Community Groups defined

Voluntary and Community Groups (VCGs) – a rough and ready definition:

- not-for-profit organisations,
- independent of government,
- benefiting from some measure of voluntarism,
- adding value to the community through such activities as:
  - o providing services;
  - o acting as advocates; and
  - o campaigning.

Other common labels

- **Voluntary sector** – preferred by the Coalition Government to 'third sector'; can seem to emphasise large household-name charities at expense of small community groups.
- **Third sector** – intended to highlight the many private bodies serving public purposes – voluntary associations, charities, foundations, NGOs – overlooked in two-sector, market/state views of the world; used by the Labour Government.
- **Civil society** – modern usage linked to reform movements in Central and Eastern Europe; very inclusive, potentially embracing all institutions that are not part of the state, market or family; for Conservatives, what the Big Society will grow from when over-expanded Big Government is rolled back.
- **Non-profit sector** – widely used internationally; misleading for pedants, suggesting that groups aim only to break even, rather than make a modest surplus: it is the underlying purpose and non-distribution of profit that are important.
- **Charity sector** – can get confused with registration with the Charity Commission. About 180,000 groups are registered, but far more are not.
- **Social enterprise sector** – also increasingly fashionable, though with different meanings for the different political parties; risks suggesting income-generation more than service provision.
- **Interest, pressure groups** – little used today in local government; much more in political science about, predominantly, national and international government. Both terms reflect a concern with groups as policy influencers, rather than potential service providers.

Some figures from the *UK Civil Society Almanac 2010* (NCVO, 2010) – see their downloadable poster at http://www.ncvo-vol.org.uk/almanac2010 (accessed 16 October 2010).

- UK 'Civil Society' comprised some 900,000 organisations in 2007/8, with a total income of £157 billion, and a workforce of 1.6 million.
- There were 171,000 VCGs, with an income of £35.5 billion, a workforce of 668,000 – 63% full-time, 68% female. Of the income, £13.1 billion comes from individuals, £12.8 billion (36%) from government sources. Nearly half the government funding is from local government, a third (and growing) from central government.
- Over half these VCGs are 'micro-organisations', with annual incomes of less than £10,000, and 75% get no grant or contract funding from government. The 438 'major' organisations (0.3% of the total) account for 44% of the sector income.

the early 1970s (1976, chs 3 and 4), which recorded 4,264 formally organ-ised voluntary associations in the city, Maloney *et al.* (2000) found 5,781 for a population of roughly 1 million, or an increase of more than a third (p. 805). If the largely non-political sports clubs were excluded, the number of groups had more than doubled, from 2,120 to 4,589.

While Putnam might have found such figures surprising, the authors did not, because of the dramatic changes in the local government environment over the intervening thirty years (Maloney *et al.*, 2000, pp. 805–6):

> For example, as local government powers and functions have been progressively eroded in traditional service delivery areas such as housing, existing or new voluntary and community organisations have taken over some of these responsibilities and developed new areas of work ... there has been a shift to a more enabling role rather than direct provision of social services. The doubling of the number of groups in the social welfare category [666 to 1,319] reflects the impact of such trends ... Local government has also moved into new policy fields, such as economic development, environmental protection and crime prevention, and has done so in co-operation with a range of 'third force' organisa-tions. (Stoker and Young, 1993)

We have here the focus of this chapter: what in the 1990s were termed 'third force' organisations and have since become generally known as the third sector – though, as in the book's previous edition, we refer to them mainly as Voluntary and Community Groups (VCGs). 'Sector' seems to play down these groups' enormous diversity and to suggest a more widely shared purpose and interest than is the case, and we prefer therefore not to use this as our principal label. Labels and definitions can be important, especially for people such as the Charity Commission and the NCVO's researchers who produce the excellent *UK Civil Society Almanac*, cited in Exhibit 18.1; also, apparently, for newly elected, image-conscious govern-ments. For us they are less so, except in so far as they confirm the immense scale and impact of group involvement at the local level. We begin with some definitions and categorisations to help make sense of this scale. The greater part of the chapter, though, looks at the differing – and changing – kinds of relationships VCGs have with their local authorities, and the nature of their influence on policy-making and service delivery.

What's in a name?

The reference above to newly elected governments serves as notice that the Office of the Third Sector, created by Tony Blair only in 2006 and point-edly located at the heart of government in the Cabinet Office, disappeared in 2010. In its place, literally, is the *Office for Civil Society*, headed by the Minister for Civil Society, Nick Hurd – previously Conservative Shadow Minister for Charities, Social Enterprise and Volunteering, and, before that, the backbench MP who sponsored the Sustainable Communities Bill (see p. 169). This re-branding was an earlier commitment thought to have been dropped, so its revival was presumed to be a boost to charities and their key role in the implementation of David Cameron's Big Society agenda. It seemed a slightly odd way, however, to win the confidence of a sector already seriously worried about losing both grants from government and contracts to the private sector. The minister had a more junior status – Parliamentary Under-Secretary – than his Labour predecessor, his office was staffed by the same civil servants, and it seems the main, and inevitably costly, change was in the headed stationery. Shakespeare's rhetorical question 'What's in a name?' referred to a rose, that by any other name would smell as sweet; some must have wondered whether an Office for Civil Society can really perform so much more sweetly than one for the Third Sector.

In fact, those who study these matters would claim there is a huge difference in the names, as indicated in Exhibit 18.1. Civil Society is a term that carries some heavy historical baggage – being most readily associated by some with the early twentieth-century Italian Marxist philosopher and politician, Antonio Gramsci. As understood today, though, it is the really big tent. For a few years now, the NCVO has used a definition-cum-explanation that David Cameron must have been tempted to plagiarise as he strove to sell us the Big Society (NCVO, 2009, p. 3):

> Civil society is where people come together to make a positive difference to their lives and the lives of others – for mutual support, to pursue shared interests, to further a cause they care about, or simply for fun and friendship. It is where me becomes we.

The NCVO's 900,000 bodies, therefore, in addition to the broadest definition of 'charities' – 127,000 sports clubs, 13,700 faith groups, 2,400 independent schools, 2,200 benevolent associations, 1,820 housing associations, 170 universities – also include trade unions, credit unions, co-operatives, employee-owned and guarantee-limited businesses, building societies, political parties and football supporters' trusts.

For VCGs – or the voluntary sector, or the third sector – it is fundamental, not optional, that the 'positive difference' should be primarily to the community or the lives of others. Our definition in Exhibit 18.1 is deliberately simple, but it serves our purposes, which differ somewhat from those of our colleagues who are writing primarily about national government, and who will prefer the terms 'pressure groups' and 'interest groups', and definitions that give greater prominence to political campaigning and policy influence, and pay less attention to working *with* government (see, for example, Leach *et al.*, 2006, ch. 8; Budge *et al.*, 2007, ch. 13; Jones and Norton, 2010, ch. 11).

As Exhibit 18.1 makes clear, campaigning counts very definitely as a public-benefiting activity, and the definition thus acknowledges that the many groups which would see themselves as either predominantly service-providing or almost entirely non-political can be drawn into the political process, if only intermittently. Thus a local gardening association resisting a proposal to build a road over its land becomes temporarily a campaigning group. At the local level, there are many such single-purpose groups, which burst into political life only when an issue such as a council planning decision affects them directly.

At the other extreme, the definition can also embrace groups which may become in effect single-issue parties, putting up candidates in local elections against those from larger, nationally-based parties. The argument would be that, while the latter are clearly seeking the responsibility of government, the single-issue groups are using the electoral process primarily as a means of publicising their cause. They may well not field enough candidates to form an administration, even if they are outstandingly successful, though they can occasionally, like the Health Concern (Kidderminster Hospital) campaigners or the Boston Bypass Independents, find themselves almost inadvertently in government (see Exhibit 13.8).

Insiders and outsiders

There are two main approaches to the categorisation of groups: according to who or what they represent, and by the nature of their relationship with government. The first categorisation would differentiate between *sectional/interest* groups, whose principal purpose is to advance the interests of their members – trade unions, business organisations, tenants', residents' and ratepayers' associations, BME (black and minority ethnic) groups, arts and cultural groups, groups for women, gays, lesbians, bisexuals – and *cause/promotional* groups, whose members and supporters are not necessarily the direct beneficiaries of their activities – groups advocating the interests of children, the elderly, the disabled, victims of violence or crime, the homeless and the unemployed.

It quickly becomes clear that even this apparently simple distinction is by no means an absolute one, with many groups obviously qualifying for both categories. That, however, goes for almost any attempted categorisation, and certainly for the one to which we shall pay greater attention: the insider/outsider distinction developed and elaborated by Grant (2000). In this case, however, the overlap serves to highlight the very point we are seeking to make.

Insider groups are those with some combination of characteristics that makes them potentially useful to government and therefore worthwhile consulting on a regular basis. *Outsider* groups either do not want to become closely involved with government or do not possess the characteristics to make them useful regular consultees.

There are several characteristics that can make groups attractive to government, or at least make them seem worth cultivating: authority, information, experience, ideological and policy compatibility, and, ultimately, sanctions. The *authority* of a group is its ability to speak on behalf of, and if necessary deliver the support of, a substantial proportion of those it purports to represent. Just how many 'Asian businesses' are members of the Birmingham Asian Business Association, a council's economic development department might reasonably ask, and from which of the city's Asian communities? Is the Midlands Vietnamese Community Association or the Vietnamese Development Centre more representative of both the Buddhist and Catholic sections of that community? Authority is likely to be closely linked with a group's possession of useful *information,* both about its own members and specialised information not necessarily otherwise accessible by policy-makers.

Local groups, their managements and leading volunteers can get to know, and be known by, council policy-makers far more easily than can their national counterparts operating on the Whitehall and Westminster stage. Reputations – good and bad – can be established and *experience* acquired much more quickly. If council officers are looking for responsive and reliable consultees, or for a group to assist in policy development or service delivery, they are naturally going to turn first to those with whom they have worked previously and who already have, in their eyes, a positive track record.

Being representative, possessing information and having experience are good – for a group that aspires to be an insider. The next test is whether its ideology, politics and policy interests are at least broadly *compatible* with those of the council, and particularly with the party or parties currently controlling the council. For the political scientists responsible for some of the early group studies in UK local government, this issue of political compatibility tended to be treated as the all-important one.

Newton, in his Birmingham study referred to above, described more and less 'respectable' and 'controversial' groups being dealt with by the Council in very different ways (1976, p. 67). Those 'so well respected and established within the community that their activity and co-operation with the [Council] is not questioned by any of the party politicians' would have their business handled by officers 'without fear of political repercussions'. In contrast, 'less respectable and more controversial organisations would be handed on to the appropriate council committee', where they would have to take their political chances. Dearlove similarly found that Kensington and Chelsea Council's response to groups revolved around councillor assessment of their demands – 'helpful' or 'unhelpful' – and their communication styles – 'acceptable' or 'unacceptable' (1973, ch. 8). Those deemed 'unhelpful', whose causes ran counter to those of the ruling Conservative administration, found themselves having to channel their demands through what the councillors saw as 'improper' routes – for example, petitions and demonstrations.

There are, of course, still plenty of outsider groups who either choose or are forced to employ 'megaphone methods' to make their voices heard: petitions and placards, letters and lobbies, marches, sit-downs and demonstrations. If you call your group the Animal Rights Militia, Reclaim the Streets, or the Disabled People's Direct Action Network, you will neither expect nor probably want the same reception as, say, the Cats' Protection League, the Bournville Village Trust, or the Birmingham Fellowship of the Handicapped.

Changing relations

It is not, then, that the insider/outsider distinction no longer has any relevance; rather, that, as Stoker (1991, ch. 5) was among the first to note, the local government world began to change significantly from the 1970s and 1980s onwards, and with it the operation of local group politics. The operational relations between groups and their respective councils appear very differently to a contemporary observer from how they did to Newton, Dearlove and colleagues. The relatively closed and inward-looking organisations they encountered have since 'opened out', as Stoker put it, in several distinct ways. There was the growth of a 'community orientation' among both councillors and officers, a greater readiness to look at services from the viewpoint of users as well as from that of the organisational providers, and an increased commitment to consultation with outside interests (Stoker, 1991, pp. 124–8). These developments were matched by a greater assertiveness and diversity among local groups themselves, and, in some cases at least, the availability of additional resources. Between them, these trends brought about 'an increased willingness on the part of interest groups and local authorities to share responsibility for the delivery of services' (p. 128).

Interestingly, this greater willingness of the two sectors to operate in concert manifested itself in councils right across the then highly politicised party spectrum, albeit in differing ways. Left-wing Labour authorities, for example, could encourage voluntary sector, cause and community groups that challenged the status quo by providing them with grant funding. Centre-right or Liberal Democrat-influenced authorities were keen to be seen to have good relations with a wide range of groups and to be listening to their concerns. And for Conservatives, voluntary groups offered an obvious alternative means of organising the delivery of services and thereby challenging the monopolistic position of the council.

Compacts – national and local

For a single-item demonstration of the extent to which councils' views of and relations with VCGs have evolved steadily since the 1970s and rapidly since the mid-1990s, one need look no further than the *Voluntary Sector Compact* that just about every English local authority now has with its own Voluntary and Community Sector (VCS). It is easy to be cynical about such documents, especially when they are so often glossy, saccharinely illustrated, and seemed at the outset about as toothless as a UN resolution. It is even easier when they derive directly from a New Labour Government initiative aimed unashamedly at persuading the sector of its role in helping it to deliver the government's own policy agenda. Here, though, it is worth also considering the other side of the case.

The 1998 *National Compact on Relations between Government and the Voluntary and Community Sector in England* was produced early in the life of the Blair Government, and based heavily on the recommendations of the highly regarded Deakin Commission Report on the Future of the Voluntary Sector (1996). Together with its series of Codes of Good Practice – on BME groups, community groups, consultation, funding and volunteering – the Compact's aim was to change the position of the VCS from one of being variously marginalised and/or patronised by government – not least by local government – to one of working in partnership with it. It thus set down, as have the ensuing local compacts, a list of rights and responsibilities or undertakings to which both sectors should adhere in order to make their relationship constructive and reciprocally beneficial. An inevitably much abbreviated illustration of the nature of those undertakings, and of the overall tone of the compacts, is provided in Exhibit 18.2.

As the compacts themselves emphasise, even though any breaches are now referable to the local ombudsman and potentially subject to judicial review, they should not be seen primarily as statutorily binding documents. Rather, they are 'frameworks' that represent the product of discussions and negotiations between the respective parties and that should be subject to regular review and amendment. Their unenforceability, however, should not detract from the significance of, in particular, some of the governmental undertakings: the explicit acknowledgement, for example, of groups' rights to receive the full cost of their service delivery, relevant information and consultation, and to criticise publicly and campaign against government policy without jeopardising any public funding. As was pointed out, this latter commitment represents a rare example of an invitation to an organisation to bite the hand that feeds it.

Our illustrative local compact in Exhibit 18.2 outlines the two principal types of council funding available to third sector organisations: relatively modest one-off grants to cover operating costs and perhaps some individual projects, and funding through a much more detailed service-level agreement

Exhibit 18.2 Outline of a Local VCS Compact

What? Why?
In 1998 the Labour Government formed a **National Compact** with the voluntary and community sector (VCS) – to improve their relationship to mutual advantage, and in recognition that VCGs were increasingly delivering services previously provided by the public sector. All English local authorities agreed to publish **Local Compacts** by 2004/5.

A typical Local Compact between Happitown BC and its VCS
Introduction – emphasises that the Compact is a negotiated, 'living' agreement, setting down shared principles, values and commitments to improve working relations between the Council and VCGs for the overall benefit of Happitowners; *not* anything threatening or legally binding.

Shared principles for joint working – for example:

- An independent, diverse VCS is vital to a democratic and inclusive society.
- In developing public policy and delivering services, the Council and VCGs have distinctive but complementary roles and accountabilities – the Council being driven by statutory duties and government policy, and VCGs by their charitable aims.
- Partnership working between the Council and VCGs will build relationships, improving policy development and service delivery.

Undertakings by Happitown Council – for example:

- To contribute two principal categories of voluntary sector funding:
  o Voluntary sector grant aid:
  o On a one-off or annual basis, usually less than £10,000; Council to publicise a clear process and framework for awarding grant funding.
  o Service-level agreements:
    For the delivery of services by VCGs for and on behalf of the Council; agreements for up to three years, subject to annual review of performance, containing clear and agreed specifications of the work involved and of monitoring and evaluation systems.
- To accept the legitimacy of VCGs, including the relevant element of overhead costs in their estimates for providing a particular service.
- To recognise and support the rights of VCGs to campaign within the law, and to challenge central and local government policy, without jeopardising any public funding.
- To consult with the VCS on major issues, wherever possible allowing affected organisations time to consult their members and beneficiaries.

Undertakings by VCGs. For example:

- To have a written constitution, and keep accurate records and financial accounts.
- To demonstrate impacts of funding: clear community benefits in terms of activities undertaken (outputs) and the results of these activities (outcomes).
- To ensure members and supporters are consulted about the group's policy positions, particularly in relation to the Council.

Resolving disagreements. For example:

- Both sides should first seek resolution through informal discussions.
- If necessary, an independent investigator/mediator should be used.
- If the VCS remains dissatisfied, the matter may be taken to the Local Government Ombudsman or the Compact Mediation Scheme run by the Government's Active Communities Unit.

Exhibit 18.3 Oxford City Council's grant funding of VCGs, 2010–11

Grants awarded through COMMISSIONING SECTION of grants programme

	Total £000s	Examples (£000s)
Advice	500	187 Oxford Citizens Advice Bureau 50 Oxfordshire Chinese Community & Advice Centre
Arts	326	72 Modern Art Oxford 52 Oxford Playhouse
Community safety	61	33 FTE domestic violence outreach worker 8 Asylum Welcome – work with young asylum seekers
Homelessness	448	96 The Gap – drop-in service for homeless 51 The Porch Steppin' Stones Centre – day centre for homeless 25 Aspire – funding for outreach worker
Specialist play	80	20 Doorstep Family Centre (Drop-in and Play Out project) 19 Blackbird Leys adventure playground

Examples of grants awarded through OPEN BIDDING section of grants programme

10	Archway Foundation – to support individuals who feel isolated and lonely through disability, low income or health problems
10	Blackbird Leys Credit Union
10	Ethnic Minority Business Service – to run ESOL/literacy training
8	Kids Enjoy Exercise Now (KEEN) – sporting opportunities for children with learning disabilities
4	Oxford Urban Wildlife Park – to maintain nature park

to undertake contractually specified work. Most councils' websites will give some indication of the approximate numbers of groups they fund and perhaps their total grant funding in the previous year. Oxford City Council is one of the commendable few to provide fuller details, and Exhibit 18.3 shows how one body of predominantly Labour councillors chose in 2010/11 to disburse more than £1.5 million, or between 1% and 2%, of the Council's total revenue expenditure. The division between the commissioning and open-bidding sections is striking, the former accounting for 94% of the total. Both sections are likely to come under pressure when the

Government's 3-year funding settlement ends in 2011, and it will be interesting to observe their respective fates.

When phrases such as 'a Compact way of working' and an upgraded 'Compact Plus' began to enter the vocabulary of local government officers, there could be little doubt of the scale of change that was overtaking the world of local group politics. Greater recognition, however, has its potential costs for all those involved, and for VCGs it can seem as if they are losing as much as they are gaining through closer involvement with their local councils and other government agencies.

There was widespread concern, for example, over the Labour Government's openly *instrumentalist* approach to the third sector: ministers' apparent belief that the sector's prime function was to contribute to the delivery of the government's agenda and to the meeting of government targets. In practice, it was argued, the Compact rhetoric about valuing a forthright and assertive voluntary and community sector can be just that: rhetoric. Some sections of government at least – local and national alike – showed little genuine interest in the sector's wider contribution to society. Groups that campaign as well as deliver services were still being viewed with suspicion, as they were in the past. Government was at best co-opting the sector; at worst, neutering it (Whelan, 1999).

In exchange for this qualification, if not sacrifice, of their independence, VCGs were expected increasingly, by government and consumers alike, to act *as if* they were in fact part of the state sector. Driven by central government's audit and performance culture, local authorities devise constricting straitjackets of regulation and accountability to safeguard grants and contracts that, groups will allege, often pay less than the full cost of service delivery in the first place. Meanwhile, politicians promise consumers quality public services and a full range of consumer choice – but from VCG staff whom they still expect to be committed volunteers, rather than properly paid professionals.

Moreover, when it comes to consultation, the very knowledge and experience that give groups their value as service deliverers may be regarded as a threat by councillors, who, as elected representatives, are inclined to see themselves as the best judges of the needs of 'their' communities. There is also the inherent problem for almost any interest group when dealing with governments: that its views can be treated in much the same way as Mandy Rice-Davies, in the 1960s' trial of Conservative minister, John Profumo, dismissed the denials of men whom she claimed to have slept with for money: 'Well, they would say that, wouldn't they?' Groups' views are sometimes presumed simply from their names.

Recent governments have seen their challenge as being in some way to move beyond groups and their spokespersons in order to reach 'ordinary people'. This creates the paradox that these groups, one of whose key functions is to provide channels of communication between citizens and their governments, are finding themselves circumvented by more innovative and government-favoured forms of consultation such as focus groups, citizens' juries, citizens' panels, deliberative opinion polls and local referendums (see Lowndes *et al.*, 2001) – devices that prioritise the involvement of individual citizens rather than organised groups (Pratchett, 2004a, pp. 227–8).

It would be quite wrong, therefore, to suppose that compacts suddenly smoothed away all the wrinkles in the relationship between VCGs and government. That relationship is inherently unequal, between sets of bodies with fundamentally different interests, values, goals and ways of working. VCGs are value-driven and non-governmental and want to stay that way. Effective working relations are bound to take time to develop, but Professor Deakin himself had little doubt that the compacts, and the culture change required to negotiate them, had helped to produce a far better two-way relationship between VCGs and councils of all political complexions than existed at the time of his report, when the Conservative Government saw voluntary groups chiefly as vehicles for delivering policy programmes that Labour councils were attempting to boycott (Brindle, 2004, p. 10):

> Labour councils would have nothing to do with voluntary sector bodies, which they associated with Tory ladies in flowery hats and that sort of stuff. The Tories were almost equally patronising – you know, 'our little helpers'. 'We can entrust you with various things; we'll contract with you to make sure you deliver [public services], but come near us to talk about policy – not a chance.'

A sea change in Conservative thinking?

In today's world, governments of all complexions insist on councils working in partnership with all other sectors. VCGs have progressed from filling public service gaps in specialist areas to the provision of mainstream services in health and social care, education and children's services, and are seen as essential to the mission to improve and cut the costs of public service delivery. The *behaviour* of councils towards their voluntary and community sectors would necessarily have had to change, but over time underlying *attitudes* have changed too. Groups and their representatives are consulted more regularly and more genuinely on policy issues that have an impact on them; they are invited to serve on advisory groups and partnership boards; and they generally have a more direct role in helping to develop as well as to deliver local government programmes.

Tomorrow's world will be different again – shaped by a Conservative-led Coalition Government committed to public spending cuts of such severity that they may amount in effect to a redefinition of which services are public, and tax-funded, and which are not. There was a souring of relations with

VCGs during Labour's final months in office. Grant-funding of local groups was already declining, as a result of increasing budgetary pressure on councils' discretionary spending, and the increasingly overt message from central government that contracts, not grants, were the best and most accountable way of engaging with all external service providers, whether private or voluntary sector. Then in November 2009 came the painful confirmation that the Commission for the Compact, set up in 2007 to promote awareness of compacts and generally oversee (but not to regulate) their operation, was as powerless as its critics had always alleged. When the Minister for the Third Sector broke the Compact by announcing, without consultation, the axing of £750,000 of grants to 32 VCGs, offered as part of the Department's own programme, the Commission confirmed it didn't 'have any more powers than anyone else to investigate this' (Plummer, 2009).

The Brown Government's 'Refreshed Compact', published the following month, did not address the enforceability issue, nor the vexed question of how partly EU-based commissioning regulations can be made more user-friendly for VCGs. It was a much shorter document, though not necessarily more accessible, than the original Compact, and was intended to lead to VCGs being more involved in policy development, rather than simply consultation. But it was also stripped of its five Codes of Good Practice, which may have overlapped in places and been hard to monitor, but which were naturally valued by those who felt their interests were being addressed directly.

The refreshed Compact prompted only a limited reaction, partly because VCGs were already turning their attentions to the Conservatives, who, under David Cameron, had been courting the voluntary sector earnestly for several years and were now seen as far more likely than Labour to form the next government. The Centre for Social Justice, established by the former Conservative leader, Iain Duncan Smith, produced two substantial reports, *Breakdown Britain* and *Breakthrough Britain* (Social Justice Policy Group, 2006 and 2007), both containing chapters on how VCGs could provide an effective alternative to state-run programmes addressing problems of worklessness, family breakdown, addiction, educational failure and indebtedness. Many of these reports' ideas and recommendations went into the Conservative Party's 2008 Green Paper, *A Stronger Society: Voluntary Action for the 21st Century*, and some eventually into the 2010 manifesto.

The Green Paper, and in particular its 20 specific policy pledges were generally well received by VCGs, and the London Voluntary Service Council (LVSC), far from a natural Conservative ally, described it as signalling 'a sea change in the Conservative Party's attitude to the VCS. It is well researched and covers many of the areas of concern identified in recent years by the VCS itself' (2009, p. 3). There is room here for only a few of the pledges, but they illustrate how far the party had travelled from the 'little helpers' view of VCGs recalled by Deakin. They also serve as a baseline against which to measure what the Coalition Government does in practice.

The proposal for an Office for Civil Society made its first official appearance in the Green Paper, coupled with a proposed Civil Society Select Committee in Parliament to provide democratic scrutiny (p. 77). There would be a drive to increase particularly local-level volunteering, with a reduction in the checks and regulations that can deter potential volunteers (pp. 21, 30). Charitable giving should become established as a social norm – of perhaps 1% of gross income (p. 17); also volunteering – starting with every central government employee being allowed eight hours' volunteering time during the year (p. 28). Government grants should remain a vital ingredient in the funding mix for VCGs, and contracts used in preference to grants only 'where there is a clear justification' (pp. 32–3). The Big Lottery Fund should be replaced by a Voluntary Action Lottery Fund, giving 100%, rather than around 70%, of funds to the VCS (p. 33). A future Conservative Government would establish a 'fair deal on funding', in which funding streams are simplified and multi-year funding is the norm (p. 39). There should be a network of Social Enterprise Zones in deprived communities, in which social enterprise investment qualifies for tax relief.

Inevitably, not all these pledges made it into the manifesto, and some eye-catching late arrivals took their place – such as an annual Big Society Day, to celebrate the work of neighbourhood groups; the National Citizen Service, a programme to give 16-year-olds the chance to develop the skills needed to be active and responsible citizens; and the transformation of the civil service into a 'civic service', by including participation in social action in civil (or civic) servants' appraisals (pp. 38–9). As with any manifesto, even one that hadn't had to be cut and pasted into a Coalition Document, there are doubts about the strength of party commitment to some of its promises – especially those that do indeed amount to a sea change in the party's thinking. There are questions too about implementability, given that, for example, well before the manifesto was even drafted, increasing numbers of Conservative councils were already openly cutting grant budgets and moving to 'commissioning only' funding regimes. For such reasons, but above all because of the centrality of the VCS to the whole Coalition project, its development and performance will be watched with unprecedented interest.

Part 3

Backward and Forward

Chapter 19

Three Decades, Two Governments, One Direction

Introduction – backward and forward, providing and deciding

As will have been apparent from the content, as well as from the regular slippage from one tense to another, this book was written before, during and immediately after the 2010 General Election. That election brought to an end 13 years of New Labour government, and produced the first national peacetime coalition since the 1930s. It would seem, therefore, an exceptionally propitious time to look both forward and backward, which is what this short final part of the book will attempt. This chapter reviews some of the major changes to, and mainly imposed on, local government since the 1970s, under first the Thatcher/Major Conservative Administrations and then the Blair/Brown Labour Administrations. Its broad thesis is that, notwithstanding the dramatic political break in 1997, when Labour gained its largest-ever parliamentary majority, there was a perceptible policy continuity across the period. To use aptly the term deployed in the later years of Comprehensive Performance Assessment (see Exhibit 10.3), the direction of travel remained fundamentally unchanged. Chapter 20 looks forward over a much shorter time period, with the help of early pronouncements from the Coalition Government, reinforced by documentation from various policy think tanks and the like.

It was suggested in Chapter 1 that readers' previous experience of local government would probably have been as customers, consumers, clients and citizens. The ordering of this short, alliterative list was not accidental. The terms cover the two fundamental functions that local government – indeed, any government – performs: the *service* function and the *political* function (Boyle, 1986), or providing and deciding. It *provides* certain goods and services, and it is the setting in which the citizenry collectively debates and *decides* the key issues concerning the public provision of those goods and services – their scale and distribution, and their quality, cost and mode of financing. Fundamental as both are, we have already argued in Chapter 14 that it is only the political function that is truly indispensable. The service function can be – and has been – contracted out, wholly or partly privatised. Remove the political function, though, and what is left is not local government, but, at most, local administration.

Yet the focus of recent national governments, of both major parties, has been disproportionately on the service function – how to provide services more efficiently, more cheaply, more homogeneously, more competitively, and more privately. For Labour, we can even quantify the disproportionality. Of 20 policy initiatives included in the official meta-evaluation of the government's 'Local Government Modernisation Agenda' (LGMA), 17 were aimed either primarily or secondarily at encouraging the improvement of services – almost twice as many as were aimed at any of the other four nominated outcomes (DCLG, 2009g, pp. 19–20). By comparison, the political function – how, collectively, it is decided what services should be provided and how they should be paid for – has been relatively neglected. Put another way, the public, already inclined to think of councils more as service providers than as *their* local government, have been seen first as customers, consumers and clients for those services, and only secondarily as citizens.

The Conservatives – CCT and the contract culture

Of the enormous quantity of local government changes introduced by the 1979–97 Conservative Administrations (see Exhibit 2.2), the most constitutionally significant were arguably those enabling ministers to intervene in the budget-making and tax-setting processes of individual councils. The most far-reaching in practice, however, were probably those associated with Compulsory Competitive Tendering (CCT) – particularly if it is seen, properly, as one strand of the 'New Right' privatisation or contracting-out strategy of those governments. Essentially, the CCT process required a comparison of the costs of continuing in-house provision of specified services with those of any interested private contractors, and the award of the contract to the most competitive bidder. That meant the *lowest* bidder, and councils were prohibited from imposing conditions on such issues as trade union rights, employment protection, sickness benefit, pensions, training and equal opportunities that might have had the effect of restricting or distorting competition. Cost was always the ultimate criterion, rather than quality.

It must be emphasised that it was the *competitive tendering* – the cost comparison – that was made compulsory, *not* the contracting-out of the service, which might or might not result, depending on the competing bids. If, after competition, no alternative bid was received or the in-house bid proved to be the lowest, the local authority continued to provide the service, but in an organisationally different way. The part of the authority carrying out the service became known as a Direct Service Organisation (DSO), and these DSOs were obliged to maintain separate trading accounts, which had to make a specified percentage surplus.

Three Local Government Acts drove the CCT process, steadily extending the services affected from the 'blue-collar' technical to the 'white-collar' managerial: 1980 – the construction and maintenance of housing and highways; 1988 – refuse collection, grounds and vehicle maintenance, building and street cleaning, school meals, sports and leisure management; 1992 – housing management, legal, personnel, financial and IT services. It sounds like an ideological policy and it was, owing much to the New Right think tanks – the Adam Smith Institute, the Institute of Economic Affairs (IEA), and the Centre for Policy Studies (CPS). Their argument, and that of like-minded Conservative politicians, was that the contracting-out of services formerly provided monopolistically by central and local government or by agencies such as the NHS would lead to both improved service quality and reduced costs. It would challenge the 'dependency culture' imbued by the Welfare State and would lead to less, and smaller, government. For local authorities, it would mean their entering a brave new world of *sharing* the provision of services with a range of other bodies – private industrial and commercial concerns, and voluntary organisations. This is how far-reaching it was: the progenitor of local governance and partnership working.

Opponents of CCT, on the other hand, noted its potential to reduce the role not only of elected local authorities but also of trade unions. It was part of the government's comprehensive attack on trade union power and public sector pay bargaining, and on the strong financial and institutional links between the public sector unions and the Labour Party. More tellingly, it was argued that claimed cost savings from CCT came in the main not from increased efficiency, but rather from cuts in employees' pay and conditions, and from safety-challenging changes in working practices.

The impact of CCT – managerial and financial

As with many innovations, the immediate impact of CCT was less dramatic than the more strident claims of either its proponents or opponents had predicted. No near-universal 'takeover' by the private sector materialised, and the overall picture was what you will by now have come to expect – extremely varied from service to service, and from one council to another. Some services were far more amenable to private sector bids than others, but only in building cleaning and construction were more than half of all contracts won by outside bidders. In all services, DSOs tended to win a disproportionate share of the larger contracts, so that, while around 40% of the total number went to private bidders, they amounted to only around 25% of the overall contract *value*. In Scotland, both figures were significantly lower, but even in England and Wales more than one in every six authorities had no outside contracts at all. What the Labour Government inherited in 1997, therefore, was, in most authorities, a mixed economy of in-house and external provision.

The financial savings or otherwise achieved by CCT were difficult to evaluate accurately. Annual cost savings were undoubtedly achieved – perhaps of around 8% overall – but neutral studies suggested that these owed more to the introduction of competition than to the awarding of contracts to private firms. The major savings came from staffing reductions, often by 20%–30%, which happened even under DSO contracts; also from the worsened pay and conditions – temporary contracts, and cuts in sick pay, holidays and pensions – of those people, disproportionately women, who hung on to their jobs. Then there were cases of service failure – some comic, others tragic (Wilson and Game, 1998, p. 349) – and councils' termination of contracts not being fulfilled satisfactorily.

It might be imagined that, with most larger contracts staying in-house, CCT left much of local government relatively unchanged. By no means. Whether retaining or 'losing' contracts, all authorities had to adapt their patterns of management and organisation quite fundamentally in response to CCT. The major change was the need to separate the roles of client and contractor within the authority. *Clients* are those responsible for the specification and monitoring of services; *contractors* are those responsible for the direct production and delivery of the service. The separation of these roles would be made within a single department or by creating separate contractor departments.

Other managerial trends

The CCT story contains within it a certain irony. It did not spell even the beginning of the end of local authorities as direct providers of services, and in one way it had almost the reverse effect because, in presenting authorities with the challenge of winning contracts in-house, it encouraged them to streamline and strengthen their management systems so that they were better able to do precisely that. The client/contractor split and creation of internal markets were an important part of this managerial reform programme, but there were also several other noteworthy strands.

Customers and charters

One of the most important developments in the public service since the 1980s has been what Skelcher termed 'the service revolution' (1992): the proclaimed commitment to put customers first, or at least to label them 'customers' and tell them they are being put first. Traditionally, local authorities have had residents, tenants, clients and claimants *to* whom, rather than *for* whom, they provided services in the way, and to the standards, that they felt most appropriate. Then, prompted to an extent by the private sector, came what was variously labelled the *public service orientation* (PSO) or *customer care*. Councils gradually came to realise that these previously passive recipients of their services should be treated more as customers, with at least a voice, if not totally free choice, and an entitlement to be consulted and even actively involved in decision-making.

The practical manifestations of a council's customer focus can be seen today in a host of ways: customer service centres, employing multi-skilled staff; one-stop telephone systems; 24/7 phone and internet access to council services; use of blogs, podcasts and social networks to communicate with residents; personal identification of 'front-line' staff; downloadable forms and leaflets; user and staff surveys; publicised complaints procedures; customer care training; neighbourhood forums and assemblies; and public question times at council meetings. And then there are *customer charters* and *service guarantees*.

Charterism came to be associated with John Major, whose 1991 White Paper, *The Citizen's Charter*, sought to empower the citizen as an individual service consumer – note the singularising apostrophe – if not more ambitiously as a participant in the collective process of government. In fact, Major's initiative was pre-dated by several mainly Labour councils developing their own charters, customer contracts and redress mechanisms. York City Council's was among the most interesting:

> not merely as an example of local government innovation anticipating a major central government initiative, but because of the way it attempts to weave together the concerns of citizens, customers and community. The commitment to citizenship – to people's *civic rights* as citizens of York – is explicitly stated in terms of rights to know; rights to be heard and to influence; rights to be treated honestly, fairly and courteously; rights to participate and be represented. These general civic rights are subsequently translated into practical entitlements, through, for example, the establishment of:
>
> • area committees where you can have your say about decisions affecting your neighbourhood;
> • special arrangements to involve some of the people who are not often listened to: people with disabilities and other special needs.
>
> (Prior, 1995, pp. 91–2, emphasis ours)

The Citizen's Charter movement, with its subsidiary charters for council tenants, parents and other groups, was part of local authorities' recognition that they should try to get 'closer' to those they served. Certainly, local charters clarified the nature of the relationship between an authority and its citizens by using the language of rights, entitlements and responsibilities that can be checked and monitored. Essentially, though, these documents – like Labour's 1998 *Service First* relaunch of *The Citizen's Charter* – were about a rather narrow, consumerist concept of citizenship, in which consumerist values are prioritised over democratic ones. For more than a hundred examples, see the website of the admirably committed Pembrokeshire CC. The Labour Government's later promotion of Neighbourhood Charters – initially in the 2006 DCLG White Paper, *Strong and Prosperous Communities* (pp. 41–2) – sought to broaden the scope of charters, to include other local service providers and a more active involvement of residents in their negotiation, but without really challenging their view of these residents as service users first and citizens second.

Quality systems and quality assurance

If 'customer first' initiatives are to be more than just pious rhetoric, there needs to be a genuine institutional commitment and capacity to translate them into service quality. This recognition prompted many authorities to develop quality control, quality assurance and total quality management systems, as means of improving their service quality. The three processes were clearly differentiated and discussed by Skelcher (1992, ch. 8)

- *Quality control* (QC) is an inspection and checking process undertaken *after* the service has been, or is ready to be, provided. Its purpose is to measure performance against pre-set standards and thereby identify any failure rate in the service provision. An example would be a post-repair tenant satisfaction survey. Knowledge of tenants' dissatisfaction will, it is hoped, help to improve the service next time.
- *Quality assurance* (QA) is an attempt to prevent sub-standard service being provided in the first place. It involves designing delivery systems and procedures so that a certain standard of service can be guaranteed every time. Originally developed in the manufacturing sector, where product standards can be measured and specified precisely, QA does not translate easily into the local government world of personal service delivery. Nevertheless, the British Standards Institute (BSI) developed a recognised benchmark (BS 5750), against which local and NHS authorities could assess their QA systems, and a number received accreditation. Developing an accreditable QA system can be a protracted and resource-intensive exercise, necessitating as it does the detailed codification of policies, procedures, performance standards and monitoring systems. On the other hand, confronted by, say, a case of alleged child abuse in a council residential home, it is not hard to see it as a worthwhile investment.
- *Total quality management* (TQM) seeks to make service quality the driving force of the authority's whole organisational culture – 'a way of involving the whole organisation; every department, every activity, every

single person at every level' in the commitment to quality (Oakland, 1989, p. 14). Its demands are obviously immense, which is why, as Stewart notes, it 'is often an aspiration imperfectly realised or perhaps understood' (1996, p. 19).

Strategic management

Self-evidently, any authority aspiring to quality management requires a *strategic approach*, ensuring that its multiplicity of activities and policies are consistent, and are all contributing to corporate objectives and values. These days, as we saw particularly in Chapter 9 (see Exhibit 9.3), this requirement is institutionalised through Local Strategic Partnerships, Sustainable Community Strategies, Local and Multi-Area Agreements. All authorities, therefore, will take stock of their activities systematically in their constantly changing environments, and either set new directions or at least state some vision of where the authority will be in a certain number of years' time, and what it will be doing.

That, in essence, is what strategic management and planning are about: providing information and developing decision-making processes that enable elected members and officers alike to set priorities, direct their energies to key issues, and thereby develop a means of coping assertively with change. It can be contrasted with, and is a means of getting away from, the limitations of operational or reactive management (see Wilson and Game, 2002, p. 334). It involves standing back from the everyday pressures of operational management and taking a broader, corporate, longer-term view of the authority and its functions.

Reflecting this emphasis on strategic leadership and the breaking down of traditional departmental and professional boundaries, most leading authorities now structure themselves around a small number of *directorates*. These are headed by *Executive/Strategic/Corporate Directors*, who may oversee several combined departments, but are freed from the day-to-day responsibility of departmental management. The intended outcome is a streamlined strategic management team, comprising the chief executive and strategic directors, who are better able to focus on major policy issues and secure co-ordination between services.

Devolved, cost centre management

An almost necessary concomitant of strategic management is a devolution of actual management responsibility. If an authority's overall objectives and policies are to be achieved, they need to be translated into clearly defined targets or key tasks for individual managers. Somebody, in short, has to be accountable. But, to make their accountability meaningful, that person has to have the necessary discretion to deploy financial and other resources in such a way as to attain the specified targets. The principle behind such devolved management is that it releases initiative among middle and junior managers, who would previously have been constrained within a steep management hierarchy, and thereby leads to greater efficiency and, in the case of a local authority, a better quality service to the public.

The managerial logic is the same as that behind the 1980s' Next Steps Initiative within the civil service, which set up separate units or executive agencies to perform the executive functions of government that were previously the responsibility of Whitehall departments. Executive Agencies – ranging from the massive Jobcentre Plus and HM Prison Service Agency to the Royal Mint and the National Archives – remain part of the civil service, but have responsibility for their own financial, pay and personnel decisions. Similarly, cost centre managers, whether within a university or local authority, remain part of the corporate body, but have the authority to use the resources they have been allocated to achieve the key tasks and standards of performance with which they have been entrusted.

Performance management

The establishment of cost centres is likely to lead in turn to performance management (PM): the specification, measurement and evaluation of the performance both of individuals and of organisations. Tasks are devolved to cost centres and expressed in measurable terms, enabling the performance of the cost centre and the cost centre manager to be reviewed regularly, appraised, and then rewarded or penalised accordingly. Generally, when it is the organisation that is being evaluated, the term used is performance review (PR); and when an individual, performance appraisal (PA).

But what, for a service-providing local authority, is 'performance'? For the Audit Commission, the body chiefly responsible for auditing and inspecting, monitoring and measuring the performance of public bodies, it meant the '3Es': economy, efficiency and effectiveness, as set out in Exhibit 19.1. Proper measurement of these '3Es', however, is a much more difficult proposition for a political, sometimes monopolistic, multi-service-delivering local authority than for a single-product, profit-maximising manufacturing company. At the very least, the council's political values and objectives have to be taken into account, and these are likely to be considerably more complex than merely the maximisation of profit. There are obvious problems too in even defining, let alone measuring, outcomes of, say, the educational experience, or some of the social services.

Controversial and provocative though they can prove, a wide selection of measures has been used over the years to assess aspects of council performance. In recent years all councils have been required annually to measure their performance against dozens – potentially hundreds – of both government- and locally-defined Performance Indicators (PIs). Initially, in

Exhibit 19.1 Performance measurement

Dimensions of performance – the Audit Commission's 3 Es

- **Economy** – concerned with *costs and inputs,* and with minimising the cost of resources involved in producing any given standard of service.
- **Efficiency** – *not* about cost per se, but the *relationship between inputs and outputs*: producing the maximum output for any given resource input.
- **Effectiveness** – about the *relationship between intended and actual outputs*, or, put another way, *between outputs and outcomes.*

These are the conventional 3Es that were at the heart of the Labour Government's whole performance management programme. The sometimes added 4th E is:

- **Equity** – a measure of how fairly resources are distributed, according to the needs of the population, not the individual.

Best Value Performance Indicators

BVPIs were an inherent part of the Best Value regime – Labour's means of getting councils continuously to improve the quality of their service provision, having regard to economy, efficiency and effectiveness. Councils were required to produce annual BV Performance Plans, assessing their performance and progress against targets set for dozens of nationally and locally determined BVPIs.

Some examples of BVPIs and their relevant Es

• Cost of adult cremation service	Economy
• Expenditure per kilometre on coastal protection	Economy
• Income generated per car parking space	Efficiency
• Benefit overpaid as percentage of total benefits paid in the year	Efficiency
• Percentage of pupils gaining places at first preference school	Effectiveness
• Percentage change from 2005 in pregnancies of 15–17-year-olds, per 1,000 15–17-year-old female residents	Effectiveness
• Percentage of pedestrian crossings with facilities for disabled persons	Equity
• Cremations conducted in such a way as to enable Hindu and Sikh families to play an active role	Equity

The National Indicator Set (NIS)

The 2007 Local Government and Public Involvement in Health Act removed the requirement for councils to produce an annual BVPP, and 2007/8 was the last year in which their performance was measured against BVPIs. In place of the 1,200+ national BVPIs, a much reduced 'suite' of 188 National Indicators was introduced, and these became the only measures by which the Government monitored the performance of councils and local partnerships. Councils' performance against the indicators was published annually as part of the Comprehensive Area Assessment, until the latter's abolition in 2010.

2000/1, there were for a unitary authority over 200 of these indicators, many, if not most, being measures of inputs or process, rather than of outcomes and effectiveness. Their numbers escalated to levels that even ministers eventually conceded were excessive, but gradually and in consultation with local authorities they were pruned back and, particularly with the introduction of the National Indicator Set (NIS) (see Exhibit 19.1), there was a significant increase in the proportions of indicators measuring progress against outcomes for local people and businesses. Not before time, councils' accountabilities to their own local electors and residents were being recognised, as well as their accountabilities upwards to their major central government funders.

New Labour – Best Value and performance plans

CCT was opposed from the outset by Labour – in Parliament and even more vehemently by Labour councils, steadily growing in number as Conservative popularity nationally went into free fall. However, while customer care, quality service, strategic and performance management may reasonably be considered to be financially and commercially driven, they are much more difficult to argue against, and the New Labour Party being primed for government by Tony Blair had no inclination to try. The Party's 1997 manifesto made clear how it would in effect transfer the first capital C from CCT to something called Best Value service provision, but that otherwise it would work with and build on other parts of the New Public Management edifice (p. 34):

> Councils should not be forced to put their services out to tender, but will be required to obtain best value. We reject the dogmatic view that services must be privatised to be of high quality, but equally we see no reason why a service should be delivered directly if other more efficient means are available. Cost counts but so does quality. Every council will be required to publish a local performance plan with targets for service improvement, and be expected to achieve them. The Audit Commission will be given additional powers to monitor performance and promote efficiency. On its advice, government will where necessary send in a management team with full powers to remedy failure.

As with most of its 1997 manifesto commitments, the Labour Government duly delivered – more completely than many of its supporters might have liked. In early 1998, one of six 'modernisation' consultation papers proposed a new duty for local authorities – to deliver services to clear standards, set nationally and locally, by the most economic, efficient and effective means available (DETR, 1998c, para. 7.2). The signals were unmistakable: the government would rid local authorities of the deeply unpopular and wholly cost-focused CCT regime, but Best Value would prove every bit as centrally prescriptive and potentially even more interventionist. It applied, moreover, to every single service and function.

CCT was repealed and Best Value introduced in the Local Government Act 1999, coming into operation in England and Wales in 2000. In Scotland these events coincided with devolution, and both the timetable and outcome were somewhat different. Scottish councils adopted a BV framework voluntarily in 1997, in exchange for an extended moratorium on CCT. But even after statutory implementation in 2003, Scotland's approach, particularly following England's embrace of CPA, contrasted significantly, with less central direction and inspection and much less scoring and compilation of league tables. Wales too marched to its own beat, and from its inception in 2002 the Wales Programme for Improvement brought the kind of risk-based/self-assessment approach to performance management that many English authorities must have envied. Exhibit 19.2 summarises how BV worked in England. It is reproduced here because, while Performance Plans and PIs came to an end in 2007/8, BV reviews lived on, asking, moreover, precisely the kinds of questions that almost all local government services will face at a time when unprecedentedly savage public spending cuts are being sought: Is this service really needed? Does this council need to provide it? Can we charge, or charge more, for it?

As with all the Labour Government's 'modernisation' initiatives, BV was officially evaluated, in this case by a team assembled by Cardiff University's Centre for Local and Regional Government Research (Entwistle *et al.*, 2003). Their verdict was highly qualified. BV had proved 'a major challenge for most authorities' (p. 4), particularly for smaller district councils with fewer corporate staff, cross-cutting reviews proving particularly demanding and time-consuming. On the 4Cs, the evaluation confirmed the widely accepted view that most councils were better at consulting and comparing than at challenging and competing. Few appeared to have examined rigorously the underlying need for a service, as opposed to thinking up ways of improving it. Competition too was a tough requirement, particularly for councils strongly committed to in-house provision, who had hoped that CCT's demise had meant the end of having to compete constantly with the private sector.

The Cardiff team raised two other issues that would prove to be recurring concerns about the government's whole top-down, inspection-heavy approach to performance management: councillors' marginalisation from most of the process and its massive costs in time and finance. Many councils reported that their elected members appeared to be generally disengaged from the whole BV exercise, and particularly from the preparation of Performance Plans. These were widely seen as officers' documents prepared for the benefit of external auditors, rather than the product of any intense political debate

Exhibit 19.2 The Best Value regime

BV's key purpose

To require councils to make arrangements – in the form of an annual Best Value Performance Plan (BVPP) and regular service-specific and cross-cutting reviews – to secure continuous improvement in their service performance, having regard to **economy, efficiency** and **effectiveness**. Councils to review all services regularly to demonstrate to the public and inspectors that they were applying principles of continuous improvement.

BV Performance Plans

Assessed existing performance through national and locally determined Performance Indicators (BVPIs), set future targets, and outlined the authority's programme of BV Reviews. Were the principal means by which an authority was held accountable for the efficiency and effectiveness of its services and for its future plans.

BV Reviews

Should consider radical approaches to service improvement, asking 'big questions' not normally addressed in day-to-day management. Reviews to follow **the 4 Cs:**

- **Challenge** why, how and by whom a service is being provided, and show that alternative approaches to service delivery have been considered.
- **Compare** its performance with that of similar authorities across a range of relevant BVPIs, taking into account the views of both service users and potential suppliers.
- **Consult** local taxpayers, service users, partners and other stakeholders in setting new and demanding performance targets and an action plan to deliver continuous improvements.
- **Compete**, wherever practicable, in order to secure efficient and effective services.

Review questions would typically include:

- What does the service do now?
- What do its customers want of it?
- How well and at what cost does it do it in comparison with other providers?
- Could the benefits of the service be obtained in some other way?
- Could another organisation provide it better and/or cheaper?
- Can we do the job better (and by how much)?
- How can we get the same benefits to the people while spending less?
- Should we be providing the service at all?

Inspection

All council functions are subject to regular inspection either by the Audit Commission or by a special inspectorate. Each inspection results in a detailed and frequently critical report, and a score for the service/function on two 4-point scales:

- **Quality of the service:** Excellent = 3 stars; Good = 2 stars; Fair = 1 star; Poor = 0 stars.
- **Prospects for improvement:** Excellent, Promising, Uncertain, Poor.

A service might be rated, therefore, 'a Fair service with promising prospects for improvement'. Like CPAs, all inspection reports are published on the Audit Commission's website and are searchable by individual authority.

Failing services

The Secretary of State has wide-ranging powers to intervene where an authority is judged by inspectors not to be delivering a BV service, and ultimately to remove responsibility for the 'failing' service from the authority altogether.

about values, priorities and resource allocation. Councillors and officers, however, were more or less at one in their questioning of the costs and time that the regime seemed to demand, particularly the inspections (p. 7):

> Many respondents believed inspection to have been a major driver of improvement in their organisations, but a large proportion felt that the added costs involved had outweighed the benefits.

Beacons and Local Innovation Awards

Best Value was New Labour's comprehensive assault on local government service provision, applying to all functional responsibilities of all councils. It was backed up, though, by other more selective initiatives, one of which was *Beacon Councils*. Launched in 1999, the Beacon scheme aimed to raise service quality by enabling all councils to learn from the best performers or 'leading lights' in a particular service area.

Each year, ministers would select service themes with a direct impact on people's quality of life – for example, affordable housing, tackling digital exclusion, dignity in care, delivering cleaner air – and councils would apply under themes where they felt they could demonstrate that they were providing an excellent service. Successful applicants were short-listed by an expert Advisory Panel, who would visit and assess them, and recommend that Beacon status be awarded to usually up to 50 councils from around 200 applicants. The scheme's key feature was that councils were required not only to show excellence in the relevant theme, but to have imaginative plans for dissemination of their good practice – through open days, workshops, publications, mentoring opportunities and the like.

Other similar schemes – Beacon Schools, NHS Beacons – had been discontinued after a few years, but Beacon Councils were both popular and successful and almost outlasted the Labour Government itself. The evaluation, this time by the University of Warwick's Local Government Centre, found much more positive reactions than to Best Value (Rashman and Hartley, 2006, p. 7): 'Authorities which have been Beacons generally indicate that the costs of their involvement are far outweighed by the benefits of raising the council's profile on the national stage and boosting staff morale.'

Ten years, however, is an eternity in the world of UK local government for even a popular programme to evade ministerial tinkering. Accordingly, in 2009 Beacons were wound up and replaced by *Local Innovation Awards* (LIAs) – 'a new, fresh and exciting award and knowledge transfer scheme ... to identify, celebrate and spread creativity and innovation' – which sounded strikingly similar to its sadly no longer new, fresh etc. predecessor. There are indeed similarities, but also differences. The scheme is jointly sponsored by the LGA and (the Department for) Communities and

Local Government, and, unlike Beacons, is for both councils and Local Strategic Partnerships. There are three categories of LIA:

- *Delivery themes* – where applicants demonstrate their strategic and innovative approach to themes such as, in 2009/10, keeping children and young people safe in the community, and empowering adults to control their own care. As with Beacons, short-listed themes are evaluated in an on-site review.
- *Challenge themes* – aimed at high-performing councils and partnerships able to bring radically novel approaches to themes such as, in 2009/10, tackling intractable local issues through inter-generational working. Assessment is at a Peer Challenge Panel Event, with short-listed applicants presenting their ideas to a panel of local government leaders.
- *Bright Ideas* – for new, untested ideas by front-line staff teams working with partners under one of the above thematic areas. Short-listed applicants try to persuade a *Dragon's Den*-style judging panel that their ideas are worth investing in.

Further differences between the two schemes are that there are fewer LIA winners – nine in 2010, four being teams from the newly unitary Northumberland County Council, obviously relishing their transformation – and the awards come in cash as well as status. Councils winning the 2009/10 delivery and challenge awards shared £2.8 million to fund learning programmes to help other service providers improve their performance. Bright Ideas winners received £50,000 each in seed-corn funding, to enable them to work up their ideas further and share them with others.

Best Value Mark II – CPA

As noted, Best Value had been introduced almost exactly as set out in the 1997 manifesto. In sharp contrast, its successor policy, Comprehensive Performance Assessment (CPA) – arguably the single policy that most characterised New Labour's approach to and relations with local government – was conspicuous in the Party's 2001 manifesto only by its absence. Its first public appearance was in the December 2001 White Paper, *Strong Local Leadership – Quality Public Services,* which explicitly acknowledged – almost as if it were news – just how strangulating central government's micro-management of local government had become: over inputs (for example, through controls over council borrowing and ring-fencing of grants), processes (by requiring the production of myriad plans or the establishment of partnerships) and decisions (DTLR, 2001, paras. 4.2–4.4).

This accumulation of central interventions and initiatives 'can become counter-productive', the White Paper admitted, as could the 'many overlapping performance measurement frameworks … to monitor local government services' (para. 3.12). In future, therefore, the government would shift its focus 'away from controls over inputs, processes and local decisions … to the assured delivery of outcomes through a national framework of standards and accountability (para 1.12). To these ends, the White Paper set out 'a *comprehensive performance framework for improvement*, coupled with a *substantial package of deregulation*' (emphases ours). The framework was fully operational within months (see Exhibit 10.3); the package – judged by most people's interpretation of 'substantial' – was indefinitely delayed.

We have termed CPA 'Best Value Mark II', which is partly accurate, partly not. CPA did not *replace* BV, but rather *incorporated* most of it. BV was a statutory regime, and the basic requirements it made of BV authorities – the Performance Plan and Performance Indicators, regular service reviews, demonstration of continuous improvement – remained largely unchanged. Most obviously incorporated by CPA was BV's dual scoring system, with 4-point scales for 'quality of the service' and 'prospects for improvement' (see Exhibit 19.2), the huge difference being that with CPA the final assessment was not of the performance of a single service, but of the whole local authority.

In the White Paper just four of these overall performance ratings were envisaged:

- *High performers*;
- *Strivers* – not top performers, but with proven capacity to improve;
- *Coasters* – not top performers, and no proven capacity to improve; and
- *Poor performers*.

Unsurprisingly, such a schema proved easy to mock. Within days the media had relabelled the categories – Thrivers, Strivers, Skivers and Divers – which, while frivolous, was arguably less misinterpretable than the original, in which 'coasting', for example, could be taken as complimentary. Almost as if prepared for it, ministers changed to a less derisible five-point scale of Excellent, Good, Fair, Weak or Poor – prompting the cynical suggestion that the whole labelling issue had been a planted concession on the part of a government nervous of its ability to sell a highly controversial policy to sceptical local authorities.

The serious disarming strategy, however, was to ensure from the start that there were more apparent winners than losers, for the point of CPA as a driver of continuous improvement was that all assessments would have consequences. The first set of CPA results, published in December 2002, were for England's 150 single-tier and county councils, and, in what struck many in local government as a barely credible coincidence, a majority – or, to be precise, 50.7% – of them were assessed as either Excellent (22) or

Good (54), with just 23% considered to be Weak (21) or Poor (13). To use an American expression: what's not to like? Whatever reservations one had about CPA in general or aspects of its methodology in particular, it was harder to make them stick when over half the nation's biggest and most important local authorities had been officially pronounced to be at least Good. And this was only the baseline year. CPA was about continuous improvement, and, if the figures didn't record improvement each year, CPA would presumably have had to be judged a failure. Fortunately, they did – to the extent that, within two years, two-thirds of these councils were Excellent or Good, the Weak had fallen to 10%, and there was just one Poor performer.

At this point, as when athletes started to throw javelins so far that they were threatening the surrounding running track, a 'harder test' had to be introduced (Wilson and Game, 2006, p. 168). The scoring system was recalibrated, which worked for about a year, and then assessments escalated again. By the time CPA was abolished in 2008, Excellent and Good (4- and 3-star) authorities comprised 83% of the total, the Weak were down to just 2%, and Poor performance had apparently been completely eradicated back in 2006. Which would have been really encouraging – indeed, amazing – if these assessment data had been based on the views and experiences of local residents and service users, and if these people recognised the same outstanding performance that the Audit Commission reported. Unfortunately, they didn't. During the CPA years, they had seen council tax rise by an average of nearly 50% – over 25% in real terms – and, while they may not have held local politicians totally responsible, their expressed satisfaction with their local councils fell on average from around 55% down to around 45% (Ipsos MORI Local, 2009, p. 12).

Freedoms, flexibilities and failures

Part of the 2001 White Paper promised 'substantial package of deregulation' would involve 'freedoms and flexibilities' for all councils: greater freedom to borrow and invest; fewer plans and strategies required by ministers; wider powers to provide services for others; and to charge for discretionary services. While such 'freedoms' were possessed already by principal authorities in most purportedly democratic countries, several were for UK councils potentially significant and were touched on earlier in this book. CPA, however, was predicated on there being significant *additional* 'rewards' for high performing councils, and these, the White Paper indicated, would include a freedom from budget- and council tax-capping, less ring-fencing of government grants, further reductions in plan requirements, greater freedom to use income from fines, and a 'much lighter touch' inspection regime.

But if, in this still obviously centrally directed system aimed at improving performance, the 'good children' were rewarded, the poor performers – the 'Poor' or 'zero-star' councils – must receive, if not punishment, at least a course of corrective therapy. Ministers initially seemed to favour a fairly heavy-handed form of *statutory intervention*, externally directed, leading possibly to the 'failing' council being placed in administration or having its functions transferred to other providers. In practice, however, they opted for a process of *engagement*, tailored to the particular needs of the individual councils – working *with* them, rather than working them over. A small team would be appointed, headed usually by a former senior local government manager, to assist the council in formulating a recovery plan, identifying external sources of support, and monitoring its implementation (Hughes *et al.*, 2004).

There was much to admire about CPA and its drive for continuous improvement, at both the high achieving and low achieving ends of the spectrum. Ministers, assisted by the Audit Commission, the LGA, the IDeA, and the generally positive commitment of local authorities themselves, created a nationally orchestrated performance management process unmatchable in any other large-scale system of local government. If you doubt it, look again at some of the numbers in the third column of Exhibit 14.3 and imagine the governments of those countries trying to run annual CPAs for their thousands of local authorities. They couldn't possibly, but, much more importantly, it wouldn't occur to them to want to. As with the wish to control individual councils' tax and spending levels, it requires both the centralist structure of local government and the centralist cast of mind.

From LPSAs to LAAs – the institutionalisation of 'new localism'

If CPA dominated Labour's second term of government, the initiative that ministers intended as the flagship of their third term were Local Area Agreements (LAAs). They would represent the move beyond the traditional ideas and inflexible institutions of elected local democracy (Travers, 2007, p. 64); or, as others saw it, from transparent and democratically accountable councils to the byzantine and largely unaccountable world of 'local governance' and quangos described in Chapter 9. Local governance, as we have seen, is characterised above all by partnerships, some statutory, some voluntary, and LAAs were the government's attempt to hitch its passion for partnership working on to Local Public Service Agreements (LPSAs), that were proving to be one of the success stories of its modernisation agenda.

LPSAs could be seen as 'old localism', in that they were a particular form of central–local partnership between government departments and *individual local authorities*. They involved specific agreed local performance goals, coupled with government cash for achieving them – 'something for some-thing' agreements, as the government put it. The 3-part LPSA set out:

- *the authority's commitment* to deliver, within about three years, a dozen or so *measurable and stretching improvements in service outcomes*, over and above any targets in its BV Performance Plan;
- *the government's commitment* to help the authority achieve these improvements, by providing interim *'pump-priming' grants* of £750,000 + £1 per resident; and
- *the government's commitment* to pay extra *Performance Reward Grants* if/when the performance improvements were verifiably attained.

The official LPSA evaluation team were impressed by the sheer scale of what was a voluntary scheme, but one taken up eventually by almost all major councils (DCLG, 2008c, p. 4): 'Negotiating a dozen or so targets covering policies owned by typically ten central government departments with each of 150 local authorities over a three-year period was a hugely ambitious undertaking'. Inevitably there were difficulties and tensions, unavoidable with a government that found it almost insuperably difficult to trust those it would publicly describe as its 'local government partners'. Local authorities thus found themselves signing up to some central government targets that they considered 'pointless if not unachievable' (p. 5). Such cases, though, were the exception, especially following the shift in emphasis to local priorities in the second generation of Agreements. Considerably more targets were exceeded than missed, and 73% triggered at least some financial reward, which no doubt helps explain why 'the overwhelming majority considered that the resulting service improve-ments and the wider benefits from the scheme had made it all worthwhile' (p. 4).

Perhaps feeling itself to be 'on a roll' with LPSAs, the government in 2004/5 decided to combine them with its increasing commitment to part-nerships, and came up with Local Area Agreements (LAAs), as outlined in Exhibit 9.3. But, if LPSAs were 'hugely ambitious', LAAs were bound to be more so, as the 'Area' in their title suggests and even their most basic defi-nition confirms: three-year agreements between central and local govern-ment, identifying how an area's policy priorities, set out in its Local Strategic Partnership's Sustainable Community Strategy, will be achieved through partnership working.

In the previous edition of this book, it was possible to refer only to the earliest evaluations of LAAs, which found pockets of considerable enthusi-asm, but rather more widespread confusion – like 'trying to eat a cloud with a knife and fork', as one bewildered respondent put it (Wilson and Game, 2006, p. 376). The confusion persisted and later evaluations also reported 'fundamental differences of understanding' (DCLG, 2006d, p. 5), not least between central and local actors. Central government's view, for example, seemed to be that LAAs were about 'everything' – comprehensive agreements setting out all key priorities for an area and thereby heralding a completely new way of doing business – while many LSP members had a perhaps more realistic sense that they should stick to identifying a few select things that partners could do differently, particularly around cross-cutting issues (p. 5). Similarly, central government saw LAAs, like LPSAs, as a contract concerning the delivery of agreed outcomes, whereas local negotiators saw them more as simply ongoing commitments to dialogue, creativity and improvement (p. 6).

As indicated in Exhibit 9.3, one of the many provisions of the 2007 Local Government and Public Involvement in Health Act was that LAAs became statutory documents, negotiated through regional Government Offices, which served at least to remove some of the previous confusion. The new LAAs were indeed about 'everything' that local government did, either on its own or in partnership with others, the government's main concession to LSPs being the major reduction of national indicators down to the 188 in the National Indicator Set (NIS) (see Exhibit 19.1), of which each LAA would have no more than 35 – negotiated with the government to reflect their respective priorities – alongside 18 statutory education and early years targets.

The proclaimed intention was that councils and their partners would be freer to determine their local spending priorities, but even the latest evaluations suggest that this was not a universally shared experience. Three-quarters of respondents felt the benefits of the LAA process outweighed the costs, but slightly more thought it had not led to any reduction in costs and bureaucracy (DCLG, 2010b, p. 9). More than 80% were critical of the lack of coverage of local issues in the NIS, and even more felt that the multiple local performance frameworks and profusion of central government priorities and targets acted as the most significant barriers to aligning mainstream programmes at the local level (pp. 8–9). That report was published less than two months before the Labour Government left office. It applied to one particular initiative, but it could almost have served as a summary verdict on the Blair/Brown Administration's whole local government record. It came as no great surprise, therefore, when, as noted in Exhibit 9.4, the Coalition Government announced that LAAs would be discontinued, along with National Performance Indicators, and would be replaced by some form of place-based budgeting and a successor framework to Total Place.

Service improvements, but under friendly fire

The second part of this chapter has focused largely on what has become known as the Local Government Modernisation Agenda (LGMA). It is an agenda without much obvious coherence, that took at least eight years to evolve, fitfully and often disconnectedly – so disconnectedly that Stoker suggested that the individual policies 'were in part deliberately designed to be a muddle, in order to ... create a dynamic for change by creating instability but also space for innovation' (2002, p. 418). True or not, the LGMA comprised more than 20 separate policies and initiatives, half of which were aimed primarily at improving services – their quality, cost-effectiveness, responsiveness, inter-connectedness and accessibility. This preponderance reflects our assertion at the start of the chapter about the government's interest in local authorities being much more in their role as providers than as deciders.

Most of these service-directed initiatives, as we have seen, were individually evaluated, but the government also commissioned from a Cardiff University research team a series of 'meta-evaluations', drawing together the evidence from the individual studies to assess the LGMA's impact on certain 'over-arching areas' or outcomes. The first of these, unsurprisingly, was service improvement, the others being: accountability, community leadership, stakeholder engagement and public confidence. It would be worrying indeed, if, after all this attention, there had no discernible improvement in local services, and fortunately the meta-evaluation was able to find some (DCLG, 2008d, pp. 6–7):

> There is strong evidence of significant improvements in many local government services between 2100 and 2006 ... analysis of a group of national performance indicators ... suggests an improvement of 21.9 per cent ... The largest improvements have been in waste and culture services. There were more modest improvements in housing, planning, community safety, benefits administration and social services ... There has been a steady increase in the numbers of authorities judged to be in the top two categories by the CPA ... interviews in case-study authorities revealed variations between services and between councils, [but] all were able to point to significant improvements in the quality and effectiveness of some services.

There were, as we shall see, some serious qualifications as well, but this service-improvement verdict was considerably more positive than those the LGMA received in respect of some of its other hoped-for outcomes – such as accountability and public confidence. Where increased local accountability was identified, the focus for many authorities was felt to be on service users rather than citizens, and, with CPA, towards central government, rather than the local community. There was 'a strong perception that partnership working compromises local accountability' (DCLG, 2008e, pp. 5–6).

In respect of public confidence, the evaluators noted that the government's Citizenship Surveys showed there to be more trust in local government than in central government and 'politicians' – not perhaps the most testing of comparisons. But they found no change in the proportion of people feeling they can influence local decisions, despite the increase in opportunities to get involved, and 'little evidence that central government policies have had a marked effect on public trust, except indirectly, in so far as these policies have encouraged local authorities to improve services and become more responsive' (DCLG, 2008e, pp. 6–7).

More important, though, even the recorded service improvements were accompanied by examples of what militarily might be termed 'friendly fire' – the inadvertent firing on one's own side while attempting to engage the enemy, or in this case examples of barriers to improvement contained within the modernisation agenda itself (DCLG, 2008d, p. 8):

> Authorities highlighted what they saw as four aspects of government policies which had been unhelpful:
>
> - initiative overload – resulting from too many central government initiatives and too many changes in policies;
> - too much central prescription and regulation;
> - insufficient joined-up working across central government; and
> - ring-fencing and other restrictions on how resources could be spent.

They finally got it – a decade late

There is an ironic postscript to this evaluation of Labour's 13 years of management change – in the form of an Action Plan, produced by the government just five months before the 2010 General Election. It was entitled *Putting the Frontline First: Smarter Government* (HM Government, 2009), and was introduced by Prime Minister Gordon Brown as a plan for reforming government to enable it to meet the 'new' fiscal and economic challenges to the future of public services. It set out proposals for strengthening the role of citizens and civic society, recasting relationships between the centre and the frontline and between the citizen and the state, and streamlining government. On examination, however, most of these proposals owed little, if anything, to the global financial crisis or Britain's own recession. They were not 'new' ideas to address a 'new' situation. Rather, as the PM himself made clear, they were about 'a radical dispersal of power', 'the diffusion of power', and 'the redirection of power from Whitehall to citizens' (pp. 6–7), that could beneficially have taken place at any time over the preceding ten years.

It was an interesting document, in several ways – one being its almost disarmingly frank style. A reader not knowing it was produced by a party that had been in government for nearly 13 years could easily take it for an opposition party's manifesto, so open was it about deficiencies and failures for which the government itself was responsible. There is space here for only some brief illustrative references, taken from the section on recasting relationships between the centre and the frontline. First, there are some examples of the problem (pp. 36–8):

- Out of 52 specific revenue grants to councils totalling £76 billion, 36 were ring-fenced;
- There were 102 different local authority revenue funding schemes, including 43 in education and children's services;
- In Leicestershire public bodies in the city and county were estimated to process over 3,000 performance datasets, reports or evaluations each year, at a cost of over £3.5 million.

Then came the Key Actions – all of which had been had been sought for years by local government, and in several cases previously promised in earlier government papers (pp. 10, 38):

- We will streamline the Government's national performance framework.
- We will significantly reduce the number of high-level priorities we set out at national level, and let local areas set priorities and guide resources.
- We will reduce the number of revenue streams to local government, which can inhibit cross-sector working.
- We will set out specific proposals to reduce the level of ring-fencing, which can inhibit strategic local spending decisions.
- We will support local authorities that wish to use their trading powers to create further commercial opportunities.
- We will reduce centrally imposed burdens on the frontline from reporting, inspection and assessment.
- We will align the different sector-specific performance management frameworks across key local agencies – the NHS, the police, schools, and local government.
- We will co-ordinate timings of all assessments, inspections and reporting arrangements where they focus on similar outcomes.

There are plenty of academic and journalistic critiques of Labour's local government record (Travers, 2007; Game, 2009c; Leach, 2010) and there will be more. Few, though, can have the force of such a lengthy 'to do' list, provided by those who for so long had had the power to do. How much of this 'post-modernisation agenda' would have materialised is obviously impossible to say, because within six months of this compelling demonstration that, finally, after all those years, ministers had really 'got it', they were out of office. Some were campaigning for their party's leadership, including David Miliband, the first Cabinet Minister for Communities and Local Government in 2005–6. He certainly got it, as his repeated campaign apologies confirmed:

We renewed schools and hospitals throughout the land, we improved public services, but people felt like consumers and not partners in the services they received. We talked about 'we', but it meant us, not them, so the workforce often felt neglected and citizens the same; the drive for managerial efficiency became seen as managerial arrogance. (Keir Hardie Lecture, 19 July 2010)

Local government did not have the prominence it should have had during our time in office [as] neither Tony nor Gordon took strengthening local government seriously enough. We devolved to Scotland and Wales but stopped there. Now is the time to look again at devolving to towns and cities across the country. (Smulian, 2010)

Indeed – but looking is all that Miliband and his former ministerial colleagues could now do. Any actual devolution would be in the hands of their successors in the Conservative–Liberal Democrat Coalition, as we see in Chapter 20.

Chapter 20

'Localism, localism, localism'?

When everyone's a localist

We opened the first chapter of this book with a quote from a professional sportsman, so there is a certain symmetry in doing the same in the last chapter. This time it's the American basketball player, John Wooden, who died aged 99 just as we had reached this point in the book's revision. Wooden is the only person inducted into the Basketball Hall of Fame as both player and coach, and it is in the latter role that he became one of the more widely quoted American sportsmen. 'When everyone is thinking the same, no one is thinking' was one of his sayings, and he might well have been talking about localism. It seems every mainstream politician today believes – or wants it believed – that they are localists, which makes it a pretty good bet that most aren't bringing that much heavyweight thought to the matter.

Take the three party leaders in the run-up to the 2010 General Election: who said what?

1 [We propose] giving local communities the power to drive real improvements in everything, from the way their neighbourhoods are policed to the way that community assets are used. I believe it will help to build the vibrant local democracies on which our society and our public services depend.
2 I am a strong localist, for one simple reason. I know that the small, the personal and the local work with the grain of human nature and not against it. But, this is not some romantic attachment to patterns of our past. Localism holds the key to economic, social and political success in the future.
3 It is vital to give people control over what goes on in their neighbourhoods. But it will never be enough while central government aggregates as much power as possible to itself. Councils can't devolve power if they don't have any themselves.

As it happens, the authors are in alphabetical order: Gordon Brown in his Foreword to the 2008 DCLG White Paper, *Communities in Control*; David Cameron is his Foreword to his party's 2009 local government Green Paper, *Control Shift: Returning Power to Local Communities*; and Nick Clegg in a speech to the 2008 LGA Annual Conference.

Several things are striking about these quotes. First, they seem more or less interchangeable, Second, they are distinctly vague about what is being 'localised' to whom and in what type of locality – just 'people' in 'neighbourhoods' and 'communities'. Yet, as we have seen throughout this book, our modern-day local authorities are far too large to represent what most people would understand as neighbourhoods, while communities can mean almost anything and are certainly not exclusively geographic. Indeed, not only is there rarely much attempt actually to define localism, it is noticeable that even the qualification of localism by 'new', widespread only a few years ago, has largely disappeared. Its obvious link with the 'New' in New Labour is probably partly responsible, but it means that a useful distinction has been lost – between New Localism, which was usually understood to be about the devolution of *managerial* power, and the Old Localism that it sought to supplant, which was primarily about the devolution of *political* power.

Old and New Localism and neighbourhood governance

It is not part of the chapter's purpose to unpick and debate concepts and their adjectival nuances, but New Localism has been too prominent in both practitioner and academic discussion of local government in recent years to be allowed to pass by completely without comment. Its early popularisation in the UK is rightly credited to the independent reformist think tank, the New Local Government Network (NLGN) (Filkin *et al.*, 2000), though their labelling it *New* Localism was stretching a point, as the term had made several appearances in the USA over the preceding quarter-century (see, for example, Morris and Hess, 1975; Goetz and Clarke, 1993). The 'catch-phrase', as Americans liked to call it, had less impact there than it did here, but they grasped quickly what we meant by it.

The Office of the Deputy Prime Minister was happy to describe New Localism as simply referring 'broadly to active participation by citizens in local democracy and decision making', and being about 'decentralised decision making, better local decision making, revitalised local democracy, civil and community renewal' (ODPM, 2005b, pp. 5, 11). In a publication actually entitled *New Localism*, though, such blandness was both unhelpful and disingenuous. New Localism might be about decentralised decision-making, but in a very definite context, as Americans recognised, often with approval: 'In policymaking in the UK, the new localism has represented a devolution of power to local governmental agencies, *but only within a framework of national priorities and goals*' (Crowson and Goldring, 2009, p. 2 – emphasis ours).

The sub-clause is key, and was from the outset, as is seen in probably the most quoted definition of New Localism, by Dan Corry and Professor Gerry Stoker (2002), NLGN's founding chair:

> a strategy aimed at devolving power and resources away from central control and towards front line managers, local democratic structures and local consumers and communities, *within an agreed framework of national minimum standards and policy priorities*. (Emphasis ours)

Pratchett elaborates (2004b, p. 369), seeing the new localism as a way of explaining what we described in Chapter 11 as the 'mixed messages' conveyed by the Labour Government's apparently inconsistent approach to local government and its balance sheet mix of centralist and localist policies (see Exhibit 11.2). The approach was not so much inconsistent, Pratchett suggests, as one that was built around a tension between increasing centralisation and enhancing local democracy:

> [The new localism] has two key features. Firstly, it recognises the importance of national standards and priorities as a driving force for public policy. Central government has a primary role in ensuring territorial justice, equity and the collective provision of public goods ... [and] can be expected to emphasise particular policy outcomes and particular priorities, especially where it has manifesto commitments. An explicit recognition of such roles and responsibilities circumscribes local autonomy, making it a secondary concern to national demands. Secondly, however, the 'new localism' also recognises the primacy of the institutions of local governance in delivering public services on behalf of the centre, as well as wider arguments for locally sensitive policy implementation and community leadership. The advocates of the 'new localism', therefore, argue that diversity, choice and local difference should lie at the heart of policy developments.

In suggesting there was a worthwhile distinction to be made between old and new localism, we described ourselves in the previous edition of this book as essentially Old Localists. We suggest that the same label fitted the book itself, with its strong emphasis on elected councils and councillors and their democratic accountability, its concern at the imbalance in central–local relations, its critique of central government's financial control and policy direction, and its scepticism about the fragmentation of local government services and their attempted re-unification through various forms of partnership.

New Localists would see most of this as pointlessly passé – more relevant to the discredited aspirations of the municipal left of the 1980s than to the dramatically changed circumstances of the 'noughties'. Though disputing some of the Labour Government's obsession with micro-management and its interventionist excesses, New Localists accepted, rather than railed against, its role as the principal driver of change at the local level. They would emphasise the 'freedoms and flexibilities' acquired by local authorities, rather than the undiluted centralism of the system in which 'earned autonomy' baubles were awarded only to approved high-performers. They accept that local 'governance' does not necessarily focus on the elected local authority, arguing that the complexity of modern-day problems requires definitions of 'locality' that are broader and more flexible than can be embraced by established democratic institutions alone.

Fairly obviously, most of what localism there has been in recent years has been new localism, managerial localism: severing schools' links with their education authorities, creating foundation hospitals, CPA, and the countless partnerships. In Chapter 19 we suggested Local Area Agreements were also very New Localist, but in fact the territorial concept that New Localists prefer is 'neighbourhood', as in neighbourhood governance, one of the topics featured in the *Communities in Control* White Paper, to which Gordon Brown contributed the foreword quoted above. As Lowndes and Sullivan record (2008, p. 53):

> neighbourhoods have been closely associated with urban regeneration policy since the mid-1990s but have now moved onto the mainstream local government agenda. The neighbourhood is promoted as the place in which local government (and other agencies) can establish new routes for citizen engagement and improved accountability ... Government statements have linked neighbourhoods to the 'practice of empowerment': enabling individuals and communities to exercise greater choice, voice and even control over services.

Lowndes and Sullivan specify four distinct, but interlocking, rationales for neighbourhood governance. The *civic* rationale is based on the simple proposition that local units of government provide more opportunities for citizens to participate effectively in decisions. The *social* rationale focuses on citizen well-being, especially in the context of 'joining up' local action to provide a more integrated approach. The *political* rationale focuses on three pivotal points: accessibility, responsiveness and accountability. The *economic* rationale is based on the proposition that local government can make more efficient and effective use of resources. As the authors observe (2008, p. 71): 'The current interest in "new localism" gets near to developing a comprehensive case for neighbourhood governance that draws upon all four rationales.' Neighbourhood governance, in its ideal form, enables 'governments to re-connect with citizens and other stakeholders to make better decisions and deliver better services'. While neighbourhoods are no panacea – they can't do everything – they do, Lowndes and Sullivan argue, offer a realistic 'bottom-up' perspective and have a central role to play in the New Localism debate.

They do not, however, meet the requirements of Old Localists such as Jones and Stewart (2005):

> Neighbourhoods cannot be the basis for local government. They are sub-local entities of towns, cities and counties. They cannot generate a broad public interest, deciding priorities over a range of concerns, and matching resources to local aspirations ... They can have a useful role in consultation and perform a few useful functions, but not as the main basis for local governing bodies.

Localism – from joke to revolution

Most politicians' attempts at public humour – at Question Time or in party conference speeches – are embarrassingly unfunny, which doesn't necessarily prevent their being received with equally embarrassing mirth. Tony Blair's 2006 Conference 'joke' was about how, relations with then Chancellor of the Exchequer Gordon Brown being what they were, at least he didn't have to worry about Cherie running off with the bloke next door – which earned him a 17-second ovation. At one of his first official public engagements, the new Coalition Communities and Local Government Secretary, Eric Pickles, produced a similar calibre of 'joke' at a reception for the Parliamentary Local Government Group:

> Our first priority is Localism ...
> And our second priority is also Localism;
> Can you guess what our third priority is?

How they laughed! In the ensuing few weeks, two things happened. First, every speech by DCLG ministers seemingly had to include the pronouncement that the government's priorities were 'Localism, localism, localism'. Second, a sub-joke was added: 'but they might occur in a different order'.

Joking aside, as they say, Pickles and his ministerial team had set the criterion by which every act by them, their department, and, indeed, other departments would in future be judged, particularly by the local government sector itself. The honeymoon period would prove brief, but early verdicts were by no means all unfavourable. The political climate helped. As Exhibit 16.4 showed, the Conservatives in 2010 controlled, in majority or minority administrations, around 60% of all English councils. This arithmetic meant they also controlled the LGA, chaired by Dame Margaret Eaton, former leader of the same Bradford City Council that was led, when she was first elected to it back in the 1980s, by Eric Pickles. None of this would guarantee Pickles applause, when he announced, for example, 2011/12 grant cuts of up to 17% for some councils, or a 'Localism Bill' containing 142 regulation-making powers, but it did mean that the LGA and much of the local government world were initially keen to be seen as positively responsive.

The Coalition's first official indications of its policy and legislative plans for local government came in its *Programme for Government* (HM Government, 2010). The document dealt with 31 policy areas in alphabetical order, so, even without further emphasis, the 'Communities and Local Government' section featured encouragingly early – unlike 'Universities and Further Education'. But there was further emphasis, immediately, in the section's preamble and first two pledges:

> The Government believes that it is time for a fundamental shift of power from Westminster to people. We will promote decentralisation and democratic engagement, and we will end the era of top-down government by giving *new powers to local councils, communities, neighbourhoods and individuals*. (Emphasis ours)
>
> - We will promote the radical devolution of power and greater financial autonomy to local government and community groups. This will include a review of local government finance.
> - We will rapidly abolish Regional Spatial Strategies (RSSs) and return decision-making powers on housing and planning to local councils.

There were 28 proposals in all, many of which went straight into the Localism Bill that was outlined in the Queen's Speech a couple of weeks later (see Exhibit 20.1). But policy was evolving fast at this time. It was not just RSSs and their regional housing targets that were to go, but the whole architecture of regionalism: Regional Development Agencies (RDAs) and all GOs. The Conservatives' election promise to freeze council tax for two years was scaled down in the Coalition Programme to one year, 2011/12, and a second if possible. Then in Chancellor of the Exchequer George Osborne's first Budget it became a selective deal, in which councils would be given additional grants for one year, if they cut or froze their own costs. By 2012/13 the government would expect to have legislation in place giving ministers the power to set an inflation-linked threshold for council tax rises each year, with any council planning to exceed it having to spend additional money holding a referendum in which voters would be able to veto the 'excessive' increase (see p. 227).

The Conservative manifesto pledge to 'give each of England's 12 largest cities the chance of having an elected mayor' made it into the Coalition Programme, with the qualification that it would be 'subject to confirmatory referendums' – a phrase that prompted suspicions of an impending ministerial U-turn. Previously, mayoral referendums had been required *before* any

Exhibit 20.1 The Localism Bill 2010

The Queen's Speech, May 2010

The Speech outlined 22 Bills to be introduced in the first parliamentary session of the new Coalition Government. Several affected local government directly, including:

- **Academies Bill,** which became the Academies Act 2010 – enabling all publicly funded schools in England to become academies, without consultation with their local authorities. Academies are still publicly funded, but with greatly increased freedom on issues such as the curriculum and teachers' salaries.
- **Education and Children's Bill** – enabling new groups, including parents, to start and run state schools, and introducing a 'pupil premium', paid to schools for teaching the poorest children.
- **Police Reform and Social Responsibility Bill** – increasing accountability through directly elected police and crime commissioners, with powers to set budgets, determine police force priorities, and hire/fire chief constables.

The Decentralisation and Localism Bill

The main Bill affecting local government, eventually to be introduced in December 2010 as the **Localism Bill.** Provisions included:

- Giving councils a **General Power of Competence** would allow councils to carry out any lawful activity or business. Should extend and clarify 'well-being' power (ch. 10), ruled in a controversial 2008 High Court case not to cover London councils' attempt to set up their own Local Authorities' Mutual Assurance company to save up to 20% on premiums for liability and property insurance.
- **Replacing Regional Development Agencies with Local Enterprise Partnerships** – joint local authority–business bodies brought forward by local authorities to promote local economic development (ch. 6).
- **Abolishing the Government Offices** for London and the regions.
- **Abolishing Regional Spatial Strategies** and returning housing and planning powers to councils – plus a **new power to stop 'garden grabbing'**: building flats and houses in back gardens, permitted through their current designation as 'brownfield' sites.
- **Replacing the Infrastructure Planning Commission** with an efficient and democratically accountable system that provides a fast-track process for major infrastructure projects.
- Introducing **new powers to help local communities save local facilities** and services threatened with closure, and enable them to bid to take over local state-run services.
- Giving **greater financial autonomy** to local government and community groups, following a review of local government finance.
- Giving residents the power to **instigate local referendums** on any local issue and the power to **veto excessive council tax increases.**
- **Abolishing Standards for England** – the former Standards Board for England that oversees investigation of the most serious alleged infringements of the Councillors' Code of Conduct.
- Requiring public bodies, including councils, to **publish online the job titles of every member of staff** and the salaries and expenses of senior officials (ch. 15).

elections took place. But, it was noted, 'confirmatory' might also mean confirmation *after* the event – after an elected mayor had been in place for a time, or after the current leader had stayed in post, but with suddenly increased mayoral status and powers.

So it proved. For 11 of the 12 largest cities, the Localism Bill 2010 set out a three-stage process of potential mayor-making: Summer 2011 – following Royal Assent, the cities' current council leaders would become 'shadow mayors' with the same powers as existing elected mayors; May 2012 – the cities would all hold mayoral referendums; May 2013 – cities voting Yes in their referendums would elect their mayors, who were promised significant, but unspecified, additional powers. The twelfth city, Leicester, chose in effect to pre-empt this process by using existing procedures to consult its electors and move directly to a mayoral election in May 2011, thereby avoiding the necessity, and cost, of a referendum.

There were other stirrings too in the policy forest. Education Secretary Michael Gove rushed his Academies Bill through Parliament as if freeing schools from any contaminating contact with local authorities was some kind of national emergency. Eric Pickles and Decentralisation Minister Greg Clark told councils and business leaders that, while Local Enterprise Partnerships (LEPs), the successors to RDAs, were expected to cover 'natural economic areas', there would be little or no ministerial intervention in their formation. But at the same time, over in the Department of Business, Innovation and Skills, Vince Cable and his ministers suggested applicants would be vetted and weeded out if their proposed boundaries failed to match ministers' ideas of natural economic areas or failed to engage sufficiently with the private sector. With the ensuing 62 applications for LEP status greatly exceeding ministerial expectations, the Business Secretary won this internal Coalition tussle and initially gave the go-ahead to just 24.

Pickles returned to one of his pre-ministerial campaigns, telling local authorities how to organise their refuse collection, by ordering the withdrawal of Audit Commission guidance encouraging fortnightly collections in the interests of recycling. The guidance, claimed Pickles, had been a 'diktat imposed from the centre', 'a clear conspiracy by Labour ministers and Whitehall bin bullies to kill off weekly bin collections'. Which made his contribution presumably a diktat imposed from the flanks, given that the department with overall responsibility for UK waste and recycling policy is not in fact DCLG, but DEFRA, the Department for Environment, Food and Rural Affairs. Back on his own turf, meanwhile, the Communities Secretary provocatively suggested that the London Borough of Newham need not replace their chief executive, as they already had a well-paid elected mayor who could surely do both jobs.

No firm conclusions could possibly be drawn from this handful of incidents, but some early impressions did emerge. First, even if DCLG ministers were signed up to localism, it didn't mean that all of their governmental colleagues were. Second, for Pickles, whatever else 'localism' might mean, it didn't mean personal non-intervention, for, as he informed the Queen's Speech Forum (10 June 2010), he sees himself as an unlikely-looking revolutionary, and revolutionaries don't tiptoe around suppressing their personal views and missing opportunities to further their cause. His revolutionary cause is constitutional change:

> We are determined to wrest control from the bureaucrats, the quangos, and central government departments. Taking power and pushing it as far away from Whitehall as possible. I am deadly serious about this. We are going to shake up the balance of power in this country. We are going to change the nature of the constitution.
>
> It won't be in a single action or a single law. It will be through dramatic and bold actions, but also small and incremental changes. Localism is the principle, the mantra, and defines everything we do.
>
> You might think, well, all governments talk like this. But we've proved it by getting on and doing it:
>
> - We've made Home Information Packs history, and already the number of homes being put up for sale has gone up by 35 per cent;
> - We've scrapped the top-down housing targets and meaningless regional spatial strategies;
> - We've put an end to 'garden grabbing', which has seen acres of land lost to intensive development;
> - We've cut the ring-fencing and red tape which comes attached to hundreds of millions of pounds' worth of central government grants;
> - We're leading by example in making central government more open, more transparent, more accountable.

He gave other examples too, but the message was already clear enough: though he himself might dismiss the idea of being associated with new anything, he was talking the language of New Localism – the devolution of power and resources away from central control towards, in the Coalition Programme's phraseology, *local councils, communities, neighbourhoods and individuals*, within a framework of national policy priorities. Councils would be just one, and probably not the major one, of the beneficiaries of this devolution. Those who saw only the centralism in Pickles' weekly bin collections, council tax referendums and other interventions were missing the point. Pushing power 'as far away from Whitehall as possible' did not necessarily mean to local councils. They could be part of the control framework too, and, if necessary, they had to be bypassed. The ultimate beneficiaries must be individuals, the people, or, as Americans would say, 'the folks'. He used the term at that same Queen's Speech Forum, contrasting the new government with the one it had displaced:

The previous Government didn't like the folks. It didn't trust them. It always believed it knew best. We've just had 13 years of the most central-ising government in history – a controlling government, obsessed with targets, inspections and micro-management. It left local government toothless, community groups out in the cold, residents powerless to change anything ...

I have three very clear priorities: localism, localism, and localism ... because we like the folks. We don't think we know better than they do. And we trust them to know what's best for them.

The LGA's dilemma

Pickles' localism presents local government, and certainly the LGA, with a dilemma. He knows more, from the inside, about the local government world for which he is politically responsible than almost any of his predecessors. Yet that world knows that, while it probably will get some of what it most wants – fewer targets and inspections and less micro-management, to quote his speech – it can expect no special favours; if anything, quite the reverse. In anticipation of the 2010 Election, the LGA had published a consultation document, *Freedom to Lead: Trust to Deliver* (2010), intended both as a reminder to, in particular, the party leaders of the 'huge strides' made by local government over the past decade in terms of performance and value for money, and as an agenda for the future to which they might respond.

The document's proposals were presented in the form of an 'offer' to government. On one side there was what local government could bring to the table, what it 'can do locally to lead a collective effort to improve the quality of life for local people and to make public money go further' – exten-sive experience of collaborative working, democratically accountable leader-ship, committed local councillors, capacity for more self-evaluation and peer scrutiny as an alternative to costly top-down inspection. On the other side was the 'ask' – a listing of the changes needed to enable local government to realise its potential fully. This listing had its predictabilities, but interestingly it was headed by and structured around the concept of *place-based budget accountability* – giving councils, or groups of councils, full commissioning responsibility for *all* the public money spent in their area, whether currently by local or central government, the NHS or any other public bodies. Getting rid of the multiple and competing funding streams, the different accounta-bility regimes, the ring-fenced budgets, the myriad quangos and other fund-ing bodies, the LGA estimated, could release savings of up to £100 billion over five years. To maximise effectiveness, the LGA 'ask' also proposed 3-year 'area financial settlements', new-style area agreements negotiated outwards with citizens, rather than upwards with Whitehall, and a single improvement framework for local public services.

Exhibit 20.2 The LG Group's offer – savings and place-based budgeting

Context

The offer was first outlined in May 2010, in response to the new government's announcement of £6.25 billion of public spending cuts in the 2010/11 financial year, a high proportion of which would fall on local government, including a £1.2 billion reduction in grants.

The 'open and comprehensive' offer

The LG Group (LGA + linked bodies) set out a three-part 'open and comprehensive offer' to the government, comprising:

1 Specific measures for swift efficiency savings:

- The LGA had identified **£4.5 billion of savings** that could be made quickly, by, for example, cutting administration costs of government departments and quangos with close links to local government; giving councils more spending flexibility; halving costs of regulating local government (LGA, 2009e).
- These savings could protect 300,000 school places, 175,000 personal care packages and 36,000 miles of road resurfacing.
- The LGA would work with government to secure these savings, and use local government expertise to identify further public sector savings that could accrue from further devolution.

2 Radical decentralisation and place-based budgets:

- Total Place pilots (see Exhibit 9.4) showed that much duplication, inefficiency and waste come from multiple public bodies trying to achieve the same goal.
- The LGA supports the government's planned finance review, but proposes a radical reshaping of the state through **Place-based Budgeting** – a system whereby all tax pounds spent in an area, whether by councils, central government, the NHS or quangos, are pooled to focus on the real needs of local citizens.
- The LGA's core proposition is that commissioning responsibility for a set of local services should rest with a **local governance body**, based probably on a city- or county-wide group of councils working together. This body should be accountable to local electors and, if partly grant-funded, directly to Parliament, rather than through the present plethora of monitors and inspectors.
- The LGA estimates this move away from command-and-control provision to more devolved managerial responsibility and decision-making could bring taxpayers **immediate annual administrative savings of £4.5 billion.**

3 Support to councils and a new improvement framework:

- The LGA accepts that this promise of a reshaped local state needs to be backed up by a guarantee that councils will deliver. The LG Group would make that pledge and commit itself to working with councils to this end.
- The LGA proposes (in place of CPA/CAA) a **new improvement framework** with streamlined inspection structures and stringent local self-regulation, including three-yearly peer reviews.
- The LGA would commit to undertaking regulation in the event of a council performing unsatisfactorily, and accepts there that may be a need for powers to be withdrawn in areas that fail to increase efficiency.

The formation of a Coalition Government took local government as much by surprise as it did the rest of the country, the more so when it became clear how urgently and fiercely it was going to attack the budget deficit and public spending. The world had changed, and it was clearly not the time for detailed negotiation of a new 'accountability framework'. If the LGA was to make its presence felt, it would have to adapt its 'offer' to the immediate demands of cuts and savings, and this is what it did (Exhibit 20.2). Place-based budgeting remained, quite rightly, at the heart of its case, but prominently up front were the 'specific measures to make substantial efficiency savings and cut waste quickly'.

Foundation Councils and other models

The LGA is a voluntary member body, dependent on the subscriptions of its more than 400 member authorities, whose interests it has to represent as fairly and inclusively as possible. It can seek to be radical – as with place-based budgeting – but it cannot easily just float ideas in the way a think tank or an individual council can. Really unusual or, in the American baseball idiom, left-field ideas have to come from other sources. Several such proposals were floating around in 2009/10. There was no knowing whether they would take off or just flutter limply to the ground, but they seemed worth recording in this book's final few pages.

Foundation Councils were introduced in an eye-catchingly titled publication – *A Magna Carta for Localism* – from the Centre for Policy Studies, the Conservative policy think tank part-founded by Margaret Thatcher. More relevantly, the authors were three prominent leaders of London councils: Colin Barrow (Westminster), Stephen Greenhalgh (Hammersmith and Fulham), and Edward Lister (Wandsworth). Their analysis of 'the central state we're in' and of the need for change resembles that presented in this book. The UK is one of the most centralised states in the developed world. Local government is shackled, because Whitehall convinces ministers that it cannot be trusted to deliver services of national importance. The barriers facing local government include its limited powers; the centrally imposed framework of legislation, targets and funding restrictions; the 'inspection industry' – 'probably the most onerous regulatory regime of any western country' (p. 3); 'service silos', whereby many local services are provided by special purpose bodies, central government and quangos, resulting in complexity, fragmentation and overlap; and financial dependency.

The Coalition Government's promised general power of competence will help, but, argue the authors, more is needed. Additional powers should be devolved to councils – initially to a few successful, well-run ones. Eventually, though, councils should be able to earn Foundation status and gain greater operational freedom in the same way as Foundation Hospitals (see Exhibit 13.6). Responsibilities that could be considered for devolution to a first generation of Foundation Councils include:

- *Local administration of benefits and tackling unemployment.* Councils are expected to tackle worklessness, yet they are responsible for less than 5% of the total expenditure, most of which is delivered through a complex and often disincentivising benefits system with too many providers. Foundation Councils could provide a one-stop shop for jobs and benefits that would yield savings in benefits administration, from the reduction in fraud and error, and from reduced welfare dependency – the total estimated at £4.4 billion if implemented nationally (p. i).
- *Improving the standard of local community care.* Primary care falls into two parts. Medical care comprises all the services commissioned by a doctor – medicines, treatments, surgery, acute and hospital care – which were currently the responsibility of PCTs and the NHS. All the rest – residential care, home care, occupational therapy, benefits and welfare payments, the direct payment regime – could be the province of local government. Rather than multiple organisations providing these services, Foundation Councils could lead and be the sole commissioning authorities for a local public health service, with long-term care services, and services for vulnerable children. Users would benefit from more joined-up provision, and the scheme could yield estimated national savings of £5.1 billion.

It takes something exceptional in local government to attract the attention of even our serious media, and sadly, whatever their future may prove to be, Foundation Councils didn't really do it in 2009/10. Two other pioneering schemes did, however, as the following headlines attest:

Barnet Council adopts easyJet and Ryanair business model (*Daily Telegraph*)

Tories to use 'easyJet' council as test for 'no frills' government (*Daily Mail*)

easyCouncil should soon be taking off (*Times Online*)

Barnet and Lambeth turn to easyJet and John Lewis (*BBC News*)

It's JohnLewis vs easyCouncil (*The Guardian*).

Barnet is a Conservative borough in north London, many of whose Finchley residents returned Margaret Thatcher numerous times to the House of Commons. With an agenda of which she would surely approve, the Council Leader from 2006, Mike Freer, began looking at changing radically the way in which services were provided. Did they have to be provided at all? Could other providers, perhaps with transferred council staff, provide them instead? Could users be charged, or charged more, for them? How could

Exhibit 20.3 easyCouncil or John Lewis council – the future of local government?

easyCouncil – as modelled by Barnet LBC

What's it about?

Potentially, much more than a budget airline way of running a council – providing basic, 'no frills' services, then charging for 'extras' traditionally considered standard – though that is part of the model. Media were fascinated by idea of charges, not for priority boarding, but for jumping the queue for planning consent; or money back for using smaller waste bins.

Rooted in a serious attempt by the 2006–9 council leader, Mike Freer (now an MP), to transform the organisation and culture of local government so that Barnet could provide a better range of services with relatively, or absolutely, less money (Barnet LBC, 2009; Mulholland, 2010).

A core idea

There are several, but one is to 'count the council in a different way' from the conventional staff numbers – for example, children's services 34%, environment and transport 23%, adult services 15%. Counting instead by **activity** – service delivery 49%, support 21%, property 1% – makes it easier to identify duplication of activity in different parts of the council, as well as potential savings.

The 3-pronged transformation strategy

1 **A new relationship with citizens** – developing a deeper understanding of community needs; connecting citizens with each other to encourage self-help; and **enabling citizens to choose and personalise services.**
2 **'One public sector'** – joint commissioning of services and merging back-office functions of various public sector bodies to cut costs and create 'one public sector' in an area.
3 **A relentless efficiency drive** – working with public, private, voluntary and community sector bodies, trading and gaining revenue through value-added services.

The John Lewis council – as modelled by Lambeth LBC

What's it about?

Services run by co-operative partnerships, modelled on the up-market department store, whose 70,000 staff/partners share the benefits and profits – council tax reductions? – of business success. Labour's apparently hurried pre-election response to easyCouncil and Conservative plans for employee-owned co-ops to deliver public services. Would build on examples of community-led services launched in the Labour-led South London borough – tenant-run housing estates, a children's centre, community sports hub, a black heritage centre, the country's first parent-promoted secondary school.

A core idea

Again, there are plenty, inspired particularly by Labour leader, Steve Reed – though here in a much more open-ended, consultative Co-operative Council Commission agenda (Lambeth Council, 2010). One is the recognition that a viable co-operative model rests on a distinction between two types of public services: **personalised services,** targeted at and shaped by individuals or families to improve their life chances, and requiring the involvement of professionals – for example, health and social care, homelessness support; and **community-based services,** where the community should take collective decisions about provision – for example, adult learning, community safety.

they be offered more choice? He produced a substantial and wide-ranging document outlining the *Future Shape of the Council*, one strand of which, as indicated in Exhibit 20.3, was the budget airline service model: providing a basic, 'no frills' service, leaving residents with more money, from their reduced council tax, to pay for 'frills' that they themselves chose.

By coincidence, the easyCouncil project received a major setback almost immediately, following Freer's resignation from the leadership in November 2009 to concentrate on his parliamentary campaign. The Council had planned to replace the live-in wardens in its sheltered accommodation with roaming carers, who would respond to residents when needed, via a telephone alarm. The new service saved £400,000, the Council's case being that it would be able to provide a better service to all the borough's elderly, rather than just the 2% in sheltered accommodation. But in a judicial review brought by the UK Pensioners' Strategy Committee, the council was judged to have failed to take into account the residents' tenancy agreements and its duties under the Disability Discrimination Act, and the wardens had to be reinstated. Under its new leadership, the Council did not appeal against the ruling, and little was heard of easyCouncil during the General Election campaign. The *Future Shape of the Council*, however, remains a serious analysis, and the timely questions it raises, particularly about councils' legal obligations and their discretion over charging for services, are certainly not going to disappear.

With easyCouncil out of the way, less was also heard than it might otherwise have been of Labour's slightly opportunistic counter-attack: the idea of branding Lambeth as Britain's first 'John Lewis Council', offering council tax rebates to residents in exchange for helping to run services. Again, the detailed thinking behind important, if controversial, ideas for alternative forms of service delivery tended to get buried under the easy and confrontational headlines. But Lambeth's plans, which had barely reached the consultation stage when they were hijacked by Labour's national leadership, raised big questions – about the extent to which most people actually want even partly to run their own services, and about the contribution this form of mutualism could make to compensating for the large drop in income councils were likely to experience in the immediate future.

Localism sings

The reformist ideas covered in the past few pages have ranged from the pragmatic through the ideological to the idealistic. We conclude with what, in the prevailing economic circumstances, must probably be classed as Utopian, but which will serve as a benchmark against which all other models and blueprints can be compared. The expression commonly applied at this stage of an event was originally a southern American proverb:

'Church isn't over until the fat lady sings'; in this case, more appropriately, it is localism that sings.

Devolution and localism have been the themes of the chapter, and Sir Simon Jenkins, author, ex-editor of *The Times*, ex-chair of the Commission for Local Democracy, is one of the most radical localists around. He writes columns on all topics, regularly including local government, in *The Guardian*, but his prospectus for the devolution of political power – what he called his attempt 'to make localism sing' (p. 7) – was best set out in the Policy Exchange pamphlet, *Big Bang Localism: A Rescue Plan for British Democracy* (Jenkins, 2004). By pamphlet standards it is lengthy and can only be summarised brutally here, but its thesis is that the deterioration of our local democratic health has become so serious in recent years that it can be rescued effectively only by a transfer of power from the centre to localities that is both comprehensive and spectacular. Hence the requirement of implementation in the form of a Big Bang – rivalling Margaret Thatcher's Big Bang reform of the City of London's financial institutions on 1 October 1986, which transformed the restrictive practices of the stock exchange and securities markets.

Compressed into eight points, Jenkins' post-Big Bang local government would comprise:

- A structure resembling that existing before the 1974/75 reorganisation (1,857 principal councils in Great Britain in place of the present 408). There would still be a mix of unitary and two-tier authorities, following the re-creation of abolished counties and the dismantling of larger rural districts (often with 'artificial' or 'compass point' names – see p. 44 above) into smaller 'real' town or parish councils with which residents can genuinely identify.
- County and city councils would regain those functions wholly or partly 'lost' to unelected quangos since the 1970s – including planning, roads, the environment, leisure, culture, the police, prison and probation, youth employment and training.
- A dismantled NHS, with health services to be taken over by counties and upper-tier authorities.
- Personal social services would become the responsibility of the most local tier of local government – in England, city, town or parish councils.
- These authorities, however small by current UK standards, would become self-governing entities for services they could reasonably supply on their own – primary schools and elderly people's homes, nurseries and day-care centres, clinics, surgeries. For provision of larger scale services, they would combine with neighbouring authorities as necessary.
- All these service-providing authorities would be elected, and led by an elected executive – a mayor, elected either directly or (as in France) as the head of a collective Cabinet.

- All authorities to be funded partly by central government through a single general or block grant, but with over half their income (as in the days before the poll tax) coming from a portfolio of local taxes on, for example, property, income, business, hotels, tourism, gambling, vehicle duty, entertainment.
- A Local Government Commission, independent of central government, would be charged with implementation: negotiating with authorities to determine their internal constitutions and electoral arrangements, and monitoring schemes for local taxes.

Jenkins would argue that, dramatic as the implementation of even half of his programme would be (say, a Big Pop's-worth), it would do no more than bring us a little closer in line with most other West European and Scandinavian systems. He is right, which is why the Big Bang is included in this chapter – even though, notwithstanding the fact that 'we're all localists now', the chances of it actually happening are substantially less than minimal.

Bibliography

Allen, H. J. B. (1990) *Cultivating the Grass Roots: Why Local Government Matters* (The Hague: IULA).

Andrews, R., Boyne, G., Chen, A. and Martin, S. (2006) *Population Size and Local Authority Performance: Final Research Report* (London: DCLG).

APSE (Association for Public Service Excellence) (2008) *Creating Resilient Economies: Exploring the Economic Footprint of Public Services* (Manchester: APSE).

Armitstead, L. (2010) 'Women Land Fewer Top Jobs', *Daily Telegraph*, 22 May.

Ashdown, P. (2001) *The Ashdown Diaries, Vol. II: 1997–1999* (Harmondsworth: Penguin).

Audit Commission (2001) *To Whom Much Is Given: New Ways of Working for Councillors Following Political Restructuring* (Abingdon: Audit Commission).

Audit Commission (2005a) *Governing Partnerships: Bridging the Accountability Gap* (London: Audit Commission).

Audit Commission (2008) *Positively Charged: Maximising the Benefits of Local Public Service Charges* (London: Audit Commission).

Audit Commission (2009) *When It Comes to the Crunch: How Councils Are Responding to the Recession* (London: Audit Commission).

Audit Commission (2010a) *Corporate Governance Inspection – Doncaster Metropolitan Borough Council, April 2010* (London: Audit Commission).

Audit Commission (2010b) *Surviving the Crunch: Local Finances in the Recession and Beyond* (London: Audit Commission).

Ayres, S. and Pearce, G. (2002) *Who Governs the West Midlands? An Audit of Government Institutions and Structures* (Telford: West Midlands Constitutional Convention).

Baggott, R. (2007) *Understanding Health Policy* (Bristol: Policy Press).

Bains, M. (Chairman) (1972) *The New Local Authorities: Management and Structure* (London: HMSO).

Baker, K. (1993) *The Turbulent Years: My Life in Politics* (London: Faber & Faber).

Barnet LBC (2009) *The Future Shape of Barnet Council: Background*. Available at: http://www.barnet.gov.uk/index/council-democracy/future-shape-of-barnet-council.htm.

Barron, J., Crawley, G. and Wood, T. (1987) *Married to the Council? The Private Costs of Public Service* (Bristol: Bristol Polytechnic).

Barrow, C., Greenhalgh, S. and Lister, E. (2010) *A Magna Carta for Localism: Three Practical Steps to Make Localism Real* (London: Centre for Policy Studies).

Be Birmingham/Ekosgen (2009) *Public Expenditure and Investment Study* (Birmingham: Be Birmingham).

BHHRG (British Helsinki Human Rights Group) (2005) *Articles on UK Postal Ballot Election by Paul Dale and Others* – with link to Commissioner Richard Mawrey QC's judgment. Available at: www.bhhrg.org/mediaYear/asp.

Birmingham City Council (2006) *Devolution and Localisation: A Report from Overview and Scrutiny* (Birmingham: Birmingham City Council).

Birmingham City Council (2009) *Budget Book 2009/10* (Birmingham: Birmingham City Council).

Blair, T. (1998) *Leading the Way: A New Vision for Local Government* (London: IPPR).

Blears, H. (2007) 'After Devolution: Building a New Contract Between Citizen and State', Speech delivered to New Local Government Network conference, 29 May. Available at: www.nlgn.org.uk/public/2007/after-devolution-building-a-new-contract-between-citizen-and-state/.

Bogdanor, V. (2001) 'Constitutional Reform', in A. Seldon (ed.), *The Blair Effect: The Blair Government 1997–2001* (London: Little, Brown), pp. 139–56.

Bogdanor, V. (ed.) (2005) *Joined-Up Government* (Oxford: Oxford University Press).

Boyle, Sir L. (1986) 'In Recommendation of Widdicombe', *Local Government Studies*, 12:6, pp. 33–9.

Brighton and Hove Community and Voluntary Sector Forum (January 2009) *Taking Account: A Social and Economic Audit of the Community & Voluntary Sector*. Available at: www.cvsectorforum.org.uk/takingaccount.

Brindle, D. (2004) 'Change Agent', *Society Guardian*, 15 September.

Brooke, R. (2005) *The Councillor – Victim or Vulgarian?* (London: LGA).

Buckinghamshire CC (2009) *A Review into Statutory, Mandatory and Discretionary Services at Buckinghamshire County Council: Phase 1 – Overview and Scrutiny Commissioning Committee Interim Report* (Aylesbury: Buckinghamshire County Council).

Budge, I., Brand, J., Margolis, M. and Smith, A. L. M. (1972) *Political Stratification and Democracy* (London: Macmillan).

Budge, I., McKay, D., Newton, K. and Bartle, J. (2007) *The New British Politics* (Harlow: Pearson Education).

Burley, K. (2005) 'Probity and Professional Conduct in Planning: A Personal Perspective', *Planning Theory and Practice*, 6:4, pp. 526–35.

Burton, M. (2005) 'A Suffolk Swansong?', *Municipal Journal*, 31 March, p. 12.

Butler, D. and Butler, G. (2006) *British Political Facts Since 1979* (Basingstoke: Palgrave Macmillan).

Butler, D., Adonis, A. and Travers, T. (1994) *Failure in British Government: The Politics of the Poll Tax* (Oxford: Oxford University Press).

Cabinet Office (1998) *Quangos: Opening the Doors* (London: HMSO).

Cabinet Office (1999) *Modernising Government*, Cm 4310 (London: HMSO).

Cabinet Office (2009) *Public Bodies 2008* (London: Cabinet Office).

Calman, Professor Sir K. (Chairman) (2009) *Final Report of the Commission on Scottish Devolution – Serving Scotland Better: Scotland and the United Kingdom in the 21st Century* (Edinburgh: Commission on Scottish Devolution).

Campbell, L. (2004) 'The Mother of All Election Campaigns', *Society Guardian*, 14 May.

CEMR-Dexia (2009) *EU Sub-national Governments: 2008 Key Figures* (Brussels: CEMR).

Centre for Policy Studies (2010) *A Magna Carta for Localism: Three Practical Steps to Make Localism Real* (London: Centre for Policy Studies).

CfPS (Centre for Public Scrutiny) (2010) *The 2009 Annual Survey of Overview and Scrutiny in Local Government* (London: CfPS).

Chandler, J. (2007) *Explaining Local Government* (Manchester: Manchester University Press).

Chandler, J. (2008) 'Liberal Justifications for Local Government in Britain: The Triumph of Expediency over Ethics', *Political Studies*, 56:2, pp. 355–73.

Chandler, J. (2010) 'A Rationale for Local Government', *Local Government Studies* 36:1, pp. 5–20.

Chisholm, M. and Leach, S. (2008) *Botched Business: The Damaging Process of Reorganising Local Government, 2006–2008* (Coleford, Glos.: Douglas McLean Publishing).

CIPFA (Chartered Institute of Public Finance and Accountancy) (2009a) *Public Library Statistics: 2007–08 Actuals* (London: CIPFA).

CIPFA (Chartered Institute of Public Finance and Accountancy) (2009b) *Finance and General Statistics* (London: CIPFA).

Citizens Advice Scotland (2007) 'Poll Tax Arrears Persist in Haunting Scots, Says Citizens Advice' – Press Release, 5 December. Available at: www.cas.org.uk/pressrelease5122007.aspx.

Clark, G. and Mather, J. (2003) *Total Politics: Labour's Command State* (London: Conservative Policy Unit).

Clarke, M. and Stewart, J. (1991) *The Choices for Local Government for the 1990s and Beyond* (Harlow: Longman).

CLD (Commission for Local Democracy) (1995) *Taking Charge: The Rebirth of Local Democracy* (London: Municipal Journal Books).

CLES (Centre for Local Economic Strategies) (2010) *Making the Most of Public Sector Spend: Procurement as Local Economic Activism – Briefing* (Manchester: CLES).

CLRD (Council of Europe Committee on Local & Regional Democracy) (2008) *Report on the Relationship Between Central and Local Authorities: Situation 2007* (Strasbourg: Council of Europe).

Cochrane, A. (1993) *Whatever Happened to Local Government?* (Buckingham: Open University Press).

Cockburn, C. (1977) *The Local State* (London: Pluto).

Compact (2009) *Refreshing the Compact: A Framework for Partnership Working – Compact on Relations between Government and the Third Sector in England* (London: Compact).

Conrad, M. (2009) '"Costly" Judicial Reviews Hit Policies, Says Healey', 2 April. Available at: LocalGov.co.uk.

Conservative Party (2008) *A Stronger Society: Voluntary Action in the 21st Century, Policy Green Paper No. 5* (London: The Conservative Party).

Conservative Party (2009) *Control Shift: Returning Power to Local Communities, Policy Green Paper No. 9* (London: The Conservative Party).

Conservative Party (2010) *Invitation to Join the Government of Britain – The Conservative Manifesto 2010* (London: The Conservative Party).

Constitution Unit (2008) *Northern Ireland Devolution Monitoring Project, September 2008* (London: Constitution Unit).

Constitution Unit (2009) *Wales Devolution Monitoring Report, May 2009* (London: Constitution Unit).

Copus, C. (2004) *Party Politics and Local Government* (Manchester: Manchester University Press).

Copus, C., Clark, A. and Bottom, K. (2008) 'Multi-Party Politics in England? Small Parties, Independents and Political Associations in English Local Politics', in M. Reiser and E. Holtmann (eds), *Farewell to the Party Model? Independent Local Lists in Eastern and Western European Countries* (Wiesbaden, Germany: VS Verlag), pp. 253–76.

Copus, C., Clark, A., Reynaert, H. and Steyvers, K. (2009) 'Minor Party and Independent Politics Beyond the Mainstream: Fluctuating Fortunes but a Permanent Presence', *Parliamentary Affairs*, 62:1, pp. 4–18.

Corina, L. (1974) 'Elected Representatives in a Party System: A Typology', *Policy and Politics*, 3:1, pp. 69–87.

Corry, D. and Stoker, G. (2002) *New Localism: Refashioning the Centre–Local Relationship* (London: NLGN).

Coulson, A. (1998) 'Town, Parish and Community Councils: The Potential for Democracy and Decentralisation', *Local Governance*, 24:4, pp. 245–8.

Coulson, A. (2005) 'The Death of a Mass Membership Party?', *Renewal – A Journal of Labour Politics*, 13:2/3, pp. 139–42.

Crowson, R. L. and Goldring, E. B. (2009) *The New Localism in American Education* (Oxford: Blackwell).

Dale, I (2010) 'In Conversation with Eric Pickles', *Total Politics*, Issue 29 – http://www.accessinterviews.com/interviews/view/21827.

Daniel, G. (2009) 'A Weapon of Mass Distraction?', *Local Government Chronicle*, 10 September.

D'Arcy, M. and MacLean, R. (2000) *Nightmare! The Race to Become London's Mayor* (London: Politico's).

Davies, S. (2008) *Taking Stock: The Future of Our Public Library Service* (London: UNISON).

Davis, H. (1996) 'Quangos and Local Government: A Changing World', *Local Government Studies*, 22:2, pp. 1–7.

DCLG (Department for Communities and Local Government) (2006a) *Developing the Local Government Services Market to Support a Long-term Strategy for Local Government* (London: DCLG).

DCLG (Department for Communities and Local Government) (2006b) *Strong and Prosperous Communities: The Local Government White Paper* (London: DCLG).

DCLG (Department for Communities and Local Government) (2006c) *Mapping the Local Government Performance Reporting Landscape – Final Report* (London: DCLG).

DCLG (Department for Communities and Local Government) (2006d) *Local Area Agreements Research: Round 2 Negotiations and Early Progress in Round 1* (London: DCLG).

DCLG (Department for Communities and Local Government) (2007) *Central–Local Concordat* (London: DCLG).

DCLG (Department for Communities and Local Government) (2008a) *Communities in Control: Real Power, Real People*, Cm 7427 (London: DCLG). Available at: ww.communities.gov.uk/documents/communities/pdf/886045.pdf.

DCLG (Department for Communities and Local Government) (2008b) *Council Tax in 2009/10 – Letter from the Minister for Local Government to Local Authority*

Leaders, 9 *December*. Available at: http://www.local.odpm.gov.uk/finance/ctax/ctax0910let.pdf.

DCLG (Department for Communities and Local Government) (2008c) *National Evaluation of Local Public Service Agreements: Summary of Final Report* (London: DCLG).

DCLG (Department for Communities and Local Government) (2008d) *Meta-evaluation of the Local Government Modernisation Agenda – The State of Local Services: Performance Improvement in Local Government: Executive Summary* (London: DCLG).

DCLG (Department for Communities and Local Government) (2008e) *Meta-evaluation of the Local Government Modernisation Agenda – The State of Local Democracy: The Impact of Policy Changes on Accountability and Public Confidence: Executive Summary* (London: DCLG).

DCLG (Department for Communities and Local Government) (2009a) 'Over Three Million People to Benefit from Historic Council Overhaul', 1 April. Available at: http://webarchive.nationalarchives.gov.uk/+/http://www.communities.gov.uk/news/corporate/1191359.

DCLG (Department for Communities and Local Government) (2009b) *Housing and Planning Statistics* (London: DCLG).

DCLG (Department for Communities and Local Government) (2009c) *Government Response to the Communities and Local Government Select Committee Report into the Balance of Power: Central and Local Government*, Cm 7712 (Norwich: TSO).

DCLG (Department of Communities and Local Government) (2009d) *Budget 2009 – Value for Money Update* (London: DCLG).

DCLG (Department for Communities and Local Government) (2009e) *Community, Opportunity, Prosperity – DCLG Annual Report 2009*, Cm 7598 (Norwich: TSO).

DCLG (Department for Communities and Local Government) (2009f) *Local Government Financial Statistics England, No. 19, 2009* (London: DCLG).

DCLG (Department for Communities and Local Government) (2009g) *Reforming Local Government: Impacts and Interactions of Central Government Policies from 2000 to 2006: Final Report of the Meta-evaluation of the Local Government Modernisation Agenda* (London: DCLG).

DCLG (Department of Communities and Local Government) (2010a) *Local Authority Private Finance Initiative (PFI) Projects* (London: DCLG).

DCLG (Department for Communities and Local Government) (2010b) *Report on the 2009 Survey of All English Local Authority Agreements: Long-term Evaluation of Local Area Agreements and Local Strategic Partnerships* (London: DCLG).

DCLG (Department for Communities and Local Government) (2010c) *Draft Structural Plan, July 2010* (London: DCLG).

DCMS (Department for Culture, Media and Sport) (2003) *Framework for the Future: Libraries, Learning and Information in the Next Decade* (London: DCMS).

Deacon, R. and Sandry, A. (2007) *Devolution in the United Kingdom* (Edinburgh: Edinburgh University Press).

Deakin Commission (1996) *Report on the Future of the Voluntary Sector* (London: NCVO).

Deal, P. (2010) 'Threat to "25,000 Council Jobs"', BBC News, 1 March. Available at: http://news.bbc.co.uk/1/hi/england/8528836.stm.

Dearlove, J. (1973) *The Politics of Policy in Local Government* (Cambridge: Cambridge University Press).

Denham, J. (2010) 'Why Total Place is the Future for Public Service Delivery across the Sectors, *Municipal Journal*, Total Place Supplement, 18 February 2010, p. 3.

Denters, B. and Rose, L. (2005) *Comparing Local Governance: Trends and Developments* (Basingstoke: Palgrave Macmillan).

DETR (Department of the Environment, Transport and the Regions) (1998a) *Modern Local Government: In Touch with the People* (London: DETR).

DETR (Department of the Environment, Transport and the Regions) (1998b) *Modernising Local Government: Local Democracy and Community Leadership* (London: DETR).

DETR (Department of the Environment, Transport and the Regions) (1998c) *Improving Local Services Through Best Value* (London: DETR).

DETR (Department of the Environment, Transport and the Regions) (1998d) *Improving Financial Accountability* (London: DETR).

DH (Department of Health) (2006) *Our Health, Our Care, Our Say: A New Direction for Community Services* (London: DH).

DH (Department of Health) (2007) *Putting People First: A Shared Vision and Commitment to the transformation of Adult Social Care* (London: DH).

DH (Department of Health) (2009) *Communities for Health: Unlocking the Energy in our Communities to Improve Health* (London: DH).

DH (Department of Health) (2010) *Equity and Excellence: Liberating the NHS*, Cm 7881 (London: TSO).

DoE (Department of the Environment) (1981) *Alternatives to Domestic Rates*, Cmnd 8449 (London: HMSO).

DoE (Department of the Environment) (1983) *Streamlining the Cities*, Cmnd 9063 (London: HMSO).

DoE (Department of the Environment) (1986) *Paying for Local Government*, Cmnd 9714 (London: HMSO).

Doig, A. (1984) *Corruption and Misconduct in Contemporary British Politics* (Harmondsworth: Penguin).

Donoughue, B. and Jones, G. (2001) *Herbert Morrison: Portrait of a Politician* (London: Orion Publishing).

Drillsma-Milgrom, D. (2009) 'Winterton Takes Local Government Role', *lgcplus*, 8 June. Available at: www.lgcplus.com/policy-and-politics/people-in-power/winterton-takes-local-government-role/5002550.article.

DTLR (Department for Transport, Local Government and the Regions) (2001) *Strong Local Leadership – Quality Public Services* (London: DTLR).

Dunton, J. (2008) 'LGA Slams Knight's U-turn', *Local Government Chronicle*, 7 February, p. 6.

Elcock, H. (1991) *Local Government* (London: Methuen).

Elcock, H., Jordan, C. and Midwinter, A. (1989) *Budgeting in Local Government: Managing the Margins* (Harlow: Longman).

Electoral Commission (2003) *The Shape of Elections to Come: A Strategic Evaluation of the 2003 Electoral Pilot Schemes* (London: The Electoral Commission).

Electoral Commission (2004) *The Cycle of Local Government Elections in England: Report and Recommendations* (London: The Electoral Commission).

Electoral Commission (2007) *Key Issues and Conclusions: May 2007 Electoral Pilot Schemes* (London: The Electoral Commission).

Electoral Commission (2010) *The Completeness and Accuracy of Electoral Registers in Great Britain* (London: The Electoral Commission).

Ellwood, S., Nutley, S., Tricker, M. and Waterston, P. (1992) *Parish and Town Councils in England: A Survey* (London: HMSO).

Entwistle, T., Dowson, L. and Law, J. (2003) *Changing to Improve: Ten Case Studies from the Evaluation of the Best Value Regime* (London: ODPM).

ESRC (Economic and Social Research Council) (2005) *Policy Making and Policy Divergence in Scotland after Devolution*, Devolution Briefing No. 21 (London: ESRC).

European Commission (n.d.) *EU Register of EMAS Organisations*. Available at: http://ec.europa.eu/environment/emas/about/participate/sites_en.htm.

European Union, Committee of the Regions (1999) *Voter Turnout at Regional and Local Elections in the EU, 1990–1999* (Brussels: CoR).

European Union, Committee of the Regions (2009) *Participation in the European Project: How to Mobilise Citizens at the Local, Regional, National, and European Levels* (Brussels: CoR).

Fenwick, J., Elcock, H. and Lilley, S. (2003) 'Out of the Loop? Councillors and the New Political Management', *Public Policy and Administration*, 18:1, pp. 29–45.

Filkin, Lord, Stoker, G., Wilkinson, G. and Williams, J. (2000) *Towards a New Localism: A Discussion Paper* (London: NLGN).

Flinders, M. (2008) *Delegated Governance and the British State: Walking Without Order* (Oxford: Oxford University Press).

Gains, F. (2004) 'The Local Bureaucrat: A Block to Reform or a Key to Unlocking Change?', in G. Stoker and D. Wilson (eds), *British Local Government into the 21st Century* (Basingstoke: Palgrave Macmillan), pp. 91–104.

Gains, F. (2009) 'Narrations and Dilemmas of Local Bureaucratic Elites: Whitehall at the Coal Face?', *Public Administration*, 87:1, pp. 50–64.

Gains, F., John, P. and Stoker, G. (2008) 'When Do Bureaucrats Prefer Strong Political Principals? Institutional Reform and Bureaucratic Preferences in English Local Government', *British Journal of Politics and International Relations*, 10:4, pp. 649–65.

Gains, F., Greasley, S., John, P. and Stoker, G. (2009) 'The Impact of Political Leadership on Organisational Performance: Evidence from English Urban Government', *Local Government Studies*, 35:1, pp. 75–94.

Galbraith, J. (1958) *The Affluent Society* (Boston, Mass.: Houghton Mifflin Co.).

Game, C. (1997) 'How Many, When, Where and How? Taking Stock of Local Government Reorganisation', *Local Government Policy Making*, 23:4, pp. 3–15.

Game, C. (2003) 'Elected Mayors: More Distraction Than Attraction', *Public Policy and Administration*, 18:1, pp. 13–28.

Game, C. (2004) 'Should the Winner Take All, or Even Quite So Much?', in A. Pike (ed.), *The Missing Modernisation: The Case for PR in Local Government Elections* (London: Make Votes Count/Electoral Reform Society), pp. 10–16.

Game, C. (2005) 'The Miscarriage of Elected English Regional Assemblies: The Future of Democratic Decentralization After the North East Shouted No!', Unpublished paper delivered at the IASIA Annual Conference, Como, Italy.

Game, C. (2006) 'Comprehensive Performance Assessment in English Local Government', *International Journal of Productivity and Performance Management*, 55:6, pp. 466–79.

Game, C. (2007a) 'Quantifiable Added Value or Just Scary Big Numbers? Partnerships and Accountability in English Local Government', Paper delivered at the National Conference of the American Society for Public Administration, Washington DC.. See linked website.

Game, C. (2007b) 'Unpacking the Ubiquitous 10 per cent: Some Facts and Figures Concerning Minor Party and Independent Local Politics in Great Britain', Paper delivered at the First Annual International Conference on Minor Parties, etc., Birmingham. Available at: www.inlogov.bham.ac.uk/seminars/minor_parties/pdfs/Game.pdf.

Game, C. (2008) 'Laying Down the Law Locally', *Municipal Journal*, 11 September, p. 17.

Game, C. (2009a) 'Twenty-nine per cent Women Councillors After a Mere 100 Years: Isn't it Time to Look Seriously at Electoral Quotas?', *Public Policy and Administration*, 24:2, pp. 149–70.

Game, C. (2009b) 'Councillors – An Endangered Species?', *c'llr.*, November, pp. 20–1.

Game, C. (2009c) 'Mayors, Monitors and Measurers: Blair's Legacy to Local Democracy', in T. Casey (ed.), *The Blair Legacy: Politics, Policy, Governance and Foreign Affairs* (Basingstoke: Palgrave Macmillan), pp. 204–18.

Gershon, Sir P. (2004) *Releasing Resources to the Front Line: Independent Review of Public Sector Efficiency* (Norwich: HMSO).

Glaister, S. (2005) 'Transport', in A. Seldon and D. Kavanagh (eds), *The Blair Effect 2001–5* (Cambridge: Cambridge University Press), pp. 207–32.

Goetz, E. G. and Clarke, S. E. (eds) (1993) *The New Localism: Comparative Politics in a Global Era* (Newbury Park, Calif.: Sage).

Golding, N. (2009) 'LGA Names Britain's Worst Quangos', *Local Government Chronicle*, 13 November. Available at: www.lgcplus.com/news/lga-names-britains-worst-quangos/5008507.article.

Gosling, P. (2004) 'Up, Up and Away', *Public Finance*, 10 December.

Goss, S. (2001) *Making Local Governance Work* (Basingstoke: Palgrave Macmillan).

Goss, S. and Corrigan, P. (1999) *Starting to Modernise: Developing New Roles for Council Members* (London: NLGN/Joseph Rowntree Foundation).

Grant, C. (2005) 'Who Has Read Lyons' Script?', *Local Government Chronicle*, 8 September, p. 14.

Grant, W. (2000) *Pressure Groups and British Politics* (London: Macmillan).

Gray, C. (2002) 'Local Government and the Arts', *Local Government Studies*, 28:1, pp. 77–90.

Griffith, J. (1985) 'Foreword', in M. Loughlin, M. D. Gelfand and K. Young (eds), *Half a Century of Municipal Decline, 1935–1985* (London: Allen & Unwin), pp. ix–xiii.

Grogan, T. (1989) *The Pickles Papers* (Bradford: 1 in 12 Publications). Available at: http://www.1in12.com/publications/library/pickles/pickles.htm.

Gyford, J. (1984) *Local Politics in Britain,* 2nd edn (London: Croom Helm).

Gyford, J., Leach, S. and Game, C. (1989) *The Changing Politics of Local Government* (London: Unwin Hyman).

Hackett, P. and Hunter, P. (2010) *Who Governs Britain? A Profile of MPs in the New Parliament* (London: The Smith Institute).

Hailstone, J. (2008) 'A Model Councillor', *Municipal Journal,* 5 June, pp. 16–17.

Hambleton, R. (2005) 'Biting the Big Apple', *Municipal Journal,* 30 June, p. 23.

Hansard Society (2010) *Audit of Political Engagement 7 – The 2010 Report* (London: Hansard Society).

Havant BC (n.d.) *Analysis of 2007/2008 Budget by Services.* Available at: http://www4.havant.gov.uk/orion1/reports/comms/stc/20080122008a.pdf.

Hebbert, M. (1998) *London: More by Fortune than Design* (Chichester: John Wiley).

Heclo, H. (1969) 'The Councillor's Job', *Public Administration,* 47:2, pp. 185–202.

Hetherington, P. (2004) 'Inspecting the Inspectors', *Society Guardian,* 15 December, p. 10.

Hexagon Research and Publishing (2005) *Survey of Scottish Councillors' Workload and Analysis of Councillors' Weight of Responsibilities.* Available at: www.hexagonresearch.co.uk/news.asp?ID=6.

Higginson, R. and Clough, C. (2010) *The Ethics of Executive Remuneration* (London: CIG).

Hill, R. (2008) 'Upping the Game on Commissioning', *Municipal Journal,* 17 July, p. 15.

HM Government (2009) *Putting Frontline Services First: Smarter Government,* Cm 7753 (Norwich: TSO).

HM Government (2010) *The Coalition: Our Programme for Government* (London: Cabinet Office), May.

HM Treasury (2007) *Review of Sub-national Economic Development and Regeneration* (London: HM Treasury).

HM Treasury (2009) *Press Notice: Public Expenditure Outturn Update, 9 December* (London: HM Treasury).

Holden, J. and Ezra, Y. (2007) 'Fact and Fiction: The Future of Public Libraries'. available at: Hantsweb, http://www3.hants.gov.uk/library/future-libraries.htm.

Hollis, P. (1987) *Ladies Elect: Women in English Local Government, 1865–1914* (Oxford: Oxford University Press).

Hope, N. (ed.) (2009) *Cities, Sub-regions and Local Alliances: MAA Forum Essay Collection* (London: NLGN).

Hope, N. and Wanduragala, N. (2010) *New Model Mayors: Democracy, Devolution and Direction* (London: NLGN).

Houlihan, B. (1988) *Housing Policy and Central–Local Government Relations* (Aldershot: Avebury).

House of Commons (2001) *Select Committee on Public Administration – Fifth Report, 2000/01: Mapping the Quango State* (London: House of Commons).

House of Commons (2002) *Select Committee on Transport, Local Government and the Regions – Fourteenth Report of Session 2001–02: How the Local Government Act 2000 is Working* (London: House of Commons).

House of Commons (2003) *Select Committee on Public Administration Fourth Report of Session 2002–03: Appendices to the Minutes of Evidence –*

Memorandum by Prof. Chris Skelcher and Dr. Helen Sullivan (PAP 70). Available at: (www.publications.parliament.uk/pa/cm200203/cmselect/cmpubadm/165/165ap55.htm).

House of Commons (2008) *EU Legislation – Standard Note SN/1A/2888* (London: House of Commons).

House of Commons (2009a) *Communities and Local Government Select Committee – Sixth Report of Session 2008–09: The Balance of Power: Central and Local Government* (London: House of Commons).

House of Commons (2009b) *Communities and Local Government Select Committee – Sixth Report of Session 2008–09: The Balance of Power: Central and Local Government – Written Evidence: Memorandum by INLOGOV (BOP 22).* Available at: (www.publications.parliament.uk/pa/cm200809/cmselect/cmcomloc/33/33we22.htm).

House of Commons (2009c) *Local Elections 2009 – Research Paper 09/54* (London: House of Commons).

House of Commons (2010a) *Communities and Local Government Select Committee Press Notice – Too Many Ministers Weakens Policy Design and Delivery,* 4 March (London: House of Commons).

House of Commons (2010b) *Communities and Local Government Select Committee – Uncorrected Transcript of Oral Evidence,* 13 September (London: House of Commons). Available at: http://www.publications.parliament.uk/pa/cm201011/cmselect/cmcomloc/uc453-i/uc45301.htm.

Hughes, M., Skelcher, C., Jas, P., Whiteman, P. and Turner, D. (2004) *Learning from the Experience of Recovery – Paths to Recovery: Second Annual Report* (London: ODPM).

Hull City Council (2009) *Partnership Annual Report 2009* (Hull: Hull City Council).

IDeA (Improvement and Development Agency) (2007a) *The Future Shape of Local Authorities' Workforces* (London: IDeA).

IDeA (Improvement and Development Agency) (2007b) 'The Role of Councillors in a Healthy Democracy', Speech delivered by Dame Jane Roberts at an IDeA conference. Available at: www.idea.gov.uk/idk/core/page.do?pageId=7581964.

IDeA (Improvement and Development Agency) (2009) *Shared Chief Executives and Joint Management: A Model for the Future?* (London: IDeA).

Illman, J. (2009) 'Spelman: Total Place Will Eclipse LAAs', *Local Government Chronicle,* 9 November. Available at: www.lgcplus.com/policy-and-politics/spelman-total-place-will-eclipse-laas/5008340.article.

Ipsos MORI Local (2009) *People, Perceptions and Place – Results of the 2008/09 Place Survey* (London: Ipsos MORI).

Jenkins, S. (2004) *Big Bang Localism: A Rescue Plan for British Democracy* (London: Policy Exchange).

Jenkins, S. (2005) 'Respect Starts With You Letting Us Run Our Lives, Godfather Blair', *The Sunday Times,* 15 May.

Jenkins, S. (2006a) 'This is an Open Invitation to Developers to Try Their Luck', *The Guardian,* 6 December.

Jenkins, S. (2006b) 'Set a Silly Target and You'll Get a Really Crazy Public Service', *The Sunday Times,* 24 September.

Jennings, R. E. (1982) 'The Changing Representational Roles of Local Councillors in England', *Local Government Studies,* 8:4, pp. 67–86.

John, P. (2001) *Local Governance in Western Europe* (London: Sage).

Jones, B. and Norton, P. (2010) *Politics UK*, 7th edn (Harlow: Pearson Education).

Jones, G. (1973) 'The Functions and Organisation of Councillors', *Public Administration*, 51, pp. 135–46.

Jones, G. (1975) 'Varieties of Local Politics', *Local Government Studies*, 1:2, pp. 17–32.

Jones, G. (2009) 'In Defence of Dame Shirley Porter', *Local Government Studies*, 35:1, pp. 143–52.

Jones, G. and Stewart, J. (1983) *The Case for Local Government* (London: Allen & Unwin).

Jones, G. and Stewart, J. (2004) 'Power Without Punch', *Local Government Chronicle*, 5 November, p. 24.

Jones, G. and Stewart, J. (2005) 'It's Big, but It's Not Clever', *Public Finance*, 9 December, pp. 28–9.

Jones, G. and Stewart, J. (2009) 'Can Local Government Learn from History?', *Municipal Journal*, 13 August, pp. 22–3.

Kamall, S. (n.d.) *Syed Kamall's Pocket Guide to the EU and Local Government*. Available at: www.syedkamall.com/EUandLocalGvt.pdf.

Kemp, R. (2009) 'Show Me the Evidence that Mayors are a Good Idea', in T. Shakespeare (ed.), *Directly Elected Mayors: Are They Appropriate for All UK Cities?* (London: Localis Research Ltd), pp. 3–11.

Kemp, R., Kemp, E., Eldridge, C. and Maxwell, B. (2009) *Council Member for Your Ward – A New Challenge for All Councillors* (London: Leadership Centre for Local Government).

King, D. (2006) 'Local Government Organization and Finance: United Kingdom', in A. Shah (ed.), *Local Governance in Industrial Countries* (Washington, DC: The World Bank), pp. 265–312.

Labour Party (1997) *New Labour – Because Britain Deserves Better* (London: The Labour Party).

Labour Party (2010) *The Labour Party Manifesto 2010 – A Future Fair for All* (London: The Labour Party).

Laffin, M. (2008) 'Local Government Modernisation in England: A Critical Review of the LGMA Evaluation Studies, *Local Government Studies*, 34:1, pp. 109–25.

Lambeth Council (2010) *The Co-operative Council: A New Settlement Between Citizens and Public Services* (London: Lambeth LBC).

Laski, H. (1934) *A Grammar of Politics,* 3rd edn (London: Allen & Unwin).

Laski, H., Jennings, W. and Robson, W. (eds) (1935) *A Century of Municipal Progress, 1835–1935* (London: George Allen & Unwin).

Laver, M. (1989) 'Theories of Coalition Formation and Local Government Coalitions', in C. Mellors and B. Pijnenburg (eds), *Political Parties and Coalitions in European Local Government* (London: Routledge), pp. 15–33.

Layfield Committee (1976) *Report of the Committee of Enquiry into Local Government Finance,* Cmnd 6543 (London: HMSO).

Leach, R. and Percy-Smith, J. (2001) *Local Governance in Britain* (Basingstoke: Palgrave Macmillan).

Leach, R., Coxall, B. and Robins, L. (2006) *British Politics* (Basingstoke: Palgrave).

Leach, S. (1999) 'Introducing Cabinets into British Local Government', *Parliamentary Affairs*, 52:1, pp. 77–93.

Leach, S. (2006) *The Changing Role of Local Politics in Britain* (Bristol: Policy Press).

Leach, S. (2008) 'Brown's Community Politics: Developments in Local Government', in Rush. M. and P. Giddings (eds), *When Gordon Took the Helm: The Palgrave Review of British Politics 2007–08* (Basingstoke: Palgrave Macmillan) pp. 180–92.

Leach, S. (2009) 'A Commentary on Seven Current Themes on the English Local Government Agenda', Seminar, July 2009, De Montfort University, Leicester.

Leach, S. (2010) 'The Labour Government's Local Government Agenda 1997–2009: The Impact on Member–Officer Relationships', *Local Government Studies*, 36:3, pp. 323–39.

Leach, S. and Copus, C. (2004) 'Scrutiny and the Political Party Group in UK Local Government: New Models of Behaviour', *Public Administration*, 82:2, pp. 331–54.

Leach, S. and Game, C. (1992) 'Local Government: The Decline of the One-Party State', in G. Smyth (ed.), *Refreshing the Parts: Electoral Reform and British Politics* (London: Lawrence & Wishart).

Leach, S. and Game, C. (2000) *Hung Authorities, Elected Mayors and Cabinet Government: Political Behaviour Under Proportional Representation* (York: Joseph Rowntree Foundation).

Leach, S. and Pratchett, L. (2007) 'Local Government: Towards Strong and Prosperous Communities', in M. Rush and P. Giddings (eds), *The Palgrave Review of British Politics 2006* (Basingstoke: Palgrave Macmillan), pp. 177–90.

Leach, S. and Stewart, J. (1992) *The Politics of Hung Authorities* (London: Macmillan).

Leach, S. and Wilson, D. (2000) *Local Political Leadership* (Bristol: Policy Press).

Leach, S. and Wilson, D. (2008) 'Diluting the Role of Party Groups? Implications of the 2006 Local Government White Paper', *Local Government Studies*, 34:3, pp. 303–21.

Leach, S., Davis. H. and Associates (1996) *Enabling or Disabling Local Government: Choices for the Future* (Buckingham: Open University Press).

Leach, S., Stewart, J. and Walsh, K. (1994) *The Changing Organisation and Management of Local Government* (London: Macmillan).

Leadership Centre for Local Government (2009) *Counting Cumbria* (London: Local Government Association).

Lee, J. (1963) *Social Leaders and Public Persons* (Oxford: Clarendon Press).

Lepine, E. and Sullivan, H. (2010) 'Realising the Public Person', *Local Government Studies* 36:1, pp. 91–108.

Lewis, D. (2005) *The Essential Guide to British Quangos, 2005* (London: Centre for Policy Studies).

Lewis, G. (2001) *Mapping the Contribution of the Voluntary and Community Sector in Yorkshire and the Humber* (Leeds: Yorkshire and the Humber Regional Forum).

LGA (Local Government Association) (2000) *Real Roles for Members – The Role of Non-executive Members in the New Structures* (London: LGA).

LGA (Local Government Association) (2001) *Electoral Reform in Local Government: A Local Government Association Consultation* (London: LGA).

LGA (Local Government Association) (2004) *The Balance of Funding – A Combination Option* (London: LGA).

LGA (Local Government Association) (2008) *The Reputation of Local Government: Literature Review to Support the 'My Council' Campaign* (London: LGA).

LGA (Local Government Association) (2009a) *Who's in Charge? The Quango Report Cards* (London: LGA).

LGA (Local Government Association) (2009b) *The Sustainable Communities Act: Shortlist of Proposals Made Under Round One* (London: LGA).

LGA (Local Government Association) (2009c) *LGA Annual Report 2009* (London: LGA).

LGA (Local Government Association) (2009d) *Local Government Earnings Survey 2008/09 – Summary Report* (London: LGA).

LGA (Local Government Association) (2009e) *Bonfire of Bureaucracy Could Save Taxpayers £4.5 billion*, LGA Press Office, 20 November 2009.

LGA (Local Government Association) (2010) *Freedom to Lead: Trust to Deliver* (London: LGA).

LGAAR (Local Government Association Analysis and Research) (2009a) *Local Government Workforce: Analysis of Job Roles* (London: LGA).

LGAAR (Local Government Association Analysis and Research) (2009b) *Local Government Workforce: Demographic Profile* (London: LGA).

LGA Group (2010) *Delivering Through People: The Local Government Workforce Strategy 2010* (London: LGA).

LGE (Local Government Employers) (2007) *Delivering a Rewarding Future: An Approach to Pay and Benefits in Local Government for the 21st Century* (London: LGE).

LGO (Local Government Ombudsman) (2009) *Annual Report 08/09: Delivering Public Value* (London: Commission for Local Administration in England).

Liberal Democrats (2010) *Liberal Democrat Manifesto 2010 – Change That Works for You* (London: The Liberal Democrats).

Lifting the Burdens Task Force (2008) *The State of the Burden – Final Report* (London: LGA).

Livingstone, K. (1987) *If Voting Changed Anything, They'd Abolish It* (London: Collins).

Local Channel, The (2005) *ICT and e-government Development for Small First-tier Councils in the EU 25*. See www.thelocalchannel.co.uk.

London Councils (2010) *Capital Crisis – Enabling Investment in London* (London: London Councils).

London Voluntary Service Council (LVSC) (2009) *Conservative Party Policy on the Voluntary and Community Sector – Policy Briefing 36* (London: LVSC).

Loughlin, J. (2001) *Subnational Democracy in the European Union: Challenges and Opportunities* (Oxford: Oxford University Press).

Loughlin, M. (1996a) *Legality and Locality: The Role of Law in Central–Local Relations* (Oxford: Clarendon Press).

Loughlin, M. (1996b) 'Understanding Central–Local Government Relations', *Public Policy and Administration*, 11:2, pp. 48–65.

Loughlin, M., Gelfand, M. D. and Young, K. (eds) (1985) *Half a Century of Municipal Decline, 1935–1985* (London: Allen & Unwin).

Lowndes, V. (1996) 'Locality and Community: Choices for Local Government', in S. Leach *et al.*, *Enabling or Disabling Local Government* (Buckingham: Open University Press), pp. 71–85.

Lowndes, V. (2002) 'Between Rhetoric and Reality: Does the 2001 White Paper Reverse the Centralising Trend in Britain?', *Local Government Studies*, 28:3, pp. 135–47.

Lowndes, V. and Sullivan, H. (2004) 'Like a Horse and Carriage or a Fish on a Bicycle: How Well Do Local Partnerships and Public Participation Go Together?', *Local Government Studies*, 30:1, pp. 52–74.

Lowndes, V. and Sullivan, H. (2008) 'How Low Can You Go? Rationales and Challenges for Neighbourhood Governance', *Public Administration*, 86:1, pp. 53–74.

Lowndes, V., Pratchett, L. and Stoker, G. (2001) 'Trends in Public Participation: Part 1 – Local Government Perspectives', *Public Administration*, 79:1, pp. 205–22.

Lynn, J. and Jay, A. (1983) *Yes, Minister: The Diaries of a Cabinet Minister, Vol. 3 – The Challenge* (London: BBC).

Lyons, Sir M. (2005) *Lyons Inquiry into Local Government: Consultation Paper and Interim Report* (Norwich: HMSO).

Lyons, Sir M. (2007) *Place-shaping: A Shared Ambition for the Future of Local Government – Final Report of the Lyons Inquiry into Local Government* (Norwich: TSO).

McIntosh, N. (Chairman) (1999) *Commission on Local Government and the Scottish Parliament,* Report (Edinburgh: Scottish Executive).

Mackenzie, W. J. M. (1961) *Theories of Local Government* (London: London School of Economics).

Macrory, P. (Chairman) (1970) *Review Body on Local Government in Northern Ireland, Report,* Cmnd 540 (NI) (HMSO: Belfast).

Mahony, C. (2005) 'Culture Vultures', *Local Government Chronicle 1855–2005,* 3 November, pp. 49–50.

Maloney, W., Smith, G. and Stoker, G. (2000) 'Social Capital and Urban Governance: Adding a More Contextualised "Top-down" Perspective', *Political Studies*, 48:4, pp. 802–20.

Marshall, A. (2008) *The Future of Regional Development Agencies* (London: Centre for Cities).

Miliband, D. (2005a) 'Power to Neighbourhoods: The New Challenge for Urban Regeneration', Speech at the Annual Conference of the British Urban Regeneration Association, 12 October.

Miliband, D. (2005b) 'Local Government Reorganisation', *Local Government Chronicle,* 1 December.

Miliband, D. (2006) 'Empowerment and the Deal for Devolution', Speech at the Annual Conference of the NLGN, 18 January (London: ODPM).

Miliband, D. (2009) 'Turning the Tide on Democratic Pessimism', John Smith Memorial Lecture, 6 July 2009.

Miliband, D. (2010) Keir Hardie Lecture, Cynon Valley, 9 July. Available at: http://www.davidmiliband.net/2010/07/09/keir-hardie-lecture-2010/.

Miller, W. (1988) *Irrelevant Elections? The Quality of Local Democracy in Britain* (Oxford: Clarendon Press).

Morris, D. and Hess, K. (1975) *Neighbourhood Power: The New Localism* (Boston, Mass.: Beacon Press).

Mulholland, H. (2010) 'Mr easyCouncil Defends his Local Government Model', *The Guardian,* 3 February.

Myerson, J. (2005) 'Lambeth Talk', *Society Guardian*, 23 February, p. 11.

NCVO (National Council for Voluntary Organisations) (2010) *The UK Civil Society Almanac 2010* (London: NCVO).

Newton, K. (1976) *Second City Politics: Democratic Processes and Decision-Making in Birmingham* (Oxford: Oxford University Press).

Newton, K. and Karran, T. (1985) *The Politics of Local Expenditure* (London: Macmillan).

NFER (National Foundation for Educational Research) (2009a) *National Census of Local Authority Councillors 2008* (Slough: NFER).

NFER (National Foundation for Educational Research) (2009b) *Members' Allowances Survey, 2008: Summary Findings and Analysis* (Slough: NFER).

Oakland, J. (1989) *Total Quality Management* (London: Butterworth Heinemann).

ODPM (Office of the Deputy Prime Minister) (2003) *The Government's Response to the Electoral Commission's Report: 'The Shape of Elections to Come'*, Cm 5975 (London: ODPM).

ODPM (Office of the Deputy Prime Minister) (2004a) *The Future of Local Government: Developing a 10-year Vision* (London: ODPM).

ODPM (Office of the Deputy Prime Minister) (2004b) *Balance of Funding Review – Report* (London: ODPM).

ODPM (Office of the Deputy Prime Minister) (2005a) *Vibrant Local Leadership* (London: ODPM).

ODPM (Office of the Deputy Prime Minister) (2005b) *New Localism – Citizen Engagement, Neighbourhoods and Public Services: Evidence from Local Government* (London: ODPM).

OECD (Organisation for Economic Co-operation and Development) (2009) *Revenue Statistics 1965–2008* (Paris: OECD).

ONS (Office for National Statistics) (2010a) *Statistical Bulletin, 20 January – Civil Service Statistics, 31 March 2009* (Newport, Wales: ONS).

ONS (Office for National Statistics) (2010b) *Statistical Bulletin, 17 March – Public Sector Employment* (Newport, Wales, ONS).

Osborne, D. and Gaebler, T. (1992) *Reinventing Government: How Entrepreneurial Spirit is Transforming the Public Sector* (Reading, Mass.: Addison-Wesley).

Parris, M. (2005) 'The Birmingham Case is Simply Vote Rigging, and at the Highest Level', *The Times*, 26 March, p. 21.

Paterson, I. V. (Chairman) (1973) *The New Scottish Local Authorities: Organisation and Management Structures* (Edinburgh: Scottish Development Department).

Perri 6, Leat, D., Seltzer, K. and Stoker, G. (2002) *Towards Holistic Governance: The New Reform Agenda* (Basingstoke: Palgrave Macmillan).

Phillips, C. (2000) *Birmingham Votes, 1911–2000* (Plymouth: LGC Elections Centre).

Pickles, E. (2010) *Address to the Queen's Speech Forum*, 10 June.

Plummer, J. (2009) 'Commission for the Compact "powerless" to investigate OTS breach', *Third Sector Online*, 19 November.

Power Inquiry (2004) *The Decline of Political Participation in Britain: An Introduction.* Available at: www.powerinquiry.org.

Pratchett, L. (2004a) 'Institutions, Politics and People: Making Local Politics Work', in G. Stoker and D. Wilson (eds), *British Local Government into the 21st Century* (Basingstoke: Palgrave Macmillan), pp. 213–29.

Pratchett, L. (2004b) 'Local Autonomy, Local Democracy and the 'New Localism'', *Political Studies*, 52:2, pp. 358–75.

Pratchett, L. and Leach, S. (2004) 'Local Government: Choice Within Constraint', *Parliamentary Affairs*, 57:2, pp. 366–79.

Pratchett, L. and Wingfield, M. (1996) 'The Demise of the Public Sector Ethos', in L. Pratchett and D. Wilson (eds), *Local Democracy and Local Government* (London: Macmillan), pp. 106–26.

Prior, D. (1995) 'Citizens' Charters', in J. Stewart and G. Stoker (eds), *Local Government in the 1990s* (London: Macmillan), pp. 86–103.

Putnam, R. (2000) *Bowling Alone: The Collapse and Revival of American Community* (New York: Simon & Schuster).

Rallings, C. and Thrasher, M. (1997) *Local Elections in Britain* (London: Routledge).

Rallings, C. and Thrasher, M. (2003) *Electoral Cycles in English Local Government* (Plymouth: LGC Elections Centre).

Rallings, C. and Thrasher, M. (2010) 'Analysis: Labour Fights Back', *Local Government Chronicle*, 13 May, pp. 16–18.

Rallings, C. and Thrasher, M. (Annual) *Local Elections Handbook* (Plymouth: LGC Elections Centre).

Rallings, C., Thrasher, M., Cheal, B. and Borisyuk, G. (2004) 'The New Deal for Communities: Assessing Procedures and Voter Turnout at Partnership Board Elections', *Environment and Planning C: Government and Policy*, 22, pp. 569–82.

Rashman, L. and Hartley, J. (2006) *Long-term Evaluation of the Beacon Scheme: Survey of Local Authorities – Final Report* (London: ODPM).

Redcliffe-Maud, J. (1932) *Local Government in Modern England* (London: Thornton Butterworth).

Redcliffe-Maud, Lord (Chairman) (1969) *Royal Commission on Local Government in England 1966–1969, Vol. 1 Report,* Cmnd 4040 (London: HMSO).

Rhodes, R. A. W. (1986) *The National World of Local Government* (London: Allen & Unwin).

Rhodes, R. A. W. (1988) *Beyond Westminster and Whitehall* (London: Allen & Unwin).

Rhodes, R. A. W. (1997) *Understanding Governance: Policy Networks, Governance, Reflexivity and Accountability* (Buckingham: Open University Press).

Rhodes, R. A. W. (1999) *Control and Power in Central–Local Government Relations* (Aldershot: Ashgate).

Rhodes, R .A. W. and Dunleavy, P. (1995) *Prime Minister, Cabinet and Core Executive* (London: Macmillan).

Richard, Lord (Chairman) (2004) *Report of the Commission on the Powers and Electoral Arrangements of the National Assembly for Wales* (Cardiff, National Assembly for Wales).

Rose, D. (2005) 'Same Goal, Different Approach', *Municipal Journal*, 21 April, p. 10.

Royal Commonwealth Society (2010) *Commonwealth Observer Team to the UK General Election 2010 – Final Report* (London: The Royal Commonwealth Society).

Saunders, P. (1980) *Urban Politics: A Sociological Interpretation* (Harmondsworth: Penguin).

Scottish Government (2010) *Joint Staffing Watch – Quarter 4, 2009* (Edinburgh: Scottish Government).

Seitz, R. (1998) *Over Here* (London: Phoenix).

Sharpe, L. J. (1970) 'Theories and Values of Local Government', *Political Studies*, 18:2, pp. 153–74.

Shaw, K. and Davidson, G. (2002) 'Community Elections for Regeneration Partnerships: A New Deal for Local Democracy?', *Local Government Studies*, 28:2, pp. 1–15.

Sherman, J. and Gilmore, G. (2009) 'Gordon Brown Orders Thousands of New Council Houses', *The Times*, 30 January 2009.

Skelcher, C. (1992) *Managing for Service Quality* (Harlow: Longman).

Skelcher, C. (2004) 'The New Governance of Communities', in G. Stoker and D. Wilson (eds), *British Local Government into the 21st Century* (Basingstoke: Palgrave Macmillan), pp. 25–42.

Skelcher, C., Weir, S. and Wilson, L. (2000) *Advance of the Quango State* (London: LGIU).

Smith, E. (2005) *On and Off the Field* (London: Penguin).

Smith, J. T. (1851) *Local Self-Government and Centralisation* (London: John Chapman).

Smulian, M. (2007) 'Community Spirit', *Local Government Chronicle*, 9 November, p. 16.

Smulian, M. (2010) 'David Miliband Admits Labour Ignored Local Government', *Local Government Chronicle*, 6 July.

Snape, S. (2004) 'Liberated or Lost Souls: Is There a Role for Non-executive Councillors?', in G. Stoker and D. Wilson (eds), *British Local Government into the 21st Century* (Basingstoke: Palgrave Macmillan), pp. 60–75.

Snape, S. and Taylor, P. (2003) 'Partnerships Between Health and Local Government: An Introduction', *Local Government Studies*, 29:3, pp 1–16.

Snape, S., Leach, S. and Copus, C. (2002) *The Development of Overview and Scrutiny in Local Government* (London: ODPM).

Social Justice Policy Group (2006) *Breakdown Britain: Interim Report on the State of the Nation* (London: Centre for Social Justice).

Social Justice Policy Group (2007) *Breakthrough Britain: Ending the Costs of Social Breakdown* (London: Centre for Social Justice).

SOLACE (Society of Local Authority Chief Executives) (2009) *Promoting Chief Executives 2009: Public and Private Sector Salaries* (London: SOLACE).

Southend-on-Sea Borough Council (2009) *Grants Strategy Working Party, Appendices 1, 2 and 4*, 5 March 2009. Available at: www.southend.gov.uk.

Stewart, J. (1990) 'The Role of Councillors in the Management of the Authority', *Local Government Studies*, 16:4, pp. 25–36.

Stewart, J. (1996) *Local Government Today: An Observer's View* (Luton: LGMB).

Stewart, J. (2000) *The Nature of British Local Government* (London: Macmillan).

Stoker, G. (1991) *The Politics of Local Government*, 2nd edn (London: Macmillan).

Stoker, G. (2002) 'Life Is a Lottery: New Labour's Strategy for the Reform of Devolved Governance', *Public Administration*, 80:3, pp. 417–34.

Stoker, G. (2004a) *Transforming Local Governance: From Thatcherism to New Labour* (Basingstoke: Palgrave Macmillan).

Stoker, G. (2004b) *How Are Mayors Measuring Up?* (London: ODPM).

Stoker, G. (ed.) (1999) *The New Management of British Local Governance* (London: Macmillan).

Stoker, G. (ed.) (2000) *The New Politics of British Local Governance* (London: Macmillan).

Stoker, G. and Wilson, D. (1986) 'Intra-Organizational Politics in Local Authorities', *Public Administration*, 64:3, pp. 285–302.

Stoker, G. and Wilson, D. (eds) (2004) *British Local Government into the 21st Century* (Basingstoke: Palgrave Macmillan).

Stoker, G. and Young, S. (1993) *Cities in the 1990s* (Harlow: Longman).

Stoker, G., Gains, F., John, P., Rao, N. and Harding, A. (2003) *Implementing the 2000 Act with Respect to New Council Constitutions and the Ethical Framework: First Report* (London: ODPM).

Stoker, G., Gains, F., Greasley, S., John, P. and Rao, N. (2004) *Operating the New Council Constitutions: A Process Evaluation* (London: ODPM).

Suffolk County Council (2010) *Implementing the New Strategic Direction*. Available at: http://apps2.suffolk.gov.uk/cgi-bin/committee_xml.cgi?p=doc&id=1_14723&format=doc.

Sullivan, H. and Skelcher, C. (2002) *Working Across Boundaries: Collaboration in Public Services* (Basingstoke: Palgrave Macmillan).

Swinford, S. (2010) 'Ballot Security "Worse than Kenya"', *The Sunday Times*, 9 May.

Taafe, P. and Mulhearn, T. (1988) *Liverpool – A City that Dared to Fight* (London: Fortress Books).

TPA (The TaxPayers' Alliance) (2009) *Towards Transparent Rewards – Research Note 55* (London: TaxPayers' Alliance).

TPA (The TaxPayers' Alliance) (2010) *Town Hall Rich List 2010 – Research Note 65* (London: TaxPayers'Alliance).

Temple, M. (1996) *Coalitions and Co-operation in Local Government* (London: Electoral Reform Society).

Travers, T. (2004) *The Politics of London: Governing an Ungovernable City* (Basingstoke: Palgrave Macmillan).

Travers, T. (2007) 'Local Government', in A. Seldon (ed.), *Blair's Britain, 1997–2007* (Cambridge: Cambridge University Press), pp. 54–78.

Travers, T. (2008) 'Ministers Need to Face the Reality of Service Delivery', *Local Government Chronicle*, 7 February, p. 5.

Vallely, P. (2009) 'Eric Pickles: The Tory Heavyweight', *The Independent*, 24 January.

Voice East Midlands (2003) *Mapping the Black and Minority Voluntary and Community Sector in the East Midlands* (Nottingham: Nottingham Research Observatory).

VONNE (Voluntary Organisations' Network North East) (2000) *The Contribution of the Voluntary and Community Sector to the Economic Life of the North East Region* (Newcastle upon Tyne: VONNE).

Wanless, D. (2002) *Securing Our Future Health: Taking a Long-term View* (London: HM Treasury).

Webb, S. and Webb, B. (1920) *A Constitution for the Socialist Commonwealth of Great Britain* (London: Longmans, Green & Co.).

Weir, S. and Beetham, D. (1999) *Political Power and Democratic Control in Britain: The Democratic Audit of Great Britain* (London: Routledge).

Westminster City Council (2009) *Our New Council Organisation* (London: Westminster City Council).

Wheatley, Lord (Chairman) (1969) *Royal Commission on Local Government in Scotland, Report,* Cmnd 4150 (Edinburgh: HMSO).

Whelan, R. (1999) *Involuntary Action: How Voluntary Is the Voluntary Sector?* (London: IEA Health and Welfare Unit).

Widdicombe, D. (Chairman) (1986a) *The Conduct of Local Authority Business: Report of the Committee of Inquiry into the Conduct of Local Authority Business,* Cmnd 9797 (London: HMSO).

Widdicombe, D. (Chairman) (1986b) *Research Volume I – The Political Organisation of Local Authorities* (by S. Leach, C. Game, J. Gyford and A. Midwinter), Cmnd 9798 (London: HMSO).

Widdicombe, D. (Chairman) (1986c) *Research Volume II – The Local Government Councillor,* Cmnd 9799 (London: HMSO).

Widdicombe, D. (Chairman) (1986d) *Research Volume III – The Local Government Elector,* Cmnd 9800 (London: HMSO).

Widdicombe, D. (Chairman) (1986e) *Research Volume IV – Aspects of Local Democracy,* Cmnd 9801 (London: HMSO).

Williams, C. (2010) 'Reaping the Benefits of Local Transparency', *Local Government Chronicle,* 24 June. Available at: http://www.lgcplus.com/5016123.article.

Wilson, D. (2003) 'Unravelling Control Freakery: Redefining Central–Local Government Relations', *British Journal of Politics and International Relations,* 5:3, pp. 317–46.

Wilson, D. and Game, C. (1994) *Local Government in the United Kingdom,* 1st edn (London: Macmillan).

Wilson, D. and Game, C. (1998) *Local Government in the United Kingdom,* 2nd edn (London: Macmillan).

Wilson, D. and Game, C. (2002) *Local Government in the United Kingdom,* 3rd edn (Basingstoke: Palgrave Macmillan).

Wilson, D. and Game, C. (2006) *Local Government in the United Kingdom,* 4th edn (Basingstoke: Palgrave Macmillan).

Young, K. (1986a) 'Party Politics in Local Government: An Historical Perspective', in Widdicombe (1986e) (London: HMSO).

Young, K. (1986b) 'The Justification for Local Government', in M. Goldsmith (ed.), *Essays on the Future of Local Government* (Wakefield: West Yorkshire Metropolitan County Council), pp. 8–20.

Young, K. and Mills, L. (1983) *Managing the Post-Industrial City* (London: Heinemann).

Index